THE
New World
Reader

THE
New World Reader

Thinking and Writing
about the Global Community

Fifth Edition

Gilbert H. Muller

The City University of New York
LaGuardia College

CENGAGE
Learning®

Australia • Brazil • Mexico • Singapore • United Kingdom • United States

CENGAGE
Learning®

The New World Reader:
Thinking and Writing about
the Global Community,
Fifth Edition
Gilbert H. Muller

Product Team Manager:
Nicole Morinon

Product Manager: Kate Derrick

Associate Content Developer:
Erin Bosco

Product Assistant: Mario Davila

Marketing Manager:
Stacey Purviance

IP Analyst: Ann Hoffman

IP Project Manager: Farah Fard

Manufacturing Planner:
Betsy Donaghey

Art and Design Direction,
Production Management,
and Composition:
Cenveo® Publisher Services

Cover Image: © Prachanart/
Getty Images

For product information and technology assistance, contact us at **Cengage Learning Customer & Sales Support, 1-800-354-9706**.

For permission to use material from this text or product, submit all requests online at **www.cengage.com/permissions**. Further permissions questions can be e-mailed to **permissionrequest@cengage.com**.

Library of Congress Control Number: 2015946509

ISBN: 978-1-305-64377-2

Loose-leaf Edition:
ISBN: 978-1-305-64552-3

Cengage Learning
20 Channel Center Street
Boston MA 02210
USA

Cengage Learning is a leading provider of customized learning solutions with employees residing in nearly 40 different countries and sales in more than 125 countries around the world. Find your local representative at **www.cengage.com**.

Cengage Learning products are represented in Canada by Nelson Education, Ltd.

To learn more about Cengage Learning Solutions, visit **www.cengage.com**.

Purchase any of our products at your local college store or at our preferred online store **www.cengagebrain.com**.

Printed in the United States of America
Print Number: 01   Print Year: 2015

For Sadie Rain and Vivian Dalia
Global Girls

Brief Contents

Contents

1 | Thinking, Reading, and Writing about the New Global Era   1

2 | New American Mosaic: Are We Becoming a Universal Nation?   28

3 | America and the World: How Do Others Perceive Us?   57

8 | The Clash of Civilizations: Is Conflict Avoidable?   222

11 | The Fate of the Earth: Can We Preserve the Global Environment?   313

Rhetorical Contents

Illustration/Exemplification

Comparison and Contrast

Definition

Classification

Process Analysis

Causal Analysis

Argument and Persuasion

Culture or Conflict?
Images of Globalization

Is Beauty Universal?
Global Body Images

PREFACE

We live in a world of transformations, affecting almost every aspect of what we do. For better or worse, we are being propelled into a global order that no one fully understands, but which is making its effects felt upon all of us.

—Anthony Giddens

Now in its fifth edition, *The New World Reader* continues to present provocative essays about contemporary global issues and challenges. The book provides students with the resources needed to think and write in ways that foster varieties of global understanding and citizenship. In an era marked by conflicts on many continents and ongoing clashes across civilizations, students need to interrogate their relationship to their home nation—whether they are from the United States or elsewhere—and also their personal place in the world. Do they agree, for example, with the controversial novelist Salman Rushdie's contention that the West has met the "Rest"? The writers in this text deal with this question as well as those global issues that increasingly shape our lives. Superlative writers from a variety of backgrounds and perspectives reveal in this new edition of *The New World Reader* that globalization is *the* big story, the most pressing issue of our times.

Students using *The New World Reader* will find interconnected chapters and selections dealing with such strategic global questions as the changing demographics of the United States, the impact of terrorism on individuals as well as entire populations, the nature of globalization, the clash of cultures and civilizations, the changing roles of women and men in the global arena, the ways in which first-world nations can successfully address global poverty and disease, and the state of the global environment. Challenged by such well-known contemporary thinkers and writers as Bharati Mukherjee, Firoozeh Dumas, Amy Tan, Ana Menendez, Henry Louis Gates, Paul Krugman, Tae Yoo, and Jane Goodall, today's students will be encouraged to come to grips with a world that is now subject to complex and often mystifying transformations.

This book demonstrates that critical thinking about our new global century begins when students consider unfamiliar perspectives and arguments, when they are open to new global ideas and perceptions. Put differently, *The New World Reader* encourages intercultural and transnational inquiry. As such, the design of the anthology encourages students to ask not only who they are in this society but also who they are in the world. Many of the diversity themes that teachers of college writing find especially productive and stimulating—gender and sexuality, race and ethnicity, class and cultural orientation—lend themselves to these issues of local and global perception. The selections in the text present a tapestry of diversity in both a local and a global light, moving from personalized encounters with cultures to analytical and argumentative treatment of topics. Students are provided the opportunity to move across cultures and continents, interrogating and assessing authors' insights into our evolving transnational society.

The writers in *The New World Reader* present keen emotional and intellectual insights into our new global era. Most of the essays are relatively brief and provocative and serve as models for the types of personal, analytical, and argumentative papers that college composition teachers ask their students to write. The vast majority of these essays were written after September 11, 2001, and many are recent, dealing with such emerging issues as the "Arab Spring," climate change, and natural disasters. Drawn from a wide variety of authorial backgrounds and sources, and offering diverse angles of opinion and perspectives, the readings in this text lend themselves to thoughtful responses, class debate, small-group discussion, and online research. Some of the longer essays—for example, "The Children Will Keep Coming" by Óscar Martínez on the crisis and violence on the southern border of the United States, "The Bilingual Imagination" by Anna Menéndez on the benefits of bilingualism, and "America's Oh Sh*t Moment" by Niall Ferguson on the rise and fall of civilizations—orient students to those forms of discourse that they will encounter in humanities and social science courses. With introductions to chapters and writers, previewing questions, a three-part apparatus following each essay, two four-color photo essays, three appendices offering guidelines on conducting research in the global era and defining rhetorical and global terms, and extensive Web resources, supported by Cengage's MindTap, *The New World Reader* can serve as the core text in composition courses.

Features

Lively Selections in Chapters That Challenge Our Understanding of Ourselves and Others

The New World Reader presents sixty-three essays in eleven interrelated chapters. This edition includes fifteen new essays, focusing on contemporary views on global issues and challenges. The first chapter introduces students to the challenges of thinking, reading, and writing about their place in the new global era. Ten subsequent chapters, each consisting of essays that move from personal and op-ed pieces to more complex selections, focus on key aspects of our increasingly globalized culture, presenting ideas and themes that radiate through the text.

- **Chapter 1. Thinking, Reading, and Writing about the New Global Era.** This concise introductory chapter offers guidelines for students as they think, read, and write about key issues in twenty-first century America and the world. Clear thinking about the "new world order" involves knowledge of both what has gone before and what lies ahead, as well as mastery of the analytical and cognitive skills at the heart of the reading and writing processes. Four brief essays permit students to practice their critical thinking, reading, and writing skills: Nicholas D. Kristof on contrasting approaches to education in the United States and China, Susan Bordo on the globalization of eating disorders, Chrystia Freeland on the rise of the super-rich, and Amy Wilentz on the checkpoints along the border between the West Bank and Israel.

- **Chapter 2. New American Mosaic: Are We Becoming a Universal Nation?** Presenting compelling insights into the new American demographics, Ellis Cose, Bharati Mukherjee, Lee C. Bollinger, and others examine the ways in which both native and "fourth wave" patterns of acculturation are changing the face of the American nation while fostering a greater appreciation of other cultures. The chapter introduces students to the idea that globalization is not only "out there" but also "here"—a phenomenon that might very well be embodied (as Dwight N. Hopkins suggests in an essay) in President Barack Obama.

- **Chapter 3. America and the World: How Do Others Perceive Us?** This chapter explores the implications (and reverberations) of America's increasingly interventionist position on the global stage. Such essays as Mehdi Hasan's "Why I Could Never Hate America" and Fouad Ajami's "The Anti-Americans" explore shifting global attitudes toward the idea of America.

- **Chapter 4. Speaking in Tongues: Does Language Unify or Divide?** Presenting essays by Amy Tan, Ana Menéndez, Jhumpa Lahiri, and other provocative writers, this chapter explores the varied ways in which language forms identity and cultural relationships in our increasingly polyglot world.

- **Chapter 5. Global Relationships: Are Sex and Gender Roles Changing?** Across the globe, the perception of gender and the larger struggle for human rights vary in the amount of change they are undergoing. Luzette Alvarez examines changing attitudes toward marriage across the globe, and Mike Ceaser opens a "dark window" on human trafficking. The last essay, by Barbara Ehrenreich and Annette Fuentes, "Life on the Global Assembly Line," is a contemporary classic, detailing the exploitation of women in factories overseas.

- **Chapter 6. The Challenge of Globalization: What Are the Consequences?** The debate over globalization, whether framed in economic, political, environmental, or cultural terms, serves increasingly to define our lives in the twenty-first century. Essays by Thomas L. Friedman, Lisa Miller, Jared Diamond, and others argue the benefits and dangers of globalization.

- **Chapter 7. Culture Wars: Whose Culture Is It, Anyway?** This chapter examines the impact of popular American culture on the nation and on the world. From American-style shopping malls in developing nations to the broadcast of American sitcoms in Islamic nations, the new American land-scape has had a global impact. Among writers offering critical appraisals of the contemporary culture wars are Henry Louis Gates Jr., Luis Alberto Urrea, and Jamaica Kincaid.

- **Chapter 8. The Clash of Civilizations: Is Conflict Avoidable?** Building on the issues raised in the first seven chapters, this unit offers a critical exami-nation of the clash-of-civilizations debate. Essays by such prominent global analysts as Amartya Sen and Niall Ferguson alert students to the fact that today's global conflicts do not spring spontaneously from September 11, 2001, but rather have deep historical and political antecedents.

- **Chapter 9. The Age of Terror: What Is the Just Response?** This chapter takes at once a broader and deeper view of the causes and consequences of international terror. Suzanne Berne offers what has already become a con-temporary classic on her response to the World Trade Center disaster, while Nobel Prize winner Shirin Ebadi recounts the moment when she discovered that forces in Iran were planning to assassinate her.

- **Chapter 10. Global Aid: Can We Reduce Disease and Poverty?** Inspired by hopeful developments in the global struggle for economic justice, this chap-ter describes the many ways in which people worldwide are working to raise the living standards of their fellow citizens. Frontline reporting by Edwidge Danticat in Haiti and Anuradha Mittal in India, among other perspectives, captures the monumental responses by ordinary citizens and workers to natural disasters, control of diseases, and economic situations.

- **Chapter 11. The Fate of the Earth: Can We Preserve the Global Environment?** From global warming to weapons of mass destruction, the Earth's ecology faces major challenges. Essays by Al Gore, Jane Goodall, Bill McKibben, and others offer insights into how we might save the environment—and the world—for future generations.

Three Distinctive Appendices

- **Appendix A. Conducting Research in the Global Era.** This unit provides students with cutting-edge, practical information on the research skills they are expected to acquire during their college careers. The appendix stresses the new world of information technology that increasingly guides research and offers extensive guidelines on locating and evaluating print and online sources.

- **Appendix B. Glossary of Rhetorical Terms.** Concise definitions of dozens of key rhetorical terms provide a handy reference for students.

- **Appendix C. Glossary of Globalization Terms.** This appendix makes the vocabulary of globalization, drawn from political science, history, econom-ics, and other disciplines, accessible to students.

A Second Table of Contents by Rhetorical Mode

This rhetorical table of contents adds flexibility for teachers who prefer to organize their syllabus around such traditional forms as narration and description, comparison and contrast, process and causal analysis, and argumentation and persuasion.

Consistent Editorial Apparatus with a Sequenced Approach to Exercises

The New World Reader provides brief introductions to all chapters, highlighting the central issues raised by the writers in each section. All readings contain substantial author headnotes followed by a prereading question. Following each essay, three carefully sequenced sets totaling ten questions provide students with the opportunity to respond to the form and content of the text in ways that promote reading, writing, discussion, group work, and Internet exploration. Added to this edition is a discussion board to provide students the opportunity to share their responses with classmates.

- **Before Reading.** One question asks students to think about their current understanding or interpretation of an event or a condition relevant to the essay.

- **Thinking about the Essay.** Five questions build on the student's ability to comprehend how the writer's ideas develop through essential rhetorical and stylistic techniques.

- **Responding in Writing.** Three writing activities reflect and expand the questions in the first section, offering opportunities for students to write personal, analytical, and argumentative responses to the text.

- **Networking.** Two questions encourage small-group and Internet work. These questions promote collaborative learning and practice in the use of Internet and library sources to conduct deeper exploration and research into issues raised by the author.

Exciting Visual Materials

Students today need to read and analyze visual as well as written texts. *The New World Reader* integrates photographs, artwork, cartoons, graphs, and maps into the chapters. The fifth edition includes a popular four-color insert devoted to examining the question of "Culture or Conflict?" as well as a four-color insert on standards of global beauty. These illustrations add a visual dimension to aid students' comprehension of the issues raised by written texts. All visual materials offer questions for informed response and analysis.

New to this Edition

For the fifth edition of *The New World Reader*, we have further strengthened the emphasis on contemporary global issues by offering essays on very recent topics, trends, and events. Students and teachers will be able to ponder the performance of Barack Obama as a new type of American president; examine climate change from competing perspectives; explore the violence of borders and uprisings across the globe; consider the impact of social media on international affairs and cultures; and interrogate the causes underlying the surge in worldwide human trafficking. Such current issues, integrated into the book's well-received and flexible pattern of organization, enhance the book's appeal.

- **Fifteen New Selections.** Provocative and compelling up-to-date essays include work by such well-known authors, commentators, public advocates, and intellectuals as Jhumpa Lahiri, Firoozeh Dumas, Atul Gawande, Niall Ferguson, and Naomi Klein.

- **Exciting New Authors.** To introduce students to emerging writers with fresh ideas and perspectives—and also to established professionals who might not be as well known—we present Michael T. Osterholm on the possibility of the uncontrolled spread of Ebola, Ana Menéndez on the impact of a second language or of several languages on the development of the brain, Óscar Martínez on the roots of the child migrant crisis, Shiraz Maher on the development and future of the Islamic State, Morgan Bazilian on the importance of energy development as a means to alleviate the problems associated with poverty, and other compelling new authors.

- **Fresh Visuals for Critical Thinking and Response.** Drawn from a wide range of modes, including photographs, advertisements, and cartoons, the new images offer students and teachers the opportunity to investigate stylistic and thematic links across print and visual dimensions in a global context.

- **An Updated Research Section (Appendix A).** The MLA citations have been updated to conform to the most current formats in the seventh edition of the *MLA Handbook for Writers of Research Papers* and on the MLA home page.

Online Resources

MindTap® English for Muller's *The New World Reader*, 5th edition engages your students to become better thinkers, communicators, and writers by blending your course materials with content that supports every aspect of the writing process.

- Interactive activities on grammar and mechanics promote application in student writing

- Easy-to-use paper management system helps prevent plagiarism and allows for electronic submission, grading, and peer review

- A vast database of scholarly sources with video tutorials and examples supports every step of the research process

- Professional tutoring guides students from rough drafts to polished writing

- Visual analytics track student progress and engagement

- Seamless integration into your campus learning management system keeps all your course materials in one place

MindTap lets you compose your course, your way.

The **Online Instructor's Resource Manual** provides an abundance of materials to give instructors maximum flexibility in planning and customizing their courses. This manual helps instructors prepare for class more quickly and effectively with such resources as discussion suggestions and suggested answers for questions on the text readings. The Instructor's Resource Manual can be downloaded by accessing cengagebrain.com.

Acknowledgments

This book is the result of very special relationships—and considerable serendipity—among friends, collaborators, reviewers, and supporters. I was first alerted to the possibility of developing a global reader by my good friend and former colleague John Chaffee, an acclaimed author and specialist in critical thinking and philosophy. To John I offer my gratitude for his faith in an old friend.

I learned long ago that any college text is only as good as the editorial staff developing it, and here there are several special people who saved me much grief, improved the book, and prevented me from sounding at times like a turgid academician. First and foremost, I want to especially acknowledge Sylvia Holladay, who made significant contributions to this edition. Sylvia, with my content developer Erin Bosco, assembled the text with incredible intelligence, grace, and agility, and kept things on track. Thanks also go to Kate Derrick, product manager, who supported *The New World Reader* from the start. I am grateful to Yashmita Hota, the content production manager, for her careful attention to detail. I am also grateful to Ann Hoffman, Farah Fard, Venkat Narayanan, and Kavitha Balasundaram for their fine work in tracking down permissions.

I would like to thank my friend and agent, John Wright, who negotiated the contract for this book. Finally, I am grateful to my wife, Laleh Mostafavi-Muller, a specialist in international relations and the Middle East, who offered support and advice as this book evolved.

Several reviewers wrote detailed appraisals of the manuscript, recommendations for changes and improvements, and praise and cautionary advice, and their collective wisdom informs this book. Thanks go to the following reviewers for the fifth edition:

Hong Ai Bai, *Long Island University Post*
Marie Hendry, *Southeastern Louisiana University*
Edward McKenna, *Pima Community College*

James McPherson, *Pima Community College*
Harvey Rubinstein, *Hudson County Community College*
Chris Seahorn, *University of Houston–Clear Lake*

We continue to be grateful for the insights of reviewers whose suggestions helped in the development of previous editions of *The New World Reader*:

Heather Akers, *University of Alabama Tuscaloosa*
Cathryn Amdahl, *Harrisburg Area Community College*
Pat Artz, *Bellevue University*
Maryam Barrie, *Washtenaw Community College*
Daniel Bergen, *Marquette University*
Elaine Bobrove, *Camden County College*
James Borton, *University of South Carolina, Sumter*
Roxana Cazan, *Indiana University Bloomington*
Julia Chavez, *Saint Martin's University*
Sandra L. Clark, *University of Wyoming*
Debra L. Cumberland, *Winona State University*
John Dailey, *New Jersey City University*
Violet Dutcher, *Eastern Mennonite University*
Marti Eads, *Eastern Mennonite University*
Stephen F. Evans, *University of Kansas*
Tyler Farrell, *Marquette University*
Eileen Ferretti, *Kingsborough Community College*
Kathleen Fitzpatrick, *Daniel Webster College*
Jeannine Fontaine, *Duquesne University*
Donna Rae Foran, *Marquette University*
Len Gougeon, *University of Scranton*
Tim Gustafson, *University of Minnesota*
Jeff Henderson, *Kalamazoo Valley Community College*
Eric Hyman, *Fayetteville State University*
Deborah Kanter, *Hudson County Community College*
Katherine Kapitan, *Buena Vista University*
Maria Keaton, *Marquette University*
William K. Lawrence, *George Mason University*
Anna Maheshwari, *Schoolcraft College*
Steven Mayers, *City College of San Francisco*
Dr. Nancy Nanney, *Chair, Humanities Division, West Virginia University at Parkersburg*
Therese Novotny, *Marquette University*
Pearlie Peters, *Rider University*
David Pryor, *University of the Incarnate Word*
Sorina Riddle, *Pfeiffer University*
Avantika Rohatgi, *San Jose State University*
Gail Samis, *Salisbury University English Department*
Hale Savard, *Golden West College*

Shelina Shariff, *Baruch College*
Ghanashyam Sharma, *University of Louisville*
Renee Schlueter, *Kirkwood Community College*
Henry Schwarz, *Georgetown University*
Karl Shaddox, *University of Alabama, Huntsville*
Micheline M. Soong, *Hawaii Pacific University*
Anne Meade Stockdell-Giesler, Ph.D., *University of Tampa*
Grace Urbanski, *Marquette University*
Randall J. VanderMey, *Westmont College*
William Vaughn, *Central Missouri State University*
Usha Wadhwani, *Hudson County Community College*
Mark Wiley, *California State University, Long Beach*
Rosemary Winslow, *Catholic University of America*
Julie Yen, *California State University, Sacramento*

—*Gilbert H. Muller*

Thinking, Reading, and Writing about the New Global Era

Global forces are shaping societies, nations, and international systems as never before. Evolving trends—among them, the spread of worldwide communications networks, the "clash of civilizations," terrorism in many regions and most continents, environmental challenges, and transnational population shifts—suggest that the last century, the "American century" as *Time* magazine's Henry Luce called it, is over and we have entered a new era. In a world where much seems increasingly interconnected, it is no longer sufficient to think locally. Instead, we need to reflect critically on new global realities, assessing the ways in which other peoples, belief systems, traditions, and cultures affect our lives. In the twenty-first century, our well-being and arguably our very survival will depend on our ability to harness the forces unleashed by the dynamics of the new global era.

Regardless of what we choose to call this emerging era—the post-9/11 world, the new world order, the post–Cold War period, the age of **globalization**, the information or digital age—we exist today in a global landscape characterized by rapid transformations. To comprehend these transformations, we should not confuse, as the historian Francis Fukuyama reminds us, our national needs with our universal ones. We must also consider what writer and *New York Times* syndicated columnist Thomas Friedman terms the "super-story." For Friedman (who asserts in one of his books that the world is "flat"), the super-story involves all the trends of globalization, including world trade, the formation of transnational economic and political alignments, the spread of **information technology**, and even new dating and marriage patterns, which affect national and transnational behavior. Writers like Fukuyama and Friedman offer insights into global challenges and the arguments surrounding them. To meet these challenges, we must recognize that we are connected to one another both in the United States and around the world. No longer isolated by two oceans and seemingly immune to the world's turmoil, we suddenly have to reexamine and reargue our complex fate.

An Azad University student uses an Internet café in Tehran, Iran. Access to the Internet is still highly restricted in some countries and by some cultures.

Thinking about the Image

1. Closely examine all of the details of this photograph. (For example, what is on the table next to this woman's elbow?) In what ways does this photograph reinforce standard images in the American media of Muslim women? In what ways is the photograph surprising?
2. Do you agree that access to the Internet provides a kind of empowerment? Why or why not?
3. In her essay "When Afghanistan Was at Peace," Margaret Atwood notes of her book *The Handmaid's Tale* (partly inspired by her travels in Afghanistan) that "there is freedom to and freedom from. But how much of the first should you have to give up in order to assure the second?" How might the woman in this photograph respond?
4. Do a search for Islamic Azad University. Visit their website and compare it to that of your own college. What are the similarities between the two schools and how they present themselves? How are they different?

In order to comprehend our complex fate and prepare for life in the twenty-first century, we will explore in this book some of the key ways we perceive and interact with our new world. In our flattened world, as Thomas Friedman terms it, where everything seems close and immediate—where cell phones, cable, and the Internet connect us instantaneously to a polyglot universe of people and events—we will try to establish parameters for what it means to exist in this global era. Family, community, state, and nation no longer suffice in the construction of our new identity, for today we are citizens of the world. As such, we have to find ways to manage change, negotiate transnational borders, understand diverse viewpoints, and defuse major **conflicts** if we are to survive and prosper in the new global era.

Critical Thinking

Are you ready for the brave new world of the twenty-first century, the new global era? Do you know enough about *globalization*—the interplay of cultures, societies, economies, and political systems—that is changing your world? Assuredly, you will study this new era in various courses, prepare for careers in it, sit next to people from around the world in your classes, and perhaps even marry into it. The three thousand people from around the world who died in the World Trade Center disaster were working, collaborating, and living in this new world. Among the dead were civilians and citizens from sixty-two countries, including 250 Indians, 200 Pakistanis, 200 Britons, and 23 Japanese. Sadly, there were other individuals—those who perpetrated this event—who felt threatened by the new international order represented by the 9/11 victims.

Your success in college hinges in part on your ability to make choices based on knowledge, experience, and careful reflection about the new world order. You will have to think critically about the global contexts that influence you and your nation. **Critical thinking** is clear thinking: it is a type of mental practice in which you respond to issues logically and, for the purposes of this course, deal with texts and the meanings they generate among class members. Often you will have to *rethink* your opinions, beliefs, and attitudes, and this, too, is a hallmark of critical thinking—the willingness to discard weak ideas or biased opinions for more mature or simply more logical intellectual opinions. For example, how do you define a *terrorist*? Why would Americans define a terrorist as anyone who takes the lives of innocent civilians, while others around the world view such individuals not as terrorists but as freedom fighters or defenders of the faith? Such questions do not admit easy or facile responses. They require deep and complex thought, for we live in a complex world.

To work effectively with the readings in this text, which deal with varieties of global experience, you need to develop a repertoire of critical thinking skills. In all likelihood, you have come to college possessing many of these skills.

But it is important to refine, strengthen, and expand these skills to achieve a degree of authority over any given body of knowledge. How, then, do you think critically about—in other words, study and interpret—any given text? How do you look closely at the ideas of writers and evaluate them? How do you respond critically in writing? Having a repertoire of critical thinking skills creates the foundation for being a critical reader and writer.

Every writer in this textbook had a project much like the projects that you will develop: to articulate clearly and convincingly a key idea or nucleus of related ideas about an aspect of human experience, whether in the United States or elsewhere. They developed their ideas by using the repertoire of critical thinking skills—which for our purposes we can associate with key rhetorical strategies. **Rhetoric** is the art of writing or speaking, often to convince an audience about a particular issue. **Rhetorical strategies** are the key patterns that writers employ in this effort to clarify ideas and opinions. We divide these patterns into three major groups: *narration* and *description*; *exposition* (consisting of definition, comparison and contrast, illustration, process analysis, causal analysis, and classification); and *argument* and *persuasion*. These are not just the classic patterns of rhetoric but also powerful ways of thinking about and understanding our world.

Research demonstrates that different people think most effectively in different ways, or **cognitive styles**. You might like to argue; however, hopefully you argue not in the style of *Crossfire* or *Hardball*, where viewpoints often are reduced simplistically to positions on the political "right" or "left," but rather with reasonableness and respect. Or you might be great at telling a story to make a point. Or perhaps you have a talent for analyzing global events. All writing reflects one or more of those cognitive styles that we see reflected in narration and description, exposition, and argumentation. You can gain control over your reading and writing practices by selecting from among these major rhetorical strategies or thinking styles.

Narration and Description

Narration can be briefly described as telling a story, and **description** as the use of vivid sensory detail—sight, sound, smell, taste, touch—to convey either a specific or an overall impression. Although narration and description are not always treated in studies of reasoning, it is foolish not to consider these strategies as aspects of the thinking process. The study of narration and description reveals that this type of thinking can produce authority in college writing.

Some composition theorists actually believe that narration and description, relying as they do on the creation of a personal voice—your personal response—is the gateway to successful student writing. For example, where were you during a recent national or global crisis? How did you feel? What was your response? How did you get through the day and the aftermath? If you were answering these questions in an essay, you would need to employ a special kind of thinking and reflection, one in which you get in touch with your feelings and find vivid ways to express and make sense of them. It would be useless to say that you are not engaged in reasoning because you are employing narration and description—perhaps even inserting **visual texts** downloaded from the Web—to arrive at your personal form of truth about the event. In all likelihood, you would also state or imply a **thesis** (a main idea) and even other generalizations about the event that go beyond pure narration or description. In fact, the vast majority of essays, while they might reflect one or two dominant rhetorical patterns or styles of organizational thought, tend to reveal mixed patterns or approaches to the writing process.

Exposition

Exposition is a relatively broad term that defines a type of writing in which you explain or convey information about a subject. Expository writing is the form of writing that in all likelihood you will be required to produce in college courses. In an **expository essay**, you set forth facts and ideas—in other words, detailed explanations—to support a thesis, or main idea. As a form of critical thinking, expository writing provides a way of clarifying many of the cultural, political, and economic forces that mold global events today.

To produce effective expository essays, you need to develop skill and fluency in the use of several key rhetorical strategies—among them, *definition*, *comparison* and *contrast*, *illustration*, *causal analysis*, *process analysis*, and *classification*. The use of any one or several of the patterns will dictate your approach to a given topic or problem, and the effective application of these strategies will help to create an authoritative voice, for the readers of your expository essay will see that you are using these rhetorical patterns to think consistently about a body of information and present it coherently. Once again, you employ specific reasoning abilities to make sense of your world.

When you consider the international events that increasingly shape both local and personal life—indeed, that are shaping your identity—it is clear that you must think critically about the best way to approach these events. The way you are able to reason about events and the perspectives you may develop on a particular problem will inform your understanding of the subject and your ability to convey this understanding in writing.

Think about a term that already has been introduced and that you will encounter in numerous essays in this collection: *globalization*. This is one of the many terms that you will have to look at closely as you come to an understanding of the global forces shaping lives, identities, **cultures**, and civilizations in the twenty-first century. How might you unravel the significance of this word, gain authority over it, explore its relevance to various texts that you will read, and ultimately express your understanding of it in writing?

To start, *definition* of a complex term like *globalization* might be in order. (Definitions for many of the key terms relating to globalization appear in Appendix C.) As a way of thinking about a subject, a **definition** is a statement about what a word or phrase means. It is always useful to be able to state this meaning in one or two sentences, as we have already done earlier in this chapter: "the interplay of cultures, societies, economies, and political systems" in the world today. But entire books have been and are being written about globalization, for it is a complex and controversial subject. We call these longer explanations **extended definitions**, which typically rely on other rhetorical strategies to expand the field of understanding. Finally, you might very well have a highly personal understanding of a term like *globalization*. Perhaps you have witnessed or read about workers in overseas factories producing Nikes for a few cents a day and consequently have mixed feelings about the Nikes you are wearing today. In this instance, globalization has a special meaning for you; we term this special meaning a **stipulative definition** because it is highly colored by your experience. Remember, as with all discussions of rhetorical strategies, you are developing and polishing critical thinking skills. With definition, you are taking abstract ideas and making them comprehensible and concrete.

A second way to approach globalization would be through comparative thinking. **Comparison and contrast** is a cognitive process wherein you consider the similarities and differences of things. Imagine that your instructor asks you to write an essay titled "Two Ways of Looking at Globalization." The title itself suggests that you have to employ a comparative method to explain and analyze this phenomenon. You would need a thesis to unify this comparative approach, and three or four key points of comparison and/or contrast to support it. The purpose of comparison and contrast is usually to state a preference for one thing over the other or to judge which one is superior. For example, if you maintain that globalization is about inclusion, while those opposing globalization define it as a new form of colonialism or exploitation, you are evaluating and judging two positions.

Any approach to a subject requires a thoughtful and accurate use of **illustration**—that is, the use of examples to support an idea. Illustration, which we also call **exemplification**, enables you to make abstract ideas concrete. Normally, several examples or one key extended example serves to illustrate your main and minor ideas about a subject. If, for example, you wanted to demonstrate that globalization is a trend that will foster understanding among nations and peoples, you would have to provide facts, statistics, examples, details drawn from personal experience, testimonials, and expert opinions to support your position. Illustration is the bedrock of virtually all ways of thinking, reading, and writing about a topic. Whether telling a story, explaining a topic, or arguing a point (which we deal with in the next section), illustration provides the evidence required to produce a powerful text. Illustration teaches the value of using the information of others—typically the texts of others—in order to build a structure for your own paper.

Causal analysis and *process analysis* are two other forms of intellectual practice that can shape your critical approaches to topics. **Causal analysis**, sometimes called **cause-and-effect analysis**, answers the basic human question *Why?* It deals with a chain of happenings and the predictable consequences of these happenings. Like all the forms of thinking presented in this introductory section, causal analysis parallels our everyday thinking patterns. When we ask why terrorists attacked some city or tourist destination, why so many people in the **Third World** oppose globalization, or why the Internet can foster international cooperation, we are looking for causes or conditions and examining consequences and results (or effects). **Process analysis**, on the other hand, answers the question *How?* It takes things apart in order to understand how they operate or function. Many varieties of process analysis deal with "how-to" subjects involving steps in a correct sequence—for example, how to prepare fajitas. But process analysis is also central to the treatment of broad global trends. How did globalization come about? How do we combat overpopulation of the planet? How do we prevent global warming? Process analysis can help explain the subtle and complex nature of relationships existing within a chain of events.

The last major form of exposition is **classification**, in which information is divided into categories or groups for the purpose of clarifying relationships among them. Some experts would term classification a "higher-order" reasoning skill. In actuality, classification again resembles a great deal of everyday thinking: we classify friends, teachers, types of music, types of cuisine, and so forth. Classification is a way of taking a large body of information and breaking it down (dividing it) into categories for better understanding. It relies on analytical ability—critical thinking that explores parts within a whole. For example, if you were to write an essay titled "Approaches to Globalization," you could establish three categories—political, economic, and cultural—to divide your subject into coherent parts. The secret to using classification effectively is to avoid the temptation to have your categories overlap excessively. (Did you notice that classification was used to organize this section on exposition?)

Writers skilled in exposition are smart and credible. They write with authority because they can think clearly in a variety of modes. With exposition you make critical thinking choices, selecting those rhetorical strategies that provide the best degree of understanding for your readers, your audience.

Argument and Persuasion

Argument is a special type of reasoning. It appears in texts—written, spoken, or visual—that express a debatable **point of view**. Stated more rigorously, argument is a process of reasoning in which the truth of some main **proposition** (or claim) is shown to be true (that is, based on the truth of other minor propositions or premises). Closely allied to argument is **persuasion**, in which you invite an audience through rational, emotional, and ethical appeals to adopt your viewpoint or embark on a course of action. Aristotle in his *Rhetoric* spoke of the appeals as *logos*, *ethos*, and *pathos*—reason, beliefs, and emotion working together to guide an audience to a proper understanding or judgment of an issue. Argument—the rational component in persuasion—enables you to think responsibly about global issues and present your viewpoints about them in a convincing fashion.

The dividing line between various forms of exposition and argumentation is a fine one. Where does a *thesis* leave off and a *claim* (the main argumentative point) begin? Some experts would say that "everything's an argument," and in the arena of global affairs this seems to be true. Issues of religion, race, class, gender, and culture are woven into the very fabric of both our local and global lives, and all of these issues trigger vigorous positions and responses. And the international environment is such that conflict and change seemingly provoke argumentative viewpoints and positions.

The distinctive feature of argumentative thinking is that you give reasons in support of a **claim** or **major proposition**. The claim is what you are trying to prove in an argument. The **reasons**, also called **minor propositions**, offer proof for the major claim. And you support each minor proposition with **evidence**—those various types of illustration mentioned in the previous section as well as logical explanations or abstract thinking used to buttress your basic reasons. If you don't "have the facts"—let's say about global inequality, the Kyoto Protocol on Climate Change, or the worldwide reach of McDonald's—you will not be able to stake a claim and defend it vigorously.

The British philosopher Steven Toulmin emphasizes that underpinning any argument or claim is a **warrant**, which he defines as an assumption, belief, or principle that is taken for granted. The warrant validates the link between the claim and the support. It might be stated or unstated. Many practices of nations, beliefs of citizens, and policies of political groups rest on such warrants. For example, if you assume that the United States is now the world's only **superpower**—a warrant—you can use this principle to claim that the United States should use its power to intervene in rogue states. Or if you believe that people have the right to free themselves from oppression—a warrant at the heart of the Declaration of Independence—you might use this warrant to claim that oppressed citizens have the right to start revolutions to break their chains.

Consider the warrants concerning the war on terrorism embedded in the following paragraph, written by Harold Hongju Koh, a former assistant secretary of state in the administration of President Bill Clinton and a professor of international law at Yale University:

> Our enemies in this war are out to destroy our society precisely because it is open, tolerant, pluralistic and democratic. In its place, they seek to promote one that is closed, vengeful, repressive and absolutist. To secure genuine victory, we must make sure that they fail, not just in their assault on our safety but also in their challenge to our most fundamental values.
>
> —"Preserving American Values"[1]

1. Harold Hongju Koh, "Preserving American Values," from *The Age of Terror: America and the World after September 11* by Strobe Talbott and Nayan Chanda (New York: Basic Books, 2002), p. 169.

Here the writer predicates his claim about the need to achieve victory over our "enemies" on an entire catalog of "fundamental values" that in essence are warrants—that is, principles and beliefs. Also notice the way in which he employs the comparative method to structure his argument in this brief but revealing paragraph.

By their explosive or contentious nature, many global subjects and international issues call for argumentative responses. Your topic might be global warming, the Patriot Act, immigration along the United States–Mexico border, outsourcing of jobs, or the possibility of peace between Israel and the Palestinians. In such instances, your opinions and beliefs will require you to recognize that other people, nations, and cultures might approach the argument from entirely different perspectives. Thus, one unique challenge when developing arguments on international topics is the need to cross cultural boundaries, understand the attitudes and assumptions held by people outside your country, and contend with diverging opinions in a global context.

Stated differently, arguments on global topics require you to recognize competing global perspectives. In all likelihood, your argumentative paper will be grounded in a Western tradition based in part on rationalism, Judeo-Christian values, and various systems of freedom and individual rights. (It will be based as well on classic Greek and Roman principles of argument.) But warrants inherent in the Western tradition do not necessarily make your claim universal. Consider that newspapers around the world use almost two dozen euphemisms for *terrorist*, including *attacker, bomber, commando, criminal, extremist, fighter, guerrilla, hostage-taker, insurgent, militant, radical, rebel,* and *separatist*. (On the website www.newssafety.com, Reuters' Nidal al-Mughrabi offers advice on this matter to fellow reporters in Gaza: "Never use the word terrorist or terrorism describing Palestinian gunmen and militants; people consider them heroes of the conflict.") How you define and interpret a word can determine the method and purpose of an argument.

Not everyone experiences the world or argues global issues from your system of opinions and beliefs. Fortunately, the Internet and the World Wide Web, various translation engines that open international newspaper sites to research, broadcast and visual clips, and even international discussion groups offer you ways to interact globally with other writers, their texts, and their arguments. By searching globally for non-U.S. viewpoints and contending with them, you will be able to write distinctive argumentative papers that go beyond mainstream propositions.

Before launching arguments over "homeland security," the pros and cons of globalization, the Arab–Israeli conflict, the rise of interracial and intercultural dating, or any other global or transnational subject, you once again have an obligation to think clearly and critically about these matters. Argumentation provides a logical way to present a viewpoint, deal fairly with opposing viewpoints, and hopefully arrive at a consensus. The psychologist Carl Rogers offers a new way of looking at argumentation when he suggests that both the communicator presenting an argument and the audience are participants in a dialogue—much like psychotherapy—in which they try to arrive at knowledge, understanding, and truth. At its best, argument results in intelligent discourse, a meeting of the minds, and even a strengthening of civic values.

Thinking about an Essay

China: The Educated Giant

NICHOLAS D. KRISTOF

Nicholas D. Kristof is a reporter and columnist for *The New York Times*. He was born in Chicago in 1959 and received a BA degree from Harvard University (1981) and a law degree from Oxford University (1983). He also has a diploma in Arabic language from the American University in Cairo. He writes: "Since my student days, when I began to travel with a backpack around Africa and Asia, I have had a fascination with foreign lands, cultures, and languages." Kristof and his wife, Sheryl WuDunn, who is also a *New York Times* reporter, won the Pulitzer Prize for their coverage of the Tiananmen Square massacre in 1989. Based in Asia for many years, Kristof and WuDunn have used their experiences there to write *China Awakes* (1994), *The Japanese Economy at the Millennium* (1999), and *Thunder from the East: Portrait of a Rising Asia* (2000). In the following essay, which appeared in *The Saturday Evening Post* in 2007, Kristof makes a provocative claim about the relative merits of the Chinese and American educational systems.

With China's trade surplus with the United States soaring, the tendency in the U.S. will be to react with tariffs and other barriers. But instead we should take a page from the Chinese book and respond by boosting education.   1

One reason China is likely to overcome the U.S. as the world's most important country in this century is that China puts more effort into building human capital than we do.   2

The area in south Guangdong Province is my wife's ancestral home 3
town. Sheryl's grandparents left villages here because they thought they
could find better opportunities for their children in "Meiguo"—"Beautiful
Country," as the U.S. is called in Chinese. And they did. At Sheryl's family
reunions, you feel inadequate without a doctorate.

But that educational gap between China and America is shrinking rap- 4
idly. I visited several elementary and middle schools accompanied by two of
my children. And in general, the level of math taught even in peasant schools
is similar to that in my kids' own excellent schools in the New York area.

My kids' school system doesn't offer foreign languages until the sev- 5
enth grade. These Chinese peasants begin English studies in either first
grade or third grade, depending on the school.

Frankly, my daughter got tired of being dragged around schools and 6
having teachers look patronizingly at her schoolbooks and say, "Oh, we do
that two grades younger."

There are, I think, four reasons why Chinese students do so well. 7

First, Chinese students are hungry for education and advancement and 8
work harder. In contrast, U.S. children average 900 hours a year in class
and 1,023 in front of a television.

Here in Sheryl's ancestral village, the students show up at school at 9
about 6:30 a.m. to get extra tutoring before classes start at 7:30. They go
home for a lunch break at 11:20 and then are back at school from 2:00
p.m. until 5:00. They do homework every night and weekend, and an hour
or two of homework each day during their eight-week summer vacation.

The second reason is [that] China has an enormous cultural respect for 10
education, part of its Confucian legacy, so governments and families alike
pour resources into education. Teachers are respected and compensated far
better, financially and emotionally, in China than in America.

Recently, I wrote about the boomtown of Dongguan, which had no 11
colleges when I first visited it 20 years ago. The town devotes 21 percent
of its budget to education, and it now has four universities. An astonishing
58 percent of the residents age 18 to 22 are enrolled in a university.

A third reason is that Chinese believe that those who get the best grades 12
are the hardest workers. In contrast, Americans say in polls that the best
students are the ones who are innately the smartest. The upshot is that
Chinese kids never have an excuse for mediocrity.

Chinese education has its own problems, including bribes and fees to 13
get into good schools, huge classes of 50 or 60 students, second-rate equipment and lousy universities. But the progress in the last quarter-century is
breathtaking.

It's also encouraging that so many Chinese will shake their heads over 14
this column and say it really isn't so. They will complain that Chinese

schools teach rote memorization but not creativity or love of learning. That kind of debate is good for the schools and has already led to improvements in English instruction, so that urban Chinese students can communicate better in English [than] Japanese or South Koreans.

After I visited Sheryl's ancestral village, I posted a video of it on the 15 Web. Soon I was astonished to see an exciting posting on my blog from a woman who used to live in that village.

Litao Mai, probably one of my distant in-laws, grew up in a house she 16 could see on my video. Her parents had only a third-grade education, but she became the first person in the village to go to college. She now works for Merrill Lynch in New York and describes herself as "a little peasant girl" transformed into "a capitalist on Wall Street."

That is the magic of education, and there are 1.3 billion more behind 17 Ms. Mai.

So let's not respond to China's surpluses by putting up trade barriers. 18 Rather, let's do as we did after the Soviet Union's launch of Sputnik in 1957: raise our own education standards to meet the competition.

Questions for Critical Thinking

1. What is *your* opinion of China as an emerging world power? What assumptions and attitudes do you bring to the subject? How open are you to an essay titled "China: The Educated Giant"? Why would such a topic invite—almost demand—careful critical thinking? What assumptions do you think Kristof makes about his readers?

2. Why does Kristof refer to his family in this essay? Do you agree or disagree with the effectiveness of this strategy? Answer these questions in groups of three or four class members.

3. Where does Kristof use narration and description to organize part of the essay? What is the effect?

4. Kristof employs numerous expository strategies in this essay. Locate and identify them, explaining what they contribute to the substance and the organization of the essay.

5. Does Kristof construct an argument in this essay, or is he simply reporting an educational or cultural development? How do you know?

Reading Critically

Most of the essays in this book were written within the last ten years, but the ideas in them run through the history of cultures and civilizations. Consequently, we have to "read" the contemporary ideas contained in these selections through lenses that scan centuries and continents. We have to read critically—analyzing, interpreting, and reassessing new and old ideas in the light of our own experience. When, for example, a writer accuses the United States of **imperialism**, we need to understand the history of this phenomenon as well as interrogate its relevance to the American experience. Is the United States the new imperial power? Are we facing the same conflicts and contradictions that imperial powers through the ages have confronted? To read actively is to be able to think critically about ideas in texts that have deep roots in world history.

As you read the selections in this book, you will discover that careful, critical reading about global issues can complement the talent you already have as a member of the generation that has grown up during the **information age**. Some say that college students have so much trouble with written texts because their culture privileges new forms of technology—call it visual or computer literacy—over older forms of print, like the essays you find in this collection. But just as you probably think critically about information acquired through electronic and visual media, you can readily acquire an ability to read written texts critically and to respond to them in discussion and writing. One of the paradoxes of our era is that although we are spending more and more time in front of our computers, we also are buying more books and magazines.

Our most respected thinkers still use the written word to convey their ideas about the issues of our day. They might post these texts on the Web in various forms ranging from online magazines to blogs, but the reality is that these texts appear before us as products of the print universe. Only print can fully convey the intricacy of ideas writers have about our contemporary lives. Speech cannot rival the power of the printed word, as our propensity for tuning out the "talking heads" on television demonstrates. Moreover, with speech we rarely have the opportunity to go back and evaluate what has been said; with written texts, we can assess the presentation of ideas. As a reader, therefore, you have an obligation to deal seriously with the ideas presented by the writers (many of them famous) in this book and to respond critically and coherently to them. You need to learn strategies that will permit you to read texts in this manner.

There are various ways in which readers can respond to any given text. You, a reader, bring varieties of personal experience—and indeed your personality—to a written text. Your social and cultural background also affects your response to texts. In short, there are several ways to respond critically to both written and visual communication.

You bring numerous personal experiences to the reading of any given text. After all, you have attitudes and opinions, likes and dislikes—a unique range of experience. You construct meaning through these personal experiences, which are rooted in your cultural background and community. If, for example, you read an essay on Islam (there are several in this book) and are Muslim yourself, you probably have personal experience of the text that might or might not be shared by other members of the class.

Along with personal experience, you also *think* about a text in special ways. Cognitive psychologists assert that when you were very young, you probably could not always distinguish fantasy from reality (which is why young children respond so powerfully to fairy tales and cartoons). When you were older—say in junior high school—you were able to seek one true meaning in a text. Then, in your high school years, you developed an ability to consider multiple meanings and interpretations. The critical intelligence that you bring to a college environment is one that must reason, hypothesize, argue, classify, define, and predict as you contend with any given text that deals with complex global issues.

Of course, the text itself is also important: you cannot center all of its meaning on your personal experience. In fact, some teachers will tell you to eliminate personal experience, moralizing, and impressionistic opinion from your writing and focus on the intrinsic meaning of the text. Thus, you become a hunter of the "truth" of a text, which reveals itself in the language, style, and structure of the work. Fortunately, there are rhetorical strategies and **conventions** that govern texts (many introduced in this book) that will help you to discover these formal truths.

The college classroom—especially the English classroom—is the place where you wrestle with the truths of a text. In this environment, you are not an isolated reader but part of a community of readers. This community or society of readers reflects the diverse features of gender, race and ethnicity, class, education, religion, politics, region, and nation. As a member of this group, you want to share insights with others for the purpose of understanding or consensus (if there is an argument framing the text and discussion). You do not surrender your personal impressions of a text as much as you become a member of what the critic Stanley Fish calls the "interpretive community." In this book, every essay contains an exercise designed to strengthen your reading and writing skills within smaller interpretative or collaborative communities.

Finally, the act of reading critically leads you into the deepest regions of culture and the forces that reveal and inform our experience of the world. Cultural theorists contend that deeply held worldviews and ideologies—for instance, **capitalism** and **socialism**, or Islam and Christianity—are the bedrock of any social configuration. Various institutions, power structures, cultural conventions, gender roles, and "fields of discourse," like medicine and law, dictate the ways we respond to a text. As you read the essays in the next chapter, "New American Mosaic," from a cultural perspective, you will have to assess the way your viewpoint on **immigration** has been formed by these deep structures of culture. Through such analysis, you can avoid biased, nationalistic, and religiously intolerant ways of thinking about a text, engaging instead in critical thought and sound, reflective argument.

When reading argumentative essays in a global context, you should consider these critical questions:

- What is the purpose of the text? What claim or main idea does the writer want to develop?
- What is the writer's background? Was the writer born in the United States or overseas?

- Who is the writer's audience? Does the writer demonstrate an awareness that U.S. and non-U.S. readers might respond differently to the content and method of the text?
- Does the writer consider the values, assumptions, and experiences of readers from other cultures?
- Does the writer treat opposing viewpoints or perspectives, especially if they come from non-U.S. sources, accurately and fairly?
- What reasons or minor propositions support the writer's claim?
- How accurate and representative is the writer's supporting evidence? Does the writer rely solely on evidence from U.S. sources, or does credible evidence from reliable global sources also appear?
- Is the shape of the writer's argument logically convincing?

Steps to Reading Critically

With a basic understanding of how ways of reading influence your approach to a text, you can now follow steps that will enable you to read critically. You should treat any "system" for critical reading flexibly, but with the conviction that it is important to extract and evaluate the meanings that professional writers want to convey to their audience. Here are guidelines for effective critical reading.

1. *Start with the conviction that critical reading, like critical thinking, requires active reading.* It is not like passively watching television. Instead, critical reading involves intellectual engagement with the text. Consequently, read with a pen or pencil in hand, underlining or circling key words, phrases, and sentences, asking questions in the margins, and making observations—a process called **annotation**. These annotations will serve as guidelines for a second reading and additional responses in writing.
2. *Pause from time to time to reflect on what you are reading.* What is the writer's main idea? What are his or her basic methods (recall the rhetorical strategies) for developing ideas? What **tone**, or voice, does the writer convey, and why? What is the writer's **purpose**? Is it to argue an issue, explain, analyze, or what? What varieties of illustration or evidence does the writer provide?
3. *Employ your critical thinking skills to interrogate the text.* Use some of the **reader response theories** to explore its deepest meanings. For example, test the text against your personal experience or against certain cultural preconceptions. Think critically about the writer's argument, if there is one, and whether it withstands the test of logic and the conventions of argumentation.
4. *Consider the implied **audience** for the text.* How does the writer address you as part of this audience? Do you actually feel that you are part of this primary audience, a secondary reader, or largely forgotten or excluded? If you feel excluded, what features of the essay have caused you to be removed from this community of readers?

How might you make yourself a part of this "universe of discourse" nevertheless?
5. *Write a **précis**, or **summary**, of the essay.* These "shorthand" techniques will help you to focus your thoughts and prepare for class discussions and subsequent writing assignments.

These five steps for critical reading should suggest that critical reading, much like critical thinking and critical writing, involves rereading. If you follow these guidelines, you will be able to enter the classroom community of readers with knowledge and authority and be prepared for productive class discussion.

Reading Visual Texts

You have to read visual texts—advertisements, tables and graphs, cartoons, artwork, photographs, and illustrations—with the same care you bring to the critical reading of written texts. Indeed, "visuals" seem like the new mother of our information age, for we are bombarded with images that invite, sometimes demand, our response. Whether dealing with spam on our computers, contending with that ubiquitous beer commercial on television, responding to a photograph of the latest disaster in a newspaper account, or trying to decipher what a graph on the federal deficit *really* means, we know that visual texts are constructions designed to influence us in carefully contrived ways.

We must, therefore, attempt to be critical readers of visual texts so that the powerful images of our culture and civilization do not seduce or overwhelm us without proper evaluation. Visual texts, after all, tend to be instruments of persuasion. A **symbol** like the American eagle, the Islamic crescent, or the red star of China can trigger powerful personal and collective responses. Similarly, political advertisements and commercials often manipulate visual texts to persuade voters to act for a candidate or against (as with negative ads) an opposing candidate. To bring this discussion to the local level, log on to your campus website. What forms of visual text do you encounter that enhance the written text? Look especially for images that suggest that your campus is culturally and globally diverse.

To read visual texts with the same critical authority you bring to scrutinizing written texts, you should consider the following questions:

- In what culture or context did the image originate? Who is the author? What is the source?
- What implicit messages are conveyed by the images and symbols?
- How is the visual designed or organized, and what is the effect of this arrangement?
- What is the purpose of the visual? What does the visual want the viewer to believe?
- What evidence is provided, and how can it be verified?
- What is the relationship of the visual to the printed text?

Visual images complement and at times overwhelm print or even make printed text unnecessary. Whether appearing on T-shirts, in ads of the glossiest fashion magazines, or marching across a computer screen, visual images usher us into a world of meaning. And we need to apply the same critical perspective to this visual universe that we do to its print counterpart.

Reading an Essay Critically

The Globalization of Eating Disorders

Susan Bordo

Susan Bordo was born in 1947 in Newark, New Jersey. She attended Carleton University (BA, 1972) and the State University of New York at Stony Brook (PhD, 1982). A well-known feminist scholar, Bordo is the Singletary Chair in the Humanities and a professor of English and Women's Studies at the University of Kentucky. In this selection, written as a preface to the tenth anniversary edition of her Pulitzer Prize–nominated book *Unbearable Weight: Feminism, Western Culture, and the Body* (2003), Bordo offers an overview of a new kind of epidemic, fueled by Western media images, that is affecting cultures around the world.

The young girl stands in front of the mirror. Never fat to begin with, 1 she's been on a no-fat diet for a couple of weeks and has reached her goal weight: 115 lb., at 5'4"—exactly what she should weigh, according to her doctor's chart. But in her eyes she still looks dumpy. She can't shake her mind free of the "Lady Marmelade" video from Moulin Rouge. Christina Aguilera, Pink, L'il Kim, and Mya, each one perfect in her own way: every curve smooth and sleek, lean-sexy, nothing to spare. Self-hatred and shame start to burn in the girl, and envy tears at her stomach, enough to make her sick. She'll never look like them, no matter how much weight she loses. Look at that stomach of hers, see how it sticks out? Those thighs—they actually jiggle. Her butt is monstrous. She's fat, gross, a dough girl.

As you read the imaginary scenario above, whom did you picture 2 standing in front of the mirror? If your images of girls with eating and body image problems have been shaped by *People* magazine and Lifetime

Susan Bordo, "The Globalization of Eating Disorders" from *Unbearable Weight: Feminism, Western Culture, and the Body*, 2003. Reprinted by permission of the author.

movies, she's probably white, North American, and economically secure. A child whose parents have never had to worry about putting food on the family table. A girl with money to spare for fashion magazines and trendy clothing, probably college-bound. If you're familiar with the classic psychological literature on eating disorders, you may also have read that she's an extreme "perfectionist" with a hyper-demanding mother, and that she suffers from "body-image distortion syndrome" and other severe perceptual and cognitive problems that "normal" girls don't share. You probably don't picture her as black, Asian, or Latina.

Read the description again, but this time imagine twenty-something   3
Tenisha Williamson standing in front of the mirror. Tenisha is black, suffers from anorexia, and feels like a traitor to her race. "From an African-American standpoint," she writes, "we as a people are encouraged to embrace our big, voluptuous bodies. This makes me feel terrible because I don't want a big, voluptuous body! I don't ever want to be fat—ever, and I don't ever want to gain weight. I would rather die from starvation than gain a single pound."[1] Tenisha is no longer an anomaly. Eating and body image problems are now not only crossing racial and class lines, but gender lines. They have also become a global phenomenon.

Fiji is a striking example. Because of their remote location, the Fiji   4
islands did not have access to television until 1995, when a single station was introduced. It broadcasts programs from the United States, Great Britain, and Australia. Until that time, Fiji had no reported cases of eating disorders, and a study conducted by anthropologist Anne Becker showed that most Fijian girls and women, no matter how large, were comfortable with their bodies. In 1998, just three years after the station began broadcasting, 11 percent of girls reported vomiting to control weight, and 62 percent of the girls surveyed reported dieting during the previous months.[2]

Becker was surprised by the change; she had thought that Fijian cul-   5
tural traditions, which celebrate eating and favor voluptuous bodies, would "withstand" the influence of media images. Becker hadn't yet understood that we live in an empire of images, and that there are no protective borders.

In Central Africa, for example, traditional cultures still celebrate volup-   6
tuous women. In some regions, brides are sent to fattening farms, to be plumped and massaged into shape for their wedding night. In a country plagued by AIDS, the skinny body has meant—as it used to among Italian,

1. From the Colours of Ana website (http://coloursofana.com//ss8.asp). [This and subsequent notes in the selection are the author's.]
2. Reported in Nancy Snyderma, *The Girl in the Mirror* (New York: Hyperion, 2002), p. 84.

Jewish, and black Americans—poverty, sickness, death. "An African girl must have hips," says dress designer Frank Osodi. "We have hips. We have bums. We like flesh in Africa." For years, Nigeria sent its local version of beautiful to the Miss World competition. The contestants did very poorly. Then a savvy entrepreneur went against local ideals and entered Agbani Darego, a light-skinned, hyper-skinny beauty. (He got his inspiration from M-Net, the South African network seen across Africa on satellite television, which broadcasts mostly American movies and television shows.) Agbani Darego won the Miss World Pageant, the first Black African to do so. Now, Nigerian teenagers fast and exercise, trying to become "lepa"—a popular slang phrase for the thin "it" girls that are all the rage. Said one: "People have realized that slim is beautiful."[3]

How can mere images be so powerful? For one thing, they are never 7 "just pictures," as the fashion magazines continually maintain (disingenuously) in their own defense. They speak to young people not just about how to be beautiful but also about how to become what the dominant culture admires, values, rewards. They tell them how to be cool, "get it together," overcome their shame. To girls who have been abused they may offer a fantasy of control and invulnerability, immunity from pain and hurt. For racial and ethnic groups whose bodies have been deemed "foreign," earthy, and primitive, and considered unattractive by Anglo-Saxon norms, they may cast the lure of being accepted as "normal" by the dominant culture.

In today's world, it is through images—much more than parents, teach- 8 ers, or clergy—that we are taught how to be. And it is images, too, that teach us how to see, that educate our vision in what's a defect and what is normal, that give us the models against which our own bodies and the bodies of others are measured. Perceptual pedagogy: "How to Interpret Your Body 101." It's become a global requirement.

I was intrigued, for example, when my articles on eating disorders 9 began to be translated, over the past few years, into Japanese and Chinese. Among the members of audiences at my talks, Asian women had been among the most insistent that eating and body image weren't problems for their people, and indeed, my initial research showed that eating disorders were virtually unknown in Asia. But when, this year, a Korean translation of *Unbearable Weight* was published, I felt I needed to revisit the situation. I discovered multiple reports on dramatic increases in eating disorders in China, South Korea, and Japan. "As many Asian countries become Westernized and infused with the Western aesthetic of a tall,

3. Norimitsu Onishi, "Globalization of Beauty Makes Slimness Trendy," *The New York Times*, Oct. 3, 2002.

thin, lean body, a virtual tsunami of eating disorders has swamped Asian countries," writes Eunice Park in *Asian Week* magazine. Older people can still remember when it was very different. In China, for example, where revolutionary ideals once condemned any focus on appearance and there have been several disastrous famines, "little fatty" was a term of endearment for children. Now, with fast food on every corner, childhood obesity is on the rise and the cultural meaning of fat and thin has changed. "When I was young," says Li Xiaojing, who manages a fitness center in Beijing, "people admired and were even jealous of fat people since they thought they had a better life. . . . But now, most of us see a fat person and think 'He looks awful.'"[4]

Clearly, body insecurity can be exported, imported, and marketed—   10 just like any other profitable commodity. In this respect, what's happened with men and boys is illustrative. Ten years ago men tended, if anything, to see themselves as better looking than they (perhaps) actually were. And then (as I chronicle in detail in my book *The Male Body*) the menswear manufacturers, the diet industries, and the plastic surgeons "discovered" the male body. And now, young guys are looking in their mirrors, finding themselves soft and ill defined, no matter how muscular they are. Now they are developing the eating and body image disorders that we once thought only girls had. Now they are abusing steroids, measuring their own muscularity against the oiled and perfected images of professional athletes, body-builders, and *Men's Health* models. Now the industries in body-enhancement—cosmetic surgeons, manufacturers of anti-aging creams, spas and salons—are making huge bucks off men, too.

What is to be done? I have no easy answers. But I do know that we   11 need to acknowledge, finally and decisively, that we are dealing here with a cultural problem. If eating disorders were biochemical, as some claim, how can we account for their gradual "spread" across race, gender, and nationality? And with mass media culture increasingly providing the dominant "public education" in our children's lives—and those of children around the globe—how can we blame families? Families matter, of course, and so do racial and ethnic traditions. But families exist in cultural time and space—and so do racial groups. In the empire of images, no one lives in a bubble of self-generated "dysfunction" or permanent immunity. The sooner we recognize that—and start paying attention to the culture around us and what it is teaching our children—the sooner we can begin developing some strategies for change.

4. Reported in Elizabeth Rosenthal, "Beijing Journal: China's Chic Waistline: Convex to Concave," *The New York Times*, Dec. 9, 1999.

Reading and Responding to an Essay

1. After reading Bordo's essay, reread and annotate it. Underline or circle key words, phrases, and sentences. Ask questions and make observations in the margins. Next to the title, write a phrase or sentence explaining what you think the title means.

2. In class groups of three or four, discuss your personal responses to this essay. Share with group members your experience of the text and why you respond to it the way you do. Would you say that your ideal image of physical beauty is based on personal or shared values? Do you know people whose ideas of beauty contrast with your own? Do you think of this difference as a matter of opinion, cultural difference, or simply personal taste?

3. Bordo claims, "In today's world, it is through images—much more than parents, teachers, or clergy—that we are taught how to be." How essential is this premise to the writer's claim? What kinds of evidence does she use to support the claim?

4. Examine the language, style, and structure of the essay. Do you find the writer's style to be engaging or accessible? Why or why not? Why does she repeat words and phrases (termed *anaphora* in rhetoric)? Where does she employ description, illustration, comparison, and the basis of case studies followed by general diagnosis—basically, a problem–solution method of essay development?

5. Explain the ways in which you could interpret this essay from psychological, cultural, and social perspectives.

Writing in Response to Reading

The distinguished writers in this book, many of them recipients of major awards, such as the Nobel and Pulitzer Prizes, are professionals. When dealing typically with local and world events—especially with the relationship of a liberal and open society like the United States to the world community—they employ a broad range of stylistic and rhetorical skills to construct meaning. They write for numerous reasons or purposes, although an argumentative edge appears in many of the essays. All engage in strategic thinking and rethinking as they tackle the promises and prospects of our new global era.

It is useful at the outset of a course in college writing to think like a professional writer, or at least a professional writer in the making. With each essay you write, imagine that you are trying to produce "publishable prose." Indeed, you will have the opportunity to write letters to the editor, post papers on the Web, pool and present research findings with other classmates, and engage in many tasks that assume the character of the professional writer who composes for a specific audience and for a specific purpose. At the least, by treating yourself as a writer capable of producing publishable prose, you will impress your instructor with your seriousness and aspirations.

Many of the issues and momentous events treated by the writers in this book demand no less than a "professional" response based on your ability to deal critically in writing with the strategic questions the essays raise. Indeed, critical thinking and writing about our common global condition is one measure of a pluralistic and tolerant society. By thinking and rethinking, writing and rewriting about your world, you contribute to the creation of open democratic discourse.

How, then, do you write about the new global era and its many challenges, or about any other topic for that matter? Globalization has changed the way people think about themselves and their relation to the world. Even ideas have become global; communication of these ideas can now span the world in milliseconds. As a writer in this brave new world of globalization, you need to apply in writing that repertoire of critical thinking skills mentioned at the outset of this chapter to make sense of contemporary life on this planet.

To start, you must have a basic understanding of the world of global interrelationships that characterizes life in the twenty-first century. The noted historian Paul Kennedy defines globalization as "the ever-growing integration of economies and societies because of new communications, newer trade and investment patterns, the transmissions of cultural images and messages, and the erosion of local and traditional ways of life in the face of powerful economic forces from abroad." Kennedy, as we might expect from a historian, is quick to note that this new world of globalization did not spring immediately from the ashes of 9/11 but can be detected in different guises in the rise and fall of great civilizations. For example, what the British Empire once termed "progress," we now call globalization. Today, the United States is the Great Power—its financial, cultural, military, and high-tech capacities unrivaled by other nations. Whether its Great Power status—its overarching control of the forces of globalization—will create new forms of "progress" for peoples and nations around the world is the central debate underlying the chapters in this book.

Writers like Paul Kennedy are "professional" in the sense that they know their subject. They are informed. But their informed essays do not result from some divinely inspired moment of creativity. When professional writers sit down to tackle an issue of importance, they know that beyond the knowledge they bring to the subject, they will have to consider various perspectives on the subject and even experiment with various methods of composition. Everyone composes differently, but it is fair to say that a good essay is the result of planning, writing, and revision, and such an essay reflects some of the key thinking strategies outlined in the first part of this chapter. There is a common consensus among professionals, including teachers of writing, that a **composing process**, consisting of *prewriting*, *drafting*, and *revision*, is the best way to approach the creation of a successful essay.

Prewriting

Prewriting is that preliminary stage in the composing process in which you map out mentally and in writing your overall approach to the subject. Prewriting in the context of this book begins when you read critically and respond to an essay. Perhaps you annotate the essay, summarize it mentally, or take notes on paper or the computer. Or maybe you take notes during class discussion. Next, you size up the nature of the writing project appearing in the exercises at the end of the essay or provided by the instructor. At this early stage, it is clear that already you are thinking, responding, and writing critically about the project at hand.

Composing processes are unique to each writer, but the prewriting process includes certain aspects that you need to consider:

- *Who is your audience?* A college writing assignment means that your primary audience will be your professor, who knows the "print code" and anticipates well-organized and grammatically correct prose. But there are secondary audiences to consider as well, and you might have to adjust your level of discourse to them. If you are working collaboratively, you have members of the group to satisfy. If you exchange papers with another class member for evaluation, this also creates a new audience. Or perhaps you will need to create an electronic portfolio of your best work as a graduation requirement; here the people who assess the quality of the portfolio become judges of your work.
- *What is your purpose?* Is your purpose to tell a story, describe, inform, argue, evaluate, or combine any number of these basic goals? Knowing your purpose in advance of actually drafting the essay will permit you to control the scope, method, and tone of the composition.
- *What is your thesis or claim?* Every paper requires a controlling idea or **assertion**. Think about and write down, either in shorthand or as a complete sentence, the main idea or claim that you plan to center your paper on.
- *How will you design your essay?* Planning or outlining your paper in advance of actually writing it can facilitate the writing process. Complete outlines, sketch outlines, sequenced notes, and visual diagrams can all serve as aids once the actual drafting begins.
- *How can you generate preliminary content?* Notes can be valuable. **Brainstorming,** in which you write without stop for a certain amount of time, can also activate the creative process. Joining online discussion groups or working collaboratively in the classroom also can result in raw content and ideas for development.

Prewriting provides both content and a plan of operation before moving to the next stage in the composing process.

Drafting

Once you have attended to the preliminary, or prewriting, stage in the composing process, you can move to the second stage, which is the actual **drafting** of the paper. Applying an Aristotelian formula, be certain to have a beginning, middle, and end. Your introduction—ideally one opening paragraph—should center the topic, be sufficiently compelling to engage your reader, and contain a thesis or claim. The body of the essay should offer a series of paragraphs supporting your main idea or central assertion. The conclusion should wrap things up in an emphatic or convincing way.

Here is a checklist for drafting an essay:

- Does your title illuminate the topic and capture the reader's interest?
- Does your opening paragraph "hook" the reader? Does it establish and limit the topic? Does it contain a thesis or claim?
- Do all body paragraphs support the thesis? Is there a main idea (called a **topic sentence**) controlling each paragraph? Are all paragraphs well developed? Do they contain sufficient examples or evidence?
- Does the body hold together? Is there a logical sequence to the paragraphs? In other words, is the body of the essay **unified** and **coherent**, with **transitions** flowing from sentence to sentence and paragraph to paragraph?
- Have you selected the best critical thinking strategies to develop the paper and meet the expectations set out in your introduction?
- Is your conclusion strong and effective?
- Think of drafting as the creation of a well-constructed plot. This plot does not begin, develop, and end haphazardly, but rather in a carefully considered sequence. Your draft should reveal those strategies and elements of the composing process that produce an interesting and logically constructed plot.

Revision

There are some professional writers who rarely, if ever, revise their work, and others who spend forever getting every word and sentence just right. Most professional writers do some amount of **revision**, either on their own initiative or in response to other experts, normally editors and reviewers. As the American poet Archibald MacLeish observed, the composing process consists of the "endless discipline of writing and rewriting and rewriting."

Think of the essay that in all likelihood you have put up on your computer screen not as a polished or final product but as a rough draft. Use the grammar and spell-checker features of your software program to clean up this draft, remembering that this software is not infallible and sometimes is even misleading. Then revise your essay, creating a second draft, with the following questions serving as guidelines:

- Is the essay long enough to satisfy the demands of the assignment?
- Is the topic suitable for the assignment?
- Is there a clear thesis or claim?
- Is the purpose or intention of the essay clear?
- Is the essay organized sensibly? Are the best rhetorical patterns used to facilitate reader interest and comprehension?

- Are all sentences grammatically correct and sufficiently varied in structure?
- Is there sufficient evidence, and is all information derived from other sources properly attributed?
- Does the manuscript conform to acceptable guidelines for submitting written work?

Successful writing blends form and content to communicate effectively with an audience. The guidelines offered in this section tap your ability to think and write critically about the global issues raised in this book. To be a global citizen, you must become aware of others, make sense of the world, and evaluate varieties of experience. To be a global writer, you have to translate your understanding of these global relationships into well-ordered and perceptive prose.

Writing in Response to an Essay

The Rich Are Different from You and Me

CHRYSTIA FREELAND

Chrystia Freeland, who is of Ukrainian extraction, was born in Peace River, Canada, in 1968. She graduated from Harvard University and attended St. Anthony's College, Oxford, as a Rhodes Scholar. Freeland has been a correspondent and editor for several publications, including Toronto's *The Globe and Mail* and the *Financial Times*, where she was Moscow bureau chief. Based on her overseas experience, she wrote *Sale of the Century: Russia's Wild Ride from Communism to Capitalism* (2000). Today she is the editor of Thomson Reuters Digital. In this article from the July/August 2011 issue of *The Atlantic*, Freeland argues that the expanding differences between the super-wealthy and the rest of the world population is a dangerous global trend.

The rich are always with us, as we learned from the Bette Davis film of   1
that name, released in the teeth of the Great Depression. The most memorable part of that movie was its title—but that terrific phrase turns out not to be entirely true. In every society, some people are richer than

others, but across time and geography, the gap between the rich and the rest has varied widely.

The reality today is that the rich—especially the very, very rich—are   2 vaulting ahead of everyone else. Between 2002 and 2007, 65 percent of all income growth in the U.S. went to the richest 1 percent of the population. That lopsided distribution means that today, half of the national income goes to the richest 10 percent. In 2007, the top 1 percent controlled 34.6 percent of the wealth—significantly more than the bottom 90 percent, who controlled just 26.9 percent.

That is a huge shift from the post-war decades, whose golden glow may   3 have arisen largely from the era's relative income equality. During the Second World War, and in the four decades that followed, the top 10 percent took home just a third of the national income. The last time the gap between the people on top and everyone else was as large as it is today was during the Roaring '20s.

The rise of today's super-rich is a global phenomenon. It is particularly   4 marked in the United States, but it is also happening in other developed economies like the United Kingdom and Canada. Income inequality is also increasing in most of the go-go emerging-market economies, and is now as high in Communist China as it is in the U.S.

These global super-rich work and play together. They jet between the   5 Four Seasons in Shanghai and the Four Seasons in New York to do business; descend on Davos, Switzerland, to network; and travel to St. Bart's to vacation. Many are global nomads with a fistful of passports and several far-flung homes. They have more in common with one another than with the folks in the hinterland back home, and increasingly, they are forming a nation unto themselves.

This international plutocracy is emerging at a moment when globaliza-   6 tion and the technology revolution are hollowing out the middle class in most Western industrialized nations. Many of today's super-rich started out in the middle and make most of their money through work, not inheritance. Ninety-five years ago, the richest 1 percent of Americans received only 20 percent of their income from paid work; in 2004, that income proportion had tripled, to 60 percent.

These meritocrats are the winners in a winner-take-all world. Among   7 the big political questions of our age are whether they will notice that everyone else is falling behind, and whether they will decide it is in their interests to do something about that.

Responding in Writing

1. As a prewriting strategy, brainstorm about this article for five minutes. Try to capture your impressions of the essay as you respond to the ideas and elements in it.

2. Working in groups of four, list everything that you know about the super-rich and the rest of the global population. Try to generate ideas not just about the United States but also about at least three other nations or geographic areas. Select one member of your group to present your findings to the class.

3. "Professional" writing is partly the result of an author's mastery of the subject and the expertise he or she brings to it. A writer's ethos may consist of a wide range of qualities: moral authority, sincerity, humility, humor, **satire**, and seriousness of purpose. Consider your response to the voice you hear in this essay. How would you characterize Freeland's tone or voice? Where do you find instances of this voice?

4. Write an analysis of this essay. What evidence suggests that Freeland has a target audience in mind, and who might this audience be? What is Freeland's claim or argument? What tone does she use to advance her claim? How does she present this argument, in terms of an introduction, body, and conclusion, and how persuasive do you find it to be? What is the nature of her evidence? What ideas about the United States and global economics and culture does she want the audience to gain from a critical reading of the text?

5. Go online and find out more about the super-rich and the rest of the global population. Write a report on your findings and summarize it in an oral presentation to the class.

2 New American Mosaic: Are We Becoming a Universal Nation?

Martin Luther King Jr. believed in the need for what he termed a "world house," a commitment to a society of global inclusion. "We are all caught up in an inescapable web of mutuality, tied in a single garment of destiny," he declared. Indeed, there are interconnected forces governing our world, and American demographic trends reflect the transnational movement of peoples on today's planet. Accelerating this transformation has been the recent arrival of tens of millions of immigrants to the United States. Instead of repeating earlier immigration patterns in which peoples arrived from Europe, these new immigrants travel here from all parts of the globe: Asia, Africa, the Caribbean, Central and South America. Today, new immigrants are changing the traditional notion of what it means to be "American." Arguably, because of the strikingly diverse nature of its citizenry, the United States is in the process of becoming a universal nation.

The writers in this chapter reflect in their own ethnic and racial origins the broad mosaic—some prefer to call it a kaleidoscope—that characterizes life in the United States today. Consider the historical magnitude of this national transformation. North America once belonged to native tribes, and the legacy of slavery, which began in 1621 when a Dutch man-of-war ship brought the first Africans to the Jamestown colony, also served to diversify the nation in ways that we continue to grapple with today. But from colonial times to 1965, the United States drew its population largely from Europe. First came the English, Scots-Irish, Germans, and French. The second great wave that began in the 1870s and continued up to World War I brought tens of millions of immigrants from southern and eastern Europe. For centuries, immigrants from non-European parts of the world were systematically excluded, with restrictive quotas preserving certain assumptions about the racial and ethnic character of the nation.

Steve Kelley/The Times - Picayune

Thinking about the Image

1. Are the people portrayed in this cartoon stereotypes? How can you tell? Do you find the stereotypes offensive, or do they help the cartoon make sense? Can you think of any comedians or hip-hop artists who use stereotypes in a way that points out an uncomfortable truth?
2. This cartoon uses **irony** to make its point. What, specifically, is ironic about this cartoon?
3. What political situation or issue is Steve Kelley, the cartoonist, responding to in this cartoon? What is his opinion? Does he make his point effectively?

The Immigration Act of 1965 abolished all such quotas and opened the United States—for the first time in the nation's history—to the world's population. Now everyone presumably had a fair opportunity to achieve the American Dream, whatever this ambiguous term might mean. And arrive they did—from Mexico, Vietnam, India, Nigeria, Cuba, the Philippines, Iran, and China—all seeking a place in the new global nation. Of course, this contemporary collision and intersection of peoples, races, and cultures is not only an American phenomenon; many countries in Europe are dealing with similar patterns. But nowhere is this new global reality more apparent than in the United States. In certain states—California, for example—and in many major American cities, "minorities" have become majorities. According to the most recent census data, by 2056 the "average" American will be as likely to trace his or her origins to the Hispanic world, Asia, or the Pacific islands as to Europe. These demographic changes are often reflected on college campuses, with students from scores of national backgrounds speaking dozens of languages sharing classes together.

The story of American civilization is still unfinished, but the authors in this chapter suggest certain directions it will take. They write about conflicts and challenges posed by the new American Dream, which is ostensibly open to, if not necessarily desired by, all the peoples of the world. They wrestle with America's complex fate. They ask collectively: How can America continue to be a beacon for peoples from around the planet seeking work, safety, security, freedom, and the right to freely practice and preserve their own customs and beliefs? Can America be—should it be—the model for a universal nation?

Red, Brown, and Blue

ELLIS COSE

Ellis Cose was born in Chicago in 1951 and grew up in one of the city's high-rise public housing projects. He attended the University of Illinois Chicago (BA, 1972) and George Washington University (MA, 1974) before embarking on a distinguished career as a writer, columnist, reporter, and editor. Cose has worked for several major publications including the *Detroit Free Press*, *New York Daily News*, *Time*, and *Newsweek*. He is also the author of many well-received and best-selling books. Several works explore the personal and political lives of black Americans—among them, *The Rage of a Political Class* (1994), *The Envy of the World* (2002), and *The End of Anger* (2011). Cose appears frequently on television shows and radio programs. In this 2010 essay from *Newsweek*, Cose examines the racial transformation taking place in American society.

Before Reading

If, as most demographers predict, blacks, Latinos, and Asian Americans will be a majority in the United States by 2050, what social, political, and economic consequences would you predict?

Would America be so different if blacks, Latinos, and people of Asian descent collectively became the new majority? It's not an idle question. According to the most recent U.S. Census projections, that's precisely where the United States is likely headed—by 2050 or thereabouts. It's important to distinguish this from concerns around the decennial Census scheduled for this year. Communities of color have a history of being undercounted, so advocates are mobilizing to make sure the new count is as accurate as possible. Those numbers, after all, confer power—via allocation of federal dollars and reapportionment of political representation. The Census projections have no power at all. And, truth be told, the future they imagine is unlikely to ever come to pass. For while the projections say much about our current racial assumptions, they are a poor measure for what lies ahead.

In America's early days, it was virtually impossible to conceive of a citizen as being other than white. The first U.S. naturalization act made whiteness a condition of gaining citizenship. So courts heard case after case from would-be white people who appeared to be something else. In 1922, a Japanese national who had lived in the United States for 20 years told the Supreme Court that most Japanese hailed from Caucasian "root stocks." The high court disagreed. Next year, a high-caste Hindu claimed he too was white. The justices found him no more persuasive.

This was during a time when even Europeans were divided into lesser and 3 better grades of white. Italians, Eastern Europeans, and Jews were, in many quarters, deemed to be of altogether different (and inferior) stock. Such ideas, though preposterous, defined debate and shaped immigration laws.

In an essay titled "How Did Jews Become White Folks?" anthropologist Karen Brodkin Sacks asks: "Did Jews and other Euroethnics become white because they became middle class? Or did being incorporated in an expanded version of whiteness open up the economic doors to middle-class status?" Both tendencies, she concluded, were at work. But her larger point is that nothing about race is static.

That's even more obvious today. A few generations back, racially mixed couples were an anomaly. But between the 1990 and 2000 census, the percentage of racially intermarried couples nearly doubled. More significantly, when Gallup's pollsters surveyed Americans' attitudes toward interracial relationships in 2005, the majority were accepting. Ninety-five percent of Americans under 30 approved, compared to roughly 45 percent of those over 64. Indeed, the majority of younger people claimed to have dated a person of a different race or ethnic background.

Census Bureau demographers are highly skilled. But there is no way they can program projections to capture the complexity of Americans' shifting attitudes. To their credit, they have tried. The 2000 Census, for instance, allowed Americans a wider range of options than did the 1990 Census. Racial categories were increased from five to six. For the first time Americans were allowed to claim more than one racial identity, and American Indians and Alaska natives were allowed to name their tribes. But there was no attempt to measure Americans' increasing propensity to propagate with partners of other races. As Census demographer Fred Hollmann told me, "We did not feel we had enough information from history to make an assumption on that particular issue."

By the same token, there is not enough information to say how quickly   7
other groups will go the route of the Italians and Jews and become more white than not. What is certain is that young people—whether choosing mates, categorizing people, or simply hanging out—are less likely than their elders to erect rigid racial walls. We also know that it's only a matter of time before DNA testing persuades many "whites" that they are much more mixed than they ever imagined.

So what does that mean for the future America? At the very least, it   8
means two things: that whites are not in danger of becoming a minority in the foreseeable future because the white category (or its equivalent) will likely expand to encompass many we now consider to be minorities. But more important, race is not going to be quite as big a deal as it is now; in the America of tomorrow—whatever people decide to call themselves—race will not be synonymous with destiny. That's a future worth embracing.

Thinking about the Essay

1. What connotations does the title of this essay raise for you? What subtle **allusion** is Cose making here, and what is the writer's purpose?

2. Consider the writer's introductory paragraph. Why is it so dense with information? Does the writer establish his claim in this introduction? Why or why not?

3. Summarize Cose's argument. How does he state the problem? What evidence does he provide? Does he offer a solution? Justify your response by referring to the text.

4. Where does Cose employ comparison and contrast? How does the comparative method reinforce Cose's claim?

5. Identify those places in the essay where the writer poses a question. What is the effect? Does the writer answer these questions or not? Explain.

Responding in Writing

6. Cose writes that young people "are less likely than their elders to erect rigid racial walls" (paragraph 7). Write an essay in which you agree or disagree with this statement, offering your own reasons and support for the position you take.

Culture or Conflict?
Images of Globalization

This portfolio of images from around the world presents a visual paradox: Is global culture a happy consumer wonderland where the fries are always crisp and the music always loud? Or has globalization simply packaged and marketed a bland, simplified version of the basics of culture, such as food and fashion, to an increasingly busy and distracted global population?

For millennia, trade between nation-states has introduced and shared aspects of culture, but the electronic telecommunication that is available now between countries has enabled instant blending of customs and has caused regional cultures and languages to fight to keep their own traditions vibrant. French-speaking Quebecois agitate for independence from the rest of English-speaking Canada. The ecotourism movement struggles to maintain the integrity of fragile cultures and environments, even as it imports Western tourists with their cash, cameras, and expectations for plumbing. The slow-food movement, which originated in Italy, calls on communities to nurture biodiversity and sustainable agriculture through renewed appreciation of their culinary heritage.

As you examine the following images, be especially attentive to the irony that lies in the details. *Irony* is a quality of being unexpected, incongruous, or out of place—juxtapositions that make something as common as a bottle of soda seem suddenly, entirely strange. That strangeness leads to a realization that there is more to the image than meets the eye: the nomad's tent topped by a satellite dish or the camel carrying an expensive mountain bicycle can be perceived either as a widening of opportunities and experiences or a flattening out of cultural vitality.

Many readings in this book describe the clashing of cultures and civilizations. Can consumer culture, based on these images, foster cooperation rather than clashes? After all, in a 1996 op-ed piece in *The New York Times*, foreign correspondent Thomas Friedman argued that no two countries that both have a McDonald's have ever fought a war against each other. What do you think?

A-1

AP Images/Enric Marti

Coca-Cola in Egypt.   An Egyptian girl drinks from a bottle of Coca-Cola in a shop in downtown Cairo, Egypt. After an Internet rumor that the Coca-Cola logo, if looked at upside-down or in a mirror, reads "No Mohammed, No Mecca" in Arabic, a top religious authority in Egypt studied the label and finally declared that "there is no defamation to the religion of Islam from near or far."

Considering the Image

1. Why would Coca-Cola be a target for such a rumor? Can you think of other examples in which consumer goods were boycotted as the symbols of a larger culture, value system, or belief?

2. What, to your eye, is particularly revealing or compelling about this image? What does the photographer want you to see? Does this image support or contradict images that you see in the media about women in the Middle East?

Joe McNally/Hulton Archive/Getty Images

Big Bird in Shanghai.   More than 90 percent of the households in the twelve major cities of the People's Republic of China have television sets. One of the favorite programs, reaching 120 million Chinese viewers, is *Sesame Street*. Here, Big Bird, known as Zhima Jie, appears on Shanghai television.

Considering the Image

1. How did the photographer capture a specific mood in this picture? What is the expression on the children's faces? Why does Big Bird loom over them? Do you think that there are universal values that make *Sesame Street* popular not just in China but throughout the world? Justify and explain your response.

2. Do you think the photographer wants to make a statement about "cultural imperialism" or the impact of globalization on national cultures, or simply capture a specific moment and scene? Explain your response. Why might globalization, which involves in part the transnational movement of media across cultures, be a force for democracy in China and elsewhere?

A-3

AfriPics.com/Alamy

Wildlife Rescue. The slaughter of prized wildlife species is one dark consequence of the forces of globalization. Here workers hoist a tranquilized elephant onto a flatbed truck for shipment to a wildlife preserve in a safer area.

Considering the Image

1. What is the dominant impression that the photographer wants to convey in this photograph? How do you know?

2. Some 100 elephants are killed in Africa every day, with elephant tusks fetching upwards of $3,000 a pound in Hong Kong. How do such facts affect your response to the content of the photograph?

© Joe McNally/Getty Images

Sophisticated Ladies.   Nakshatra Reddy is a biochemist who is married to a prosperous businessman in Mumbai (formerly Bombay). Her daughter, Meghana, dressed in a PVC suit of her own design, is a model and former host on a local music channel.

Considering the Image

1. How does the photographer stage or set up this scene? How does the photographer emphasize certain cultural contrasts between mother and daughter, and what is the purpose? Why is it important for viewers to know that mother and daughter represent a wealthy Indian family rather than a middle-class or poor one?

2. The daughter in this family represents a familiar Western type. How would you describe her? What are her sources of imitation? Do you think that the daughter has succumbed to the lure of Western popular culture, or might she be making a statement about her global identity? Explain your response.

B.Henry/Travel-Images.com

Globalization Protest.   Women lead an anti-globalization march against the World Trade Organization (WTO) in Hong Kong, China.

Considering the Image

1. What elements stand out in this photograph? How does the artist create a sense of perspective among these elements? What is the dominant impression?

2. Does the photographer hope to make a statement about globalization or simply record an anti-globalization protest without editorializing? Justify your response.

© Michael Benanav

Modern Conveniences.   The *ger* is the traditional, portable home of the nomadic people of Mongolia. A cone-shaped structure of felt stretched over a timber frame, with an opening in the top or a pipe to vent smoke from the stove, the *ger* is a symbol both of freedom and of hospitality. Many residents of Mongolia's capital, Ulaan Baatar, still live in traditional *gers*, and in keeping with their nomadic routes, any visitor is warmly greeted and offered shelter and food, as well as many modern conveniences. Here, a *ger* is outfitted with a satellite dish.

Considering the Image

1. This photo suggests not so much a clash of cultures as a fusion of ancient ways and modern technology. Why might a nomadic culture, like that of rural Mongolia, value the latest in communications technology?

2. Many writers define the so-called electronic gap or digital divide as one of the great challenges—and opportunities—for the twenty-first century. What does this image suggest to you about the digital divide? Granted, we do not know from this photograph if that satellite dish is being used to watch CNN or MTV; should that even matter? Why or why not?

Buena Vista Images/The Image Bank/Getty Images

Mixing Cultures.   Sadhu (Hindu ascetic) uses a mobile phone in the Pashupatinath (Hindu temple) in Kathmandu, Nepal, 2005.

Considering the Image

1. What impression do you think this photograph conveys? What sensory images and elements, such as sight and colors, stand out? How do these elements highlight the impact of Western popular culture on traditional Indian culture? How is the photograph composed so as to illustrate the blending (or conflict) of cultures?

2. What point do you think the photographer is attempting to make? Does the photographer advance a thesis or claim about the clash of civilizations, or the viability of old cultural practices in an age of globalization? Justify your response.

7. Write an essay titled "The New Majority" in which you discuss the same demographic patterns that Cose raises in his article.

8. In considering the demographic changes already occurring in the United States, are you optimistic or pessimistic about the nation's future? Respond to this question in a personal essay.

Networking

9. In small groups, discuss the issues raised by Cose's essay and whether or not you think his approach is fair and balanced. Offer a summary of your discussion to the class.

10. Access the U.S. Census Bureau's website, and examine the most recent data on race and ethnicity. What do these data suggest about future demographic trends? Write a brief summary of your findings.

American Dreamer

Bharati Mukherjee

Bharati Mukherjee was born in Calcutta, India, in 1940. She attended the universities of Calcutta and Baroda, where she received a master's degree in English and ancient English culture. In 1961 she came to the United States to attend the Writer's Workshop at the University of Iowa, receiving a PhD degree in English and comparative literature. Mukherjee became an American citizen in 1988; she is married to the writer Clark Blaise, with whom she has published two books, *Days and Nights in Calcutta* (1977) and *The Sorrow of the Terror* (1987). Mukherjee's books of fiction include *The Middleman and Other Stories*, which won the 1988 National Book Critics Circle Award for fiction; *Jasmine* (1989); *The Holder of the World* (1993); and *The Tree Bride* (2004). She is currently professor of English at the University of California at Berkeley. In the following essay, which was published in 1993 in *Mother Jones*, Mukherjee displays both narrative power and keen analytical strength in rejecting any hyphenated status as an American.

Before Reading

Mukherjee, writing in 1993, hyphenates such words as African-American and Asian-American. As a matter of style, why don't we use hyphenated race compounds today? Why do these terms even exist?

The United States exists as a sovereign nation. "America," in contrast,   1
exists as a myth of democracy and equal opportunity to live by, or as
an ideal goal to reach.

I am a naturalized U.S. citizen, which means that, unlike native-born   2
citizens, I had to prove to the U.S. government that I merited citizenship.
What I didn't have to disclose was that I desired "America," which to me is
the stage for the drama of self-transformation.

I was born in Calcutta and first came to the United States—to Iowa City,   3
to be precise—on a summer evening in 1961. I flew into a small airport surrounded by cornfields and pastures, ready to carry out the two commands my
father had written out for me the night before I left Calcutta: Spend two years
studying creative writing at the Iowa Writers' Workshop, then come back
home and marry the bridegroom he selected for me from our caste and class.

In traditional Hindu families like ours, men provided and women were   4
provided for. My father was a patriarch and I a pliant daughter. The neighborhood I'd grown up in was homogeneously Hindu, Bengali-speaking,
and middle-class. I didn't expect myself to ever disobey or disappoint my
father by setting my own goals and taking charge of my future.

When I landed in Iowa 35 years ago, I found myself in a society in which   5
almost everyone was Christian, white, and moderately well-off. In the women's
dormitory I lived in my first year, apart from six international graduate students
(all of us were from Asia and considered "exotic"), the only non-Christian was
Jewish, and the only nonwhite an African-American from Georgia. I didn't
anticipate then, that over the next 35 years, the Iowa population would become
so diverse that it would have 6,931 children from non-English-speaking homes
registered as students in its schools, nor that Iowans would be in the grip of a
cultural crisis in which resentment against immigrants, particularly refugees
from Vietnam, Sudan, and Bosnia, as well as unskilled Spanish-speaking workers, would become politicized enough to cause the Immigration and Naturalization Service to open an "enforcement" office in Cedar Rapids in October
for the tracking and deporting of undocumented aliens.

In Calcutta in the '50s, I heard no talk of "identity crisis"—communal or   6
individual. The concept itself—of a person not knowing who he or she is—was
unimaginable in our hierarchical, classification-obsessed society. One's identity
was fixed, derived from religion, caste, patrimony, and mother tongue. A Hindu
Indian's last name announced his or her forefathers' caste and place of origin. A
Mukherjee could *only* be a Brahmin from Bengal. Hindu tradition forbade
intercaste, interlanguage, interethnic marriages. Bengali tradition even discour-
aged emigration: To remove oneself from Bengal was to dilute true culture.

Until the age of 8, I lived in a house crowded with 40 or 50 relatives.   7
My identity was viscerally connected with ancestral soil and genealogy.
I was who I was because I was Dr. Sudhir Lal Mukherjee's daughter, because
I was a Hindu Brahmin, because I was Bengali-speaking, and because my
desh—the Bengali word for homeland—was an East Bengal village called
Faridpur.

The University of Iowa classroom was my first experience of coeduca-   8
tion. And after not too long, I fell in love with a fellow student named
Clark Blaise, an American of Canadian origin, and impulsively married
him during a lunch break in a lawyer's office above a coffee shop.

That act cut me off forever from the rules and ways of upper-middle-   9
class life in Bengal, and hurled me into a New World life of scary improvi-
sations and heady explorations. Until my lunch-break wedding, I had seen
myself as an Indian foreign student who intended to return to India to live.
The five-minute ceremony in the lawyer's office suddenly changed me into
a transient with conflicting loyalties to two very different cultures.

The first 10 years into marriage, years spent mostly in my husband's   10
native Canada, I thought of myself as an expatriate Bengali permanently
stranded in North America because of destiny or desire. My first novel, *The
Tiger's Daughter*, embodies the loneliness I felt but could not acknowledge,
even to myself, as I negotiated the no man's land between the country of
my past and the continent of my present. Shaped by memory, textured with
nostalgia for a class and culture I had abandoned, this novel quite naturally
became an expression of the expatriate consciousness.

It took me a decade of painful introspection to put nostalgia in perspec-   11
tive and to make the transition from expatriate to immigrant. After a
14-year stay in Canada, I forced my husband and our two sons to relocate
to the United States. But the transition from foreign student to U.S. citizen,
from detached onlooker to committed immigrant, has not been easy.

The years in Canada were particularly harsh. Canada is a country that   12
officially, and proudly, resists cultural fusion. For all its rhetoric about a
cultural "mosaic," Canada refuses to renovate its national self-image to
include its changing complexion. It is a New World country with Old
World concepts of a fixed, exclusivist national identity. Canadian official
rhetoric designated me as one of the "visible minority" who, even though I
spoke the Canadian languages of English and French, was straining "the
absorptive capacity" of Canada. Canadians of color were routinely treated
as "not real" Canadians. One example: In 1985 a terrorist bomb, planted
in an Air-India jet on Canadian soil, blew up after leaving Montreal, killing
329 passengers, most of whom were Canadians of Indian origin. The prime
minister of Canada at the time, Brian Mulroney, phoned the prime minister
of India to offer Canada's condolences for India's loss.

Those years of race-related harassments in Canada politicized me and   13
deepened my love of the ideals embedded in the American Bill of Rights. I
don't forget that the architects of the Constitution and the Bill of Rights
were white males and slaveholders. But through their declaration, they
provided us with the enthusiasm for human rights, and the initial framework from which other empowerments could be conceived and enfranchised communities expanded.

I am a naturalized U.S. citizen and I take my American citizenship very   14
seriously. I am not an economic refugee, nor am I a seeker of political asylum. I am a voluntary immigrant. I became a citizen by choice, not by
simple accident of birth.

Yet these days, questions such as who is an American and what is   15
American culture are being posed with belligerence, and being answered
with violence. Scapegoating of immigrants has once again become the politicians' easy remedy for all that ails the nation. Hate speeches fill audito-
riums for demagogues willing to profit from stirring up racial animosity.
An April Gallup poll indicated that half of Americans would like to bar
almost all legal immigration for the next five years.

The United States, like every sovereign nation, has a right to formulate   16
its immigration policies. But in this decade of continual, large-scale diasporas, it is imperative that we come to some agreement about who "we"
are, and what our goals are for the nation, now that our community
includes people of many races, ethnicities, languages, and religions.

The debate about American culture and American identity has to date   17
been monopolized largely by Eurocentrists and ethnocentrists whose rhetoric has been flamboyantly divisive, pitting a phantom "us" against a
demonized "them." All countries view themselves by their ideals. Indians
idealize the cultural continuum, the inherent value system of India, and are
properly incensed when foreigners see nothing but poverty, intolerance,
strife, and injustice.

Americans see themselves as the embodiments of liberty, openness, and   18
individualism, even as the world judges them for drugs, crime, violence,
bigotry, militarism, and homelessness. I was in Singapore in 1994 when the
American teenager Michael Fay was sentenced to caning for having spray-
painted some cars. While I saw Fay's actions as those of an individual, and
his sentence as too harsh, the overwhelming local sentiment was that van-
dalism was an "American" crime, and that flogging Fay would deter
Singapore youths from becoming "Americanized." Conversely, in 1994, in
Tavares, Florida, the Lake County School Board announced its policy (since
overturned) requiring middle school teachers to instruct their students that
American culture, by which the board meant European-American culture, is
inherently "superior to other foreign or historic cultures." The policy's

misguided implication was that culture in the United States has not been affected by the American Indian, African-American, Latin-American, and Asian-American segments of the population. The sinister implication was that our national identity is so fragile that it can absorb diverse and immigrant cultures only by recontextualizing them as deficient.

Our nation is unique in human history in that the founding idea of 19 "America" was in opposition to the tenet that a nation is a collection of like-looking, like-speaking, like-worshipping people. The primary criterion for nationhood in Europe is homogeneity of culture, race, and religion—which has contributed to blood-soaked balkanization in the former Yugoslavia and the former Soviet Union.

America's pioneering European ancestors gave up the easy homogene- 20 ity of their native countries for a new version of Utopia. Now, in the 1990s, we have the exciting chance to follow that tradition and assist in the making of a new American culture that differs from both the enforced assimilation of a "melting pot" and the Canadian model of a multicultural "mosaic."

The multicultural mosaic implies a contiguity of fixed, self-sufficient, 21 utterly distinct cultures. Multiculturalism, as it has been practiced in the United States in the past 10 years, implies the existence of a central culture, ringed by peripheral cultures. The fallout of official multiculturalism is the establishment of one culture as the norm and the rest as aberrations. At the same time, the multiculturalist emphasis on race- and ethnicity-based group identity leads to a lack of respect for individual differences within each group, and to vilification of those individuals who place the good of the nation above the interests of their particular racial or ethnic communities.

We must be alert to the dangers of an "us" vs. "them" mentality. In 22 California, this mentality is manifesting itself as increased violence between minority, ethnic communities. The attack on Korean-American merchants in South Central Los Angeles in the wake of the Rodney King beating trial is only one recent example of the tragic side effects of this mentality. On the national level, the politicization of ethnic identities has encouraged the scapegoating of legal immigrants, who are blamed for economic and social problems brought about by flawed domestic and foreign policies.

We need to discourage the retention of cultural memory if the aim of 23 that retention is cultural balkanization. We must think of American culture and nationhood as a constantly reforming, transmogrifying "we."

In this age of diasporas, one's biological identity may not be one's only 24 identity. Erosions and accretions come with the act of emigration. The experience of cutting myself off from a biological homeland and settling in an adopted homeland that is not always welcoming to its dark-complexioned citizens has tested me as a person, and made me the writer I am today.

I choose to describe myself on my own terms as an American, rather   25 than as an Asian-American. Why is it that hyphenation is imposed only on non-white Americans? Rejecting hyphenation is my refusal to categorize the cultural landscape into a center and its peripheries; it is to demand that the American nation deliver the promises of its dream and its Constitution to all its citizens equally.

My rejection of hyphenation has been misrepresented as race treachery   26 by some India-born academics on U.S. campuses who have appointed themselves guardians of the "purity" of ethnic cultures. Many of them, though they reside permanently in the United States and participate in its economy, consistently denounce American ideals and institutions. They direct their rage at me because, by becoming a U.S. citizen and exercising my voting rights, I have invested in the present and not the past; because I have committed myself to help shape the future of my adopted homeland; and because I celebrate racial and cultural mongrelization.

What excites me is that as a nation we have not only the chance to   27 retain those values we treasure from our original cultures but also the chance to acknowledge that the outer forms of those values are likely to change. Among Indian immigrants, I see a great deal of guilt about the inability to hang on to what they commonly term "pure culture." Parents express rage or despair at their U.S.-born children's forgetting of, or indifference to, some aspects of Indian culture. Of those parents I would ask: What is it we have lost if our children are acculturating into the culture in which we are living? Is it so terrible that our children are discovering or are inventing homelands for themselves?

Some first-generation Indo-Americans, embittered by racism and by   28 unofficial "glass ceilings," construct a phantom identity, more-Indian-than-Indians-in-India, as a defense against marginalization. I ask: Why don't you get actively involved in fighting discrimination? Make your voice heard. Choose the forum most appropriate for you. If you are a citizen, let your vote count. Reinvest your energy and resources into revitalizing your city's disadvantaged residents and neighborhoods. Know your constitutional rights, and when they are violated, use the agencies of redress the Constitution makes available to you. Expect change, and when it comes, deal with it!

As a writer, my literary agenda begins by acknowledging that America   29 has transformed me. It does not end until I show that I (along with the hundreds of thousands of immigrants like me) am minute-by-minute transforming America. The transformation is a two-way process: It affects both the individual and the national-cultural identity.

Others who write stories of migration often talk of arrival at a new 30
place as a loss, the loss of communal memory and the erosion of an original culture. I want to talk of arrival as a gain.

Thinking about the Essay

1. What is the significance of the title? How is Mukherjee a dreamer? Why does
   the idea of America inspire dreams? What impact does the American Dream
   have on one's identity? For example, Mukherjee says in paragraph 7 that she
   had a clear sense of identity when she was in India. How has this sense of identity changed now that she is an American?

2. What is Mukherjee's purpose in writing this essay? Does she want to tell a story,
   analyze an issue, or argue a position? Remember that this article appeared in
   Mother Jones, a progressive or left-of-center magazine. What does her primary
   audience tell you about her intentions?

3. Why does Mukherjee divide her essay into four parts? What are the relationships
   among these sections? Why has she used this pattern of organization? Where
   does she employ comparison and contrast and definition to achieve coherence
   among these parts?

4. Mukherjee refers to Eurocentrics and ethnocentrics. What do these terms mean to
   you? Discuss your understanding of these terms with other members of the class.

Responding in Writing

5. Write a summary of Mukherjee's essay, capturing as many of her major ideas as
   possible in no more than 300 words.

6. Write your own essay titled "American Dreamer," referring specifically to the
   dreams that immigrants—perhaps even you or members of your family—have
   had about coming to this country.

7. Mukherjee asserts, "We must be alert to the dangers of an 'us' vs. 'them' mentality" (paragraph 22). Write an argumentative essay responding to this statement, referring to other assertions by Mukherjee to amplify your own position.

Networking

8. In small groups, develop a summary of Mukherjee's essay. Next, compose a list
   of outstanding questions you still might have about her essay. For example, has
   she overlooked or diminished the importance of a specific topic, or has she personalized the subject too much? Finally, collaborate on a letter to the author in
   which you lay out your concerns.

9. Using a search engine, compile all the information that you can find about
   Bharati Mukherjee. Then compose a brief analytical profile of the author in which
   you highlight her career and the impact that living in several cultures has had on
   her work. Use "American Dreamer" as a foundation for this presentation, and be
   certain to provide citations for your Web research. (For information on citing
   online sources, see Appendix A: Conducting Research in the New Global Era.)

Why Diversity Matters

Lee C. Bollinger

> Lee C. Bollinger is currently the president of Columbia University and an acclaimed First Amendment scholar. Born in Santa Rosa, California, in 1946 and raised there and in Bend, Oregon, Bollinger attended the University of Oregon (BS, 1968) and subsequently received his law degree from Columbia University Law School (1971). As president of two distinguished universities—Michigan and then Columbia—Bollinger has been in the front lines in the debate over college diversity and affirmative action. Bollinger's support for an open, pluralistic educational culture and society is inherent in his scholarship, notably *The Tolerant Society: Freedom of Speech and Extremist Speech in America* (1968), *Images of a Free Press* (1991), and *Uninhibited, Robust, and Wide-Open: A Free Press for a New Century* (2010). In the following essay from the June 1, 2007, issue of *The Chronicle of Higher Education*, Bollinger claims that we cannot understand America—or the world—without being exposed to a full spectrum of peoples and beliefs.

Before Reading

Do you think that affirmative action is still relevant to college life today, or have we moved into what some call a "postracial" environment that makes affirmative action unnecessary? Explain.

During this frantic admissions season it is easy for our applicants to   1
think that the most important moment in their college career is when they rip open the mail to find out where they got in and where they didn't. But we in higher education understand that the admissions process has less to do with rewarding each student's past performance—although high performance is clearly essential—than it does with building a community of diverse learners who will thrive together and teach one another.

When it comes to creating the kinds of diversity we sorely need in this   2
country, however, disturbing trends and setbacks are making it difficult for many public schools and universities to succeed. The reality is that as much as we may want to believe that racial prejudice is a relic of history, conscience and experience tell us better.

Lee C. Bollinger, "Why Diversity Matters," *The Chronicle of Higher Education*, Washington: June 1, 2007, Vol. 53, Iss. 39, pg. B20. © 2007 Lee C. Bollinger. Reprinted by permission of the author.

Even now, the Supreme Court is considering two public-school cases out   3
of Washington and Kentucky that would subvert the resounding principle
that *Brown v. Board of Education* established 53 years ago on May 17, 1954,
that "separate is inherently unequal." If successful, both cases would ban local
districts from developing voluntary desegregation programs that seek to
maintain racial balance in our schools and counteract the worst resegregation
crisis we have faced since the early days of the civil-rights movement.

According to the 2000 census, only 14 percent of white students attend   4
multiracial schools, while nearly 40 percent of both black and Latino students attend intensely segregated schools where 90 percent to 100 percent
are from minority groups. Further, almost half of all black and Latino students attend schools where three-quarters or more students are poor, compared with only 5 percent of white students; in extremely poor schools, 80
percent of the students are black and Latino.

Beyond elementary and secondary schools, higher education continues   5
to face its own challenges, including statewide bans on affirmative action.
Recent news reports have noted how hard some of our leading public universities are working to revise recruitment and admissions policies to comply with those bans without jeopardizing the diversity of the students who
attend their campuses. What's important, however, is why those universities are trying so hard to maximize diversity—even though no law requires
it, and in several states affirmative action is explicitly forbidden.

I have been deeply involved in two U.S. Supreme Court cases—*Gratz v.*   6
Bollinger and *Grutter v. Bollinger* (2003)—that ultimately upheld the con-
stitutionality of affirmative-action policies at public universities. Let me
suggest why, having vindicated the legality of affirmative action, higher
education must not lose the practical and political battles to maintain
racially, ethnically, and socioeconomically diverse student bodies.

Universities understand that to remain competitive, their most impor-   7
tant obligation is to determine—and then deliver—what future graduates
will need to know about their world and how to gain that knowledge.
While the last century witnessed a new demand for specialized research,
prizing the expert's vertical mastery of a single field, the emerging global
reality calls for new specialists who can synthesize a diversity of fields and
draw quick connections among them. In reordering our sense of the earth's
interdependence, that global reality also cries out for a new age of exploration, with students displaying the daring, curiosity, and mettle to discover and learn entirely new areas of knowledge.

The experience of arriving on a campus to live and study with class-   8
mates from a diverse range of backgrounds is essential to students' training
for this new world, nurturing in them an instinct to reach out instead of
clinging to the comforts of what seems natural or familiar. We know that

connecting with people very—or even slightly—different from ourselves stimulates the imagination; and when we learn to see the world through a multiplicity of eyes, we only make ourselves more nimble in mastering—and integrating—the diverse fields of knowledge awaiting us.

Affirmative-action programs help achieve that larger goal. And the uni-   9
versities that create and carry them out do so not only because overcoming longstanding obstacles to people of color and women in higher education is the right thing to do, but also because policies that encourage a comprehensive diversity help universities achieve their mission. Specifically, they are indispensable in training future leaders how to lead all of society, and by attracting a diverse cadre of students and faculty, they increase our universities' chances of filling in gaps in our knowledge with research and teaching on a wider—and often uncovered—array of subjects.

At the same time, such policies foster a greater spirit of community on   10
campuses as well as between universities and the cities and town they call home. The days of the gated university are past, and affirmative action is crucial to making our universities welcoming places for community members to visit, take classes, and inspire their children to dream.

Opponents of affirmative action forget that broader purpose in their   11
demand for what they see as a "pure" admissions meritocracy based on how students perform in high school and on standardized tests. But it is far less important to reward past performance—and impossible to isolate a candidate's objective talent from the contextual realities shaping that performance—than to make the best judgment about which applicants can contribute to help form the strongest class that will study and live together. For graduate schools and employment recruiters, that potential is the only "merit" that matters because in an increasingly global world, it is impossible to compete without already knowing how to imagine, understand, and collaborate with a diverse and fluid set of colleagues, partners, customers, and government leaders.

By abolishing all public affirmative-action programs, voters in California   12
and Michigan (and other states if affirmative-action opponents are successful) have not only toppled a ladder of equal opportunity in higher education that so many of us fought to build and the Supreme Court upheld in 2003. They will almost assuredly make their great public universities less diverse—and have, in fact, done so in California, where the impact has become clear—and therefore less attractive options to potential students and, ultimately, less valuable contributors to our globalized society.

As the president of a private university, I am glad that independent   13
institutions retain the autonomy to support diversity efforts that make our graduates more competitive candidates for employers and graduate schools, as well as better informed citizens in our democracy and the world. But as

an alumnus of one public university and a former president of another, I worry about a future in which one of America's great success stories slides backward from the mission of providing generations of young Americans with access to an affordable higher education.

From the establishment of the land-grant colleges in the 1860s to the   14 GI Bill after World War II to the Higher Education Act of 1965, our public universities have advanced the notion that in educating college students for the world they will inhabit, it is necessary to bring people together from diverse parts of society and to educate them in that context. Far from being optional or merely enriching, it is the very essence of what we mean by a liberal or humanistic education.

It is also vital for establishing a cohesive, truly national society—one in   15 which rising generations learn to overcome the biases they absorb as children while also appreciating the unique talents their colleagues bring to any equation. Only education can get us there.

As Thurgood Marshall knew so well: "The legal system can open doors   16 and sometimes even knock down walls. But it cannot build bridges. . . . We will only attain freedom if we learn to appreciate what is different and muster the courage to discover what is fundamentally the same." Cutting affirmative action short now only betrays that history of social progress. And, in the process, it threatens the core value of academically renowned public universities at a time when many Americans list rising tuition costs as one of their gravest economic concerns.

All of this leads to the conclusion that diversity—one of the great   17 strengths of American education—is under siege today. At the elementary- and secondary-school levels, resegregation is making it exceedingly difficult for minority students to get the resources that inspire rising generations to apply to and then attend college. At the same time, the elimination of affirmative action programs at our public universities is keeping admissions officials from lifting those same students up to offset the structural inequalities they had to face in getting there.

As we honor the parents, students, lawyers, and nine justices who spoke   18 with one voice in *Brown* on that May day 53 years ago, we would all do well to remember that when it comes to responsible diversity programs— those that help our public schools and our great public universities fulfill their historic roles as avenues of economic and cultural mobility—what is wise is also what is just.

Thinking about the Essay

1. What is Bollinger's claim, and where does he state it? On what warrant does Bollinger base his claim? Discuss why you agree or disagree with his claim and the warrant underpinning it.

2. Where and why does Bollinger use emotional and ethical appeals in his approach to his primary audience? At what points does he stress his authority in addressing this audience?

3. What minor propositions does Bollinger use to buttress his claim?

4. What forms of evidence does Bollinger use to support his argument?

5. How does Bollinger refute the arguments of those opposed to affirmative action? Do you find his strategy to be effective? Justify your response.

Responding in Writing

6. Summarize the main points of reasoning that inform Bollinger's claim, and then discuss the extent to which you find his argument reasonable and convincing.

7. Bollinger asserts that students must be educated for twenty-first-century realities. Write an essay in which you explore the relevance of diversity and affirmative action to this challenge.

8. Write a response to Bollinger explaining why you agree (or disagree) with his premise, and how his essay reflects life and conditions on your college campus.

Networking

9. Form small groups and debate the merits of diversity and affirmative action in higher education. Select one member of each group to join a class forum presenting the results of your debate.

10. Go online and read about the decision of the Supreme Court in the two public-school cases that Bollinger alludes to in paragraph 3. How do these decisions relate to Bollinger's conclusion that diversity is under siege today?

Deportation Order

RANDA JARRAR

Randa Jarrar was born in Chicago in 1978. Of Egyptian and Jordanian heritage, she grew up in Kuwait and Egypt. At the age of thirteen, she moved back to the United States. She is an award-winning writer and translator living in Austin, Texas. Her first novel is *A Map of Home* (2008). In this essay from a 2010 issue of *The Progressive*, Jarrar recounts a family crisis rooted in the complexities of US immigration policy.

Before Reading

Should the children of documented or undocumented families residing in the United States be deported for any legal infraction? Why or why not?

Just after New Year's of 2005, my younger brother, Raed, then a senior   1
at the University of Maryland, came home to D.C. after visiting our
parents in Kuwait. The security people at Dulles Airport detained and
questioned him for hours, then told him he was a deportable alien. He had
two weeks to surrender to authorities. Once he did, he was sent to a jail in
Virginia.

A few days after his imprisonment, I got an e-mail from his lawyer that   2
he needed contact lens solution. I rushed out and bought it, sent it off with
his prisoner ID number on the envelope, went home, and spent the rest of
the day in bed.

Unlike my brother, I was born in the U.S., and never had to work for   3
my little blue passport. My Egyptian/Jordanian family did; they all took
tests and held little flags and swore to do or not do things—all but my
brother, who was too flaky at eighteen to fill out the proper forms or take
buses to the right offices. He was left behind in our family's Becoming
American journey. In 2001, he was living with students who sold pot.
When they got busted, he went to jail for five days, and did a few dozen
hours of community service. And he was being deported four years later
because that had been "a crime of moral turpitude."

My brother called me collect, and I got up the courage to ask him what   4
the jail in Virginia looked like.

"They let us congregate for religious reasons inside a small strip. They   5
seal it off with yellow tape. You can pray or talk inside the yellow line."

A few days later, my father called me in a panic.   6

"Your brother is turning into a fundie," he said.   7

"Don't be ridiculous."   8

"He told mom he is writing a sermon for this Friday's prayers."   9

I pictured my brother reading a sermon in the small space, his hand   10
resting on the yellow tape on the floor.

"That's so sweet," I said.   11

"It is not sweet; it is crazy. Please stop him. He will come out of that jail   12
a fanatic!"

"That'll never happen," I said. "Don't you know him at all? He is just   13
finding a way to cope." I couldn't tell my father that my brother liked
liquor and women too much to become religious.

In order to get the government to reverse the deportation, we hired a   14
psychologist to determine the level of hardship my brother's absence would
cause us. By the time the therapist called me, the lawyer had written me an
e-mail saying I was the only sane person in my family.

Randa Jarrar, "Deportation Order" from *The Progressive*, March 2010. Used by permission of
The Progressive.

His final court date was March 22. I met my parents in a hotel in the 15
same building as the courthouse. At dinner the night before the hearing, my
father couldn't figure out how to work the pepper shaker. He kept trying
to find the magic way, and, finally, I reached over and twisted the top. "It's
simple," he said, shocked. He always thinks things are much harder than
they actually are.

After dinner, we took the elevator up to our rooms. "I'm sick," my 16
father said. "The therapist gave me my file today. I need help."

I'd been waiting to hear those words all my life. 17

My mother, who has always hated therapists because she thinks all 18
people talk about in therapy is what a terrible person she is, interrupted. "I
passed the test. The doctor said I was severely depressed. I wanted him to
think so! I wanted to prove the hardship!" She smiled and danced around
the hotel room.

The morning of the hearing, we all sat in the waiting area with other 19
families. The rows of white plastic chairs faced a wall. It felt like we were
all on a plane, being deported. Inside the courtroom, my brother was on a
monitor, defending his moral fiber. An hour passed. "Maybe the judge will
just let him out after this," I said.

"That is wishful thinking," my father said, closing his eyes. Everything 20
had to be like that pepper shaker.

Less than fifteen minutes later, the judge stopped the hearing. "I've 21
heard enough," he said, leafing through dozens of family photos.

He released my brother and reversed the deportation order. 22

But it wasn't over. I had to map the jail, print out the directions, and sit 23
in the car with my parents as they screamed at each other all the way from
D.C., through traffic, across Virginia.

Four hours after we set out, we reached the jail. We parked outside the 24
entrance and waited. My brother's silhouette appeared against the electric
fence. Soon we were embracing him. His hair was shaved close. In the car,
he told us stories of the men he'd been living with.

As we approached College Park, my father grew impatient with the 25
printed map and the unfamiliar roads. He ignored my brother's directions,
and soon we were going the wrong way up a highway road. After all we'd
done, my father jeopardized our lives out of impatience. Or maybe he was
determined that he wouldn't let the government do the destruction for him.
In any case, by the time we reached my brother's apartment, we were all
anxious to leave the small prison of the rental car. We stood awkwardly
around Raed's coffee table, reluctant to admit that we got along a lot easier
in crisis. A few minutes passed, and we shuffled our feet and said goodbye.
My brother waved to us from the doorway, as though we'd just spent the
last few hours visiting, and were now heading home.

When my brother was four, he broke into a parked Cadillac in our 26
apartment building's parking lot. He and his best friend hung out in the big
American car's velvety seats and pretended to drive, their short legs dan-
gling high above the floor. A neighbor saw them and brought my brother
home. My father yelled all that night. Then, he stood up, knowing what he
had to do. He would take my brother to the police; he would put him in
jail. To teach him a lesson. He would.

"Get ready," he told my brother.   27

I watched as my brother went to the front door, bent down, and silently, 28
without the smallest murmur of resistance, strapped on his small, leather shoes.

Then he straightened up, looked down the hallway, and waited.   29

Inside the courtroom, my brother was on a monitor, defending his 30
moral fiber.

Thinking about the Essay

1. How does the writer characterize various members of her family? What tone does she take in describing her mother, father, and brother? What causal connections do you detect between their behavior and the deportation order that Raed receives?

2. What elements of narration does Jarrar utilize in order to create a dramatic plot?

3. Would you say that Jarrar's main purpose is simply to tell a tale about her family, or does she have a broader purpose in mind? Might she be advancing an argument? Why or why not?

4. Many of the writer's paragraphs are very brief one-sentence units. What is your response to this strategy? Does this technique aid or damage the overall coherence and unity of the essay? Explain.

5. The last five paragraphs constitute Jarrar's conclusion. How does this end unit reinforce the issues raised in the body of her essay?

Responding in Writing

6. Argue for or against the proposition that anyone violating immigration policy should be eligible for deportation.

7. Compose an argumentative essay in which you support or oppose a "dream act" that provides a pathway to citizenship for undocumented immigrants.

8. Should the children of undocumented immigrants be eligible for in-state college tuition? Respond to this question in an argumentative essay.

Networking

9. Exchange your essay based on this reading with another class member. Then peer critique your partner's paper, focusing on the relative effectiveness of the argument.

10. Go online to find out more about deportation policies in the United States. Based on your findings, write a brief action report in which you advocate changes in specific policies.

Beyond Black and White:
The Hawaiian President

DWIGHT N. HOPKINS

> Dwight N. Hopkins, who was born in Richmond, Virginia, in 1953, is a professor of theology at the University of Chicago. He holds degrees from Harvard University (BA, 1976), Union Theological Seminary (MDiv, 1984), and the University of Cape Town (PhD, 2000). Much of Hopkins's work deals with the intersection of race and religion in the modern world. Among his books are *Shoes That Fit Our Feet: Sources for a Constructive Black Theology* (1993), *Heart and Head: Black Theology—Past, Present, and Future* (2002), *Being Human: Race, Culture, and Religion* (2005), and *Walk Together Children: Black and Womanist Theologies, Church and Theological Education* (2010). In this essay, which appeared in the February 10, 2009, issue of *The Christian Century*, Hopkins offers a provocative assessment of Barack Obama as a new type of American.

Before Reading

Do you think that Americans will ever transcend their preoccupation with race? Why or why not?

Since the November presidential election, friends, colleagues and casual   1
acquaintances throughout the United States and across the world have written me and claimed Barack Obama as the son of their state, race, country or region. Of course, countless black Americans have celebrated the fact that "in our lifetime, one of us is in the White House."

How is it possible that Hawaii claims Obama as its own; Indonesia   2
and parts of Asia perceive him as reflective of their experiences; Kenya cries in ecstasy to have a blood relative on 1600 Pennsylvania Avenue; all of Africa embraces him as a close kin of that continent; Kansans believe his roots sink deep within their soil; and black Americans, without much critical self-reflection, relish the idea that the 44th president is black like them?

The fact that Obama is perceived as belonging in a variety of ways to such disparate groups points up at least one persistent and absurd concept in race relations in America: the one-drop rule.   3

Coming out of slavery and segregation, the one-drop rule was one of the most egregious dimensions of white supremacy. When Africans arrived in the New World in chains, all of their children were called black and thus were enslaved, even if one biological parent was white. If it was determined that a person who looked white had any African or black ancestors, that white person was reclassified as black. A drop of black blood in one's genealogy could instantly transform a white citizen into a black slave.   4

Long after slavery the one-drop rule persisted in racial classification, and oddly enough, was eventually accepted by black Americans. This led to all manner of absurdities. Walter White, a pioneering leader of the NAACP, was so white-looking that he once attended a high-society function where some of the whites present wondered why he had brought his "black" wife. The irony was that White was, according to the one-drop rule, black, and his so-called black wife was actually white.   5

The one-drop-of-black-blood rule is unique to the U.S. It presupposes a black-white paradigm. On one extreme are "white" people, on the other, "black" people. Lost in these absolutes is the kaleidoscope of Asian Americans, Caribbean Americans, African Americans, Pacific Islander Americans, Latino-Hispanic Americans, Middle Eastern Americans, European Americans, American Indians and all the complexities of identity that make us unique human beings.   6

What race is Obama? Shortly after the election, the venerable John Lewis, a member of Congress from Georgia, stated that no black person who had come out of segregation and the civil rights movement could have been elected the first black president. And in fact Obama did not. Obama redefines what it means to be black. His ancestors did not come from the glorious West African empires of centuries ago. To my knowledge, he has no biological connection to those empires' encounter with the European slave trade. His family history does not flow from de jure and de facto segregation. During the civil rights struggle, the black power movement and reparation efforts, he was living in Asia and the Pacific Islands. He has never lived in the (segregated or nonsegregated) southern U.S. In his major speeches, he has not mentioned two heroic icons of black manhood—Martin Luther King Jr. and Malcolm X. He was not born into nor did he grow up in a black church. He did not assemble black preachers and civil rights stalwarts together and from that base launch his presidential campaign.   7

Obama is Hawaiian. He is familiar with flip-flops, surfing, snorkeling, Aloha Spirit and 'Ohana family values. Before he lived in Chicago's segregated black community, his social reality was Asia and the Pacific more   8 than the southern U.S. Born in Hawaii in 1961, he grew up alongside Japanese Hawaiians, Chinese Hawaiians, Filipino Hawaiians, Pacific Island Hawaiians, Native Hawaiians and white Hawaiians. The black-white paradigm of the mainland did not dominate his reality. In fact, whites were and still are a minority in Hawaii, and except for the occasional vacationer and military personnel, blacks were and are a rarity.

Obama spent ages six to ten in Indonesia, going to school and speaking   9
Indonesian. His Indonesian stepfather gave him an ape as a pet. This pet was not caged but lived in their backyard.

Obama was nurtured in a white environment. His Kansan white mother   10
(not from the South) reared him with the help of his white grandparents. (All accounts indicate that no black men or women, boys or girls ever lived in his home until he married and had his own children.) To illustrate how different his upbringing was from that of most black Americans, who call their grandmothers Big Mama, Ma Dear or Grandma, Obama's intimate name for his white grandmother was Toot—the Hawaiian endearment for grandmother.

Obama has never identified himself as an Afrocentric person or a   11
pan-Africanist. Yet he is more African than the overwhelming majority of black Americans. There need be no genetic test to find out what West African "tribe" his ancestors came from centuries ago. His ancestry is from Kenya, a country in East Africa from which the enslaved rarely came. His father voluntarily came to the U.S. as a student in 1959. Before that, he was a goat herder in Kenya. President Obama has visited the exact location where his father and other ancestors were born. He understands the "tribal" language, politics, economics, religions, foods, songs, indigenous names, folktales, clothing, dances, illnesses, personalities and gravesites. When he pours libations (spilling liquids on the ground in memory of the dead), he is not talking about unknown Africans lost in the slave trade. Like Africans born on the continent, he can pour libations to his specific blood family members and directly on family gravesites. Some of those burial grounds are still next to family compounds in Kenya. Obama doesn't have to change his English "slave master's" name to an African one; his name is already African.

Growing up, Obama was certainly aware of the mainland's obsession   12
with race. Witness the Afro hairstyle he adopted at Punahou, one of the most elite private schools in the U.S., and his idolizing of NBA star Julius "Dr. J" Erving. But it wasn't until he was 22 and came to the heavily segregated South Side of Chicago that, for the first time in a sustained manner, he engaged the particularities (and some might say the peculiarities) of traditional black-white race relations, including the one-drop rule.

Segregated Chicago offered Obama three things: a black family through   13
marriage, a black community through grass roots organizing and a black
church through baptism.

While black Americans may not be quite right in their declaration that   14
Obama is only "one of us," the 44th president does symbolize a change in
the U.S. If not going so far as to redefine race in America, Obama might
expand what race means. Perhaps he will help the millions of Americans
with black and white parents, black and Asian parents and black and
Latino/Hispanic parents integrate the various tuggings of their identities—
identities that have been too often forced into narrow racial options.

Like all American citizens, this Hawaiian, Polynesian, Indonesian,   15
Asian, white, Kenyan and black human being is caught up in the narrative
of the black-white paradigm, a structure still rooted in the absurdity of the
one-drop-of-black-blood rule. Yes, he is black. But no one can understand
him deeply who does not appreciate the rainbow racial mixtures of his
Hawaiian origins.

Thinking about the Essay

1. How does Hopkins's title reveal his purpose? What is his claim, and where does
   he state it?

2. Why does Hopkins begin in a personal mode? Which paragraphs constitute his introduction, and how does he use this introduction to structure the body of the essay?

3. Hopkins is writing for a specialized group of readers. Why would these readers
   be especially interested in his essay? Would a more general audience be equally
   absorbed by this article? Why or why not?

4. How successful do you think Hopkins is in explaining the paradox of race in
   America and how Barack Obama transcends conventional notions of black and
   white? Justify your assessment by referring to specific passages and **motifs** in
   the essay.

5. In part, this essay is about the limitations of racial categorization, but Hopkins is
   also interested in the causal connections that have perpetuated such classification throughout American history. Where in the essay does Hopkins analyze the
   reasons why Americans are so preoccupied with race and the effects of this
   obsession?

Responding in Writing

6. Hopkins argues that the election of Barack Obama to the presidency in 2008 is
   a watershed in America's history of racial classification. In an argumentative
   essay, agree or disagree with the writer's claim.

7. In an **analytical essay**, explore the reasons why you think Americans have
   been so preoccupied with race. Do you think that today's younger Americans

are moving beyond racial classification? Justify your response with compelling reasons.

8. Hopkins claims that Barack Obama is a "Hawaiian President." Explain why you agree or disagree with this notion.

Networking

9. Form two groups and debate the proposition that the election of Barack Obama to the presidency means that Americans have finally transcended the politics of race.

10. Go online and find out more about Barack Obama's life in Hawaii. Then construct your own profile of Obama based on this information.

Mall Together Now

FIROOZEH DUMAS

Firoozeh Dumas is an Iranian American, born in Abadan, Iran, in 1965. In 1972 her family immigrated to California, though they briefly moved back to Iran. She began to write to earn money to go to college, and attended UC Berkeley where she met and married her husband. She writes of love, family, country, and heritage, stressing the similarities instead of the differences across cultures. She has contributed to various newspapers and magazines and has published several books, including a memoir, *Funny in Farsi: A Memoir of Growing Up Iranian in America* (2003), and *Laughing Without an Accent: Adventures of a Global Citizen* (2008). Scheduled for publication in 2016 is *It Ain't So Awful, Falafel*, a tween novel based on her experiences in middle and high school. She has been nominated for various awards, including the Thurber Prize for American Humor, the first Iranian author to receive this honor, and in 2008 she received the Spirit of America Award from the National Council for the Social Studies. In this article she relates a trip to the mall on her daughter's thirteenth birthday.

Before Reading

Think of the last time you visited a large mall. Recall the diversity of shoppers you observed. How would the mall you visited be similar to and different from a mall in another country?

For her 13th birthday, my daughter wanted to go to the mall with her friend Jacqueline. This was not the mall near our house, but a discount mall we had never visited. We don't have a TV (my husband and I choose not to), but my daughter heard about the place from the girls at school. She looked it up on the Internet, repeatedly went over all the stores, made a list of the ones she wanted to visit and decided that it was indeed worth the half-hour drive.

I hate malls, but I was not about to drop the girls off by themselves. I invited Jacqueline's mom to come with us. I didn't tell her that I was inviting her because I hated malls and needed someone to listen to me complain about malls. I just told her that lunch was on me. I like Jacqueline's mom, and I would have preferred taking her somewhere where I would not be in a prolonged bad mood, but daughters turn 13 only once, and it was hard to say no to her one birthday request.

My aversion to malls goes back to when I was 7. That was the year we moved to America from Iran. One of the first times we went to a mall, a man approached us, talking with urgency. We didn't speak English, but my brother Farid said this man was selling a religion. We let him know that we spoke only Persian, but then he pulled out a sheet of paper, in Persian! He wanted to tell us about Jesus Christ. We told him we were Muslim, which felt like cheating since we never practiced Islam. My dad even ate ham. But this man was not deterred. He was pumped up! We finally got rid of him, but from then on I decided that malls were places to approach with caution, and maybe with a Koran, a Bible and the Torah for good measure.

Thirty years later, my dislike for malls has nothing to do with religion but with culture. Right around the time junior-high-school girls started wearing thongs, I decided that there was something very wrong with the choices being offered to young girls and that malls epitomized this wrong something. At one point I sat my daughter down for a talk about it. I explained to her that my dream for her was that she would do whatever she wanted in life. I told her that my beloved Aunt Sedigeh had to marry when she was 14, even though she was the smartest person in the family. That was life In Iran back then, I said, but this is America! Girls can do, in theory, anything they want. But there are so many bad choices to navigate, and as far as I'm concerned, I told her, certain clothing and the mindless desire for it are the beginning of the end. My daughter told me that she understood about my aunt because, Lord knows, this was not the first time she had heard that story, but that she still liked going to the mall.

On the day of our big excursion, I packed two protein bars and timed our trip to get there right when it opened to avoid any parking drama.

Firoozeh Dumas, "Mall Together Now," *The New York Times Magazine*, July 13, 2008.

The Mall of America, the largest mall in the United States, contains more than 500 stores and is visited by around 100,000 shoppers daily, 4 million annually.

When we arrived there were almost no other cars. The girls could barely contain their excitement, so we decided to let them go off by themselves for an hour. This particular indoor mall had not only endless stores but also rows of portable kiosks in front of and in between the stores. It reminded me of a science experiment in grade school: the teacher put big rocks in a jar; then when you thought it was full, she added some smaller rocks. Then when you thought it was full, she added water. This mall was just missing the water. The kiosks were in every nook and cranny, selling key chains shaped like the 50 states, costumes for pets, bamboo plants, personalized lollipops and nail decals.

"Can't you just see the trajectory from dressing your pug in faux leopard to wearing palm-tree nail decals to deciding you don't want to go to college?" I asked Jacqueline's mom. She couldn't quite see it, but she could see the Neiman Marcus outlet. 6

We went in, and the next thing I knew I was on my third trip to the fitting room, arms loaded with clothes I could not normally afford. That's when Jacqueline's mom told me that we had forgotten to meet the girls. "Let's come back," I said, parting with the clothes longingly, experiencing a feeling usually reserved for loved ones leaving on trips overseas. 7

The mall was crowded by this time, and we passed groups of teenage 8
girls with too much makeup; sari-clad Indian women shopping with multiple generations of their families; Hispanic guys checking out Hispanic
girls who were all dolled up; and moms with toddlers, strollers, diaper bags
and sippy cups. We found the girls at our designated meeting spot. "You're
15 minutes late," my daughter said. "We were worried." I apologized to the
responsible members of our party, explaining how I'd gotten caught up in
all the great Dana Buchman outfits.

In the end, my daughter gave me a lesson not only in punctuality but 9
also in restraint, buying one pair of jeans and one blouse and no nail decals.
Which is less than I can say.

Thinking about the Essay

1. What is the origin of Dumas's aversion to malls? Why does she still dislike
   malls? How does her attitude change during this visit to the discount mall?

2. What advice does she give her daughter? Why? Is she a typical or atypical
   mother? How are mother–daughter relationships in this country different
   or the same as in other countries?

3. Dumas goes beyond just telling what happened to her; she adds her
   responses and insights into what occurred. Her essay is a typical op-ed piece.
   Read a few op-ed pieces in current newspapers. Why do authors write such
   pieces? Who is the audience for such columns? Why do editors choose to
   print them?

4. Dumas uses several metaphors in her essay. Find and analyze her metaphors,
   and think about their meaning and what they add to the essay. Why does Dumas
   use these implied comparisons in her essay?

5. Another technique that Dumas uses in her essay is cataloguing. Find several
   of her cataloguing lists. Do you feel they effectively illustrate the point Dumas
   is trying to make? Look around the classroom, and write a sentence or more
   using this technique to describe what you observe. Share your description with
   the class.

Responding in Writing

6. Write an essay in which you relate some advice you received from a parent or
   another older person. Explain the situation in which you received this advice,
   and how you responded.

7. Write a cause-and-effect essay in which you explain how the displays in a mall
   affect customers. Be sure to provide specific examples to support your
   assertions.

8. In paragraph 4, Dumas tells her daughter, "certain clothing and the mindless desire for it are the beginning of the end." Write an essay in which you explain what she means and then take a clear stance on whether you agree or disagree with her. Be sure that you use specific evidence to support your position.

Networking

9. Go to this author's home page and read some of her recent postings. With a group of your classmates, discuss what these postings tell you about the author. Did you each draw the same conclusions?

10. With a small group of classmates, research malls in several other countries. Find some images of international malls, and discuss what these images indicate about shopping malls in other cultures. Compare and contrast what you discover with shopping malls in the United States. Summarize your findings, and share them with the class.

America and the World: How Do Others Perceive Us?

One of the key elements supporting the idea of America is a belief in freedom, democracy, and human rights—what we often term American exceptionalism. This ideal, as we saw in the previous chapter, has been a motivating impulse in all waves of immigration, especially for the flood of peoples from around the world who have found their way to the United States since 1965, transforming the nation into a global village. But does the rest of the world believe that the United States is truly a "city upon a hill" as President Ronald Reagan (borrowing a phrase from one of the nation's first immigrants, Governor John Winthrop of Massachusetts Bay Colony) declared? Are we truly a beacon of democratic promise for other nations? Do we promote democracy and human rights everywhere? Or are we "ugly Americans" constantly meddling in the affairs of other nations? What ideals and values—especially when projected by American foreign policy or even American tourists abroad—do we actually represent?

Today the conflicts inherent in the "war on terror" and "clash of civilizations"—framed by a suspicion of American-style capitalism, democracy, and imperialism—fuel a widespread belief that the world's reigning superpower acts out of self-interest rather than altruism. For many, the United States is not a bastion of democracy but a destructive element—a Great Satan in the minds of some. That we led the wars of the last century against the totalitarian forces of Nazism, fascism, and communism apparently has become a historic footnote. That we provide international aid today to developing nations and victims of natural disasters, that we share information and technology openly, and that we promote democracy at great human and material cost all seem lost in a maelstrom of anti-Americanism. In a world of predators, the United States appears to many as the most insatiable enemy. Yet with the election of Barack Obama to the presidency in 2008, there emerged a degree of hope for a revival of American exceptionalism around the world.

Kevin Lee/Newsmakers/Getty Images

Chinese customers buy snacks from a store decorated with ads for an American soft drink company in Beijing, China.

Thinking about the Image

1. What is your response to this image? Is it positive or negative? Explain your response.
2. Identify and analyze the elements in this photograph that contribute to the dominant impression or overall effect. What point of view, if any, does the photographer want to convey?
3. How is this image divided into three parts? What relationships do you detect among the units? What is the dominant impression?
4. Research the Pepsi Cola Corporation in China and its impact on local culture. Write a summary of your findings.

The truth, of course, is that the image America projects to the world has always been a function of what others have projected onto it. As the world's superpower, the United States today faces the option not only of inspiring ideals of democracy and freedom in the rest of the world but also of trying to remake nations and regions—as in the case of Iraq and the broader Middle East— according to those ideals. The problem is that the very idea of America is symbolically saturated with conflicting aspirations and associations. The ideals that America would transmit to the world will inevitably clash with rival ideals that have been projected from afar. If, for example, we are guardians of the free world, then what forces are we guarding the world *against*? How can the United States unilaterally pursue debatable policies and still maintain moral authority on the world stage? What ideals, beyond self-interest, would justify intervention in the affairs of other nations? For instance, recent administrations have promoted democracy in the Middle East; but many in the area view Washington's actions as an amoral attempt to control the region, destroy traditional societies, and guarantee access to oil.

Of course, not everyone hates the United States or is cynical about its role in the world. The Islamic Republic of Iran and the Islamic State of Syria and the Levant might denounce America as the Great Satan (and England as the Lesser Satan), but Iranians and Syrians love Americans in particular and the West in general. Again, the truth lies in the beholder and the ways in which we construct national mythologies for ourselves. Some might engage in a frenzy of anti-Americanism and even want to harm the United States for what they perceive America does to the rest of the world; but many others around the world, especially in moments of crisis, are thankful for American food during famine, tents and medical supplies after earthquakes and tsunamis, the promotion of human rights, and even military intervention (as in Libya) to prevent genocide. The global village does admire America's political and economic freedoms, along with its wealth, culture, and technology, even as it might be appalled by certain foreign policy doctrines and behavior on the world stage.

The essays in this chapter deal with America's complex relationship with the rest of the world and with the psychological factors behind both anti-American and pro-American attitudes. The wars in Afghanistan and Iraq and the repercussions of the "Arab Spring" have affected the image of America in ways that we are only beginning to understand. ("As the savagery of the images coming out of Iraq demonstrate all too well," writes Sasha Abramsky in an essay appearing in this chapter, "we live in a world where image is if not everything, at least crucial.") The famous film footage of the cavalry charge up San Juan Hill that made Theodore Roosevelt's reputation during the Spanish-American War was, as we now know, a staged reenactment filmed after the real charge took place. Today, more than a hundred years after Roosevelt's charge, it is no easy task to alter the perception of America as an aggressive imperialist power; but it is still possible, after the fact, to examine and learn from the images, actions, and mythologies that are at its source.

The Children Will Keep Coming

ÓSCAR MARTÍNEZ

Óscar Martínez, a journalist in El Salvador, is the author of the acclaimed *The Beast: Riding the Rails and Dodging Narcos on the Migrant Trail*. Every year thousands of people from Honduras, Guatemala, Nicaragua, and El Salvador make a perilous overland journey to the United States through Mexico, riding atop cargo trains known as "La Bestia." In 2010

Martinez rode the Beast eight times himself, interviewing people on their way to the United States and
reporting his discoveries in this book, published in
English in 2013. In the following 2014 article from
The Nation, he explores the violence that children in
particular face at home and why they continue to
make the risky trip.

Before Reading

When you read the title of this article, how do you respond? Is the title an effective attention getter? Does it make you want to read the article? Why or why not?

On Friday, June 11, David de la O disappeared. He was walking home   1
from school in rural Santa Cruz Michapa, a small city in El Salvador about an hour's drive from San Salvador, the nation's capital. David's
family searched for him all night, without success. The next morning, his
remains were found buried in an abandoned field outside town. He had
been stabbed four times in the torso; his head, arms and legs had been severed. David was only 11 years old. In fourth grade, he had been learning
long division and multiplication and practicing verb tenses. With no leads
to go on, the police speculated that David was killed and dismembered by
gang members because he refused to join their ranks. (He went to school
in an area controlled by one gang and lived in a neighborhood dominated
by another.)

David's murder wasn't widely reported in the country. It was yet another   2
incident of violence—a terrible one, but one of many. The day before David
was killed, two other teenagers, 15 and 16, had their throats slit and were
dumped in another abandoned field on the outskirts of the capital.

To avoid becoming the victims of gang violence, tens of thousands of   3
children like David have fled El Salvador, Guatemala and Honduras for
the United States. As their numbers skyrocket, lawmakers in Washington
have sought to "repatriate" these refugees as quickly as possible. The
Obama administration initially sought to change the 2008 Trafficking
Victims Protection Reauthorization Act to allow the 52,000 or so child
migrants who have arrived on US soil in the last nine months to be
deported without going before an immigration judge. (Under the TVPRA,
unaccompanied minors from countries that do not share a border with the
United States are handed over to the Department of Health and Human
Services, then go before an immigration court that will determine their
fate; those hailing from Mexico, on the other hand, can accept "voluntary

Oscar Martinez, "The Children Will Keep Coming", *The Nation* (August 18/25, 2014), pp. 12–16 deportation" and return immediately.) The White House has since backed off this proposal and has instead asked Congress for $3.7 billion to ramp up enforcement and hire more judges to expedite the removal process. Republicans in the House of Representatives—including the GOP's standard-bearer on immigration issues, Ted Cruz—continue to press for the TVPRA to be changed.

Little consideration has been given to the violence that children from these countries face upon returning home. But those who doubt that their lives are at risk are either deeply misinformed or, more likely, turning a blind eye to the epidemic of violence for the sake of political expedience. In the northern triangle of Central America, children are not only being killed but brutally so—stabbed to death, cut into pieces, tortured.   4

But the violence in El Salvador, as in neighboring Guatemala and Honduras, has been going on for years. When President George W. Bush signed the TVPRA into law in 2008, there were fifty-two murders per 100,000 people in El Salvador. The number shot up to seventy-one in 2009 before plateauing at sixty-five. Then, thanks in part to a truce between the government and the gangs, it dropped sharply in 2012. That year, the Salvadoran government transferred thirty leaders of the two biggest gangs in the country, the 18th Street Gang and the Mara Salvatrucha, from maximum-security prisons to gang-segregated minimum-security prisons where inmates are allowed conjugal visits and visits from their children. As a result, in 2012 and 2013, the murder rate fell to around forty per 100,000. But the truce has been slowly falling apart as police have employed more aggressive tactics to deal with the still-rampant violence. This year, El Salvador has typically seen at least eight people murdered every day.   5

Violence is no less prevalent to the north or west. In 2013, the United Nations identified neighboring Honduras, which had ninety murders per 100,000 people in 2012, as the most violent country in the world. El Salvador was the fourth most violent; Guatemala, with forty murders per 100,000 people in 2012, the fifth.   6

Let's put those numbers in perspective. The United Nations considers a rate of ten murders per 100,000 people an epidemic. If we were to apply the Honduran murder rate to New York City, where the yearly homicide rate is five per 100,000, more than 7,000 New Yorkers would be murdered per year. The rate of violence in Honduras is nearly twice that of America's most violent city, Detroit, which has a homicide rate of fifty-five per 100,000.   7

Just as striking as these statistics is the consistent young age of the victims. According to El Salvador Institute of Legal Medicine, 38 percent of those murdered in the country every year are between the ages of 15 and 24. In the first three months of 2014 alone, 790 Salvadorans were killed, 306 of them between 15 and 24.   8

In a country with more than 6 million inhabitants, the 18th Street Gang and 9
Mara Salvatrucha have some 60,000 members, according to El Salvador's
Ministry of Security and Justice. Their presence is felt everywhere; they control entire neighborhoods, extorting regular fees from residents and business owners alike. In June, residents abandoned three apartment buildings
in the capital because they could not afford to make monthly payments to
the gangs. Gang violence is such a fixture of life here that the legislative
assembly recently approved a change in the law that would allow those
accused of murder—who, under Salvadoran law, are typically held in jail
until police finish investigating the crime—to go free as the investigation
proceeds if they can show that they acted to protect themselves from harm.
Lawmakers said the change was necessary to provide the public with the
"tools for self-defense." Altogether, gang violence accounts for 40 percent of
the murders in El Salvador and 27 percent of the overall crime.

The gangs not only recruit heavily among children, who act as mes- 10
sengers or drug runners because they are better able to evade detection by
police; they are also recruiting younger and younger children. According
to El Salvador's National Public Security Council, the typical age at which
children enter the gangs has dropped from 14 to 12. The Mara Salvatrucha
recruits children as young as 8 or 9.

El Salvador's minister of education has attributed the high dropout 11
rate at many schools to gang recruitment. The gangs' constant turf wars
also keep some kids out of school. If a school is in an area controlled
by the Mara, the gang will not allow children who live in neighborhoods
controlled by the 18th Street Gang (known in El Salvador as Barrio 18) to
attend. Students in some areas must carry backpacks made of transparent
plastic to ensure that they are not carrying weapons, and they are searched
by police before entering classrooms.

As the case of David de la O shows, saying no to a gang can be dan- 12
gerous, and hiding is nearly impossible. For many, the best option—and in
some cases, the only option—is to flee.

In 2009, I met three brothers traveling through Mexico on their way to 13
the United States. Auner, the eldest, was 20. His siblings, who went by Chele
and Pitbull, were 16 and 17. They had decided to flee El Salvador after
violence came knocking at their door. First, two gang members were killed
right outside of their home. Then their mother, who sold snacks on the sidewalk and had witnessed the murder, was killed by a gunshot wound to the
head a few months later. Auner's explanation for leaving is straightforward:
"I'm running because I'm scared they're going to kill me." As with many
of the children I met during the three years I spent reporting on migration
through Mexico, Auner and his siblings had nowhere near the $7,000 to
pay a coyote to take them to a relative in the United States. They had to

leave El Salvador on their own, traveling by bus, staying in hostels, and navigating the treacherous journey on the advice of fellow migrants. I accompanied them until they reached the city of Oaxaca in south-central Mexico. Last I heard, they were on the outskirts of Mexico City; without a peso in their pockets, they planned to hop aboard a cargo train headed north.

As thousands of children like Auner, Chele and Pitbull arrive at the US   14 border, it is important to remember the role the United States has played in creating this mass migration. In the 1970s and '80s, El Salvador, Guatemala and Honduras were in the midst of either bloody civil wars or fierce government repression in which the United States played an iron-fisted role. Fearing the spread of communism in Latin America, the United States supported the autocratic military governments of these three countries, which in turn generated thousands of northbound migrants. Some of these migrants went on to join gangs in California. The 18th Street Gang and the Mara Salvatrucha were not formed in El Salvador, Honduras or Guatemala but in the United States. Some fifty years ago, the 18th Street Gang splintered off from Clanton 14 in Southern California. The Mara Salvatrucha formed in Los Angeles in the late 1970s. At the end of the '80s and the start of the '90s, the United States deported close to 4,000 gang members. When they arrived back in Central America, they found fertile conditions in which to increase their numbers: countries devastate by war and poverty, with thousands upon thousands of corruptible and abandoned children.

But it would be an oversimplification to say that the flight of children   15 to the United States is the product of violence alone.

Rubén Zamora is currently the Salvadoran ambassador to the UN and,   16 until a month ago, El Salvador's ambassador to the United States. With his replacement awaiting confirmation by the Saldoran Senate, Zamora has been left to address the international implications of the child migrant crisis. Zamora explains that there is no single cause of the surge in child migrants. In addition to gang activity, Zamora says that the improving economic conditions experienced by Salvadoran migrants to the United States have acted as a draw. "From sharing a single room with a group of people, now some migrants can pay $1,000 a month and rent a two-bedroom apartment for themselves in the suburbs," he says. And that means "more people can pay to bring their children to the US."

Thousands of migrants from Central America are ineligible for tempo-   17 rary protected status—not because they've violated any law but because they missed the cutoff dates. The United States offers a mere 5,000 visas for low-skilled workers every year. For many, the only chance for gaining legal status in the United States is the asylum process, and it's a long shot. Over the last few decades, in part as a response to the wave of Central American migrants fleeing the civil wars, the United States has narrowed the definition of who qualifies for asylum. Because most of those fleeing Central America are not doing so because of their "race, religion, nationality, membership in a particular social group, or political opinion," they are ineligible.

I recently asked two immigration lawyers from California and North   18 Carolina how many requests for asylum they file each week. "At least ten," they said. They've lost track of how many migrants they've represented over the years. But the tally of those who have been successful is easy to remember: none.

"Parents don't see any chance of bringing their children legally to the   19 US," Zamora says, "so what options are left for them?"

The case of Sandra, a Salvadoran woman who migrated to the United   20 States eleven years ago, is typical. She crossed without papers and remains undocumented. Working at a laundromat in Maryland, she isn't wealthy. But she has been able to save enough money to bring her children across. Two years ago, she paid a coyote $7,000 to bring her 15-year-old daughter to the States. A month ago, Sandra hired another to bring her 12-year-old son as well. The coyote gave her two options: she could pay $7,500 for her son to be brought to Maryland, or $4,500 for him to be taken to the US-Mexico border, where he would be handed over to the US Border Patrol. The coyote assured Sandra that he knew how the laws worked and that her son would eventually be turned over to her. Sandra chose the cheaper option. But the child was caught by authorities in southern Mexico and deported back to El Salvador.

Sandra knows she doesn't have a chance to get papers legally. She   21 wouldn't even qualify for a visa if comprehensive immigration reform were to pass. And yet she is a mother who wants to be close to the child she hasn't seen in eleven years.

Sandra is originally from La Unión in eastern El Salvador, where gang   22 members have begun charging extortion fees in her former neighborhood. The gangs, she hears, are closing in on her son.

I asked her if she would try again to bring her son to the United States.   23 "Yes," Sandra said.

The root of the child migrant crisis is simple: undocumented Central   24 American mothers and fathers want to be reunited with their children. And because they don't see an end to the violence that is rapidly encroaching on their kids in Honduras, El Salvador or Guatemala, these parents have only one option—coyotes.

On Wednesday, July 9, I paid a visit to a coyote at his house in Chalatenango   25 in northern El Salvador. This coyote, who wishes to remain anonymous—I'll call him "José"—is one of the oldest veterans of his profession. A man of over 50, stout like a tree, José explains that coyotes used to be beloved figures in their communities rather than vilified. "People would greet you on the streets, bring you gifts," he says. "Today, many see you as a criminal because so many new coyotes engage in deception."

José started guiding people to the United States when it wasn't illegal   26 to do so—at least not in El Salvador. His career took off in 1979 amid the escalating civil war. At the time, he would publish ads promoting his business in newspaper classified sections. SAFE TRIPS TO THE UNITED STATES, a typical ad announced. This coyote has never used the train known as "The Beast" to cross Mexico and reach the US border; his methods are safer and his services more expensive. He ferries migrants north using a chain of Central American and Mexican coyotes whose movements he coordinates by phone. They travel by bus and pay bribes to Mexican police officers and Border Patrol agents with whom they have established "agreements." He charges $7,500 per person.

I ask José how he would explain this new wave of migrant children. "I   27 laugh when the media says children are going by themselves. Not one of them goes alone—all of them are taken by coyotes," he boasts. "If I were undocumented in the US, how am I going to tell my kid, 'Come on over!' No, that's not how it goes."

José no longer advertises in the papers; these days, his clients are   28 referred to him by word of mouth, which has an astounding power in the world of migrants. Despite the tremendous distances traveled by them—and the dozens of US cities in which they live and hide without papers—these migrants seek each other out, they congregate, they gather at the same restaurants and send remittances to their families in Central America. Most working-class Central Americans either know a coyote personally or know someone who knows one. If a mother in Los Angeles sees that her neighbor's children have made it into the States, she will want her own kids to come as well; then another mother will do the same, and then another and then another, until you have 52,000 children crossing the border.

In the United States, coyotes are generally perceived as ruthless crim-   29 inals on the level of narco-traffickers. But those fleeing the violence in their native countries would make that trek with or without them; what the coyotes do is make the journey easier. They are part of our communities, and often they're our only hope. Tragically, evidence suggests that for most Central American families separated by the treacherous expanse of Mexico, the possibilities for reunification remain almost nil.

José thinks there will be a mass crackdown on coyotes in Central   30 America, triggered by US pressure. Ambassador Zamora confirms that Salvadoran President Sánchez Cerén has circulated instructions for such a crackdown in his country. José thinks the United States might call for the extradition of certain Central American coyotes, an idea that to Ambassador Zamora does not seem outside the realm of possibility. One thing is certain: the Obama administration's record number of deportations has only given coyotes like José new customers.

Of the $3.7 billion President Obama has requested from Congress to deal with the child migrant crisis, only $295 million will be set aside for the governments of El Salvador, Honduras and Guatemala to better control their borders and create conditions to ameliorate the lead causes of mass migration. If we assume that a budget represents a government's vision, then the US government believes that its responsibility to Central America in this crisis amounts to less than 8 percent. But the violence in Central America is far more than 8 percent of the problem. 31

The United States is not looking into creating a family reunification visa, nor has it announced any plans to grant asylum or refugee status to thousands of children who risk death in Central America if they return. Instead, the US government plans to continue deporting immigrants and financing Central American governments to combat their coyotes and better patrol their borders. 32

Cracking down on coyotes will surely slow the flood of children coming to the United States for a time. The Obama administration may also approve quicker methods for deporting children, which will diminish the flow as well. But none of these policies get to the heart of the matter. Central American mothers and fathers will continue to seek ways to be reunited with their children; they will continue to try to get them out of violent places and keep them safe. And if no one offers a better alternative, coyotes will continue to be their only way to do this. The children will not stop coming. 33

Thinking about the Essay

1. Martínez begins his essay with an anecdote about one El Salvadorian boy, David de la O. Is this introduction an effective way to begin the essay? Why or why not? He uses several other examples of people he has talked with. What do these interviews and direct quotations add to the essay?

2. What is Martínez's thesis? What do the statistics Martínez cites add to the personal anecdotes? What other evidence does he present to support his claim? Does he present sufficient evidence to support his stance? Does he convince you to agree with his position?

3. In Paragraph 14, Martínez makes the claim that the United States has played a role in this mass immigration of children. According to the author, what is the United States doing to try to solve the problem? Are these actions helping?

4. What does Martínez claim is the major reason that so many Central American children are coming to the United States and that the children will continue to come? Does he suggest any solution to this problem?

5. Who are the coyotes? What is the connotation of this word *coyote*? What is the history of the coyotes?

Responding in Writing

6. Write an essay in which you identify and explain the causes of this immigration issue, according to Martínez.

7. Write an essay in which you propose some actions that would mitigate the situation of the migration of children into the United States. Explain and support your proposals.

8. Write a letter to your congressman or senator in which you state, explain, and support your position on the issues of immigration, and ask him or her to take legislative action in support of your position.

Networking

9. Discuss with a small group of your classmates how the people attempting to migrate to the United States are similar to and different from the Palestinians attempting to enter the checkpoints into Israel.

10. What is the current news about immigration into the United States from Central American countries? What are the conflicts between President Obama and Congress regarding this situation? Do some research on the current controversies and proposed solutions, and share what you discover with a small group of your classmates. Discuss how you think some of the immigration problems might be solved. Present a summary of your group discussion to the class.

Why I Could Never Hate America

Mehdi Hasan

Mehdi Hasan graduated from Christ Church College, Oxford, in 2000 with a degree in Philosophy, Politics, and Economics. He began his career as a journalist by answering phones, conducting research, and serving in several progressively important positions at newspapers and television studios in London. Previously senior editor of politics at the *New Statesman*, today Hasan is the political director of the *Huffington Post* UK. He is the coauthor of a biography of Ed Miliband, a British Labour Party politician; has contributed articles to the *Evening Standard*, *Daily Mail*, and

The New York Times; and has appeared on a variety
of television news shows. In this posting from his blog
at the *New Statesman*, Mehdi recounts a difficult
personal episode at Bush Intercontinental Airport
in Houston that tested his faith in the American
experience.

Before Reading

Have you ever had a problem while boarding a flight or coming off one at an
American airport? In a more general sense, what is your experience of security
policies at airports, bus terminals, or train stations? Why might the conflicts that
overseas travelers experience in the United States contribute to a sense of
anti-Americanism?

"Any jokes or inappropriate remarks may result in your arrest," says   1
a robotic voice over the Tannoy at Bush Intercontinental Airport in
Houston, as I join the silent procession of bleary-eyed passengers disem-
barking from the plane after a ten-hour transatlantic flight. Welcome, as
they say, to the United States.

I'm in Texas on holiday, making the annual pilgrimage to see my   2
in-laws. I married an American in 2003, and each time we return to her

A security officer searches a businessman at the airport.

Mehdi Hasan, "Why I Could Never Hate America," *New Statesman*. (March 22, 2010). Reprinted
with permission by *New Statesman*.

homeland I'm reminded of the *New Yorker* journalist Hendrik Hertzberg's description of the "brutal fuck-you that greets foreigners arriving in the United States," and his call to U.S. immigration officials to stop making "preventive war" on innocent tourists. "It might make us more friends."

But making friends isn't high on the agenda at Bush Intercontinental. 3 This is my ninth trip to Houston since 2000, and it doesn't get any easier. I attributed a rare smooth entry in March last year to the change in administration, from bellicose Bush to benign Barack. My mistake.

"What is the purpose of your trip?" asks a morose airport official, 4 thumbing through my passport and refusing to look me in the eye. The badge on his arm says "U.S. Customs and Border Patrol," part of the department of homeland security. Perhaps I don't look happy enough to be here on holiday. Moments later, I'm deposited in a homeland security "holding lounge." "Why am I here?" I ask the nearest uniformed officer. "Random check," he grunts. Random? I'm sitting in a room filled exclusively with black, Hispanic and Asian passengers.

Name and shame

Nor is it my first time in this "lounge." A few years ago I spent several 5 hours here, detained because my surname matched that of a wanted insurgent inside Iraq. Yes, "Hasan"—the Middle Eastern equivalent of "Smith" or "Jones." Incidentally, I note an addition to the waiting room in the form of a giant map of Afghanistan and Pakistan. Iraq is so 2003.

Why does my detention matter? Isn't my inconvenience far less impor- 6 tant than U.S. airport security? Of course, but as the former secretary of state Colin Powell remarked in 2007: "We are taking too much counsel of our fears . . . Let's make sure people come to Disney World and not throw them up against the wall in Orlando simply because they have a Muslim name . . . Let's show the world a face of openness and what a democratic system can do."

Time and again we have been told that the "war on terror" is at its core 7 a struggle for hearts and minds. Not so on U.S. borders, where foreigners are met, in Hertzberg's words, with "delays, ugliness, sullen contempt and near chaos while being treated alternately as cattle or potential terrorists." Despite Hollywood's best efforts, millions of people across the world no longer consider the U.S. to be "the land of the free and the home of the brave" (to quote the national anthem), the "shining city upon a hill" (Ronald Reagan), or the "indispensable nation" (Madeleine Albright).

Indeed, anti-Americanism is rife. Some argue it has a long and shameful 8 history, pre-dating even the founding of the United States in 1776. In the mid-18th century, the French naturalist the Comte de Buffon—together with Voltaire and the Dutch philosopher Cornelius de Pauw, among others—condemned the "degeneracy" of the inhabitants of the Americas. But as the British historian Tony Judt points out, anti-Americanism today is not confined to smug intellectuals—European or otherwise. Most foreigners are untroubled by the cultural dominance of the U.S., and many even aspire to the so-called American way of life. "Most of them don't despise America, and they certainly don't hate Americans," Judt writes. "What upsets them is U.S. foreign policy. . . ."

There is evidence to support this. During the eight years of the Bush   9 administration, with its lawless and bloody wars, positive opinion of the U.S. declined in most European countries. A Pew Global Attitudes Project poll showed how, between 2000 and 2006, "favourable opinions" of the U.S. dropped from 83 percent to 56 percent in the UK, from 62 percent to 39 percent in France and from 78 percent to 37 percent in Germany. In the Middle East, Zogby International found that negative attitudes towards the U.S. jumped between 2002 and 2004, from 76 percent to 98 percent in Egypt, from 61 percent to 88 percent in Morocco and from 87 percent to 94 percent in Saudi Arabia—and these are allies of Uncle Sam. Respondents in most of these countries said they objected, above all, to U.S. foreign policies that they considered unjust.

Love, actually

In *Destiny Disrupted: a History of the World Through Islamic Eyes*, the   10 Afghan-American writer Tamim Ansary shows how the Middle Eastern view of the U.S. in the early 20th century was much more positive than negative. Wilsonian idealism was seductive to Arabs living under colonial rule but craving self-determination. It was, Ansary argues, only after the CIA-funded coup against the secular, democratically elected prime minister of Iran, Muhammed Mossadeq, that anger and disillusionment with the U.S. spread across the region.

Noam Chomsky, bête noire of the right, has long argued that the   11 notion of anti-Americanism itself seeks to excuse the crimes of U.S. elites and "identify state policy with the society, the people, the culture." It is an important point. I condemn the actions of the U.S. government in Iraq, Afghanistan and Yemen, without attacking my American friends in Houston, LA or New York.

"I am willing to love all mankind," Samuel Johnson said, "except an   12 American." I cannot agree. I may be considered anti-American, in that I abhor many U.S. foreign policies, but the person I love most happens to be an American. America is not the American government. Nor is it the U.S. border patrol.

Thinking about the Essay

1. What is Hasan's claim, and where does he state it? How does he support his argument?

2. How does the writer establish a specific tone and mood in the opening paragraph?

3. Do you think that Hasan engages in **refutation** in this essay? Why or why not?

4. Hasan divides his essay into brief sections. Explain whether or not you think this strategy detracts from the unity of the selection.

5. What allusions do you find in this essay? List these references, identify each one, and then explain the writer's purpose in presenting them.

Responding in Writing

6. Write an analysis of the argumentative style, structure, and tone that Hasan employs in this essay.

7. Argue for or against the proposition that anti-Americanism is an improper or overblown reaction to current US foreign policy.

8. Basing your essay on the statement by Noam Chomsky in paragraph 11, write a paper in which you offer a strategy whereby one can be critical of certain American foreign policy initiatives but at the same time maintain a pro-American perspective.

Networking

9. In small groups, debate the proposition that anti-American attitudes ignore or undermine the efforts of the American government and American people to do good around the world. Present the outcome of this debate to the class.

10. Locate Hasan's blog on the Internet, and provide a profile based on your reading of at least three of his postings.

The America I Love

ELIE WIESEL

Elie Wiesel was awarded the Nobel Peace Prize in 1986. Born in Romania in 1928, he was sent at the age of fifteen to a Nazi concentration camp along with his mother, father, and sister. Only Wiesel survived. He was liberated by American forces at Buchenwald in 1945. Wiesel's first book, *Night* (1960), recounted his experience at Buchenwald; he has written more than forty books since then and has become a major voice in the campaign for global peace and security. Wiesel became a US citizen in 1963. In the following essay, published in *Parade* magazine in 2004, Wiesel takes issue with critics of American foreign policy.

Before Reading

Do you think that the positive role of the United States in foreign affairs is often unappreciated by peoples and nations that benefit from our aid? Why or why not?

The day I received American citizenship was a turning point in my life. I had ceased to be stateless. Until then, unprotected by any government and unwanted by any society, the Jew in me was overcome by a feeling of pride mixed with gratitude. 1

From that day on, I felt privileged to belong to a country which, for two centuries, has stood as a living symbol of all that is charitable and decent to victims of injustice everywhere—a country in which every person is entitled to dream of happiness, peace and liberty; where those who have are taught to give back. 2

Grandiloquent words used for public oratory? Even now, as America is in the midst of puzzling uncertainty and understandable introspection because of tragic events in Iraq, these words reflect my personal belief. For I cannot forget another day that remains alive in my memory: April 11, 1945. 3

That day I encountered the first American soldiers in the Buchenwald concentration camp. I remember them well. Bewildered, disbelieving, they walked around the place, hell on earth, where our destiny had been played out. They looked at us, just liberated, and did not know what to do or say. Survivors snatched from the dark throes of death, we were empty of all hope—too weak, too emaciated to hug them or even speak to them. Like lost children, the American soldiers wept and wept with rage and sadness. And we received their tears as if they were heartrending offerings from a wounded and generous humanity. 4

Ever since that encounter, I cannot repress my emotion before the flag and the uniform—anything that represents American heroism in battle. That is especially true on July Fourth. I reread the Declaration of Independence, a document sanctified by the passion of a nation's thirst for justice and sovereignty, forever admiring both its moral content and majestic intonation. Opposition to oppression in all its forms, defense of all human liberties, celebration of what is right in social intercourse: All this and much more is in that text, which today has special meaning. 5

Granted, U.S. history has gone through severe trials, of which anti-black   6
racism was the most scandalous and depressing. I happened to witness it in
the late Fifties, as I traveled through the South. What did I feel? Shame. Yes,
shame for being white. What made it worse was the realization that, at that
time, racism was the law, thus making the law itself immoral and unjust.

Still, my generation was lucky to see the downfall of prejudice in many   7
of its forms. True, it took much pain and protest for that law to be changed,
but it was. Today, while fanatically stubborn racists are still around, some
of them vocal, racism as such has vanished from the American scene. That
is true of anti-Semitism too. Jew-haters still exist here and there, but organized anti-Semitism does not—unlike in Europe, where it has been growing
with disturbing speed.

As a great power, America has always seemed concerned with other   8
people's welfare, especially in Europe. Twice in the 20th century, it saved
the "Old World" from dictatorship and tyranny.

America understands that a nation is great not because its economy is   9
flourishing or its army invincible but because its ideals are loftier. Hence
America's desire to help those who have lost their freedom to conquer it
again. America's credo might read as follows: For an individual, as for a
nation, to be free is an admirable duty—but to help others become free is
even more admirable.

Some skeptics may object: But what about Vietnam? And Cambodia? And   10
the support some administrations gave to corrupt regimes in Africa or the
Middle East? And the occupation of Iraq? Did we go wrong—and if so, where?

And what are we to make of the despicable, abominable "interrogation   11
methods" used on Iraqi prisoners of war by a few soldiers (but even a few
are too many) in Iraqi military prisons?

Well, one could say that no nation is composed of saints alone. None is   12
sheltered from mistakes or misdeeds. All have their Cain and Abel. It takes
vision and courage to undergo serious soul-searching and to favor moral
conscience over political expediency. And America, in extreme situations,
is endowed with both. America is always ready to learn from its mishaps.
Self-criticism remains its second nature.

Not surprising, some Europeans do not share such views. In extreme   13
left-wing political and intellectual circles, suspicion and distrust toward
America is the order of the day. They deride America's motives for its
military interventions, particularly in Iraq. They say: It's just money. As if
America went to war only to please the oil-rich capitalists.

They are wrong. America went to war to liberate a population too long   14
subjected to terror and death.

We see in newspapers and magazines and on television screens the   15
mass graves and torture chambers imposed by Saddam Hussein and his

accomplices. One cannot but feel grateful to the young Americans who leave their families, some to lose their lives, in order to bring to Iraq the first rays of hope—without which no people can imagine the happiness of welcoming freedom.

Hope is a key word in the vocabulary of men and women like myself   16 and so many others who discovered in America the strength to overcome cynicism and despair. Remember the legendary Pandora's box? It is filled with implacable, terrifying curses. But underneath, at the very bottom, there is hope. Now as before, now more than ever, it is waiting for us.

Thinking about the Essay

1. Where does Wiesel make his claim? Why doesn't he place it in his introductory paragraph?

2. Consider that the writer published this essay in the July Fourth edition of a popular magazine. How does Wiesel adjust his tone to a broad readership and to the occasion? Do you find his tone to be effective? Justify your response with reference to the text.

3. From the start of this essay, Wiesel fashions a specific mood. How would you describe the emotional impact he attempts to project? Why, for example, does he mention the day he became an American citizen; the Declaration of Independence; and April 11, 1945? Does he combine emotional appeals with logical ones? Why or why not?

4. Explain the writer's use of cause-and-effect analysis to structure his essay.

5. Do you find Wiesel's conclusion to be effective? Why or why not?

Responding in Writing

6. Wiesel asserts that "Americans are taught to give back." Write a paper defending or criticizing this proposition. Provide at least three reasons in support of your position.

7. Do you think that citizens can criticize their country while at the same time remaining loyal and patriotic? Respond to this question in an argumentative essay.

8. Compose an extended definition of patriotism, using Wiesel's ideas as a point of departure.

Networking

9. As a class, debate the proposition that Wiesel is being too patriotic in his "love" of America. (We call this excessive patriotism *jingoism*.)

10. Conduct online research on a debatable, ambiguous, or regrettable aspect of recent U.S. policy—for instance, the invasion of Iraq, the use of drones, resistance to climate change, and so forth. Then write an argumentative essay explaining why this action was justified or unjustified and what this says about the America you love.

Americans Are Tuning Out the World

ALKMAN GRANITSAS

Alkman Granitsas is an American-born journalist who has reported on global issues in Asia and Europe for more than ten years. He is based in Athens and is currently the bureau chief for Greece and Cyprus at *The Wall Street Journal*; he has contributed articles to *Business Week*, the *Far Eastern Economic Review*, and numerous other journals. In the following essay, from the November 24, 2005, issue of the online journal *Yale Global*, Granitsas warns against the consequences of a trend toward cultural and political isolationism in the United States.

Before Reading

Do you believe that America is "a shining city on the hill"? Why or why not?

For all the talk about a global village, there are actually two communities in the world today: Americans and everyone else. The average Frenchman, Brazilian, or Pakistani is becoming more attuned to the American way of life, but Americans themselves are increasingly tuning out the rest of the globe. At a time when U.S. power, benefiting from globalization, is unchallenged in the world, a disinterested electorate could be a recipe for trouble. 1

Foreigners have long bemoaned the "isolationist" attitude of Americans—safely protected by two oceans and their tabula rasa history. But over the last several decades, that isolation has deepened. Americans now pay less attention to international affairs, and read less foreign news than at any time in the last two generations. Relative to the global boom in international travel, tourism, and business, fewer Americans go overseas or study a foreign language at university. The truth is that Americans are becoming relatively less—not more—engaged with the world in general. 2

A few facts. Since the early 1970s, the American public has paid less and less attention to foreign affairs. According to Gallup polls from presidential election years 1948 through 1972, Americans used to rank foreign affairs as the most important issue facing the nation. Since then, however, with the single exception of the 2004 elections, the economy has been ranked first. 3

Over the same period, the percentage of American university students 4
studying a foreign language has steadily declined. According to a report
funded by the U.S. Department of Education, in 1965, more than 16 percent of all American university students studied a foreign language. Now
only 8.6 percent do.

It has long been known that fewer Americans have passports, and travel 5
less, than their counterparts in other developed economies. And while a
record 21 percent of all Americans now have passports and are traveling
more, the number going overseas in the past 20 years—not just to neighboring Canada and Mexico—has grown at a slower rate than the number
of overseas visitors to America or the growth in international tourism in
general. And indeed, during the late 1980s and early 1990s, the number of
Americans even applying for a passport declined in several years.

American media coverage of foreign affairs has also been diminish- 6
ing. For example, according to a 2004 Columbia University survey, the
presence of foreign news stories in American newspapers has been dropping since the late 1980s. In 1987, overseas news accounted for about
27 percent of front page stories in American newspapers—about the same
as a decade earlier. By 2003, foreign news accounted for just 21 percent of
front page stories, while coverage of domestic affairs more than doubled
over the same period. On television, both the number of American network
news bureaus overseas and the amount of air-time spent on foreign news
fell by half in the 1990s.

Why are Americans progressively tuning out the rest of the world? The 7
reason is twofold. But both confirm the cherished belief of most Americans:
that their country is a "shining city on the hill." And the rest of the world
has relatively little to offer.

Consider first, that for the past 45 years, Americans have witnessed a 8
massive immigration boom. Since 1960, more than 20 million immigrants
have come to the United States—the greatest influx of newcomers in the last
hundred years, surpassing even the wave of immigrants that arrived in the
first three decades of the 20th century. Two-thirds of these newcomers—
more than 15 million—have come in just the past 25 years.

That they should come bears out the myth that America is a melt- 9
ing pot of peoples. Indeed, the iconic images of the first Plymouth Rock
Pilgrims and the Ellis Island immigrants of the early 1900s are at the very
center of American popular mythology. More recently, news footage of
Mexican-Americans rushing the fences on the southern borders shows
that America attracts all comers. And every single American—from the
mid-western blue collar worker to the pedigreed New England blueblood—
knows their forebears came from someplace else. Chances are they've met
or know someone—the Bangladeshi working at the 7-Eleven, the Chinese

scientist on TV, the Somali cab driver at the airport—who has come even more recently.

With the whole world apparently trying to get to America, the average   10 American can only ask: why look to the rest of the world? After all, why would everyone try to come here if there was anything worthwhile over there? It is telling that according to a 2002 National Geographic survey, 30 percent of Americans believed the population of America to be between 1 and 2 billion people. For most Americans, it must seem like everyone is rushing the fences these days.

The second reason is that for much of the last two decades most (but   11 not all) Americans have seen their economic well-being grow relative to the rest of the world. Through much of the 1990s, American consumer confidence and real disposable income have risen at their fastest levels since the relatively golden age of U.S. economic growth of the 1960s. These have been matched by perceptions of increased wealth from a stock market rally that, with interruptions, lasted from the early 1980s until three years ago.

Why should that matter? Because since the days of ancient Rome, it is   12 an axiom of political science that economic well-being dulls the appetite of citizens to participate in civil affairs. It is something that de Tocqueville observed more than a hundred years ago.

"There is, indeed, a most dangerous passage in the history of a demo-   13 cratic people," de Tocqueville observed. "When the taste for physical grat-ifications among them has grown more rapidly than their education and their experience of free institutions . . . the discharge of political duties appears to them to be a troublesome impediment which diverts them from their occupations and business."

Long before 9/11, the Asian tsunami, SARS, the bird flu, and the rela-   14 tively weaker dollar, Americans were already growing less interested in the rest of the world. Since then, they have found even more reasons to tune out.

The implications, however, are disturbing. Because of America's preem-   15 inent position in world affairs—and its role in "globalization," its foreign policy matters more than any other country on earth. But can America shape a responsible foreign policy with such an uninformed electorate? The world may be turning into a "global village," but the average American has moved to the suburbs.

Thinking about the Essay

1. What is Granitsas's claim, and where does he state it? Do you detect any war-rant underpinning his claim? Explain.

2. How does Granitsas connect perceptions about immigration to the United States to the isolationist attitude of the average American?

3. Where does the essay shift from factual support of a claim to the causal analysis and attribution of psychological motives?

4. Why does Granitsas quote Alexis de Tocqueville at length (paragraph 13)? Who was de Tocqueville, and what does quoting him add to the argument of the essay?

5. Where in the essay does the author provide answers immediately following the question he has posed? Are there rhetorical questions anywhere in the essay? Why are these questions left unanswered, and what function do they serve in the essay?

Responding in Writing

6. In a brief essay, critique the "axiom" that economic well-being dulls the appetite of citizens to participate in civil affairs. Can you think of exceptions to this rule?

7. Write down your response to the popular view that Americans have a "tabula rasa history." Why would non-Americans view American history in this way?

8. Make a list of the factual indicators Granitsas mentions in the essay as measures of the engagement of the American public. What are the diagnostic limitations of each indicator? Analyze these indicators in an essay.

Networking

9. Do you rank foreign affairs as the most important issue facing the United States? Poll members of your class and, in a class discussion, attempt to explain the majority opinion.

10. Compare the coverage of one foreign affairs issue over the course of a week in two online journals, one published in the United States and one published in a foreign country (the French *Le Monde*, for example, or the British *Guardian*).

Waking Up from the American Dream

Sasha Abramsky

Sasha Abramsky is a freelance journalist and author who writes on politics and culture. He was born in England, studied politics, philosophy, and economics at Balliol College, Oxford, and moved to New York in 1993 to study journalism at Columbia University. His first book, *Hard Time Blues: How Politics Built a Prison Nation* (2002), examines the American prison system. Abramsky's most recent book, *The American Way of Poverty*, was published in 2013. Abramsky is currently a Senior Fellow at the New York City–based

Demos Foundation. In the following essay, published in the July 23, 2004, issue of *The Chronicle of Higher Education*, Abramsky asks why foreign sympathy for America, inspired by faith in the American Dream, dissipated at the turn of the new century.

Before Reading

Do you feel that the recent crisis of confidence in the United States among other nations also reflects a global loss of confidence in the ideal of the American Dream?

Last year I visited London and stumbled upon an essay in a Sunday paper written by Margaret Drabble, one of Britain's pre-eminent ladies of letters. "My anti-Americanism has become almost uncontrollable," she wrote. "It has possessed me, like a disease. It rises up in my throat like acid reflux, that fashionable American sickness. I now loathe the United States and what it has done to Iraq and the rest of the helpless world." 1

The essay continued in the same rather bilious vein for about a thousand words, and as I read it, two things struck me: The first was how appalled I was by Drabble's crassly oversimplistic analysis of what America was all about, of who its people were, and of what its culture valued; the second was a sense somewhat akin to fear as I thought through the implications of the venom attached to the words of this gentle scribe of the English bourgeoisie. After all, if someone whose country and class have so clearly benefited economically from the protections provided by American military and political ties reacts so passionately to the omnipresence of the United States, what must an angry, impoverished young man in a failing third world state feel? 2

I grew up in London in the 1970s and 1980s, in a country that was struggling to craft a postcolonial identity for itself, a country that was, in many ways, still reeling from the collapse of power it suffered in the post–World War II years. Not surprisingly, there was a strong anti-American flavor to much of the politics, the humor, the cultural chitchat of the period; after all, America had dramatically usurped Britannia on the world stage, and who among us doesn't harbor some resentments at being shunted onto the sidelines by a new superstar? 3

Today, however, when I talk with friends and relatives in London, when I visit Europe, the anti-Americanism is more than just sardonic asides, rueful Monty Python–style jibes, and haughty intimations of superiority. 4

Sasha Abramsky, "Waking Up from the American Dream," from *The Chronicle of Higher Education*, 7/23/04. Reprinted by permission of the author.

A public display of anti-American sentiment in Tehran.

Today something much more visceral is in the air. I go to my old home and I get the distinct impression that, as Drabble put it, people really *loathe* America somewhere deep, deep in their gut.

A Pew Research Center Global Attitudes Project survey recently found   5
that even in Britain, America's staunchest ally, more than 6 out of 10 people polled believed the United States paid little or no attention to that country's interests. About 80 percent of French and German respondents stated that, because of the war in Iraq, they had less confidence in the trustworthiness of America. In the Muslim countries surveyed, large majorities believed the war on terror to be about establishing U.S. world domination.

Indeed, in many countries—in the Arab world and in regions, such as   6
Western Europe, closely tied into American economic and military structures—popular opinion about both America the country and Americans as individuals has taken a serious hit. Just weeks ago, 27 of America's top

retired diplomats and military commanders warned in a public statement, "Never in the 2¼ centuries of our history has the United States been so isolated among the nations, so broadly feared and distrusted."

If true, that suggests that, while to all appearances America's allies con- 7
tinue to craft policies in line with the wishes of Washington, underneath the surface a new dynamic may well be emerging, one not too dissimilar to the Soviet Union's relations with its reluctant satellite states in Eastern Europe during the cold war. America's friends may be quiescent in public, deeply reluctant to toe the line in private. Drabble mentioned the Iraq war as her primary *casus belli* with the United States. The statement from the bipartisan group calling itself Diplomats and Military Commanders for Change focused on the Bush administration's recent foreign policy. But to me it seems that something else is also going on.

In many ways, the Iraq war is merely a pretext for a deeper discontent 8
with how America has seemed to fashion a new global society, a new economic, military, and political order in the decade and a half since the end of the cold war. America may only be riding the crest of a wave of modernization that, in all likelihood, would have emerged without its guiding hand. But add to the mix a discontent with the vast wealth and power that America has amassed in the past century and a deep sense of unease with the ways in which a secular, market-driven world divvies up wealth and influence among people and nations, and you have all the ingredients for a nasty backlash against America.

I'm not talking merely about the anti-globalism of dispossessed Third 9
World peasants, the fears of the loss of cultural sovereignty experienced by societies older and more traditional than the United States, the anger at a perceived American arrogance that we've recently been reading so much about. I'm talking about something that is rooted deeper in the psyches of other nations. I guess I mean a feeling of being marginalized by history; of being peripheral to the human saga; of being footnotes for tomorrow's historians rather than main characters. In short, a growing anxiety brought on by having another country and culture dictating one's place in the society of nations.

In the years since I stood on my rooftop in Brooklyn watching the 10
World Trade Center towers burn so apocalyptically, I have spent at least a part of every day wrestling with a host of existential questions. I can't help it—almost obsessively I churn thoughts over and over in my head, trying to understand the psychological contours of this cruel new world. The questions largely boil down to the following: Where has the world's faith in America gone? Where is the American Dream headed?

What is happening to that intangible force that helped shape our mod- 11
ern world, that invisible symbiotic relationship between the good will of

foreigners and the successful functioning of the American "way of life," that willingness by strangers to let us serve as the repository for their dreams, their hopes, their visions of a better future? In the same way that the scale of our national debt is made possible only because other countries are willing to buy treasury bonds and, in effect, lend us their savings, so it seems to me the American Dream has been largely facilitated by the willingness of other peoples to lend us their expectations for the future. Without that willingness, the Dream is a bubble primed to burst. It hasn't burst yet—witness the huge numbers who still migrate to America in search of the good life—but I worry that it is leaking seriously.

Few countries and cultures have risen to global prominence as quickly   12
as America did in the years after the Civil War. Perhaps the last time there was such an extraordinary accumulation of geopolitical, military, and economic influence in so few decades was 800 years ago, with the rise of the Mongol khanates. Fewer still have so definitively laid claim to an era, while that era was still unfolding, as we did—and as the world acknowledged— during the 20th century, "the American Century."

While the old powers of Europe tore themselves apart during World   13
War I, the United States entered the war late and fought the fight on other people's home terrain. While whole societies were destroyed during World War II, America's political and economic system flourished, its cities thrived, and its entertainment industries soared. In other words, as America rose to global pre-eminence during the bloody first half of the 20th century, it projected outward an aura of invulnerability, a vision of "normalcy" redolent with consumer temptations and glamorous cultural spectacles. In an exhibit at the museum on Ellis Island a few years back, I remember seeing a copy of a letter written by a young Polish migrant in New York to his family back home. Urging them to join him, he wrote that the ordinary person on the streets of America lived a life far more comfortable than aristocrats in Poland could possibly dream of.

In a way America, during the American Century, thus served as a safety   14
valve, allowing the world's poor to dream of a better place somewhere else; to visualize a place neither bound by the constraints of old nor held hostage to the messianic visions of revolutionary Marxist or Fascist movements so powerful in so many other parts of the globe.

Throughout the cold war, even as America spent unprecedented   15
amounts on military hardware, enough was left over to nurture the mass-consumption culture, to build up an infrastructure of vast proportions. And despite the war in Vietnam, despite the dirty wars that ravaged Latin America in the 1980s, despite America's nefarious role in promoting coups and dictatorships in a slew of countries-cum-cold-war-pawns around the globe, somehow much of the world preserved a rosy-hued vision of

America that could have been culled straight from the marketing rooms of Madison Avenue.

Now something is changing. Having dealt with history largely on its 16 own terms, largely with the ability to deflect the worst of the chaos to arenas outside our borders (as imperial Britain did in the century following the defeat of Napoleon in 1815, through to the disastrous events leading up to World War I in 1914), America has attracted a concentrated fury and vengeful ire of disastrous proportions. The willingness to forgive, embodied in so much of the world's embrace of the American Dream, is being replaced by a rather vicious craving to see America—which, under the Bush administration, has increasingly defined its greatness by way of military triumphs—humbled. Moreover, no great power has served as a magnet for such a maelstrom of hate in an era as saturated with media images, as susceptible to instantaneous opinion-shaping coverage of events occurring anywhere in the world.

I guess the question that gnaws at my consciousness could be rephrased 17 as: How does one give an encore to a bravura performance? It's either an anticlimax or, worse, a dismal failure—with the audience heading out the doors halfway through, talking not of the brilliance of the earlier music, but of the tawdriness of the last few bars. If the 20th century was the American Century, its best hopes largely embodied by something akin to the American Dream, what kind of follow-up can the 21st century bring?

In the immediate aftermath of September 11, an outpouring of genu- 18 ine, if temporary, solidarity from countries and peoples across the globe swathed America in an aura of magnificent victimhood. We, the most powerful country on earth, had been blindsided by a ruthless, ingenious, and barbaric enemy, two of our greatest cities violated. We demanded the world's tears, and, overwhelmingly, we received them. They were, we felt, no less than our due, no more than our merit. In the days after the trade center collapsed, even the Parisian daily *Le Monde*, not known for its pro-Yankee sentimentality, informed its readers, in an echo of John F. Kennedy's famous "Ich bin ein Berliner" speech, that "we are all Americans now."

Perhaps inevitably, however, that sympathy has now largely dissipated. 19 Powerful countries under attack fight back—ruthlessly, brutally, with all the economic, political, diplomatic, and military resources at their disposal. They always have; like as not, they always will. In so doing, perhaps they cannot but step on the sensibilities of smaller, less powerful dare I say it, less *imperial* nations and peoples. And as Britain, the country in which I grew up, discovered so painfully during the early years of World War II, sometimes the mighty end up standing largely alone, bulwarks against history's periodic tidal waves. In that fight, even if they emerge successful, they ultimately emerge also tarnished and somewhat humbled, their power and drive and confidence at least partly evaporated on the battlefield.

In the post–September 11 world, even leaving aside Iraq and all the dis-   20
tortions, half-truths, and lies used to justify the invasion, even leaving aside the cataclysmic impact of the Abu Ghraib prison photographs, I believe America would have attracted significant wrath simply in doing what had to be done in routing out the Taliban in Afghanistan, in reorienting its foreign policy to try and tackle international terror networks and breeding grounds. That is why I come back time and again in my mind to the tactical brilliance of Al Qaeda's September 11 attacks: If America hadn't responded, a green light would have been turned on, one that signaled that the country was too decadent to defend its vital interests. Yet in responding, the response itself was almost guaranteed to spotlight an empire bullying allies and enemies alike into cooperation and subordination and, thus, to focus an inchoate rage against the world's lone standing super-power. Damned if we did, damned if we didn't.

Which brings me back to the American Dream. In the past even as   21
our power grew, much of the world saw us, rightly or wrongly, as a moral beacon, as a country somehow largely outside the bloody, gory, oft-tyrannical history that carved its swath across so much of the world during the American Century. Indeed, in many ways, even as cultural elites in once-glorious Old World nations sneered at upstart, crass, consumerist America, the masses in those nations idealized America as some sort of Promised Land, as a place of freedoms and economic possibilities simply unheard of in many parts of the globe. In many ways, the American Dream of the last 100-some years has been more something dreamed by foreigners from afar, especially those who experienced fascism or Stalinism, than lived as a universal reality on the ground in the United States.

Things look simpler from a distance than they do on the ground. In the   22
past foreigners might have idealized America as a place whose streets were paved if not with gold, at least with alloys seeded with rare and precious metals, even while those who lived here knew it was a gigantic, complicated, multifaceted, continental country with a vast patchwork of cultures and creeds coexisting side by messy side. Today, I fear, foreigners slumber with dreamy American smiles on their sleeping faces no more; that intangible faith in the pastel-colored hue and soft contours of the Dream risks being shattered, replaced instead by an equally simplistic dislike of all things and peoples American.

Paradoxically these days it is the political elites—the leaders and policy   23
analysts and defense experts—who try to hold in place alliances built up in the post–World War II years as the *pax Americana* spread its wings, while the populaces shy away from an America perceived to be dominated by

corporations, military musclemen, and empire-builders-in-the-name-of-democracy; increasingly they sympathize with the unnuanced critiques of the Margaret Drabbles of the world. The Pew survey, for example, found that sizable majorities in countries such as Jordan, Morocco, Turkey, Germany, and France believed the war on terror to be largely about the United States wanting to control Middle Eastern oil supplies.

In other words, the *perception*—never universally held, but held by 24 enough people to help shape our global image—is changing. Once our image abroad was of an exceptional country accruing all the power of empire without the psychology of empire; now it is being replaced by something more historically normal—that of a great power determined to preserve and expand its might, for its own selfish interests and not much else. An exhibit in New York's Whitney Museum last year, titled "The American Effect," presented the works of 50 artists from around the world who portrayed an America intent on world dominance through military adventurism and gross consumption habits. In the run-up to the war in Iraq, Mikhail Gorbachev lambasted an America he now viewed as operating in a manner "far from real world leadership." Nelson Mandela talked of the United States as a country that "has committed unspeakable atrocities in the world."

Maybe the American Dream always was little more than marketing 25 hype (the author Jeffrey Decker writes in *Made in America* that the term itself was conjured up in 1931 by a populist historian named James Truslow Adams, perhaps as an antidote to the harsh realities of Depression-era America). But as the savagery of the images coming out of Iraq demonstrate all too well, we live in a world where image is if not everything, at least crucial. Perhaps I'm wrong and the American Dream will continue to sweeten the sleep of those living overseas for another century. I certainly hope, very much, that I'm wrong—for a world denuded of the Dream, however far from complex reality that Dream might have been, would be impoverished indeed. But I worry that that encore I mentioned earlier won't be nearly as breathtaking or as splendid as the original performance that shaped the first American century.

Thinking about the Essay

1. Why does Abramsky wait until paragraph 3 to inform the reader that he grew up in London? What effect does this strategic withholding of information have upon you as a reader?

2. List some of the illustrations that Abramsky invokes as "barometers" of public sentiment.

3. According to Abramsky, why is it important for the future of America that foreigners continue to idealize the country and believe in some concept of an American Dream?

4. How does Abramsky characterize American power as being the result of a symbiotic relationship or exchange with the rest of the world?

5. The concluding sentence picks up an extended **metaphor** (or conceit) that was introduced earlier in the essay. How effective is this metaphor as a structuring device?

Responding in Writing

6. Do you feel that the Iraq war was merely a pretext for a deeper discontent with America? In a brief essay, speculate on the nature of the discontent underlying one critique of the Iraq war that you have heard expressed.

7. Reread the no-win scenario outlined in paragraph 20. Do you agree with Abramksy's statement that America "would have attracted significant wrath simply in doing what had to be done"? Defend your opinion in an argumentative essay.

8. Have you ever felt "marginalized by history" as a result of your place of birth, time of birth, or other factors beyond your control? Write an essay explaining some of the factors that would contribute to that feeling.

Networking

9. In groups of three or four, list some key features of the American Dream, and share these lists with the class. Is there a concept of the American Dream common to everyone in the class?

10. Go online and view (or read about) some of the works that were on display in "The American Effect" exhibit at New York's Whitney Museum. Do you detect a "party line" in the way these artists view America? Are there perceptions of America that Abramsky might consider "nuanced"?

The Anti-Americans

Fouad Ajami

Fouad Ajami (1945–2014), of Lebanese Shiite Muslim ancestry, became an influential commentator and writer on Middle Eastern issues. He was educated at the University of Washington and Eastern Oregon University, was a senior fellow at Stanford University's Hoover Institution, Director of Middle East Studies at Johns Hopkins University's School of Advanced International Studies, and won a MacArthur Fellowship. He straddled different worlds, and in a time of much strife between Western and Arab societies he was an important, yet controversial, interpreter of the Middle East and helped American audiences understand Arab history and culture. In this article he discusses the roots of anti-Americanism across the globe, not just in Middle Eastern countries.

Before Reading

Do you think the United States is disliked by people in many countries? Or is the claim of anti-Americanism a myth, or is it often blown out of proportion? Why or why not?

America is unloved in the alleyways of Nablus and Karachi, and in the cafes of Paris: The Pew Research Center for the People and the Press came forth last month with news of anti-Americanism in foreign lands. Its Global Attitudes Project, directed by the pollster Andrew Kohut, and chaired and advised by former Secretary of State Madeleine Albright, told us that the "bottom has fallen out" of support for America in the Muslim world, that the rift has widened between Americans and Europeans. From 20 countries, pollsters returned with what they took to be evidence of a growing animus toward the U.S. Only 1% of Palestinians think "favorably" of the U.S.; the numbers are not much better in Jordan and Pakistan. Turkey, once reliably anchored in the Pax Americana, is now of a piece with its neighbors: only 15% of Turks now report positive views of the U.S. Leave the Muslim lands behind, and this anti-Americanism has infected other places and peoples—all the way from South Korea, where American power underpins Korean security, to France and Russia. 1

Americans ache to be loved in foreign places, and now the world denies us. But a mix of partisanship and naivete runs through this survey. Consider this leading question and the trail it opens: What's the problem with the U.S.?, the pollsters ask. Is it "mostly Bush," or "America in general," or both? Not surprisingly, President Bush is the culprit in France and Germany (74% attribute their anti-Americanism to him). 2

What does all this mean? What are we to make of the hatred in Egypt, for instance? Vast American treasure has been invested there, thousands of that crowded country's citizens have made it to America's shores and escaped destitution. But we are never benevolent in Egyptian eyes, and a kind of generalized anger toward America has taken hold there. 3

"Nations follow the religion of their kings," an Arab expression has it. The anti-Americanism of Egypt is the malignant strain that leaders wink at. You can't rail against Hosni Mubarak; so anti-Americanism is the permissible politics. Where the dream of modernism atrophies, as it has in Egypt, and a culture of abdication settles in, a people are easy prey to any doctrine 4

Reprinted from Fouad Ajami, "The Anti-Americans," *The Wall Street Journal*, July 3, 2003.

that absolves them of responsibility for their own world. Anti-Americanism is the placebo. There is no need in a culture of this kind to ask the crowd for consistency, to query the academic who does well by American foundation grants why he harbors such hate for America. The Pew pollsters fall for a legend and an evasion that those who rail against America often put forth to pretty up their anti-Americanism: It is not individual Americans they hate, but the United States! This is pure sophistry, but the pollsters report it as credible sentiment.

Consider Turkey next. It is odd among the Turks, this anti-Americanism. In their modern history, the Turks have been serious and empirical, not given to the cluster of sentiments that give anti-Americanism its potency in France or among the intellectuals of the Third World. Years ago, Mustafa Kemal Ataturk pointed Turkey westward, gave it a dream of renewal and self-help, and distanced it from its Arab-Muslim hinterland. But that was then, and now Kemalism has come apart. The secular, modernist dream in Turkey has cracked; and anti-Americanism blows Turkey's way from the Arab lands, and from Brussels and Berlin. 5

The fury of the Turkish protests against America's war plans in Iraq had a pathology all its own. It was nature imitating art: The Turks burning American flags, superimposing swastikas on portraits of President Bush, went at it, it seemed, in the hope that Europeans (real Europeans, that is) would take Turkey into the fold. The American presence had been benign and benevolent in Turkey. Americans have been Ankara's advocates in the European councils of power, and have been free of the Turkophobia just beneath the surface of European life. But suddenly this relationship that served Turkey so well was no longer good enough. The "soft" Islamists (there is no such thing, we should know by now) hacked at the Pax Americana; secularists averted their gaze and let stand this new anti-Americanism. Pollsters calling on the Turks found a people in distress, their economy on the ropes, their polity in an unfamiliar world beyond the simple certainties of Kemalism. 6

Running through the Pew survey is the explicit assumption that it had been better for America before the "unilateralism," and our campaign in Iraq: We called up this anti-Americanism. But leave the false empiricism of these numbers, and there is nothing new in Amman, and Cairo, and Paris. No one said good things about America in Egypt in the 1990s, either. It was then that the Islamists of Egypt had taken to the road, to Hamburg and Kandahar, to hatch a monstrous conspiracy against the U.S. And it was then, during our fabled stock market run, when globalizers were celebrating the triumph of our economic model over the protected versions in places like France, when anti-Americanism became the uncontested ideology of French public life. We were barbarous, a threat to their cuisine, 7 to their language. Our pension funds were acquiring their assets. We executed too many criminals. All this during a decade when we were told that we were loved abroad.

Much has been made of the sympathy that the French expressed for 8
America in the immediate aftermath of Sept. 11, and of the speed with which America presumably squandered that sympathy. Much has been made of that editorial in Le Monde, "Nous Sommes Tous Americains"— We Are All Americans—penned after Sept. 11. But it took the paper precious little time to revoke the sympathy it had expressed on Sept. 12. To maintain France's sympathy, and that of Le Monde, we would have had to turn the other cheek to al Qaeda, and engage the Muslim world in some high civilizational dialogue. Anti-Americanism flatters France, and gives its unwanted Muslims a claim on the political life of a country that knows not what to do with them.

"America is everywhere," Ignazio Silone once observed. An idea of it, a 9
fantasy of it, hovers over distant lands. In the days that followed the attacks of Sept. 11, a young Palestinian gave expression to the image America holds out in places where its shadow falls: the boy passing out sweets in celebration of America's grief wondered aloud as to the impact of the bombings on his ability to get a U.S. visa. He felt no great contradiction. He had no feeling of affection or loyalty for the land he yearned to migrate to. He grew up to the familiar drums of anti-Americanism. He had implicated America in his life's circumstances. You can't reason with his worldview. You can only wish for him deliverance from his incoherence—or go there, questionnaire in hand, and return with dispatches of people at odds with American policies. You can make foreigners say the sort of things about America you wanted to say yourself. It is an old literary trick. Everyone knew that Montesquieu's "Persian Letters" were indeed Parisian letters, a writer's device to chronicle France's foibles in the early 18th century. His "Persians," Rhedi and Usbek, spoke of France. It is our American pollsters we hear speaking to us through those Turks and Arabs and Frenchmen who, on cue, were ready to speak of America's alienation from the rest of the world.

Thinking about the Essay

1. Look up the definition of *statistical validity*. Does Ajami consider the Pew Research survey on anti-Americanism statistically valid? Why or why not? What evidence does he provide to support his position?

2. Identify and analyze the specific countries that the Pew Research Center and Ajami cite in the discussion of anti-Americanism. How and why did people in each of these countries react? How are their attitudes and actions similar? How are they different? What does Ajami assert as the causes of these attitudes?

3. In paragraph 4, Ajami states, "Where the dream of modernism atrophies, as it has in Egypt, and a culture of abdication settles in, a people are easy prey to any doctrine that absolves them of responsibility for their own world. [In this case] Anti-Americanism is the placebo." What is the meaning of this statement? Identify other situations in which people may use a doctrine to absolve themselves of responsibility for their situation.

4. What is the irony in the example of the young Palestinian in the last paragraph? Can you identify other examples of irony in recent news events or in your own life?

5. In the middle of the last paragraph, the author uses the second person *you* to address the readers. Why does Ajami address the readers at this point in the essay? Is this shift to *you* effective? Rephrase the sentences in which Ajami uses *you* by changing *you* to *people* or readers and *they*. Does the change make the section more or less effective? Why?

Responding in Writing

6. Think of a time when you visited another country and talked with someone, or when you talked with someone from another country who was in the United States. What can you deduce to be this person's opinion of America? Write a narrative in which you state and explain his or her attitudes toward America.

7. Write an essay in which you analyze Ajami's explanation of the causes and effects of anti-Americanism.

8. Choose a situation, an attitude, or a stereotype that you believe is based on a misunderstanding or misconception. Write an argumentative essay in which you try to convince your readers that this belief is inaccurate and perhaps even harmful.

Networking

9. Visit the Pew Research Center's website. This organization states that it is a nonpartisan, non-advocacy public opinion fact tank that conducts public opinion polling to inform the public about the issues, attitudes, and trends shaping America and the world. Study the center's description of its methods. Analyze how well the center followed its methods to present objective, statistically valid and reliable information in the opinion poll about anti-Americanism around the globe.

10. With a small group of your classmates, construct a poll about an issue on your campus or in your city. Be careful to avoid biased or leading questions in your poll. Then distribute your poll to 20 or more people (perhaps your classmates), tabulate the results, and write a report in which you summarize and interpret these results. Then share your findings with your class.

Speaking in Tongues: Does Language Unify or Divide Us?

CHAPTER 4

The diverse voices in the previous chapters reflect some of the numerous ethnic and racial aspects of the new American mosaic—as well as global perceptions of American exceptionalism. Part of this mosaic is the variety of languages we hear on American streets and college campuses. Of course, you have been taught to speak and write the same language—that standard variety of English that places you in the college classroom today. Knowing the standard English "code" provides you with a powerful tool, offering pragmatic and liberating ways to gain control over your world.

However, other languages might compete for your attention at home or in your community. Powerful constituencies—politicians and advertisers among them—exploit this fact. For example, some Anglo politicians try to speak Spanish to Latino crowds (often to the amusement of native Spanish speakers). Other constituencies, threatened by our multilingual world, try to enact English-only laws in various states. Moreover, governments often use language—for example, words like "patriotism" or "Islamic fascism"—to advance political goals. Language can unify or divide a community or nation, but basically it remains a mark of your identity. To know a language or languages permits you to navigate your community, culture, and even global society.

Imagine, for example, what it would be like if you were illiterate. For one thing, you wouldn't be in college. You might not be able to read a menu or fill out a job application. You might not be interested in voting because you cannot read the names of the candidates. Illiteracy is common around the world—and far more common in the United States than you might think.

We have vivid reminders of both the cost of illiteracy and the power of literacy in film and literature. In the film *Driving Miss Daisy*, the character played by Morgan Freeman goes through most of his life pretending to read the daily newspaper. When Daisy (played by Jessica Tandy) teaches him to read, his world—and his comprehension of it—expands. Or consider one of

91

the memorable sequences in *The Autobiography of Malcolm X*. Malcolm teaches himself to read and write when he is in prison. He starts at the beginning of the dictionary and works his way to the end. Going into prison as Richard Little, he comes out as Malcolm X, his identity reconstructed not only by the acquisition of a new system of belief—Islam—but also by a newly acquired literacy. In his writing and in his recovered life, Malcolm X harnessed the power of language to transform himself and his understanding of the world.

AP Photo/Robert Mecca

The neighborhood of Elmhurst, Queens, in New York City, is one of the most ethnically and linguistically diverse places in the world. At Elmhurst's Newtown High School, students come from more than a hundred countries and speak at least thirty-nine languages. In this photograph, local schoolchildren take part in the neighborhood's annual International Day Festival on May 27, 1999.

Thinking about the Image

1. Recall a class photograph from your childhood. Was your school as diverse as this group of schoolchildren? What are the advantages of being exposed to so many nationalities and languages at such a young age? What are the disadvantages?
2. News photographers often shoot many images of the same event and then decide with their editors which unique image best captures the spirit of the event. Why do you think this photo was selected?
3. Are there parades for various ethnic or social groups in your community? How are those events covered in the local news media?
4. Would this parade have achieved its purpose, or appealed to its audience, as effectively if the marchers were adults instead of children? Why or why not? Would the message (or purpose) have been different? In what way?

Think of language, then, as a radical weapon. Language permits you to share experiences and emotions, process information, analyze situations and events, defend a position, advocate a cause, and make decisions. Language contributes to the growth of the self. Language is the bedrock of our academic, social, and professional lives. Language is a liberating force—but some writers in this chapter remind us that language can also be culturally and politically divisive.

The idea that language is the key to our identity and our perception of the world is not new. Early Greek and Roman philosophers believed that you could not be a good thinker or writer unless you were a good person. Assuming that you are a good person, you possess a repertoire of mental skills that you can bring to bear on various situations and dimensions of your life. You can draw inferences, interpret conditions, understand causal relationships, develop arguments, make intelligent choices, and so forth. But have you ever found yourself in a situation where you know what you mean but not how to say it? Or think of how difficult it must be for people acquiring a second language; they know what they mean in their primary language but cannot express it in their new one. The essays in this chapter deal with precisely this situation.

The writers in this chapter illuminate the power and paradox of language. They link language, culture, politics, identity, imagination, and creativity. They use language with skill, intelligence, and emotion. They work with the problems and contradictions of language, seeking answers to the question "Who am I, and where do my words—my languages—fit into the American as well as the world mosaic?"

Tweet Like an Egyptian

KEVIN CLARKE

> Kevin Clarke is a writer living in New York City. He contributes articles on religion, culture, and politics to uscatholic.org. Clarke is also a senior editor and chief correspondent at the publication *America: The National Catholic Weekly*. In this article from the April 2011 issue of *U.S. Catholic*, Clarke examines the impact of social networking on recent upheavals and revolutions in the Arab world.

Before Reading

What is your response to the assertion that the "Arab Spring" would not have been possible without various forms of social networking and new ways of communicating with people demanding political change?

In the early days of the World Wide Web, HTML wizards maintained the 1
googly eyed optimism of people who thought they were changing the
world. Here was a civically electrifying form of communication that would
obliterate time and space and the distance between people. Agonizing over
our 2,400 baud TCP connections, and sharing strategies over regional bul-
letin board systems, there was a brief shining moment of giddy joy in the
very new and unironic enthusiasm for the very bold.

Then the retailers and the marketers and the pornographers arrived. In 2
the space of just a few months the Internet transformed from the electronic
marketplace of new ideas and experiences into, well, just the same old
marketplace of crud nobody really needed.

But since January in the Arab world that early promise of revolution 3
and real change that drove the first Internet reasserted itself. It was not just
that the protesters for human freedom, civil rights, economic justice, and
the end of soul-crushing oligarchy in Egypt and elsewhere used the latest
social networking technologies of the Internet to organize themselves and
outmaneuver the entrenched authority in their respective societies. It was
not just that they used the Internet to get their message out to the rest of
the world and to inspire likeminded protests in other nations.

The young people who took to the streets in Egypt and Tunisia were 4
not demanding a freedom they could only imagine, they were demanding
the freedom they had already experienced in their virtual lives, a freedom
they wanted to translate into their actual daily lives. On the Internet they
had already learned what it looked and felt like to inhabit a society where
opinions were welcome and thoughts could be freely expressed, an alternative reality that encouraged the limitlessness of imagination and the
life-affirming energy of human freedom.

But the Internet did even more. It empowered them with the information 5
they needed to question and challenge authority in their nonvirtual societies.

Wikileaks has endured white-hot criticism for its purported irrespon- 6
sibility in releasing U.S. classified documents and diplomatic cables that
capture what U.S. officials really think about conditions and political
characters around the world. The data dump orchestrated by Wikileaks,
a new kind of communication outlet that could only have been brought
to life via the infrastructure, capability, and spirit of the Internet, has been
condemned as a threat to the lives of confidential sources and to diplomacy as we know it. So far, however, what it has mostly proved to be is a
regime-shattering tool of information sharing.

Most people in Tunisia endured a begrudging awareness of the lar- 7
cenous leadership of the Ben Ali regime. But something about seeing the
depth of that larceny and civic indifference spelled out in a U.S. State
Department cable was the electronic straw that broke the camel's back and
propelled people into the streets.

No one knows where this new era of Internet-generated people power 8
may ultimately lead. In chaos there is both opportunity and danger. It's
still possible that the energy for change and thirst for freedom on the Arab
streets today could be subverted. Revolutions have been co-opted before.
But it is at least as likely that the Internet will continue to be a viaduct of
energy and information that empowers and enlightens rather than degrades
and distracts. It maintains its potential to be a force that makes real the
spiritual connectedness of all people.

Maybe it will be a force strong enough to rouse the democratic 9
impulses of the people in a nation which, though materially better off
than many other states, maintains levels of income and resource inequity
and poverty that rival any demoralized society in the developing world.
If you're wondering what state I'm talking about, get online and explore
a little bit.

Thinking about the Essay

1. What is Clarke's claim in this essay? Does he state this claim or imply it? Explain your response.

2. How do the title and opening paragraph grasp and hold the reader's interest?

3. This essay appeared in a journal affiliated with the Catholic Church. What can we assume about the writer's audience and the values of the writer and his readership? How are these values reflected in the essay?

4. What examples does Clarke use to support his claim?

5. Clarke's closing paragraphs attempt to prompt his audience to action. How does he develop this persuasive technique?

Responding in Writing

6. Do you agree or disagree with the claim that social networking empowers people around the world with the information they need "to question and challenge authorities in their nonvirtual societies" (paragraph 5)? Write an argumentative essay in response to this question.

7. The writer presents several examples to support his claim. Do you find these examples to be sufficient, effective, and persuasive? Justify your response in an analytical essay.

8. Clarke discusses WikiLeaks in paragraph 6. Find out more about WikiLeaks, and then write an argument either in favor of or opposed to the release of classified documents.

Networking

9. Work in small groups of four or five. Pool your knowledge about the impact of the Internet and social networking on global political change. After discussing this

topic as a group, report to the class on your findings, using specific evidence to support your conclusions.

10. Go online with another student and—as Clarke recommends—"explore a little bit." In your exploration, research the impact of Twitter on one specific protest movement. Take notes on your findings, and report them to the class.

Mother Tongue

Amy Tan

Amy Tan was born in Oakland, California, in 1952, only two and a half years after her parents emigrated from China to the United States. She was educated at San Jose State University and the University of California at Berkeley and then worked as a reporter and technical writer. Tan is best known as a novelist whose fiction focuses on the conflict in culture between Chinese parents and their Americanized children. Her first novel, *The Joy Luck Club* (1989), was highly popular and adapted by Hollywood as a feature film. Tan's other novels are *The Kitchen God's Wife* (1991), *The Hundred Secret Senses* (1995), *The Bonesetter's Daughter* (2001), *Saving Fish from Drowning* (2006), and *The Valley of Amazement* (2013). Tan published a nonfiction work, *The Opposite of Fate: A Book of Musings*, in 2003. Tan's complicated relationship with her mother, Daisy, who died of Alzheimer's disease in 1999 at the age of eighty-three, is central to much of her fiction. In this essay, published in 1990 in *The Threepenny Review*, Tan, who has a master's degree in linguistics, invokes her mother in exploring the "Englishes" that immigrants employ as they navigate American culture.

Before Reading

How many "Englishes" do you speak, and what types of English do you speak in various situations? Is the English you speak in the classroom the same as you speak in your home or dormitory?

I am not a scholar of English or literature. I cannot give you much more   1
than personal opinions on the English language and its variations in this country or others.

I am a writer. And by that definition, I am someone who has always 2
loved language. I am fascinated by language in daily life. I spend a great
deal of my time thinking about the power of language—the way it can
evoke an emotion, a visual image, a complex idea, or a simple truth. Language is the tool of my trade. And I use them all—all the Englishes I grew
up with.

Recently, I was made keenly aware of the different Englishes I do use. 3
I was giving a talk to a large group of people, the same talk I had already
given to half a dozen other groups. The nature of the talk was about my
writing, my life, and my book, *The Joy Luck Club*. The talk was going
along well enough, until I remembered one major difference that made
the whole talk sound wrong. My mother was in the room. And it was
perhaps the first time she had heard me give a lengthy speech, using the
kind of English I have never used with her. I was saying things like, "The
intersection of memory upon imagination" and "There is an aspect of
my fiction that relates to thus-and-thus"—a speech filled with carefully
wrought grammatical phrases, burdened, it suddenly seemed to me, with
nominalized forms, past perfect tenses, conditional phrases, all the forms of
standard English that I had learned in school and through books, the forms
of English I did not use at home with my mother.

Just last week, I was walking down the street with my mother, and 4
I again found myself conscious of the English I was using, the English I do
use with her. We were talking about the price of new and used furniture
and I heard myself saying this: "Not waste money that way." My husband
was with us as well, and he didn't notice any switch in my English. And
then I realized why. It's because over the twenty years we've been together
I've often used that same kind of English with him, and sometimes he even
uses it with me. It has become our language of intimacy, a different sort of
English that relates to family talk, the language I grew up with.

So you'll have some idea of what this family talk I heard sounds like, 5
I'll quote what my mother said during a recent conversation which I video-
taped and then transcribed. During this conversation, my mother was talking about a political gangster in Shanghai who had the same last name as her
family's, Du, and how the gangster in his early years wanted to be adopted
by her family, which was rich by comparison. Later, the gangster became
more powerful, far richer than my mother's family, and one day showed up
at my mother's wedding to pay his respects. Here's what she said in part:

"Du Yusong having business like fruit stand. Like off the street kind. 6
He is Du like Du Zong—but not Tsung-ming Island people. The local people call putong, the river east side, he belong to that side local people. That
man want to ask Du Zong father take him in like become own family. Du
Zong father wasn't look down on him, but didn't take seriously, until that

man big like become a mafia. Now important person, very hard to inviting him. Chinese way, came only to show respect, don't stay for dinner. Respect for making big celebration, he shows up. Mean gives lots of respect. Chinese custom. Chinese social life that way. If too important won't have to stay too long. He come to my wedding. I didn't see, I heard it. I gone to boy's side, they have YMCA dinner. Chinese age I was nineteen."

You should know that my mother's expressive command of English   7
belies how much she actually understands. She reads the Forbes report, listens to *Wall Street Week*, converses daily with her stockbroker, and reads all of Shirley MacLaine's books with ease—all kinds of things I can't begin to understand. Yet some of my friends tell me they understand 50 percent of what my mother says. Some say they understand 80 to 90 percent. Some say they understand none of it, as if she were speaking pure Chinese. But to me, my mother's English is perfectly clear, perfectly natural. It's my mother tongue. Her language, as I hear it, is vivid, direct, full of observation and imagery. That was the language that helped shape the way I saw things, expressed things, made sense of the world.

Lately, I've been giving more thought to the kind of English my mother   8
speaks. Like others, I have described it to people as "broken" or "fractured" English. But I wince when I say that. It has always bothered me that I can think of no way to describe it other than "broken," as if it were damaged and needed to be fixed, as if it lacked a certain wholeness and soundness. I've heard other terms used, "limited English," for example. But they seem just as bad, as if everything is limited, including people's perceptions of the limited English speaker.

I know this for a fact, because when I was growing up, my mother's   9
"limited" English limited *my* perception of her. I was ashamed of her English. I believed that her English reflected the quality of what she had to say. That is, because she expressed them imperfectly her thoughts were imperfect. And I had plenty of empirical evidence to support me: the fact that people in department stores, at banks, and at restaurants did not take her seriously, did not give her good service, pretended not to understand her, or even acted as if they did not hear her.

My mother has long realized the limitations of her English as well.   10
When I was fifteen, she used to have me call people on the phone to pretend I was she. In this guise, I was forced to ask for information or even to complain and yell at people who had been rude to her. One time it was a call to her stockbroker in New York. She had cashed out her small portfolio and it just so happened we were going to go to New York the next week, our very first trip outside California. I had to get on the phone and say in an adolescent voice that was not very convincing, "This is Mrs. Tan."

And my mother was standing in the back whispering loudly, "Why he 11
don't send me check, already two weeks late. So mad he lie to me, losing
me money."

And then I said in perfect English, "Yes, I'm getting rather concerned. 12
You had agreed to send the check two weeks ago, but it hasn't arrived."

Then she began to talk more loudly. "What he want, I come to New 13
York tell him front of his boss, you cheating me?" And I was trying to calm
her down, make her be quiet, while telling the stockbroker, "I can't tolerate
any more excuses. If I don't receive the check immediately, I am going to
have to speak to your manager when I'm in New York next week." And
sure enough, the following week there we were in front of this astonished
stockbroker, and I was sitting there red-faced and quiet, and my mother, the
real Mrs. Tan, was shouting at his boss in her impeccable broken English.

We used a similar routine just five days ago, for a situation that was 14
far less humorous. My mother had gone to the hospital for an appointment, to find out about a benign brain tumor a CAT scan had revealed a
month ago. She said she had spoken very good English, her best English,
no mistakes. Still, she said, the hospital did not apologize when they said
they had lost the CAT scan and she had come for nothing. She said they
did not seem to have any sympathy when she told them she was anxious
to know the exact diagnosis, since her husband and son had both died
of brain tumors. She said they would not give her any more information
until the next time and she would have to make another appointment for
that. So she said she would not leave until the doctor called her daughter.
She wouldn't budge. And when the doctor finally called her daughter, me,
who spoke in perfect English—lo and behold—we had assurances the CAT
scan would be found, promises that a conference call on Monday would
be held, and apologies for any suffering my mother had gone through for
a most regrettable mistake.

I think my mother's English almost had an effect on limiting my possi- 15
bilities in life as well. Sociologists and linguists probably will tell you that a
person's developing language skills are more influenced by peers. But I do
think that the language spoken in the family, especially in immigrant families which are more insular, plays a large role in shaping the language of the
child. And I believe that it affected my results on achievement tests, IQ tests,
and the SAT. While my English skills were never judged as poor, compared
to math, English could not be considered my strong suit. In grade school
I did moderately well, getting perhaps B's, sometimes B-pluses, in English
and scoring perhaps in the sixtieth or seventieth percentile on achievement
tests. But those scores were not good enough to override the opinion that
my true abilities lay in math and science, because in those areas I achieved
A's and scored in the ninetieth percentile or higher.

This was understandable. Math is precise; there is only one correct   16
answer. Whereas, for me at least, the answers on English tests were always
a judgment call, a matter of opinion and personal experience. Those tests
were constructed around items like fill-in-the-blank sentence completion,
such as, "Even though Tom was _____, Mary thought he was _____."
And the correct answer always seemed to be the most bland combinations
of thoughts, for example, "Even though Tom was shy, Mary thought he
was charming," with the grammatical structure "even though" limiting the
correct answer to some sort of semantic opposites, so you wouldn't get
answers like, "Even though Tom was foolish, Mary thought he was ridiculous." Well, according to my mother, there were very few limitations as to
what Tom could have been and what Mary might have thought of him. So
I never did well on tests like that.

The same was true with word analogies, pairs of words in which you   17
were supposed to find some sort of logical, semantic relationship—for
example, "*Sunset* is to *nightfall* as _____ is to _____." And here you would
be presented with a list of four possible pairs, one of which showed the
same kind of relationship: *red* is to *stoplight*, *bus* is to *arrival*, *chills* is to
fever, *yawn* is to *boring*. Well, I could never think that way. I knew what the
tests were asking, but I could not block out of my mind the images already
created by the first pair, "*sunset* is to *nightfall*"—and I would see a burst of
colors against a darkening sky, the moon rising, the lowering of a curtain
of stars. And all the other pairs of words—red, bus, stoplight, boring—
just threw up a mass of confusing images, making it impossible for me to
sort out something as logical as saying: "A sunset precedes nightfall" is
the same as "a chill precedes a fever." The only way I would have gotten
that answer right would have been to imagine an associative situation, for
example, my being disobedient and staying out past sunset, catching a chill
at night, which turns into feverish pneumonia as punishment, which indeed
did happen to me.

I have been thinking about all this lately, about my mother's English,   18
about achievement tests. Because lately I've been asked, as a writer, why
there are not more Asian Americans represented in American literature.
Why are there few Asian Americans enrolled in creative writing programs?
Why do so many Chinese students go into engineering? Well, these are
broad sociological questions I can't begin to answer. But I have noticed in
surveys—in fact, just last week—that Asian students, as a whole, always
do significantly better on math achievement tests than in English. And
this makes me think that there are other Asian-American students whose
English spoken in the home might also be described as "broken" or "limited." And perhaps they also have teachers who are steering them away
from writing and into math and science, which is what happened to me.

Fortunately, I happen to be rebellious in nature and enjoy the challenge 19
of disproving assumptions made about me. I became an English major
my first year in college, after being enrolled as pre-med. I started writing
non-fiction as a freelancer the week after I was told by my former boss that
writing was my worst skill and I should hone my talents toward account
management.

But it wasn't until 1985 that I finally began to write fiction. And at 20
20 first I wrote using what I thought to be wittily crafted sentences, sentences that would finally prove I had mastery over the English language.
Here's an example from the first draft of a story that later made its way into
The Joy Luck Club, but without this line: "That was my mental quandary
in its nascent state." A terrible line, which I can barely pronounce.

Fortunately, for reasons I won't get into today, I later decided I should 21
envision a reader for the stories I would write. And the reader I decided
upon was my mother, because these were stories about mothers. So with
this reader in mind—and in fact she did read my early drafts—I began to
write stories using all the Englishes I grew up with: the English I spoke to
my mother, which for lack of a better term might be described as "simple";
the English she used with me, which for lack of a better term might be
described as "broken"; my translation of her Chinese, which could certainly be described as "watered down"; and what I imagined to be her
translation of her Chinese if she could speak in perfect English, her internal language, and for that I sought to preserve the essence, but neither an
English nor a Chinese structure. I wanted to capture what language ability
tests can never reveal: her intent, her passion, her imagery, the rhythms of
her speech and the nature of her thoughts.

Apart from what any critic had to say about my writing, I knew I had 22
succeeded where it counted when my mother finished reading my book
and gave me her verdict: "So easy to read."

Thinking about the Essay

1. Explain the multiple meanings of Tan's title and how they illuminate the essay.
   What are the four ways Tan says language can work?

2. What is Tan's thesis, and where does it appear? How do we know her point
   of view about other "Englishes"? Does she state it directly or indirectly, and
   where?

3. How do narration and description interact in this essay? How does Tan describe
   her mother? What is the importance of dialogue?

4. What is Tan's viewpoint about language? Does she state that language should
   always be "simple"? Why or why not? To the extent that Tan's mother is an
   intended audience for her essay, is her language simple? Explain your answer

by specific reference to her words and sentences. Finally, why does Tan's mother find her daughter's writing easy to understand?

5. How and where does Tan use humor in this essay? Where does Tan employ amusing anecdotes? What is her purpose in presenting these anecdotes, and how do they influence the essay's overall tone?

Responding in Writing

6. Tan suggests that the way we use language reflects the way we see the world. Write an essay based on this observation. Feel free to present an analytical paper or a narrative and descriptive essay, or to blend these patterns as does Tan.

7. Should all Americans speak and write the same language? Answer this question in an argumentative essay.

8. Tan writes about having felt "ashamed" because of her mother's speech (paragraph 9). Write an essay about the dangers of linking personality or behavior to language. Can this linkage be used to promote racist, sexist, or other discriminatory ideas?

Networking

9. With two other class members, draw up a list of all the "Englishes" you have encountered. For example, how do your parents speak? What about relatives? Friends? Classmates? Personalities on television? Share your list with the class.

10. Conduct Internet or library research on the role of stereotyping by language in American radio and/or film. You might want to look into the popularity of the *Charlie Chan* series or *Amos and Andy*, or focus on a particular film that stereotypes a group. Present your information in an analytical and evaluative essay.

The Bilingual Imagination

ANA MENÉNDEZ

Ana Menéndez was born in 1970 to Cuban exile parents who fled to California in 1964 and expected to return to Cuba at any time. She spoke only Spanish until she went to kindergarten. The family eventually moved to Florida, where Menéndez went to high school and received her BA from Florida International University. She worked as a journalist for six years in Florida and California and then entered the Creative Writing Program at New York University. Shortly after her graduation, she published a collection of short stories, *In Cuba I Was a German Shepherd* (2001), and the title story won the Pushcart Prize for

Short Fiction. In 2008 she accepted a Fullbright grant to teach at the American University in Cairo. Her other publications include *Loving Che* (2003), *The Last War* (2009), and *Adios, Happy Homeland!* (2011). In this essay, Menendez remembers her early fascination with language—"its possibilities as well as its limitations"—and discusses the impact of early bilingualism.

Before Reading

Are you or someone you know bilingual? What are some of the advantages of knowing more than one language?

My first memory is about language. I'm two years old and being carried by my mother. She is holding me in one arm and with the other is opening the freezer. "Esto se llama hielo," she says, taking out a tray of ice. "Así es como se dice amarillo en Inglés." 1

This is called ice. That is how you say 'yellow' in English. I don't know what my toddler mind made of this riddle. But it shocked and delighted me enough that I still remember it, almost forty years later. I think it was there in that kitchen in Tampa that my lifelong fascination with language—its possibilities as well as its limitations—was born. 2

My sister and I grew up in a bilingual family. And though my parents spoke Spanish almost exclusively, my mother (aware that we were, after all, living in the United States) made an effort to slip in an English word now and then. I think she was worried I might be lost when I started school. And I was. I remember my first day at preschool, where the other kids were speaking a fast, hard language that I could not really understand. 3

I don't remember suffering from my inability to communicate. If I felt anything, it was more a fascination before the enormous mystery of language. How was it that these people could make their feelings and desires known simply by manipulating a set of unintelligible syllables? The fascination, of course, soon gave way to comprehension. By kindergarten, my English was fluent enough for me to play along with the others. And by first grade I began experimenting with language, writing a short story (in crayon) about how the butterfly got its name—naturally, the etymology involved a vat of butter. 4

In grade school, as my grasp of grammar rules and vocabulary grew, an unease began to gnaw at me. One day in the car, I presented my mother with the dilemma. How was it, I demanded to know, that in Spanish not 5

Ana Menendez, "The Bilingual Imagination", *Poets and Writers* (Jan/Feb 2011), pp. 23–26 just people, but also things—chairs, desks, refrigerators—were either male or female, but in English they seemed to be neither? Was una mesa still female when you translated it to table? I don't really remember my mother's response. I suspect it was something along the lines of, "That's just the way it is, dear." Like most parents of young children, my mom had by this time grown weary of my endless questions.

But she might have also been a little concerned about my apparent confusion. In the 1970s, when I was growing up, hearing more than one language as a child was said to delay language ability and possibly interfere with general cognitive development.   6

Following a series of national rulings, Florida was debating bilingual education in the schools at that time. Tampa was still something of a backwater, and my father was accosted one day at work by a colleague demanding to know if he was in favor of bilingual education. My father, sensing a trap, responded: "Absolutely not. My children are already bilingual." Then he added, mischievously: "Your children, however, might benefit."   7

In fact, the benefits of bilingualism have since been widely studied. Aside from encouraging the development of a more worldly and educated citizen, early bilingualism may confer other advantages. Since the dark ages of my childhood, researchers seem to have revised warnings about the horrible dangers that a second language poses to a young brain. In fact, knowing more than one language as a child seems to set you up for a smarter adulthood. Alison Mackey and Kendall King summed up some of the new research in *The Bilingual Edge* (HarperCollins, 2007). People who are fluent in two or more languages from early childhood are better able to perform multiple tasks while distracted, tend to score higher on IQ tests, and exhibit greater creativity. And the dividends are not confined to young adulthood. Those exposed to multiple languages as children show fewer signs of mental decline as they age. Perhaps not surprisingly, they also tend to show greater cultural empathy as well as an ability to learn still more languages. In one widely quoted study, first reported in *Nature*, bilingual children were shown to have more gray matter in their brains than children who had not been exposed to a second language. The earlier the exposure, the more they had.   8

But all the research in the world won't persuade a skeptic. And anyway, it's not my aim to convert anyone. I'm proof that bilingualism is no ticket to success or exceptional intelligence. I still haven't managed to master the multiplication tables. For me this early exposure to two languages was simply a wedge that opened a wider world, that primed me to adapt to difference and change. I think what all bilingual children know instinctively—even if they're not consciously aware of it—is that there is more than one way to interpret the world. This is a significant insight, especially for a child, by nature a self-centered being.   9

If there is more than one way to express colors, if inanimate objects 10
can acquire different properties, if one girl's mesa is another boy's table,
then increasingly the idea of a single truth becomes harder to accept.
Since childhood I have been obsessed with the search for the real and
the true. No doubt my misgivings about the possibility of ever discovering them hinged on my early exposure to two languages. These concerns
were deepened by the effects of memory and story on the interpretation
of history.

My parents are exiles from Cuba. When I was born, my parents had 11
been in the United States for just a few years. They were from different
towns in Cuba and met in Los Angeles. No doubt the key to their attraction lay in their nicely matched memories and the mutual language they
used to recount them.

The stories my parents told of Cuba were always full of superlatives: 12
Their homeland had the best people, the finest music, the loveliest beaches.
The chocolate was better; the fruit actually tasted like fruit. As children,
my sister and I mocked our parents for their rosy nostalgia. But we also
believed it, or at least wanted to. As I grew older, it became harder to
reconcile their Garden of Eden view of history with the more nuanced
reality. I began to read everything I could about Cuba and found more and
more to complicate my certainties. From then on, there were at least two
languages in which to tell Cuba's story. Multiple truths became the only
possible truth.

If the idea of certainty was never resolved for me, its pursuit became a 13
constant in my work. In this way, writing was a kind of problem solving.
So I wrote stories about memories that later come into doubt, or turn out
to be gentle fabrications. In my first novel, history itself is mutable. In
my second, personal memories are repressed and redrawn. Through all of
them, the real protagonist is language: shifting and imprecise.

Inevitably language, being so intimate an appendage of consciousness, 14
comes to reflect the best and worst in us. It is tyrant and victim, obfuscator
and clarifier. Hundreds of indigenous languages are disappearing from the
earth, plowed under by the relentless march of English. The loss in possible
worlds—in expressions, philosophies, and thought patterns—is incalcula-
ble. But even this is not a new development. We moderns may believe we
invented globalization. But humans have been accommodating their habits
to the demands of power and trade for a long time: Before the dominance
of English, language empires stretched from Mesopotamia to South Asia.
The empires of Arabic and Latin remain alive in my own native Spanish,
though purists would have us believe that the language as spoken now can
and should be protected from further foreign contamination; hence, the
insistence of ordenador over the anglicized computadora.

The range of emotion attending language—from the protective to the   15
hysterical—suggests that it has always been more than a means of communication. Identity and national pride are, for better and worse, intimately
wrapped up in it. The average citizen of Amsterdam may be able to speak
multiple languages, but if you wish to immigrate to the Netherlands, you
must prove fluency in Dutch. Next door, in Belgium, four governments have
fallen in the last three years because of the tensions between the country's
Dutch and French speakers. In France, a recent book, *Mélancolie Française*
(French Melancholy) by Éric Zemmour, bemoans what the author sees as
the decline of the French language. Suspicion of the other often translates
into suspicion of his language, and vice versa. It has been like this since
long before the Greeks invented the term barbaros to describe their unintelligible neighbors. And it will probably always be like this. A mother
tongue connects us to creation. It both shapes and is shaped by the speaker's understanding of reality. As the means by which to recount history, it
becomes history itself. Such an idealized connection to the past, of course,
tends to resist innovation. François Le Lionnais—one of the founders of
the French avant-garde literary group Oulipo—humorously illustrated this
point in the group's first manifesto:

Do you remember the polemic that accompanied the invention of lan-   16
guage? Mystification, puerile fantasy, degeneration of the race and decline
of the State, treason against Nature, attack on affectivity, criminal neglect
of inspiration; language was accused of everything (without, of course,
using language) at that time.

And the creation of writing, and grammar—do you think that that   17
happened without a fight? The truth is that the Quarrel of the Ancients and
the Moderns is permanent. It began with Zinjanthropus (a million seven
hundred and fifty thousand years ago) and will end only with humanity—
or perhaps the mutants who succeed us will take up the cause.

Thinking about the Essay

1. Does Menéndez's title draw you into the essay? Is her childhood anecdote an effective introduction? Does it make you want to read the essay?

2. What is Menéndez's thesis? What are the sections of her essay? How does she connect all these sections? Is her combination of personal and academic information effective?

3. This article was published in a journal titled *Poets & Writers*. Who would read this journal? Is Menéndez's essay appropriate for this audience of readers? Explain.

4. What are the benefits or advantages of bilingualism, according to linguistic researchers? What is Menéndez's perspective on these benefits, and how do her feelings relate to the title of this article?

5. In the conclusion of her essay, she quotes from Oulipo that "the Quarrel of the Ancients and the Moderns is permanent." What does this quotation mean, and how does it relate to various countries' attempting to preserve the "purity" of their language?

Responding in Writing

6. What are some of your early memories of childhood or of your early days in school? How did you learn to talk? How did you learn to read? To recognize and write the alphabet? To express your emotions and ideas in compositions? Write a narrative essay about one or several of your earliest memories about language and how you learned language. Be sure that you have a thesis or main idea to unify the memories and make a point about their significance.

7. Write an essay analyzing and explaining the advantages that Menéndez states about knowing more than one language.

8. Write an argumentative essay in which you try to convince elementary teachers, school boards, and/or parents that young children should study another language in elementary school. Include in your essay a refutation of those who would disagree with your position.

Networking

9. Working with a small group of your classmates, interview several people who know more than one language. Before you interview them, in your group prepare a list of questions to ask them, such as the age at which they learned another language, what difficulties they experienced, what benefits they have experienced, what advice they have for others, and so on. Write a group report and share it with your class.

10. Read a research study in an academic or scientific journal on learning a second language. Write a summary of the study and of your responses to your findings.

Mute in an English-Only World

Chang-rae Lee

Chang-rae Lee was born in 1965 in Seoul, South Korea. He and his family immigrated to the United States in 1968. Lee attended public schools in New Rochelle, New York; graduated from Yale University (BA, 1987); and received an MFA degree from the University of Oregon (1993). His first novel, *Native Speaker* (1995), won several prizes, including the Ernest Hemingway Foundation/PEN Award for First Fiction. His other works include *A Gesture Life* (1999); *Aloft* (2004); *The Surrendered* (2010), a finalist for the 2011 Pulitzer Prize for Fiction; and

On Such a Full Sea (2014). He has also published fiction and nonfiction in many magazines, including *The New Yorker* and *Time*. Lee has taught in the creative writing programs at the University of Oregon and Hunter College; today he is a professor of creative writing at Princeton University. In the following essay, which appeared on the op-ed page of *The New York Times* in 1996, Lee remembers his mother's efforts to learn English, using literary memoir to comment on recent laws passed by certain towns in New Jersey requiring English on all commercial signs.

Before Reading

Should all commercial signs have English written on them, in addition to any other language? What about menus in ethnic restaurants?

When I read of the troubles in Palisades Park, N.J., over the proliferation of Korean language signs along its main commercial strip, I unexpectedly sympathized with the frustrations, resentments and fears of the longtime residents. They clearly felt alienated and even unwelcome in a vital part of their community. The town, like seven others in New Jersey, has passed laws requiring that half of any commercial sign in a foreign language be in English. 1

Now I certainly would never tolerate any exclusionary ideas about who could rightfully settle and belong in the town. But having been raised in a Korean immigrant family, I saw every day the exacting price and power of language, especially with my mother, who was an outsider in an English-only world. 2

In the first years we lived in America, my mother could speak only the most basic English, and she often encountered great difficulty whenever she went out. 3

We lived in New Rochelle, N.Y., in the early '70s, and most of the local businesses were run by the descendants of immigrants who, generations ago, had come to the suburbs from New York City. Proudly dotting Main Street and North Avenue were Italian pastry and cheese shops, Jewish tailors and cleaners and Polish and German butchers and bakers. If my mother's marketing couldn't wait until the weekend, when my father had free time, she would often hold off until I came home from school to buy the groceries. 4

Though I was only 6 or 7 years old, she insisted that I go out shopping with her and my younger sister. I mostly loathed the task, partly because it meant I couldn't spend the afternoon playing catch with my friends but 5 also because I knew our errands would inevitably lead to an awkward scene, and that I would have to speak up to help my mother.

I was just learning the language myself, but I was a quick study, as   6
children are with new tongues. I had spent kindergarten in almost complete silence, hearing only the high nasality of my teacher and comprehending little but the cranky wails and cries of my classmates. But soon, seemingly mere months later, I had already become a terrible ham and mimic, and I would crack up my father with impressions of teachers, his friends and even himself. My mother scolded me for aping his speech, and the one time I attempted to make light of hers I rated a roundhouse smack on my bottom.

For her, the English language was not very funny. It usually meant trou-   7
ble and a good dose of shame, and sometimes real hurt. Although she had a good reading knowledge of the language from university classes in South Korea, she had never practiced actual conversation. So in America, she used English flashcards and phrase books and watched television with us kids. And she faithfully carried a pocket workbook illustrated with stick-figure people and compound sentences to be filled in.

But none of it seemed to do her much good. Staying mostly at home   8
to care for us, she didn't have many chances to try out sundry words and phrases. When she did, say, at the window of the post office, her readied speech would stall, freeze, sometimes altogether collapse.

One day was unusually harrowing. We ventured downtown in the new   9
Ford Country Squire my father had bought her, an enormous station wagon that seemed as long—and deft—as an ocean liner. We were shopping for a special meal for guests visiting that weekend, and my mother had heard that a particular butcher carried fresh oxtails—which she needed for a traditional soup.

We'd never been inside the shop, but my mother would pause before   10
its window, which was always lined with whole hams, crown roasts and ropes of plump handmade sausages. She greatly esteemed the bounty with her eyes, and my sister and I did also, but despite our desirous cries she'd turn us away and instead buy the packaged links at the Finast supermarket, where she felt comfortable looking them over and could easily spot the price. And, of course, not have to talk.

But that day she was resolved. The butcher store was crowded, and as   11
we stepped inside the door jingled a welcome. No one seemed to notice. We waited for some time, and people who entered after us were now being served. Finally, an old woman nudged my mother and waved a little ticket, which we hadn't taken. We patiently waited again, until one of the beefy men behind the glass display hollered our number.

My mother pulled us forward and began searching the cases, but   12
the oxtails were nowhere to be found. The man, his big arms crossed,

sharply said, "Come on, lady, whaddya want?" This unnerved her, and she somehow blurted the Korean word for oxtail, soggori.

The butcher looked as if my mother had put something sour in his 13 mouth, and he glanced back at the lighted board and called the next number.

Before I knew it, she had rushed us outside and back in the wagon, 14 which she had double-parked because of the crowd. She was furious, almost vibrating with fear and grief, and I could see she was about to cry.

She wanted to go back inside, but now the driver of the car we were 15 blocking wanted to pull out. She was shooing us away. My mother, who had just earned her driver's license, started furiously working the pedals. But in her haste she must have flooded the engine, for it wouldn't turn over. The driver started honking and then another car began honking as well, and soon it seemed the entire street was shrieking at us.

In the following years, my mother grew steadily more comfortable with 16 English. In Korean, she could be fiery, stern, deeply funny and ironic; in English, just slightly less so. If she was never quite fluent, she gained enough confidence to make herself clearly known to anyone, and particularly to me.

Five years ago, she died of cancer, and some months after we buried her 17 I found myself in the driveway of my father's house, washing her sedan. I liked taking care of her things; it made me feel close to her. While I was cleaning out the glove compartment, I found her pocket English workbook, the one with the silly illustrations. I hadn't seen it in nearly 20 years. The yellowed pages were brittle and dog-eared. She had fashioned a plain-paper wrapping for it, and I wondered whether she meant to protect the book or hide it.

I don't doubt that she would have appreciated doing the family shop- 18 ping on the new Broad Avenue of Palisades Park. But I like to think, too, that she would have understood those who now complain about the Korean-only signs.

I wonder what these same people would have done if they had seen 19 my mother studying her English workbook—or lost in a store. Would they have nodded gently at her? Would they have lent a kind word?

Thinking about the Essay

1. What is the author's purpose? Is he trying to paint a picture of his mother, describe an aspect of the immigrant experience, convey a thesis, argue a point, or what? Explain your response.

2. What is unusual about Lee's introduction? How does his position on the issue raised defy your expectations?

3. Lee offers stories within stories. How are they ordered? Which tale receives greatest development, and why?

4. Lee uses colloquial language in this essay. Identify some examples. What is the effect?

5. What is the dominant impression that you have of Lee's mother? How does he bring her to life?

Responding in Writing

6. Construct a profile of the writer. What do we learn about Lee? What are his values? What is his attitude toward English? How does this son of immigrant parents establish himself as an authority? How does he surprise us with his perspective on language?

7. In a personal essay, tell of a time when you were embarrassed either by the language of someone close to you or by your own use of language in a social or business situation.

8. Both Amy Tan and Chang-rae Lee focus on their mothers' handling of their second language—English. Write a comparative essay in which you explain the similarities and differences in the authors' approaches to their subject.

Networking

9. With two other class members, discuss the emotional appeal of Lee's essay. Look especially at his conclusion. Share your responses with the class.

10. Write an email to your instructor, suggesting two additional questions you would ask about Lee's essay if you were teaching it.

My Two Lives

Jhumpa Lahiri

Jhumpa Lahiri was born in 1967 in London to Bengali parents who emigrated from Calcutta, India. Her father, a university librarian, relocated the family to the United States, and she grew up in Rhode Island. She studied English literature at Barnard College in New York and then transferred to Boston University, where she earned three literary master's degrees before she received her doctorate in Renaissance Studies and completed a Provincetown, Cape Cod, residency. Her first collection of short stories, *Interpreter of Maladies* (1999), which provided glimpses into the lives of characters in both India and the States, won several honors, including the Pulitzer Prize and the PEN/Hemingway Award. In 2003 she published a novel, *The Namesake*, and in 2008 another collection of short stories, *Unaccustomed Earth*, both of which focused on the lives of immigrant clans and US-raised children. In this essay from *Newsweek* in 2006, Lahiri explores her experiences as an immigrant offspring, torn between two cultures.

Before Reading

Have you ever felt that you were living two separate lives? What were your emotional and intellectual responses to this situation?

I have lived in the United States for almost 37 years and anticipate growing old in this country. Therefore, with the exception of my first two years in London, "Indian-American" has been a constant way to describe me. Less constant is my relationship to the term. When I was growing up in Rhode Island in the 1970s I felt neither Indian nor American. Like many immigrant offspring I felt intense pressure to be two things, loyal to the old world and fluent in the new, approved of on either side of the hyphen. Looking back, I see that this was generally the case. But my perception as a young girl was that I fell short at both ends, shuttling between two dimensions that had nothing to do with one another. 1

At home I followed the customs of my parents, speaking Bengali and eating rice and dal with my fingers. These ordinary facts seemed part of a secret, utterly alien way of life, and I took pains to hide them from my American friends. For my parents, home was not our house in Rhode Island but Calcutta, where they were raised. I was aware that the things they lived for—the Nazrul songs they listened to on the reel-to-reel, the family they missed, the clothes my mother wore that were not available in any store in any mall— were at once as precious and as worthless as an outmoded currency. 2

I also entered a world my parents had little knowledge or control of: school, books, music, television, things that seeped in and became a fundamental aspect of who I am. I spoke English without an accent, comprehending the language in a way my parents still do not. And yet there was evidence that I was not entirely American. In addition to my distinguishing name and looks, I did not attend Sunday school, did not know how to ice-skate, and disappeared to India for months at a time. Many of these friends proudly called themselves Irish-American or Italian-American. But they were several generations removed from the frequently humiliating process of immigration, so that the ethnic roots they claimed had descended underground whereas mine were still tangled and green. According to my parents I was not American, nor would I ever be no matter how hard I tried. I felt doomed by their pronouncement, misunderstood and gradually defiant. 3

Jhumpa Lahiri, "My Two Lives", *Newsweek* (March 6, 2006), p. 43.

In spite of the first lessons of arithmetic, one plus one did not equal two but zero, my conflicting selves always canceling each other out.

When I first started writing I was not conscious that my subject was 4 the Indian-American experience. What drew me to my craft was the desire to force the two worlds I occupied to mingle on the page as I was not brave enough, or mature enough, to allow in life. My first book was published in 1999, and around then, on the cusp of a new century, the term "Indian-American" has become part of this country's vocabulary. I've heard it so often that these days, if asked about my background, I use the term myself, pleasantly surprised that I do not have to explain further. What a difference from my early life, when there was no such way to describe me, when the most I could do was to clumsily and ineffectually explain.

As I approach middle age, one plus one equals two, both in my work 5 and in my daily existence. The traditions on either side of the hyphen dwell in me like siblings, still occasionally sparring, one outshining the other depending on the day. But like siblings they are intimately familiar with one another, forgiving and intertwined. When my husband and I were married five years ago in Calcutta we invited friends who had never been to India, and they came full of enthusiasm for a place I avoided talking about in my childhood, fearful of what people might say. Around non-Indian friends, I no longer feel compelled to hide the fact that I speak another language. I speak Bengali to my children, even though I lack the proficiency to teach them to read or write the language. As a child I sought perfection and so denied myself the claim to any identity. As an adult I accept that a bicultural upbringing is a rich but imperfect thing.

While I am American by virtue of the fact that I was raised in this 6 country, I am Indian thanks to the efforts of two individuals. I feel Indian not because of the time I've spent in India or because of my genetic composition but rather because of my parents' steadfast presence in my life. They live three hours from my home; I speak to them daily and see them about once a month. Everything will change once they die. They will take certain things with them—conversations in another tongue, and perceptions about the difficulties of being foreign. Without them, the back-and-forth life my family leads, both literally and figuratively, will at last approach stillness. An anchor will drop, and a line of connection will be severed.

I have always believed that I lack the authority my parents bring to 7 being Indian. But as long as they live they protect me from feeling like an impostor. Their passing will mark not only the loss of the people who created me but the loss of a singular way of life, a singular struggle. The immigrant's journey, no matter how ultimately rewarding, is founded on departure and deprivation, but it secures for the subsequent generation a sense of arrival and advantage. I can see a day coming when my American side, lacking the counterpoint India has until now maintained, begins to gain ascendancy and weight. It is in fiction that I will continue to interpret the term "Indian-American," calculating that shifting equation, whatever answers it may yield.

Thinking about the Essay

1. What is Lahiri's subject in this article? What is her purpose? Who are her intended audience? How do the three relate and influence the author's rhetorical and linguistic choices in this article?

2. How has Lahiri felt her two worlds pulling her in different directions? How has her being "Indian-American" changed as she has grown older? How does she say her situation will change again when her parents die? Why?

3. What is the organizational pattern of Lahiri's essay—chronological or logical, or a combination of the two? Is it easy to follow? Is it effective?

4. What does the author mean when she states that her ethnic roots were "tangled and green." How did her responses to her ethnic roots differ from those of her parents? Why?

5. What does she mean by her "conflicting selves"? Identify and analyze specifically what she says in the essay to explain this phrase.

Responding in Writing

6. Write an essay in which you relate a time in your life when you felt pulled between two ways of life or between two directions for the future. Explain what you decided and why.

7. Why does Lahiri say she writes? Find, read, and write a synopsis of one of her short stories. Then write an analysis of how her fiction differs from her nonfiction.

8. Write an essay in which you explain how transitioning from one way of life to another (such as from one job to another, from high school to college, from living in one city to moving to another) can be made easier or simpler. Use specific evidence to convince your readers that your plan is workable.

Networking

9. With a small group of your classmates, study Lahiri's use of the colon and the dash in Paragraphs 2, 3, and 6. Discuss how and why the author uses these two punctuation marks and the effects of this punctuation.

10. Lahiri states, "What drew me to my craft [of writing] was the desire to force the two worlds I occupied to mingle on the page as I was not brave enough, or mature enough, to allow in life." Choose a writer whom you admire, and research the reason he or she began to write or what the writer says is the reason he or she writes. Write a summary of what you learn, and share it with your class.

The Power of Words in Wartime

ROBIN TOLMACH LAKOFF

Robin Tolmach Lakoff was born in Brooklyn, New York, in 1942 and educated at Radcliffe College (BA, 1964), Indiana University (MA, 1965), and Harvard University (PhD, 1967). An influential linguist who serves on the faculty at the University of California at Berkeley, Lakoff has written several studies focusing on the influence of language on social attitudes—especially attitudes toward women and "others." Among her most important works are *Language and Women's Place* (1975), *Talking Power: The Politics of Language in Our Lives* (1990), and *The Language of War* (2000). The following essay appeared in *The New York Times* on May 18, 2004.

Before Reading

What does *stereotyping* mean? What is the relationship between stereotyping and such words in wartime as *terrorist, jihadist, invader,* and *infidel*?

An American soldier refers to an Iraqi prisoner as "it." A general speaks   1
not of "Iraqi fighters" but of "the enemy." A weapons manufacturer doesn't talk about people but about "targets."

Bullets and bombs are not the only tools of war. Words, too, play their part.   2

Human beings are social animals, genetically hard-wired to feel compas-   3
sion toward others. Under normal conditions, most people find it very difficult to kill.

But in war, military recruits must be persuaded that killing other people   4
is not only acceptable but even honorable.

The language of war is intended to bring about that change, and not   5
only for soldiers in the field. In wartime, language must be created to enable combatants and noncombatants alike to see the other side as killable, to overcome the innate queasiness over the taking of human life. Soldiers, and those who remain at home, learn to call their enemies by names that make them seem not quite human—inferior, contemptible and not like "us."

The specific words change from culture to culture and war to war. The   6
names need not be obviously demeaning. Just the fact that we can name them gives us a sense of superiority and control. If, in addition, we give

them nicknames, we can see them as smaller, weaker and childlike—not worth taking seriously as fully human.

The Greeks and Romans referred to everyone else as "barbarians"— 7 etymologically those who only babble, only go "bar-bar." During the American Revolution, the British called the colonists "Yankees," a term with a history that is still in dispute. While the British intended it disparagingly, the Americans, in perhaps the first historical instance of reclamation, made the word their own and gave it a positive spin, turning the derisive song "Yankee Doodle" into our first, if unofficial, national anthem.

In World War I, the British gave the Germans the nickname "Jerries," 8 from the first syllable of German. In World War II, Americans referred to the Japanese as "Japs."

The names may refer to real or imagined cultural and physical differ- 9 ences that emphasize the ridiculous or the repugnant. So in various wars, the British called the French "Frogs." Germans have been called "Krauts," a reference to weird and smelly food. The Vietnamese were called "slopes" and "slants." The Koreans were referred to simply as "gooks."

The war in Iraq has added new examples. Some American soldiers refer 10 to the Iraqis as "hadjis," used in a derogatory way, apparently unaware that the word, which comes from the Arabic term for a pilgrimage to Mecca, is used as a term of respect for older Muslim men.

The Austrian ethologist Konrad Lorenz suggested that the more clearly 11 we see other members of our own species as individuals, the harder we find it to kill them.

So some terms of war are collective nouns, encouraging us to see the 12 enemy as an undifferentiated mass, rather than as individuals capable of suffering. Crusaders called their enemy "the Saracen," and in World War I, the British called Germans "the Hun."

American soldiers are trained to call those they are fighting against "the 13 enemy." It is easier to kill an enemy than an Iraqi.

The word "enemy" itself provides the facelessness of a collective noun. 14 Its non-specificity also has a fear-inducing connotation; enemy means simply "those we are fighting," without reference to their identity.

The terrors and uncertainties of war make learning this kind of lan- 15 guage especially compelling for soldiers on the front. But civilians back home also need to believe that what their country is doing is just and necessary, and that the killing they are supporting is in some way different from the killing in civilian life that is rightly punished by the criminal justice system. The use of the language developed for military purposes by civilians reassures them that war is not murder.

The linguistic habits that soldiers must absorb in order to fight make 16 atrocities like those at Abu Ghraib virtually inevitable. The same language that creates a psychological chasm between "us" and "them" and enables American troops to kill in battle, makes enemy soldiers fit subjects for torture and humiliation. The reasoning is: They are not really human, so they will not feel the pain.

Once language draws that line, all kinds of mistreatment become imaginable, and then justifiable. To make the abuses at Abu Ghraib unthinkable, we would have to abolish war itself.   17

Thinking about the Essay

1. Lakoff wrote this essay as an op-ed article for a newspaper. What aspects of style, thesis placement, paragraph organization, length, and tone does she employ to satisfy the demands of an op-ed contribution?

2. What is Lakoff's purpose in this essay? Does she want to inform readers about language, analyze words in wartime, argue about the Iraq war, or what?

3. Lakoff organizes her essay around causes and effects, using a series of examples to support her causal analysis. Trace this strategy through the essay, trying to determine where language is a cause, an effect, or both.

4. How logical do you find Lakoff's article, and why? Do you think that she succumbs to any logical fallacies or exaggerates in order to make a point? Justify your response.

5. How effective do you find Lakoff's attempt to link the language stemming from the war in Iraq with that of the language used to invoke the "enemy" in wars stretching back in history to ancient Greece? Is this sufficient support for her thesis or claim? Explain.

Responding in Writing

6. Select one word that appears prominently in discussions of the war in Afghanistan (or Iraq, or both), and demonstrate the ways in which government and the press invoke this word to influence public attitudes.

7. Write a cause-and-effect essay in which you demonstrate the ways in which language can stereotype certain types of people—for example, immigrants, Muslims, gays, Africans.

8. Argue for or against the proposition that Lakoff presents a convincing argument in "The Power of Words in Wartime." Refer to specific strategies she employs to support your position.

Networking

9. Lakoff refers to Konrad Lorenz in paragraph 11. With one other class member, go online and find out more about this person. Then explain in class discussion why you think Lakoff refers to him in her essay.

10. Go online to find out more about Abu Ghraib, a topic that Lakoff injects into her essay. Download at least three images of this episode, and then write a brief essay, with illustrations, highlighting Lakoff's claim about the "psychological chasm between 'us' and 'them.'"

CHAPTER 5

Global Relationships: Are Sex and Gender Roles Changing?

As we move into the twenty-first century, the roles of men and women in the United States and around the world are in flux. In the United States, there are increasing numbers of women in many professional fields—medicine, law, education, politics, and corporate life. And with more men—"Mr. Moms"—staying home and caring for their children, either by preference or by necessity, there is greater equality in domestic responsibilities. At the same time, a woman's right to choose or even obtain social services is under attack. And it was only in the summer of 2003 that the United States Supreme Court struck down a Texas law that had made sex between consenting adult males in the privacy of their homes a crime.

This national opposition in certain quarters to equality of rights in human relations is reflected in reactionary global attitudes and practices. Issues of race, sexual orientation, and ethnicity complicate the roles of women and men on a global scale. In certain nations, women can still be stoned to death for sexual "crimes"; in others, homosexuality can be punished by incarceration and even execution. Slave trafficking in women and children fuels a vibrant sex industry here and around the world. And children—stolen, bought, or extorted from poor parents from South America to Southeast Asia—can wind up in the United States as "adopted" boys and girls.

American women do seem to have advantages over many of their global counterparts, for when we consider the situation of women globally, the issue of equal rights and human rights becomes acute. From increasing acquired immunodeficiency syndrome (AIDS) rates among global women, to their exploitation as cheap labor or sex workers, to female infanticide, to the continuing resistance of men in traditional societies to any thought of gender equality, the lives of women in many parts of the world are perilous. Gendered value systems in traditional societies change glacially, and often under only the most extreme conditions. For example, before the massacre of more than 800,000 Tutsi by their Hutu neighbors in Rwanda in 1993, women could not

Jonathan Player/The New York Times/Redux

Hindu women take part in a speed-dating event at a London nightclub. Daters meet for a few minutes before moving on to the next date. Traditionally, relationships and marriages in this community were arranged by the families of the potential bride and groom.

Thinking about the Image

1. You probably know how awkward it can be to meet someone new. How do you think this photographer captured such an intimate, difficult moment between these two people?
2. What key characteristics do you see that distinguish groups of people or ethnicities in this photograph?
3. This photograph originally accompanied "Arranged Marriages Get a Little Reshuffling" by Lizette Alvarez, the first reading in this chapter. How accurately does the photograph illustrate the article? Newspaper editors have a limited amount of space to fill each day—why do you think this newspaper's editors wanted to include a photograph with this story?
4. If you could take a snapshot of dating culture in your own social group, what would you need to include in order to best capture its essence? Describe the image using very specific language.

work or appear alone in the market; with the killing of so many men, Rwandan women suddenly had to assume responsibility for tasks from which they had formerly been excluded. Women are the ones who are displaced disproportionately by wars, ethnic conflicts, famine, and environmental crises.

In this new global era, the destinies of women and men around the world are intertwined. Global forces have brought them together. The role of democracy in promoting human rights, the challenge to spread wealth from North to South and West to East, the need to prevent wars, and even the degradation of the environment have notable implications for men and women. Some argue that global forces—which we will detect in some essays in this chapter and study in detail in the next chapter—are notably hostile to women. Others argue that to the extent that nations can promote peace and democracy, produce prosperity, improve health and the environment, and reduce racism and ethnocentrism, both women and men will be the beneficiaries.

The essays in this chapter present insights into the roles of men and women around the world. The writers inquire into the impact of economics, politics, race, gender and sexual orientation, and culture on the lives of women and men. They invite us to reconsider the meaning of human rights, self-determination, and equality from a gendered perspective. In the twenty-first century, new ideas have emerged about the roles and rights of women and men. The essays that follow reveal some of the challenges that must be overcome before the concept of equal rights and opportunities for women and men can be realized.

Arranged Marriages Get a Little Reshuffling

LIZETTE ALVAREZ

Lizette Alvarez, born in Miami in 1964, currently serves as the Miami bureau chief for *The New York Times*. While working at *The Miami Herald*, she was part of a team that won the 1993 Pulitzer Prize for Public Service for coverage of Hurricane Andrew. In the following article, which appeared in *The New York Times* in 2003, Alvarez examines changing attitudes and rituals concerning the traditional practice of arranged marriages. Writing from London, she focuses on "young, hip, South Asians." These young people do not reject traditions governing relations between the sexes. Instead, they "reshuffle" these conventions so that they may work successfully for them in the twenty-first century.

Before Reading

What is your attitude toward arranged marriage? In many Western nations, divorce rates approach 50 percent. Why not try arranged marriage if choosing your own mate is so frustrating and perilous?

They are young, hip, South Asians in their 20s who glide seamlessly   1
between two cultures, carefully cherry picking from the West to modernize the East.

They can just as easily listen to Justin Timberlake, the pop star, as Rishi   2
Rich, the Hindu musical dynamo. They eat halal meat but wear jeans and T-shirts to cafes.

Now these young Indians and Pakistanis are pushing the cultural   3
boundaries created by their parents and grandparents one step further: they are reshaping the tradition of arranged marriages in Britain.

While couples were once introduced exclusively by relatives and   4
friends, the Aunt Bijis, as Muslims call their matchmakers, are now being slowly nudged out by a boom in Asian marriage Web sites, chat rooms and personal advertisements. South Asian speed dating—Hindus one night, Muslims the next—is the latest phenomenon to hit London, with men and women meeting each other for just three minutes at restaurants and bars before moving on to the next potential mate.

Arranged marriages are still the norm within these clannish, tight-knit   5
communities in Britain, but, with the urging of second- and third-generation children, the nature of the arrangement has evolved, mostly by necessity.

What the young Indians and Pakistanis of Britain have done, in effect,   6
is to modernize practices that had evolved among the urban middle class in India in recent decades, allowing the prospective bride and groom a little more than one fleeting meeting to make up their minds.

The relaxation that had crept in since the 1960s allowed the couple,   7
after an initial meeting before their extended families, to meet alone several times, either with family members in another room or at a restaurant, before delivering a verdict. Now, the meetings take place in public venues without the family encounter first.

"The term we use now is 'assisted' arranged marriage," said Maha   8
Khan, a 23-year-old London Muslim woman. "The whole concept has changed a lot. Parents have become more open and more liberal in their concept of marriage and courtship."

Gitangeli Sapra, a trendy, willowy British Sindhu who at 25 jokes that   9
she is on her way to spinsterhood, is an avid speed dater with no qualms about advertising her love of modern arranged marriages. She even wrote a column about it for *The Sunday Times*.

"It's not based on love," she said, "which can fizzle out."   10

Ms. Sapra had attended 10 of the more formal arranged meetings— 11
awkward, drawn-out affairs in which the young man, his mother and several other relatives came over to meet the young woman and her family.
She wore her best Indian outfit, a sari or elegant Indian pants and top. She
sat quietly, which is almost impossible to fathom, considering her chat-
tiness. When called upon, she poured tea, and then talked briefly to her
potential mate in a side room.

"The matriarchs do the talking," she said over a glass of wine at an 12
Italian restaurant. "You sit there looking cute and like the ideal housewife."

"To be honest, it's an easy way to get a rich man, with my mother's 13
blessing," she added, with a laugh.

None of them worked out, though, and Ms. Sapra has moved on to 14
speed dating with the blessings of her mother.

The very concept raises the hackles of some more old-fashioned parents, 15
but many are coming around, in part out of desperation. If Ms. Sapra finds
someone on a speed date, she will quickly bring him home to her mother.

The abiding principles behind an arranged marriage still remain 16
strong—lust does not a lasting marriage make and family knows best. But
parents and elders, eager to avoid alienating their children, making them
miserable or seeing them go unmarried, have shown considerable flexibility. This is especially pronounced among the middle class, whose members
tend to have integrated more into British life.

"The notion of arrangement has become more fluid," said Yunas 17
Samad, a sociology professor at Bradford University, who has studied marriage in the Muslim community. "What is happening is that the arranged
marriage is becoming a bit more open and children are getting a bit more
say in this so it becomes a nice compromise. There is the comfort of family
support and a choice in what they are doing."

"It's a halfway house, not completely traditional and not completely 18
the same as what is happening in British society," he added.

To the surprise of parents and elders, this new hybrid between East and 19
West has actually stoked enthusiasm for an age-old tradition that many
young people privately viewed as crusty and hopelessly unhip.

Now they see it as an important way to preserve religion and identity, 20
not to mention a low-maintenance way of finding a mate. "It's like your
parents giving you a black book of girls," said Ronak Mashru, 24, a London comedian whose parents are from India.

The young people also recognize that arranged marriages—in which 21
similar education and income levels, religious beliefs and character outweigh
the importance of physical attraction—can well outlast love marriages.

"The falling-in-love system has failed," said Rehna Azim, a Pakistani 22
family lawyer who founded an Asian magazine, *Memsahib.*

South Asian unions are viewed as marriages between families, not 23
individuals. Divorce is anathema, while respect and standing within a
community are paramount. A lot of people have much invested in making
a match work.

Similarly, several customs have survived dating: decisions have to be made 24
relatively quickly, often after the second or third meeting, and, Ms. Sapra
said, "once you've said yes, there is no turning back."

Dowries remain common and background still matters, too. 25

"Our mums look at the C.V.'s," said Vani Gupta, 30, a speed dater." 26
They figure out whether we're compatible on paper—right job, right background, right caste. It's nice to know your parents have done the work for
you. You feel more secure."

These middle-class women, most of them educated professionals or uni- 27
versity students, are looking for more modern men, who accept working
wives and help around the house. But a "mechanic won't try for a lawyer
and a lawyer would not look for a mechanic," she said.

Ms. Sapra, for example, is looking for a fellow Sindhu, and a Gujarati 28
Indian typically seeks another Gujarati.

Muslims still keep it mostly within the family and the same region of 29
Pakistan. Cousins still frequently marry cousins, or at least second or third
cousins, and many British Pakistanis still find their brides back in Pakistan.
But now more men are marrying white British women who convert to Islam,
and others insist on finding a Muslim bride there who speaks English, eats
fish and chips and watches *East Enders*, a popular soap opera.

Parents and elders have had to adapt, in large part because the number 30
of potential partners is much smaller here than in their home countries.
Rather than see an educated daughter go unwed, parents and elders have
accepted these more modern approaches, "Women are not going to be put
back in some kind of bottle," Professor Samad said.

Ms. Azim said, "Parents can say my child had an arranged marriage, 31
and he can say, 'Yeah, it's arranged. But I like her.'"

Thinking about the Essay

1. Writing for *The New York Times*, Alvarez knows her primary audience. What
   assumptions does she make about this audience? What secondary audiences
   would be interested in her topic, and why?

2. Does this article have a thesis? If so, where is it? If not, why not?

3. How does this essay reflect journalistic practice? Point to aspects of style,
   paragraph organization, article length, and other journalistic features. Is the
   tone of the article strictly neutral and objective (one aspect of journalistic
   method), or does it shade toward commentary or perhaps even contain an
   implicit argument? Explain.

4. How many people were interviewed for this article? Who are they, and what are their backgrounds? Taken together, how do they embody some of the main points that Alvarez wants to make about courtship practices among some Asians today?

5. What rhetorical practices—for example, definition, comparison and contrast, process and causal analysis—can you locate in this essay? Toward what purpose does the writer use them?

Responding in Writing

6. What is the difference between people who use Internet dating sites to make their own contacts and establish their own relationships and people from traditional societies who use the Internet to "cherry pick" prospective mates, whom they then present to their parents for appraisal? Which method strikes you as safer or potentially more successful, and why?

7. What is so great about "modern" dating and courtship practices if they often end in frustration and failure? Why not try something old, tried, and tested—like arranged marriage? Imagine that your parents insist on an arranged marriage for you. Write a personal response to this situation. Do not write that you would try to subvert the entire ritual. Instead, explain how you might "manage" this process to make the outcome acceptable.

8. Alvarez, presenting one principle behind the need for arranged marriages, writes that "lust does not a lasting marriage make" (paragraph 16). Do you agree or disagree with this claim? Provide at least three reasons to justify your response.

Networking

9. In class discussion, design a questionnaire about attitudes toward arranged marriage. Aim for at least five questions that can be answered briefly. Then have each class member obtain several responses to the questionnaire from other students. Compile the results, discuss them, and arrive at conclusions.

10. Investigate an Internet dating site. Sign up for it if you feel comfortable, or simply monitor the site for information. Report your findings to the class.

In Africa, AIDS Has a Woman's Face

KOFI A. ANNAN

Kofi A. Annan was born in the Gold Coast, as Ghana was known under British rule, in 1938. The son of a Fante nobleman, he graduated in 1957 from Mfantsipim, a prestigious boarding school for boys that had been founded by the Methodist Church; Ghana won its independence from Great Britain that same year. After studies at the University of Science and Technology in Kumasi, Annan came to the United States on a Ford

Foundation fellowship in 1959, completing his degree in economics at Macalester College in St. Paul, Minnesota. He also has a master's degree in management from the Massachusetts Institute of Technology (1972). Annan has worked for the United Nations in various capacities for four decades and was secretary-general of the United Nations from 1997 to 2006. He shared the Nobel Peace Prize in 2001 with the United Nations. In the following essay, which appeared in *The New York Times* in 2002, he writes about one of the many "problems without borders" that he believes we must deal with from an international perspective.

Before Reading

Consider the impact that AIDS has on a developing nation or an entire region. What are the economic consequences of the AIDS epidemic in these countries? What happens to the condition of women in such societies?

A combination of famine and AIDS is threatening the backbone of Africa— 1 the women who keep African societies going and whose work makes up the economic foundation of rural communities. For decades, we have known that the best way for Africa to thrive is to ensure that its women have the freedom, power and knowledge to make decisions affecting their own lives and those of their families and communities. At the United Nations, we have always understood that our work for development depends on building a successful partnership with the African farmer and her husband.

Study after study has shown that there is no effective development 2 strategy in which women do not play a central role. When women are fully involved, the benefits can be seen immediately: families are healthier; they are better fed; their income, savings and reinvestment go up. And, what is true of families is true of communities and, eventually, of whole countries.

But today, millions of African women are threatened by two simultane- 3 ous catastrophes: famine and AIDS. More than 30 million people are now at risk of starvation in southern Africa and the Horn of Africa. All of these predominantly agricultural societies are also battling serious AIDS epidemics. This is no coincidence: AIDS and famine are directly linked.

Because of AIDS, farming skills are being lost, agricultural develop- 4 ment efforts are declining, rural livelihoods are disintegrating, productive capacity to work the land is dropping and household earnings are shrinking—all while the cost of caring for the ill is rising exponentially. At the same time, H.I.V. infection and AIDS are spreading dramatically and disproportionately among women. A United Nations report released last month shows that women now make up 50 percent of those infected with H.I.V. worldwide—and in Africa that figure is now 58 percent. Today, AIDS has a woman's face.

AIDS has already caused immense suffering by killing almost 2.5 million   5
Africans this year alone. It has left 11 million African children orphaned since the epidemic began. Now it is attacking the capacity of these countries to resist famine by eroding those mechanisms that enable populations to fight back—the coping abilities provided by women.

In famines before the AIDS crisis, women proved more resilient than   6
men. Their survival rate was higher, and their coping skills were stronger. Women were the ones who found alternative foods that could sustain their children in times of drought. Because droughts happened once a decade or so, women who had experienced previous droughts were able to pass on survival techniques to younger women. Women are the ones who nurture social networks that can help spread the burden in times of famine.

But today, as AIDS is eroding the health of Africa's women, it is eroding   7
the skills, experience and networks that keep their families and communities going. Even before falling ill, a woman will often have to care for a sick husband, thereby reducing the time she can devote to planting, harvesting and marketing crops. When her husband dies, she is often deprived of credit, distribution networks or land rights. When she dies, the household will risk collapsing completely, leaving children to fend for themselves. The older ones, especially girls, will be taken out of school to work in the home or the farm. These girls, deprived of education and opportunities, will be even less able to protect themselves against AIDS.

Because this crisis is different from past famines, we must look beyond   8
relief measures of the past. Merely shipping in food is not enough. Our effort will have to combine food assistance and new approaches to farming with treatment and prevention of H.I.V. and AIDS. It will require creating early-warning and analysis systems that monitor both H.I.V. infection rates and famine indicators. It will require new agricultural techniques, appropriate to a depleted work force. It will require a renewed effort to wipe out H.I.V.-related stigma and silence.

It will require innovative, large-scale ways to care for orphans, with   9
specific measures that enable children in AIDS-affected communities to stay in school. Education and prevention are still the most powerful weapons against the spread of H.I.V. Above all, this new international effort must put women at the center of our strategy to fight AIDS.

Experience suggests that there is reason to hope. The recent United   10
Nations report shows that H.I.V. infection rates in Uganda continue to
decline. In South Africa, infection rates for women under 20 have started to
decrease. In Zambia, H.I.V. rates show signs of dropping among women in
urban areas and younger women in rural areas. In Ethiopia, infection levels
have fallen among young women in the center of Addis Ababa.

We can and must build on those successes and replicate them elsewhere.   11
For that, we need leadership, partnership and imagination from the international community and African governments. If we want to save Africa from
two catastrophes, we would do well to focus on saving Africa's women.

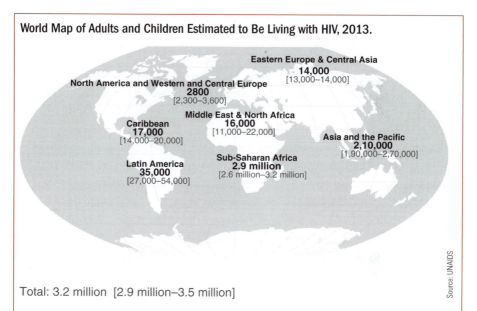

World Map of Adults and Children Estimated to Be Living with HIV, 2013.

Total: 3.2 million [2.9 million–3.5 million]

Source: UNAIDS, 2013 World AIDS Day Report. Reprinted with permission.

Thinking about the Image

1. The preceding map was produced by a United Nations group formed to educate people about, and actively combat, HIV/AIDS. In what ways does this map visually represent the trends Annan describes? How does the map make the urgency of his argument more immediate?
2. Is there any information on the map that surprises you?
3. If you were a delegate to the United Nations from an African or Asian nation, what questions or responses would you have for Secretary-General Kofi Annan?
4. Use the information in this map to support your answer to any of the "Responding in Writing" questions.

Thinking about the Essay

1. What is the tone of Annan's introductory paragraph and the entire essay? What is his purpose? Point to specific passages to support your answer.

2. Annan employs causal analysis to develop this essay. Trace the causes and effects that he presents. What are some of the primary causes and effects? What secondary causes and effects does he mention?

3. This essay is rich in the use of examples. What types of illustration does Annan present to support his thesis?

4. Locate other rhetorical strategies—for example, comparison and contrast—that appear as structuring devices in this essay.

5. This essay presents a problem and offers a solution. Explain this strategy, paying careful attention to how the pattern evolves.

Responding in Writing

6. In a brief essay, explain what you have learned about AIDS in Africa from Annan's essay. Do you share his sense of optimism about the ability of the nations involved and the international community to solve the problem? Why or why not?

7. Explain your personal viewpoint on the increase of AIDS among the women of the world—not just in Africa but in Asia, Russia, Europe, and elsewhere.

8. Write an essay on another threat to women—either in a particular country or region, or around the world.

Networking

9. Form working groups of four or five class members, and draw up an action plan to solicit funds on your campus for United Nations AIDS relief efforts in Sub-Saharan Africa. Then create a master plan based on the work of other class groups. Decide if you want to present this plan to the campus administration for approval.

10. Search the Internet for information on the United Nations programs to alleviate the AIDS epidemic around the world. Then write a letter to your congressional representative explaining why Congress should (or should not) support these efforts.

Naked

ATUL GAWANDE

Atul Gawande, an American surgeon, researcher, and author, was born in Brooklyn, New York, in 1965 to immigrant Indian parents, both of whom were doctors, and he grew up in Athens, Ohio. He received a bachelor's degree from Stanford University (1987), and as a Rhodes Scholar he studied philosophy, politics, and economics at Balliol College, Oxford, England (PPE, 1989). He graduated from Harvard Medical School (MD, 1993) and received a Master of Public Health from the Harvard School of Public Health (MPH, 1999). He is a surgeon at Brigham and Women's Hospital in Boston and a professor in public health and in surgery at Harvard. He is also Executive Director of Ariadne Labs, a center for health systems innovation, and chair of Lifebox, a nonprofit organization working to reduce deaths in surgery around the globe. He has published four best-selling books, has been a staff writer for *The New Yorker* since 1998, and frequently contributes to *Slate* magazine. His wide-ranging interests are reflected in his writings, for which he has received various awards, including the Lewis Thomas Prize for Writing about Science, a MacArthur Fellowship, and two National Magazine Awards. His most recent book is *Being Mortal: Medicine and What Matters in the End* (2014). In this article, Gawande explores the clash between professional ethics and international cultural beliefs.

Before Reading

Remember one of your visits to a doctor or a dentist. How did you feel? Were you nervous? Were you anxious? Why did you feel as you did? How did you feel when the visit was over?

There is an exquisite and fascinating scene in *Kandahar*, the 2001 movie set in Afghanistan under the Taliban regime, in which a male physician is asked to examine a female patient. They are separated by a dark blanketlike screen hung between them. Behind it, the woman is covered from head to foot by her burka. The two do not talk directly to each other. The patient's young son—he looks to be about six years old—serves as the go-between. She has a stomachache, he says.   1

"Does she throw up her food?" the doctor asks.   2

"Do you throw up your food?" the boy asks.   3

"No," the woman says, perfectly audibly, but the doctor waits as if he has not heard.   4

Atul Gawande, "Naked", *The New England Journal of Medicine* 353.7 (Aug. 18, 2005), pp. 645–648.

"No," the boy tells him.   5

For the purposes of examination, there is a two-inch circle cut in the   6
screen. "Tell her to come closer," the doctor says. The boy does. She brings
her mouth to the opening, and through it he looks inside. "Have her bring
her eye to the hole," he says. And so the exam goes. Such, apparently, can
be the demands of decency.

When I started in my surgical practice, I was not at all clear what my   7
etiquette of examination should be. There are no clear standards in the
United States, expectations are murky, and the topic can be fraught with
hazards. Physical examination is deeply intimate, and the way a doctor
deals with the naked body—particularly when the doctor is male and the
patient female—inevitably raises questions of propriety and trust.

No one seems to have discovered the ideal approach. An Iraqi surgeon   8
told me about the customs of physical examination in his home country.
He said he feels no hesitation about examining female patients completely
when necessary, but because a doctor and a patient of opposite sex cannot
be alone together without eyebrows being raised, a family member will
always accompany them for the exam. Women do not remove their clothes
or change into a gown. Instead, only a small portion of the body is uncovered at any one time. A nurse, he said, is rarely asked to chaperone: if the
doctor is female, it is not necessary, and if male, the family is there to ensure
that nothing unseemly occurs.

In Caracas, according to a Venezuelan doctor I met, female patients vir-   9
tually always have a chaperone for a breast or pelvic exam, whether the
physician is male or female. "That way there are no mixed messages," the
doctor said. The chaperone, however, must be a medical professional. So the
family is sent out of the examination room, and a female nurse brought in.
If a chaperone is unavailable or the patient refuses to allow one, the exam
is not done.

A Ukrainian internist from Kiev told me that she has not heard of doc-   10
tors there using a chaperone. I had to explain to her what a chaperone was.
If a family member is present at an office visit, she said, he or she will be
asked to leave. Both patient and doctor wear their uniforms—the patient
a white examining gown, the doctor a white coat. Last names are always
used. There is no effort at informality to muddy the occasion. These practices, she believes, are enough to solidify trust and preclude misinterpreta-
tion of the conduct of care.

A doctor, it appears, has a range of options.   11

In October 2003, I posted my clinic hours, and soon my first patients   12
arrived to see me. For the first time, I realized, I was genuinely alone
with patients. No attending physician supervising in the room or getting
ready to come in; no bustle of emergency room personnel on the other

side of a curtain. Just a patient and me. We'd sit down. We'd talk. I'd ask about whatever had occasioned the visit, about past medical problems, medications, the family and social history. Then the time would come to have a look.

There were, I will admit, some inelegant moments. I had an instinctive 13 aversion to examination gowns. At our clinic they are made of either thin, ill-fitting cloth or thin, ill-fitting paper. They seem designed to leave patients exposed and cold. I decided to examine my patients while they were in their street clothes, for the sake of dignity. If a patient with gallstones wore a shirt she could untuck for the abdominal exam, this worked fine. But then I'd encounter a patient in tights and a dress, and the next thing I knew, I had her dress bunched up around her neck, her tights around her knees, and both of us wondering what the hell was going on. An exam for a breast lump one could manage, in theory: the woman could unhook her brassiere and lift or unbutton her shirt. But in practice, it just seemed weird. Even checking pulses could be a problem. Pant legs could not be pushed up high enough to check a femoral pulse. (The femoral artery is felt at the crease of the groin.) Try pulling them down over shoes, however, and . . . forget it. I finally began to have patients change into the damn gowns. (I haven't, however, asked men to do so nearly as often as women. I asked a female urologist friend of mine whether she had her male patients change into a gown for a genital or rectal examination. No, she said. Both of us just have them unzip and drop.)

As for having a chaperone present with female patients, I hadn't settled 14 on a firm policy. I found that I always asked a medical assistant to come in for pelvic exams and generally didn't for breast exams. I was completely inconsistent about rectal exams.

I surveyed my colleagues about what they do and received a variety 15 of answers. Many said they bring in a chaperone for all pelvic and rectal exams—"anything below the waist"—but only rarely for breast exams. Others have a chaperone for breast and pelvic exams but not for rectal exams. Some do not have a chaperone at all. Indeed, an obstetrician-gynecologist I talked to estimated that about half the male physicians in his department do not routinely use a chaperone. He himself detests the word *chaperone* because it implies that mistrust is warranted, but he offers to bring in an "assistant" for pelvic and breast exams. Few of his patients, however, find the presence of the assistant necessary after the first exam, he said. If the patient prefers to have her sister, boyfriend, or mother stay for the exam, he does not object—but he is under no illusion that a family chaperone offers protection against an accusation of misconduct. Instead, he relies on his reading of a patient to determine whether bringing in a nurse witness would be wise.

One of our residents, who was trained partly in London, said he found   16
the selectivity here strange. "In Britain, I would never examine a woman's
abdomen without a nurse present. But in the emergency room here, when I
asked to have a nurse come in when I needed to do a rectal exam or check
groin nodes on a woman, they thought I was crazy. 'Just go in there and
do it!' they said." In England, he said, "if you need to do a breast or rectal
exam or even check femoral pulses, especially on a young woman, you
would be either foolish or stupid to do it without a chaperone. It doesn't
take much—just one patient complaining, 'I came in with a foot pain and
the doctor started diving around my groin,' and you could be suspended
for a sexual harassment investigation."

Britain's standards are stringent: the General Medical Council, the   17
Royal College of Physicians, and the Royal College of Obstetricians and
Gynaecologists specify that a chaperone of the appropriate gender must
be offered to all patients who undergo an "intimate examination" (that is,
involving the breasts, genitalia, or rectum), irrespective of the gender of the
patient or of the doctor. A chaperone must be present when a male physician performs an intimate examination of a female patient. The chaperone
should be a female member of the medical team, and her name should be
recorded in the notes. If the patient refuses a chaperone and the examination is not urgent, it is supposed to be deferred until it can be performed
by a female physician.

In the United States, where we have no such guidelines, our patients have   18
little idea of what to expect from us. To be sure, some minimal standards
have been established. The Federation of State Medical Boards has spelled
out that touching a patient's breasts or genitals for a purpose other than
medical care is a sexual violation and a disciplinable offense. So are oral
contact with a patient, encouraging a patient to masturbate in one's presence, and providing services in exchange for sexual favors. Sexual impropriety—which involves no touching but is no less proscribed—includes asking
a patient for a date, criticizing a patient's sexual orientation, making sexual
comments about the patient's body or clothing, and initiating discussion of
one's own sexual experiences or fantasies. I can't say anyone taught me these
boundaries in medical school, but I would like to think that no one needed
to teach them.

The difficulty for doctors who behave properly is that medical exams   19
remain inherently ambiguous. Any patient can be led to wonder: Did the
doctor really need to touch me there? And when doctors simply inquire
about patients' sexual history, can anyone be certain of the intent? The
fact that all medical professionals have blushed or found their thoughts
straying in unwanted directions during a patient visit reveals the potential
for impropriety.

The tone of an office visit can turn on a single word, a joke, a com- 20
ment about a tattoo in an unexpected place. One surgeon told me of a
young patient who expressed concern about a lump in her "boob." But
when he used the same word in response, she became extremely uncomfortable and later made a complaint. A woman I know left her gynecol-
ogist after he let slip an offhand admiring comment about her tan lines
during a pelvic exam.

The examination itself—the how and where of the touching—is, of 21
course, the most potentially dicey territory. If a patient even begins to
doubt the propriety of what a doctor is doing, something must not be right.
So what then should our customs be?

There are many reasons to consider setting tighter, more uniform pro- 22
fessional standards. One is to protect patients from harm. About 4 percent
of the disciplinary orders that state medical boards issue against physicians
are for sex-related offenses. One of every two hundred physicians is dis-
ciplined for sexual misconduct with patients sometime during his or her
career. Some of these cases have involved such outrageous acts as having
intercourse with patients during pelvic exams. The vast majority of cases
involved male physicians and female patients, and virtually all occurred
without a chaperone present. In one state, about a third of cases involved
dating patients or sexual touching of them; two-thirds involved sexual
impropriety or inappropriate touching short of sexual contact.

Clearer standards could also reduce false accusations against physi- 23
cians. Chaperones in particular provide physicians with a stronger defense
when such accusations are made. Inappropriate patient behavior might
be averted, too. A 1994 study found that 72 percent of female medical
students and 29 percent of male medical students experienced at least one
instance of patient-initiated sexual behavior. Twelve percent of the females
were sexually touched or grabbed by patients.

Yet, all this said, eliminating misconduct and accusations seems like 24
the wrong priority to drive how doctors proceed when examining patients'
bodies. The trouble is not that problems are rare (though the statistics
suggest they are) or that total prevention of impropriety—zero tolerance—
is impossible. It is that the measures required to achieve total prevention
inevitably approach the Talibanesque and risk harming patients by dis-
couraging complete and thorough examinations.

Instead, the most important reason to consider tightening standards 25
of medical protocol is simply to improve trust and understanding between
patients and doctors. The new informality of medicine—with white coats
disappearing and patient and doctor sometimes on a first-name basis—has
blurred boundaries that once guided us. If physicians are unsure about
what the etiquette of the examination room should be, is it any surprise

that patients are, too? Or that misinterpretations occur? We have jettisoned our old customs but we have not managed to replace them.

My father, a urologist, has thought carefully about how to avert such   26
uncertainties. From the start, he told me, he felt the fragility of his standing as an outsider, an Indian immigrant practicing in our small southern Ohio town. In the absence of guidelines to reassure patients that what he does as a urologist is routine, he made painstaking efforts to avoid any question.

The process begins before the examination. He always arrives in a tie   27
and white coat. He is courtly. Although he often knows patients socially and doesn't hesitate to speak with them about private matters (the subjects can range from impotence to sexual affairs), he keeps his language strictly medical. If a female patient must put on a gown, he steps out while she undresses. He makes a point of explaining what he is going to do during the examination and why. If the patient lies down and needs further unzipping or unbuttoning, he is careful not to help. He wears gloves even for abdominal examinations. If the patient is female or under eighteen years of age, he brings in a female nurse as a chaperone, whether the examination is "intimate" or not.

His approach works. He has a busy practice. There have been no   28
unseemly rumors. I grew up knowing many of his patients, and they seemed to trust him completely.

I find, however, that some of his practices are not quite right for me.   29
My patients are as likely to have problems above the waist as below, and having a chaperone present for a routine abdominal exam or an examination of enlarged lymph nodes under an arm seems absurd to me. I don't don gloves for nongenital exams, either. Nonetheless, I have tried to emulate the spirit of my father's visits—the decorum in language and attire, the respect for modesty, the precision of examination. And as I thought further about his example, I made changes: I now routinely bring in a female assistant not just for pelvic exams but also for female breast and rectal exams. "If it's all right, I'll go get Janice," I say. "She can be our chaperone."

Thinking about the Essay

1. When you first read the title "Naked," what was your response? What did you think the essay might be about? Why do you think the author uses this title for his essay?

2. Who is the primary audience for this essay? What clues to the audience does the author provide in the essay? Are there other audiences who might be interested in reading this essay?

3. What rhetorical strategies does the author use to develop and organize the essay? Identify specific examples of the use of narration, comparison and contrast, causal analysis, illustration, and problem to solution.

4. What is the author's argumentative claim? How does the author use the three appeals for argument—emotional, rational, and ethical—to articulate and bolster his argument?

5. What is the author's conclusion about the etiquette of medical examination and policies that might be set up to systemize the relationship between doctor and patient? Do you agree or disagree with his conclusion?

Responding in Writing

6. In a brief personal essay, narrate an experience in which you felt either comfortable or uncomfortable in a medical situation. Use specific descriptions and images to recreate your experience, and choose words and images that will help you create the tone of the experience (how you felt and responded to what was happening).

7. Write an expository essay in which you compare and contrast what a doctor or other medical personnel might do to make a patient feel comfortable in a medical situation and what those same medical professionals might do to make a patient feel uncomfortable.

8. Write an argumentative essay in which you support the claim that uniform policies of ethical behavior are or are not advisable for medical personnel.

Networking

9. Working with three or four of your classmates, create a scenario to illustrate how a doctor should or should not behave in examining a patient. Write a summary of the conclusions and recommendations that result from the scenario. With your group, act out the scenario for the rest of the class, and lead a discussion of the conclusions and recommendations of your scenario.

10. Search the Internet for information on the history of medical ethics and the current Code of Medical Ethics of the American Medical Association. Write a summary of what you discover.

The French, the Veil, and the Look

ELAINE SCIOLINO

Elaine Sciolino currently lives in Paris and is a writer for *The New York Times*. After receiving an MA from New York University in 1971, she began a distinguished career in journalism, first working for *Newsweek* from 1972 to 1984 as a foreign correspondent and Rome bureau chief. Since 1985, Sciolino has been employed by *The New York Times* as a reporter, senior writer, and chief diplomatic correspondent—the first woman to hold that position at the newspaper. Sciolino has covered the Iranian revolution, the Iran hostage crisis, the

Iran–Iraq War, the US invasion of Grenada, and other global crises. Her books include *Outlaw State: Saddam Hussein's Quest for Power and the Gulf Crisis* (1991), *Persian Mirrors* (2000), and *La Seduction: How the French Play the Game of Life* (2011). In this essay from the April 17, 2011, issue of *The New York Times*, Sciolino examines the causes behind French hostility to the facial veil.

Before Reading

Should women and men be permitted by law to dress as they wish in any society, or should restrictions be placed on the ways in which people dress in public?

P ARIS—Many scholars of Islam will tell you that nothing in the Koran   1
requires a Muslim woman to cover her face—that its rules for proper Islamic dress are ambiguous and limited. "Say to the believing women that they should lower their gaze and guard their modesty," it says. It adds, "They should draw their veils over their bosoms and not display their ornaments."

Even Khadija, the first wife of the prophet Muhammad and a successful   2
businesswoman, who surely guarded her modesty, is believed to have bared her face in public. Historically, in the Middle East, it was often tribal Bedouin women who covered their faces, sometimes with decorative masklike veils dripping with coins that announced the value of their bank accounts.

Westerners became sensitive to the image of faceless Muslim women   3
largely through the use of the burqa by the Taliban to oppress women in Afghanistan. That garment functions like a body tent, with an eye screen to allow some vision. Years before it became an issue in the United States, French feminists fulminated against the burqa, and later against other radical interpretations of Islam in Afghanistan, including public stoning for adultery, the demolition of Buddhist shrines and the banning of music. And now, the French government has officially banned the wearing of full-face veils.

But the face-covering veils in France are different. Even though many   4
here mistakenly call it a burqa, the garment worn by women here is a niqab, an improvised cover in black with no religious or traditional significance beyond what a wearer or observer gives it. Some of these women may be rebels, demanding control over their bodies and recognition within

The naqib is a veil worn by conservative Muslim women which exposes only a woman's eyes. However, some European countries, France in particular, have banned wearing the naqib on the streets. In 2010, a popular Muslim cleric in Saudi Arabia, Sheik Aedh al-Garni, issued a ruling, or fatwa, saying it is permissible for Muslim women to reveal their faces in countries where the Islamic veil is banned, while criticizing efforts in Europe to outlaw the garment.

a Western culture whose social values they reject. Some may have been forced into covering their faces by domineering men; others may believe they are better Muslims because they hide their faces in public. Some are French converts from Christianity.

France's ideal of a secularized republic theoretically leaves it blind to   5
color, ethnicity and religion, and makes everyone equal under the law; there is no census or reliable poll data on why these women veil, or even how many do. (The government's best estimate is 2,000 at most.)

So why all the fuss, on both sides of this question, about a tiny minor-   6
ity of women who wear odd-looking dress in a country that is the world's creative headquarters for odd-looking fashion? One explanation is cultural. In French culture, the eyes are supposed to meet in public, to invite a conversation or just to exchange a visual greeting with a stranger. Among Muslims, the eyes of men and women are not supposed to meet, even by chance, and especially not in public or between strangers.

"Le regard"—the look exchanged by two people—is a classic compo-   7
nent of French literature, developed centuries ago in the love poetry of the troubadours. Especially in Paris, a stare in public is not usually taken as a

sign of rudeness, and can be accepted as a warm compliment. You never walk alone here, it seems. "The visual marketplace of seduction" is how Pascal Bruckner and Alain Finkielkraut define public space in their 1977 book, "The New Love Disorder."

In another book, "Galanterie Française," Claude Habib, a specialist in   8
18th-century literature, argues that the centuries-old French tradition of gallantry "presupposes a visibility of the feminine" and "a joy of being visible—the very one that certain young Muslim girls cannot or do not want to show."

French tradition has also long encouraged mixing of the sexes in social   9
situations. "The veil," Ms. Habib continues, "interrupts the circulation of coquetry and of paying homage, in declaring that there is another possible way for the sexes to coexist: strict separation."

A more familiar explanation for French antagonism to the facial veil is   10
historical and political: the deep-rooted French fear, resentment and rejection of the "other"—the immigrant, the invader, the potential terrorist or abuser of human rights who eats, drinks, prays and dresses differently, and refuses to assimilate in the French way. Some of the French, particularly on the far right, still believe that France's colonial "civilizing mission" was a noble one, and that the people of former colonies, including the Arabs of North Africa, have clung to backward ways that they are now exporting to France. "The veil's presence reminds French people daily that that mission failed," said Rebecca Ruquist, an American scholar of race and religion in modern France. "It has been seen as a sartorial rejection of the values of the French republic."

By donning an all-encompassing black garment that covers all but   11
the eyes, these women seem to want their coverings, not their faces, to be noticed. Their veils are generally fixed in place, cut or shaped in such a way that they hide all but their eyes.

In some parts of the Islamic world, however, women opt for more flu-   12
idity. In Saudi Arabia, for example, where Muslim women are required to keep their bodies and hair under wraps in public, facial covering is neither obligatory nor banned and can be used in a kind of cat-and-mouse game with strangers. One favorite head covering is a long black scarf that becomes opaque when doubled over. It is worn with one end hanging down in front, the other over the shoulder. Should a strange man look at her, a woman might take the hanging end of the scarf and flip it up to cover her face. She can see out, but no one can see in.

France's officials and legislators have used an amalgam of arguments to   13
defend their new law. Interior Minister Claude Guéant said it defends "two fundamental principles: secularism and the principle of equality between man and woman." A stronger argument is that any hidden face is a potential security risk, and it is on that basis that the law does not single out Islamic veils by name, but rather all facial coverings in public.

In theory, that means that anyone wearing a balaclava, a fencing mask 14 or a motorcycle helmet with a full-face visor could be punished. But will they? The French might be shocked if they were. And there are exemptions, for Santa Clauses and carnivalgoers, for example.

Here's another question: Will lavish-spending female tourists from 15 gulf Arab states be forced to bare their faces on the Champs-Elysées? (In Switzerland, Justice Minister Eveline Widmer-Schlumpf wants to ban facial veils, but has said that gulf tourists will be exempt.) Perhaps, as some have suggested, it will be rare for anyone to be penalized in France, given how difficult it is to enforce the law fairly and uniformly.

Meanwhile, France will remain France—the land where the uncovered 16 body is celebrated. Billboards and posters on Paris streets regularly feature naked breasts and buttocks. To encourage women over the age of 40 to get mammograms, 10 prominent women, including the two-starred Michelin chef Hélène Darroze and Nathalie Rykiel, director of the Sonia Rykiel fashion house, posed topless in Marie Claire magazine two years ago.

And one of the most colorful images of protest against labor reform in 17 2006 was of a flag-waving student in Bordeaux dressed as Marianne, in a red Phrygian cap and white peasant blouse. As in the 19th-century painting by Eugène Delacroix that hangs in the Louvre, her breasts were exposed. Marianne remains, as she has always been, the French republic's idealized national symbol.

Thinking about the Essay

1. What is Sciolino's thesis? Where does she state her main idea, or does she imply it? Explain.

2. Why does Sciolino begin her essay with a discussion of the Koran and Islam? Which paragraphs constitute her introduction, and what facts does she present?

3. The writer uses several comparative methods in this essay. Identify the paragraphs where comparison and contrast exist, and explain the purpose of this strategy. What types of evidence does she use to support her comparative strategy?

4. Trace the pattern of cause and effect that Sciolino develops.

5. Where does Sciolino use definition as a rhetorical strategy? Do you find this strategy effective? Why or why not?

Responding in Writing

6. Compose an argumentative essay in which you defend or support the proposition that a secular society should have the right to impose dress restrictions on residents who dress according to religious guidelines.

7. Write your own extended definition of "the look," connecting it to a specific ethnic, racial, or national culture.

8. In an essay, analyze the impact of religion on relationships between men and women. Focus on one religious group—for example, Catholics, Christian Evangelicals, fundamentalist Muslims—and explain how these groups attempt to regulate moral behavior.

Networking

9. Exchange your essay with another class member. Peer critique your partner's essay, focusing on his or her use of various rhetorical strategies to develop the paper.

10. Locate online at least three reviews of Elaine Sciolino's most recent book, *La Seduction*. Then write a summary presenting your findings.

A Dark Window on Human Trafficking

MIKE CEASER

Mike Ceaser is a journalist based in Bogotá, Colombia, who writes frequently for *The Chronicle of Higher Education*. He specializes in Latin American affairs. Ceaser has also written for *Americas*, *The Lancet*, *National Catholic Reporter*, and other publications. In the following essay, published in the *Chronicle* on July 25, 2008, Ceaser investigates the unsavory world of human trafficking of young girls across South American and North American borders.

Before Reading

How would you define "human trafficking"? Why has this phenomenon recently become such a problem worldwide?

Police-car lights flashed and prostitutes, pimps, reporters, and police officers milled about. One by one, the neon signs displaying scantily clad women went dark. Finally, the police sealed the gates beneath the billboard of two naked women amid the moon and stars.

While the police closed the La Luna nightclub for employing underage girls as prostitutes, a pair of graduate students from Dominican University, near Chicago, stood by urging them on. For the students, the shuttering of the club was a personal victory.

"I don't think that prostitution can be a choice that you make," said   3
Tracy O'Dowd, who, along with Sergio Velarde, had assisted in winning
the court battle against the owners of the nightclub. "I think you're brought
there one way or another."

Ms. O'Dowd and Mr. Velarde, both master's-degree students in social   4
work, had come here three months earlier, in late January, to work as
interns at the Our Youth Foundation, which is based in Ecuador and battles the exploitation of children. Concerned about human trafficking and
interested in Latin America, both had studied the issue of trafficking at
Dominican. Before leaving home, they learned that the sexual exploitation
of minors was common in Ecuador, and that the country's corrupt and
inefficient legal system rarely took action against those responsible.

Only in 2005 did Ecuador pass its first major law against human traf-   5
ficking; in 2007 the United States' "Trafficking in Persons Report" said
that Ecuador "does not fully comply with the minimum standards for the
elimination of trafficking," though the report also noted improvements in
prosecutions, public education, and support for victims.

Mr. Velarde, whose parents and grandparents emigrated from Mexico   6
to the United States, speaks passionately about the challenges faced by
migrants, who are often exploited even when they are not the victims of
traffickers. Once, while visiting relatives in the Mexican state of Chihua-
hua, his family encountered immigrants from Central America who had
been abandoned there and told they were in the United States. The many
fast-food restaurants made the locale resemble a U.S. city.

Mr. Velarde believes that in "individualistic" American society, people   7
are leery of supporting and assisting immigrants—even those who were
brought to the United States against their will.

"Once the stigma is placed on immigrants, it doesn't matter how you   8
got there," Mr. Velarde says. "If you got there on your free will or against
your free will, you're always going to have that stigma."

But he and Ms. O'Dowd found that human trafficking in Ecuador   9
differs fundamentally from what they'd read about in other nations, and
soon found themselves swept up in a landmark legal battle against traffickers. Human trafficking generally refers to the carrying of people across
borders deceitfully or against their will, for prostitution or forced labor.
While that happens to Ecuadoreans, here the crime most commonly consists of forcing young girls into brothels, through coercion or outright kid-
napping. Sometimes young men seek out girls from poor, troubled families
and pretend to fall in love with them—and then "sell" them to brothel
owners.

"Here, they do this whole fantasy couple, fantasy relationship, and   10
then all of a sudden, 'I don't have any more money, so you have to work,'"

says Mr. Velarde. "But the girl still believes they're a couple, and he still kind of treats them as a couple."

It's an often-invisible crime. 11

Mr. Velarde says that in his visits to poor communities, he discovered 12 that people often don't know that such cases involve human trafficking, or are so poor that they assume their absent daughters must be better off.

Most families never imagine that their daughters have ended up at 13 a place like La Luna, a complex of three huge nightclub-brothels, which had come to represent both the crime and the legal invulnerability often enjoyed by the perpetrators. Adult prostitution is legal in Ecuador, but La Luna was notorious for employing underage girls. In January 2006, pressured by the Our Youth Foundation and others, the police finally raided the club and rescued 11 girls ages 13 through 17, who were taken to a safe house operated by the foundation.

The trial of the club's five owners, repeatedly postponed, dragged 14 on until this March. Ms. O'Dowd and Mr. Velarde met three of the victims, now ages 15 through 17, when the girls prepared to testify for the prosecution. Then the two demonstrated in front of the courthouse in support of the victims—and faced off against a group backing the brothel owners.

"We stood outside the courtroom for three hours," Ms. O'Dowd wrote 15 in the blog she posted as part of her course work. "There were about 50 people there to support these girls, and there were about 20 supporting the traffickers. We waited with posters saying 'No to sexual exploitation,' 'Justice that comes late isn't justice.'"

In the first days of April, the court issued its verdict: All the men were 16 guilty.

"The five men on trial were sentenced to 16 years," Mr. Velarde blogged 17 on April 4, "and it was a huge win."

Children's-rights advocates called the club's shuttering in April a land- 18 mark because of its size and wealth. And officials present at the closing vowed that it was the start of a crackdown on brothels employing minors.

But while La Luna became the face of exploitation here, the crime's 19 roots lie in the city's poor and socially troubled barrios. And it was there that the Dominican interns did the nitty-gritty and often frustrating work intended to prevent the children of vulnerable families from ever being misled into prostitution.

The interns did this in places like a nondescript neighborhood of brick 20 and concrete houses that Ms. O'Dowd visited one overcast day.

She knocked on the door of a home where the father had been impris- 21 oned for sexually abusing one of his daughters. Then, surrounded by children, Ms. O'Dowd sat on a couch with the mother in the tidy living room and asked about the family's situation and needs: How were they doing financially? Did the children need notebooks for school? Would they like counseling? But the woman seemed resigned and hopeless. Between sobs, she described how the absence of her husband, an auto mechanic, had left the family financially devastated. She was even hostile to the Our Youth Foundation, which she blamed for taking him away.

"What I want is for you to help me, to get my husband out of jail," she   22
pleaded. Ms. O'Dowd left feeling frustrated by the mother's attitude and lack of appreciation for the danger to her daughters.

Even united families face the threat of trafficking because of the pov-   23
erty and social dislocation caused by Ecuador's heavy migration from the country side to the wealthier cities.

Another morning, Mr. Velarde rode a series of buses and then a pickup   24
truck up a dirt road to a neighborhood of crude homes scattered among bushes on a mountainside high above Quito, the capital. In a house of uninsulated brick and concrete lived an indigenous family who had migrated from the coast in search of work. The mother cleans houses when pain from a kidney stone permits, while the children's stepfather earns about $30 per month as a security guard.

Inside the home, Mr. Velarde and an intern from an Ecuadorean univer-   25
sity interviewed the family and left satisfied that they were making do with their limited resources. But while the group waited for a bus back down the mountainside, the mother unexpectedly mentioned that two years earlier her daughter, now 14 years old, was kidnapped by a family acquaintance, who raped her and held her captive for eight days while trying to "sell" her to a brothel.

Although the family succeeded in rescuing the girl, she is still afraid to   26
leave the house. Then the mother described how the local schoolteacher accosts female students, forcing the family to send their daughters to a more distant school—which means a perilous walk back home every evening.

"Sometimes I think about the other girls who are getting bigger," their   27
mother worried, "that the same thing could happen to them."

The interns reported the family's situation to the foundation, for   28
follow-up assistance. "That her daughter was kidnapped—that just changes the whole situation," Mr. Velarde observed afterward. "Research says that if they've had such a thing with a sister, a cousin, . . . then they're vulnerable."

Ms. O'Dowd and Mr. Velarde returned to Chicago this spring feeling   29
hopeful that Ecuador was taking real steps against trafficking, through both police actions and new laws. But the court case against the club fell short of being a complete victory: The owners' sentences were slashed from 16 years to six.

Their Ecuadorean experience left the Dominican students with hopes   30
of continuing to fight human trafficking, either in the United States, where
they feel the problem has received too little attention, or back in Latin
America. But the visit to Ecuador also changed them both, making them
more interested in preventing the circumstances that make people vulnerable to trafficking. Although thousands of people are believed to be victims
of human trafficking into the United States each year, the United States
does not include itself in its own annual trafficking report.

"As a country, I think we've focused more on everyone else," says   31
Mr. Velarde, "and when you have eyes on everybody else, you don't have
eyes on your own situation."

Thinking about the Essay

1. How does Ceaser devise his introduction? What techniques does he use to create a dramatic situation throughout the essay? Are these strategies effective?
   Why or why not?

2. Ceaser profiles two students. Who are they, and what do we learn about them?
   What is the writer's attitude toward them? Justify your response.

3. Does Ceaser have a thesis or claim in this essay? Explain.

4. Ceaser wrote this article for a specialized audience—college teachers and
   administrators. Why would this readership be interested in the subject? Why
   might the essay appeal to a broader audience?

5. In analyzing the trafficking of young South American girls to the United States
   for the purpose of prostitution, Ceaser relies on causal analysis. Examine the
   causes and effects—both primary and secondary—that the writer traces.

Responding in Writing

6. In an investigative essay, analyze the causes behind the increase in the trafficking of women across international borders.

7. Argue for or against the proposition that American society is too tolerant of
   human trafficking for the purpose of prostitution, especially if the victims are
   undocumented immigrants.

8. Do you believe that we are collectively responsible for such realities as human
   trafficking? Write a persuasive essay in which you respond to this question.

Networking

9. In small groups, discuss Ceaser's assertion that "individualistic" American society creates the conditions that foster a tolerance for human trafficking.

10. Go online and find out more about human trafficking in girls and young women
    from South America to the United States. Write an investigative report based on
    your findings.

Life on the Global Assembly Line

BARBARA EHRENREICH AND ANNETTE FUENTES

Barbara Ehrenreich was born in 1941 in Butte, Montana. She attended Reed College (BA, 1963) and Rockefeller University (PhD in biology, 1968). A self-described socialist and feminist, Ehrenreich uses her scientific training to investigate a broad range of social issues: health care, the plight of the poor, and the condition of women around the world. Her scathing critiques of American health care in such books as *The American Health Empire* (with John Ehrenreich, 1970), *Complaints and Disorders: The Sexual Politics of Sickness* (with Deirdre English, 1973), and *For Her Own Good* (with English, 1978) established her as an authority in the field. A prolific writer during the 1980s and 1990s, Ehrenreich's more recent works include the award-winning book *Nickel and Dimed: On (Not) Getting By in America* (2001), *Bait and Switch: The (Futile) Pursuit of the American Dream* (2005), and *This Land Is Their Land: Reports from a Divided Nation* (2008). She is also a frequent contributor to magazines, including *The Nation*, *Esquire*, *Radical America*, *The New Republic*, and *The New York Times*, while serving as a contributing editor to *Ms.* and *Mother Jones*. The classic essay that appears here, written for *Ms.* in 1981 with Annette Fuentes, an American journalist who has written for publications such as *The New York Times*, *The Progressive*, and *USA Today*, was among the first articles to expose the plight of working women around the world.

Before Reading

What experiences or expectations do you bring to a new job? What happens if you discover you are being exploited?

Every morning, between four and seven, thousands of women head out for the day shift. In Ciudad Juárez, they crowd into ruteras (run-down vans) for the trip from the slum neighborhoods to the industrial parks on the outskirts of the city. In Penang they squeeze, 60 or more at a time, 1 into buses for the trip to the low, modern factory buildings of the Bayan Lepas free trade zone. In Taiwan, they walk from the dormitories—where the night shift is already asleep in the still-warm beds—through the checkpoints in the high fence surrounding the factory zone.

This is the world's new industrial proletariat: young, female, Third World. Viewed from the "first world," they are still faceless, genderless "cheap labor," signaling their existence only through a label or tiny imprint "made in Hong Kong," or Taiwan, Korea, the Dominican Republic, Mexico, the Philippines. But they may be one of the most strategic blocs of womanpower in the world. Conservatively, there are 2 million Third World female industrial workers employed now, millions more looking for work, and their numbers are rising every year.

It doesn't take more than second-grade arithmetic to understand what's happening. In the U.S., an assembly-line worker is likely to earn, depending on her length of employment, between $3.10 and $5 an hour. In many Third World countries, a woman doing the same work will earn $3 to $5 a day.

And so, almost everything that can be packed up is being moved out to the Third World: garment manufacture, textiles, toys, footwear, pharmaceuticals, wigs, appliance parts, tape decks, computer components, plastic goods. In some industries, like garment and textile, American jobs are lost in the process, and the biggest losers are women, often black and Hispanic. But what's going on is much more than a matter of runaway shops. Economists are talking about a "new international division of labor," in which the process of production is broken down and the fragments are dispersed to different parts of the world, while control over the overall process and technology remains safely at company headquarters in "first world" countries.

The American electronics industry provides a classic example: circuits are printed on silicon wafers and tested in California; then the wafers are shipped to Asia for the labor-intensive process by which they are cut into tiny chips and bonded to circuit boards; final assembly into products such as calculators or military equipment usually takes place in the United States. Garment manufacture too is often broken into geographically separated steps, with the most repetitive, labor-intensive jobs going to the poor countries of the southern hemisphere.

So much any economist could tell you. What is less often noted is the gender breakdown of the emerging international division of labor. Eighty to 90 percent of the low-skilled assembly jobs that go to the Third World are performed by women in a remarkable switch from earlier patterns of foreign-dominated industrialization. Until now, "development" under the aegis of foreign corporations has usually meant more jobs for men and—compared to traditional agricultural society—a diminished economic status for women. But multinational corporations and Third World governments alike consider assembly-line work—whether the product is Barbie dolls or missile parts—to be "women's" work.

It's an article of faith with management that only women can do, or will   7
do, the monotonous, painstaking work that American business is exporting to the Third World. The personnel manager of a light assembly plant in Taiwan told anthropologist Linda Gail Arrigo, "Young male workers are too restless and impatient to do monotonous work with no career value. If displeased, they sabotage the machines and even threaten the foreman. But girls? At most, they cry a little."

A top-level management consultant who specializes in advising   8
American companies on where to relocate, gave us this global generalization: "The [factory] girls genuinely enjoy themselves. They're away from their families. They have spending money. Of course it's a regulated experience too—with dormitories to live in—so it's a healthful experience."

Dorigny Marie/SIPA

This three-year-old in India helps her mother and sisters make soccer balls—for 75 cents a day.

What is the real experience of the women in the emerging Third World   9
industrial work force? Rachael Grossman, a researcher with the Southeast Asia Resource Center, found women employees of U.S. multinational
firms in Malaysia and the Philippines living four to eight in a room in
boarding-houses, or squeezing into tiny extensions built onto squatter huts
near the factory. Where companies do provide dormitories, they are not of
the "healthful," collegiate variety. The American Friends Service Committee reports that dormitory space is "likely to be crowded—while one shift
works, another sleeps, as many as twenty to a room."

Living conditions are only part of the story. The work that multina-   10
tional corporations export to the Third World is not only the most tedious,
but often the most hazardous part of the production process. The countries
they go to are, for the most part, those that will guarantee no interference
from health and safety inspectors, trade unions, or even freelance reformers.

Consider the electronics industry, which is generally thought to be the   11
safest and cleanest of the exported industries. The factory buildings are
low and modern, like those one might find in a suburban American industrial park. Inside, rows of young women, neatly dressed in the company
uniform or T-shirt, work quietly at their stations. There is air conditioning
(not for the women's comfort, but to protect the delicate semiconductor
parts they work with), and high-volume piped-in Bee Gees hits (not so
much for entertainment, as to prevent talking).

For many Third World women, electronics is a prestige occupation, at   12
least compared to other kinds of factory work. They are unlikely to know
that in the United States the National Institute on Occupational Safety and
Health (NIOSH) has placed electronics on its select list of "high health-risk
industries using the greatest number of toxic substances." If electronics
assembly work is risky here, it is doubly so in countries where there is no
equivalent of NIOSH to even issue warnings. In many plants toxic chem-
icals and solvents sit in open containers, filling the work area with fumes
that can literally knock you out. "We have been told of cases where ten
to twelve women passed out at once," an AFSC field worker in northern
Mexico told us, "and the newspapers report this as 'mass hysteria.'"

Some of the worst conditions have been documented in South Korea,   13
where the garment and textile industries have helped spark that country's
"economic miracle." Workers are packed into poorly lit rooms, where summer temperatures rise above 100 degrees. Textile dust, which can cause
permanent lung damage, fills the air. Management may require forced overtime of as much as 48 hours at a stretch, and if that seems to go beyond
the limits of human endurance, pep pills and amphetamine injections are
thoughtfully provided. In her diary (originally published in a magazine
now banned by the South Korean government), Min Chong Suk, 30, a

sewing-machine operator, wrote of working from 7 A.M. to 11:30 P.M. in a garment factory: "When [the apprentices] shake the waste threads from the clothes, the whole room fills with dust, and it is hard to breathe. Since we've been working in such dusty air, there have been increasing numbers of people getting tuberculosis, bronchitis, and eye diseases. Since we are women, it makes us so sad when we have pale, unhealthy, wrinkled faces like dried-up spinach. It seems to me that no one knows our blood dissolves into the threads and seams, with sighs and sorrow."

In all the exported industries, the most invidious, inescapable health   14
hazard is stress. Lunch breaks may be barely long enough for a woman to stand in line at the canteen or hawkers' stalls. Visits to the bathroom are treated as privileges. Rotating shifts—the day shift one week, the night shift the next—wreak havoc with sleep patterns. Because inaccuracies or failure to meet production quotas can mean substantial pay losses, the pressures are quickly internalized; stomach ailments and nervous problems are not unusual.

As if poor health and the stress of factory life weren't enough to drive   15
women into early retirement, management actually encourages a high turnover in many industries. "As you know, when seniority rises, wages rise," the management consultant to U.S. multinationals told us. He explained that it's cheaper to train a fresh supply of teenagers than to pay experienced women higher wages. "Older" women, aged 23 or 24, are likely to be laid off and not rehired.

The lucky ones find husbands. The unlucky ones find themselves at the   16
margins of society—as bar girls, "hostesses," or prostitutes.

There has been no international protest about the exploitation of Third   17
World women by multinational corporations—no thundering denunciations from the floor of the United Nations' General Assembly, no angry resolutions from the Conference of the Non-Aligned Countries. Sociologist Robert Snow, who has been tracing the multinationals on their way south and eastward for years, explained why. "The Third World governments want the multinationals to move in. There's cutthroat competition to attract the corporations."

The governments themselves gain little revenue from this kind of   18
investment—especially since most offer tax holidays and freedom from export duties in order to attract the multinationals in the first place. Nor do the people as a whole benefit, according to a highly placed Third World woman within the U.N. "The multinationals like to say they're contributing to development," she told us, "but they come into our countries for one thing—cheap labor. If the labor stops being so cheap, they can move on. So how can you call that development? It depends on the people being poor and staying poor." But there are important groups that do stand to gain

when the multinationals set up shop in their countries: local entrepreneurs who subcontract to the multinationals; "technocrats" who become local management; and government officials who specialize in cutting red tape for an "agent's fee" or an outright bribe.

In the competition for multinational investment, local governments 19 advertise their women shamelessly. An investment brochure issued by the Malaysian government informs multinational executives that: "the manual dexterity of the Oriental female is famous the world over. Her hands are small, and she works fast with extreme care. . . . Who, therefore, could be better qualified by nature and inheritance, to contribute to the efficiency of a bench-assembly production line than the Oriental girl?"

Many "host" governments are willing to back up their advertising with 20 whatever brutality it takes to keep "their girls" just as docile as they look in the brochures. Even the most polite and orderly attempts to organize are likely to bring down overkill doses of police repression:

- In Guatemala in 1975 women workers in a North American–owned 21 garment factory drew up a list of complaints that included insults by management, piecework wages that turned out to be less than the legal minimum, no overtime pay, and "threats of death." In response, the American boss called the local authorities to report that he was being harassed by "Communists." When the women reported for work the next day they found the factory surrounded by two fully armed contingents of military police. The "Communist" ringleaders were picked out and fired.
- In the Dominican Republic in 1978, workers who attempted to organize 22 at La Romana industrial zone were first fired, then obligingly arrested by the local police. Officials from the AFL-CIO have described the zone as a "modern slave-labor camp," where workers who do not meet their production quotas during their regular shift must stay and put in unpaid overtime until they do meet them, and many women workers are routinely strip-searched at the end of the day. During the 1978 organizing attempt, the government sent in national police in full combat gear armed with automatic weapons. Gulf & Western supplements the local law with its own company-sponsored motorcycle club, which specializes in terrorizing suspected union sympathizers.
- In Inchon, South Korea, women at the Dong-II Textile Company (which 23 produces fabrics and yarn for export to the United States) had succeeded in gaining leadership in their union in 1972. But in 1978 the government-controlled, male-dominated Federation of Korean Trade Unions sent special "action squads" to destroy the women's union. Armed with steel bars and buckets of human excrement, the goons broke into the union office, smashed the office equipment, and smeared the excrement over the women's bodies and in their hair, ears, eyes, and mouths.

Crudely put (and incidents like this do not inspire verbal delicacy), 24
the relationship between many Third World governments and the multinational corporations is not very different from the relationship between a
pimp and his customers. The governments advertise their women, sell them,
and keep them in line for the multinational "johns." But there are other
parties to the growing international traffic in women—such as the United
Nations' Industrial Development Organization (UNIDO), the World Bank,
and the United States government itself.

UNIDO has been a major promoter of "free trade zones." These are 25
enclaves within nations that offer multinationals a range of creature comforts, including: freedom from paying taxes and export duties; low-cost
water, power, and buildings; exemption from whatever labor laws may
apply in the country as a whole; and, in some cases, such security features
as barbed-wire, guarded checkpoints, and government-paid police.

Then there is the World Bank, which over the past decade has lent sev- 26
eral billion dollars to finance the roads, airports, power plants, and even
the first-class hotels that multinational corporations need in order to set up
business in Third World countries.

But the most powerful promoter of exploitative conditions for Third 27
World women workers is the United States government itself. For example, the notoriously repressive Korean textile industry was developed with
the help of $400 million in aid from the U.S. State Department. Malaysia
became a low-wage haven for the electronics industry thanks to technical
assistance financed by AID and to U.S. money (funneled through the Asian
Development Bank) to set up free trade zones.

But the most obvious form of United States involvement, according to 28
Lenny Siegel, the director of the Pacific Studies Center, is through "our consistent record of military aid to Third World governments that are capitalist, politically repressive, and are not striving for economic independence."

What does our government have to say for itself? According to AID 29
staffer Emmy Simmons, "we can get hung up in the idea that it's exploitation
without really looking at the alternatives for women. These people have to
go somewhere."

Anna, for one, has nowhere to go but the maquiladora. Her family left 30
the farm when she was only six, and the land has long since been bought
up by a large commercial agribusiness company. After her father left to
find work north of the border, money was scarce for years. So when the
factory where she now works opened, Anna felt it was "the best thing that
had ever happened" to her. As a wage-earner, her status rose compared
to her brothers with their on-again, off-again jobs. Partly out of her new
sense of confidence she agreed to meet with a few other women one day
after work to talk about wages and health conditions. That was the way

she became what management called a "labor agitator" when, six months later, 90 percent of the day shift walked out in the company's first south-of-the-border strike.

Women like Anna need their jobs desperately. They know the risks of   31 organizing. Beyond that—if they do succeed in organizing—the company can always move on in search of a still-docile, job-hungry work force. Yet thousands of women in the Third World's industrial work force have chosen to fight for better wages and working conditions.

One particularly dramatic instance took place in South Korea in 1979.   32 Two hundred young women employees of the YH textile-and-wig factory staged a peaceful vigil and fast to protest the company's threatened closing of the plant. On the fifth day of the vigil, more than 1,000 riot police, armed with clubs and steel shields, broke into the building where the women were staying and forcibly dragged them out. Twenty-one-year-old Kim Kyong-suk was killed during the melee. It was her death that touched off widespread rioting throughout Korea that many thought led to the overthrow of President Park Chung Hee.

So far, feminism, first-world style, has barely begun to acknowledge the   33 Third World's new industrial womanpower. Jeb Mays and Kathleen Connell, cofounders of the San Francisco–based Women's Network on Global Corporations, are two women who would like to change that: "There's still this idea of the Third World woman as 'the other'—someone exotic and totally unlike us," Mays and Connell told us. "But now we're talking about women who wear the same styles in clothes, listen to the same music, and may even work for the same corporation. That's an irony the multinationals have created. In a way, they're drawing us together as women."

Saralee Hamilton, an AFSC staff organizer says: "The multinational corporations have deliberately targeted women for exploitation. If feminism is   34 going to mean anything to women all over the world, it's going to have to find new ways to resist corporate power internationally." She envisions a global network of grass-roots women capable of sharing experiences, transmitting information, and—eventually—providing direct support for each other's struggles. It's a long way off; few women anywhere have the money for intercontinental plane flights or even long-distance calls, but at least we are beginning to see the way. "We all have the same hard life," wrote Korean garment worker Min Chong Suk. "We are bound together with one string."

Thinking about the Essay

1. Describe the writers' argumentative purpose in this essay. Is it to convince or persuade—or both? Explain.

2. Who is the intended audience for this essay? What is the level of diction? How are the two connected?

3. Examine the writers' use of illustration in this essay. How do they use these illustrations to support a series of generalizations? Ehrenreich and Fuentes cite various studies and authorities. Identify these instances and explain the cumulative effect.

4. Ehrenreich and Fuentes draw on a number of rhetorical strategies to advance their argument. Explain their use of comparison and cause-and-effect analysis.

5. Evaluate the writers' conclusion. Does it effectively reinforce their argument? Why or why not?

Responding in Writing

6. Ehrenreich and Fuentes wrote this article originally for *Ms.* magazine. Why would the essay appeal to the *Ms.* audience? What elements would also appeal to a general audience? Write a brief essay that answers these questions, providing specific examples from the text.

7. Write a personal essay in which you describe a job that you had (or have) in which you were exploited. Provide sufficient illustrations to support your thesis.

8. The writers imply that workforce women around the world are exploited more than men. Write an essay in which you agree or disagree with their claim.

Networking

9. Form small groups and read the drafts of each other's essays. After general comments about how to improve the first draft, concentrate on ways to provide even greater illustration to support each writer's thesis or claim.

10. Do a Web search for new examples of the global exploitation of working women. Limit your focus to one of the countries mentioned by Ehrenreich and Fuentes. Think about whether the conditions that the two writers exposed more than thirty years ago are better or worse today. Share your conclusions with the rest of the class.

6

CHAPTER

The Challenge of Globalization: What Are the Consequences?

Quick! Where was your cell phone manufactured? What is the origin of the clothes you are wearing today—and how much do you think the workers were paid to produce it? What will your lunch or dinner consist of: pizza, fried rice, tacos, a California roll? The ordinary features of our daily lives capture the forces of globalization that characterize our new century and our changed world. *The New York Times* columnist Thomas Friedman, who writes persuasively on the subject—and who has an essay in this chapter—terms globalization the "super-story," the one all-embracing subject that dominates national and transnational developments today. As we see from the essays in this chapter, the concept of globalization already influences many major trends in economic, social, cultural, and political life in the twenty-first century.

It could be argued, of course, that globalization is nothing new: after all, Greece "globalized" much of the known world as far as India. Then Rome created its global dominion from England to Persia. More recently, for almost three centuries—from the seventeenth to the twentieth— England ruled the waves and a majority of the world's nations. And from the twentieth century to the present, the United States has assumed the mantle of the world's major globalizing power. (Some critics claim that globalization might simply be a mask for "Americanization.") With anti-globalization demonstrations and riots now commonplace in the United States, Europe, and the Third World, we have to acknowledge that there *is* something about contemporary globalization that prompts debate and demands critical analysis. Lawyer, consumer advocate, writer, and three-time presidential candidate Ralph Nader states the case against globalization boldly: "The essence of globalization is a subordination of human rights, of labor rights, consumer rights, environmental rights, democracy rights, to the imperatives of global trade and investment." But is Nader correct? Robert Rubin, who was secretary of the treasury during the

154

A multiethnic group of protesters, representing a wide range of causes, marches in Richmond, California, to protest globalization.

Thinking about the Image

1. How many different ideas or causes do you see represented in this photograph? What does that suggest about this particular protest? About the antiglobalization movement in general?
2. What is the photographer's perspective on this event? Is anyone looking directly at the lens? Would your response to the photograph—or the story it tells—be different if there was a focus on just one or two people? If the photographer was farther away and captured a larger crowd in the frame?
3. What other kinds of images do you associate with street protests? Based on the fact that this one photograph was chosen to represent an entire day of protest, what can you infer about the tone of the protest and the response of the community?
4. Street protest is a kind of rhetoric, in that the demonstrators have a purpose and an audience. How clear is the purpose of these protesters? Who is their audience? Do you think such protests will make a difference?

Clinton administration and a prominent figure in the financial community, objects: "I think a healthy economy is the best environment in which to pursue human rights." The oppositional viewpoints of Nader and Rubin suggest that discussion of globalization often produces diverse opinions and that consequently we must think carefully and openly about the globalizing trends molding our lives today.

One trend that is clear today in the twenty-first century is that capitalism has triumphed over all its main rivals: communism, fascism, and socialism. Thus capitalism is the dominant if not the sole model of development for the nations of the world. Where capitalism collides with alternative visions of development—for example, Islamic economics in the Middle East—the result proves disastrous. The question that many people—especially young people in college and university campuses around the world—ask is whether capitalism can meaningfully address the numerous questions of social justice raised by globalization. If, for example, the environmental policy of the United States aids the interests of its energy companies, can this policy benefit others in the developing world? Or does the policy exclude almost everyone in a developing nation? Such questions can be asked about virtually every key issue raised by Ralph Nader and others who are skeptical of globalization as an overpowering economic force around the world.

The writers in this chapter and the next offer a variety of perspectives and critical insights into the nature and effects of globalization trends. Because of developments in information technology, people in the most distant parts of the world now are as close to us as someone in the dorm room next door—and perhaps more compelling. We certainly see poverty, famine, the degradation of the environment, and civil wars close-up. But is all this suffering the result of predatory multinational corporations and runaway capitalism? After all, both globalization *and* civil society are increasing worldwide, and the connections between the two require subtle critical analysis. The writers in this chapter bring such critical ability to their treatment of the social implications of current globalization trends.

Prologue: The Super-Story

Thomas L. Friedman

A noted author, journalist, and television commentator, and currently an op-ed columnist for *The New York Times*, Thomas L. Friedman writes and speaks knowledgeably about contemporary trends in politics and global development. He was born in Minneapolis, Minnesota, in 1953, and was educated at Brandeis University (BA, 1975) and St. Anthony's College (MA, 1978). Friedman covered the Middle East for

The New York Times for ten years, and for five years he was bureau chief in Beirut, writing about both the Lebanese civil war and the Israel–Palestine conflict. He recorded these experiences in *From Beirut to Jerusalem* (1989), for which he won the National Book Award for nonfiction. A strong proponent of American intervention to solve seemingly intractable problems like the Arab–Israeli conflict, Friedman writes at the end of *From Beirut to Jerusalem*, "Only a real friend tells you the truth about yourself. An American friend has to help jar these people out of their fantasies by constantly holding up before their eyes the mirror of reality." In 2002, Friedman received the Pulitzer Prize for Commentary for his reports on terrorism for *The New York Times*, in addition to his previous two Pulitzer Prize wins for International Reporting in 1983 and 1988. His other books include *The Lexus and the Olive Tree: Understanding Globalization* (2000), *The World Is Flat* (2005), *Hot, Flat, and Crowded* (2008), and *That Used to Be Us: How America Fell Behind in the World It Invented and How We Can Come Back* (2011). Friedman has also published a collection of articles and essays, *Longitudes and Attitudes: Exploring the World After September 11* (2002); the following selection serves as the book's **prologue**.

Before Reading

How would you define the word *globalization*? Is it simply a trend in which nations interrelate economically, or are other forces involved? Do you think that globalization is good or bad? Justify your response.

I am a big believer in the idea of the super-story, the notion that we all   1
carry around with us a big lens, a big framework, through which we look at the world, order events, and decide what is important and what is not. The events of 9/11 did not happen in a vacuum. They happened in the context of a new international system—a system that cannot explain everything but *can* explain and connect more things in more places on more days than anything else. That new international system is called globalization. It came together in the late 1980s and replaced the previous

international system, the cold war system, which had reigned since the end of World War II. This new system is the lens, the super-story, through which I viewed the events of 9/11.

I define globalization as the inexorable integration of markets, trans- 2 portation systems, and communication systems to a degree never witnessed before—in a way that is enabling corporations, countries, and individuals to reach around the world farther, faster, deeper, and cheaper than ever before, and in a way that is enabling the world to reach into corporations, countries, and individuals farther, faster, deeper, and cheaper than ever before.

Several important features of this globalization system differ from those 3 of the cold war system in ways that are quite relevant for understanding the events of 9/11. I examined them in detail in my previous book, *The Lexus and the Olive Tree*, and want to simply highlight them here.

The cold war system was characterized by one overarching feature— 4 and that was *division*. That world was a divided-up, chopped-up place, and whether you were a country or a company, your threats and opportunities in the cold war system tended to grow out of who you were divided from. Appropriately, this cold war system was symbolized by a single word— *wall*, the Berlin Wall.

The globalization system is different. It also has one overarching 5 feature—and that is *integration*. The world has become an increasingly interwoven place, and today, whether you are a company or a country, your threats and opportunities increasingly derive from who you are connected to. This globalization system is also characterized by a single word—*web*, the World Wide Web. So in the broadest sense we have gone from an international system built around division and walls to a system increasingly built around integration and webs. In the cold war we reached for the hotline, which was a symbol that we were all divided but at least two people were in charge—the leaders of the United States and the Soviet Union. In the globalization system we reach for the Internet, which is a symbol that we are all connected and nobody is quite in charge.

Everyone in the world is directly or indirectly affected by this new sys- 6 tem, but not everyone benefits from it, not by a long shot, which is why the more it becomes diffused, the more it also produces a backlash by people who feel overwhelmed by it, homogenized by it, or unable to keep pace with its demands.

The other key difference between the cold war system and the global- 7 ization system is how power is structured within them. The cold war system was built primarily around nation-states. You acted on the world in that system through your state. The cold war was a drama of states confronting states, balancing states, and aligning with states. And, as a system, the cold war was balanced at the center by two superstates, two superpowers: the United States and the Soviet Union.

The globalization system, by contrast, is built around three balances,   8 which overlap and affect one another. The first is the traditional balance of power between nation-states. In the globalization system, the United States is now the sole and dominant superpower and all other nations are subordinate to it to one degree or another. The shifting balance of power between the United States and other states, or simply between other states, still very much matters for the stability of this system. And it can still explain a lot of the news you read on the front page of the paper, whether it is the news of China balancing Russia, Iran balancing Iraq, or India confronting Pakistan.

The second important power balance in the globalization system is   9 between nation-states and global markets. These global markets are made up of millions of investors moving money around the world with the click of a mouse. I call them the Electronic Herd, and this herd gathers in key global financial centers—such as Wall Street, Hong Kong, London, and Frankfurt—which I call the Supermarkets. The attitudes and actions of the Electronic Herd and the Supermarkets can have a huge impact on nation-states today, even to the point of triggering the downfall of governments. Who ousted Suharto in Indonesia in 1998? It wasn't another state, it was the Supermarkets, by withdrawing their support for, and confidence in, the Indonesian economy. You also will not understand the front page of the newspaper today unless you bring the Supermarkets into your analysis. Because the United States can destroy you by dropping bombs, but the Supermarkets can destroy you by downgrading your bonds. In other words, the United States is the dominant player in maintaining the globalization game board, but it is hardly alone in influencing the moves on that game board.

The third balance that you have to pay attention to—the one that is   10 really the newest of all and the most relevant to the events of 9/11—is the balance between individuals and nation-states. Because globalization has brought down many of the walls that limited the movement and reach of people, and because it has simultaneously wired the world into networks, it gives more power to *individuals* to influence both markets and nation-states than at any other time in history. Whether by enabling people to use the Internet to communicate instantly at almost no cost over vast distances, or by enabling them to use the Web to transfer money or obtain weapons designs that normally would have been controlled by states, or by enabling them to go into a hardware store now and buy a five-hundred-dollar global positioning device, connected to a satellite, that can direct a hijacked airplane—globalization can be an incredible force-multiplier for individuals. Individuals can increasingly act on the world stage directly, unmediated by a state.

So you have today not only a superpower, not only Supermarkets, but   11
also what I call "super-empowered individuals." Some of these super-empowered individuals are quite angry, some of them quite wonderful—but all of them are now able to act much more directly and much more powerfully on the world stage.

Osama bin Laden declared war on the United States in the late 1990s.   12
After he organized the bombing of two American embassies in Africa, the U.S. Air Force retaliated with a cruise missile attack on his bases in Afghanistan as though he were another nation-state. Think about that: on one day in 1998, the United States fired 75 cruise missiles at bin Laden. The United States fired 75 cruise missiles, at $1 million apiece, at a person! That was the first battle in history between a superpower and a super-empowered angry man. September 11 was just the second such battle.

Jody Williams won the Nobel Peace Prize in 1997 for helping to build   13
an international coalition to bring about a treaty outlawing land mines. Although nearly 120 governments endorsed the treaty, it was opposed by Russia, China, and the United States. When Jody Williams was asked, "How did you do that? How did you organize one thousand different citizens' groups and nongovernmental organizations on five continents to forge a treaty that was opposed by the major powers?" she had a very brief answer: "E-mail." Jody Williams used e-mail and the networked world to super-empower herself.

Nation-states, and the American superpower in particular, are still hugely   14
important today, but so too now are Supermarkets and super-empowered individuals. You will never understand the globalization system, or the front page of the morning paper—or 9/11—unless you see each as a complex interaction between all three of these actors: states bumping up against states, states bumping up against Supermarkets, and Supermarkets and states bumping up against super-empowered individuals—many of whom, unfortunately, are super-empowered angry men.

Thinking about the Essay

1. Friedman constructs this essay and entitles it a "prologue." What is the purpose of a prologue? What subject matter does the writer provide in his prologue?

2. The writer is not afraid to inject the personal "I" into his analysis—a strategy that many composition teachers will warn you against. Why does Friedman start

with his personal voice? Why can he get away with it? What does the personal voice contribute to the effect of the essay?

3. In addition to his personal voice, what other stylistic features make Friedman's essay, despite its complicated subject matter, accessible to ordinary readers? How does he establish a colloquial style?

4. This essay offers a series of definitions, comparisons, and classifications as structuring devices. Locate instances of these three rhetorical strategies and explain how they complement each other.

5. Friedman uses September 11 as a touchstone for his essay. Why does he do this? What is the effect?

Responding in Writing

6. Write a 250-word summary of Friedman's essay, capturing all the important topics that he presents.

7. Take one major point that Friedman makes in this essay and write a paper on it. For example, you might want to discuss why September 11 represents a key transition point in our understanding of globalization. Or you might focus on the concept of the Supermarket or the Electronic Herd.

8. Think about the world today, and write your own "super-story" in which you define and classify its primary features.

Networking

9. Divide into two roughly equal groups, and conduct a debate on whether globalization is a good or bad phenomenon. Use Friedman's essay as a reference point. Your instructor should serve as the moderator for this debate.

10. Develop a list of links to sites that deal with globalization. Combine your list with those generated by other class members to create a superlist for possible future use.

Brave, New Social World

DENNIS MCCAFFERTY

Dennis McCafferty is a technology writer living in Washington, DC. Currently a freelance writer for *Baseline* magazine, he also contributes to the "Society" page of the professional journal *Communications of the ACM*, where this article featuring the use of Facebook, Twitter, and other social media tools in three countries—Brazil, Egypt, and Japan—originally appeared in July 2011.

Before Reading

List the ways in which social media tools promote globalization trends.

Today, social media is emerging as a dominant form of instant global   1
communication. Growing more addictively popular by the day—nearly
two thirds of Internet users worldwide use some type of social media, according to an industry estimate—Facebook, Twitter, and other easily accessible
online tools deepen our interaction with societies near and far.

Consider these numbers: Facebook is poised to hit 700 million users   2
and, as seven of 10 Facebook members reside outside the U.S., more than
70 global-language translations. Twitter's user numbers will reportedly hit
200 million later this year, and users can tweet in multiple languages. In
terms of daily usage, Facebook generates the second-most traffic of any site
in the world, according to Alexa.com, a Web information company, at press
time. (Google is number one.) As for blogging, which now seems likes a relatively old-fashioned form of social media, the dominant site, blogger.com,
ranks eighth. As for Twitter, it's now 11th—and climbing.

The top five nations in terms of social media usage are the U.S., Poland,   3
Great Britain, South Korea, and France, according to the Pew Research
Center. But beyond international rankings and traffic numbers, there's
much diversity in the manner in which the citizens of the world take advantage of these tools, according to *Blogging Around the Globe: Motivations,
Privacy Concerns and Social Networking*, an IBM Tokyo research report.
In Japan, blogs often serve as outlets for personal expression and diary-
style postings. In the U.S., it's mostly about earning income or promoting
an agenda. In the U.K., it's a combination of these needs, as well as professional advancement and acting as a citizen journalist.

Communications connected with three citizens in three different   4
nations, each of whom are finding their own individual voice through these
resources. In fact, we depended primarily upon social media to initially
reach them. One is a Japanese female blogger who segues seamlessly from
pop-culture observations to revealing reflections on the nation's recent
earthquake, tsunami, and nuclear disaster. Another is a Brazilian businesswoman who uses multiple digital outlets to expand her marketing reach
throughout the world. The third is an Egyptian newsman who is helping
record history with his dispatches of daily life in a region undergoing dramatic political change. (In terms of social media usage, Brazil ranks eighth,
Japan 12th, and Egypt 18th, according to Pew.) Here are their stories.

Dennis McCafferty "Brave, New Social World," *Communications of the ACM*, Vol. 54:7, © 2011
Association for Computing Machinery, Inc. Reprinted by permission. http://dl.acm.org/citation.
cfm?doid=1965724.1965732.

Blogs: Motivations for Writing and Readership Levels by Region		
Region	**Motivation**	**Readership**
Japan	Personal diary, self-expression	74% Internet users, average 4.54 times/week, 25% daily, highest in world
Korea	Personal diary, personal scrapbook, online journalism	43% Internet users, average 2.03 times/week, ages 8–24: 4 times/week ages 25–34: 3 times/week
China	96% personal blogs loaded with photos, audio, animations	Highest for ages 18–24 (less than 3 times/week), probably friends
U.S.	Make money, promote political or professional agenda	27% Internet users, average 0.9 times/week, lower than Asia, higher than Europe
Germany	For fun, like to write, personal diary	Bloggers are regular readers of other blogs on average 21.15 (std. dev. 39, med. 10)
U.K.	Connect with others, express opinions/vent, make money, citizen journalist, validation, professional advancement	23% Internet users, average 0.68 times/week
Poland	Self-expression, social interaction, entertainment	Not available

Source: Mei Kobayashi, *Blogging Around the Globe: Motivations, Privacy Concerns and Social Networking*, IBM Research-Tokyo, 2010.

Me and Tokyo

The contrast is striking: Before March 11, Mari Kanazawa's blog, Watashi   5
to Tokyo (translation: Me and Tokyo), waxes whimsically about a recent
tweet in Japanese by the band Radiohead, as well as consumer products
such as Wasasco, a wasabi-flavored Tabasco.

    After March 11, however, the conversation takes an abrupt turn. The   6
day after the devastating Tohoku earthquake and tsunami, Kanazawa
writes this unsettling passage: "Earthquake, tsunami, fire and now we have
a nuclear meltdown . . . I was in the Midtown Tower when it happened.

Japanese people are used to earthquakes, we can usually sense them because the building sways, but this time it was shaking up and down. Some people screamed and some hid under their desks."

Within a week, Kanazawa casts a sense of humor about the situation: "I really don't need to check Geiger counters and don't need a lot of toilet paper because earthquakes [don't] make me [go to the bathroom] more than usual."   7

A high-profile cyberpersonality in Japan, Kanazawa has always perceived her blog as equal parts diary and cultural commentary. She was one of the rare Japanese citizens who wrote a blog in English when she started in 2004, so her traffic numbers have spiked to a healthy 2,000 unique visitors a day. A Web site manager, Kanazawa prefers the freeform creativity of a blog, as opposed to the restrictive 140-character count of Twitter. "It doesn't fit me," she says of the latter. "My blog is an information hub for Japanese subculture. That's my style. I wanted to tell people that we have more interesting, good things than sushi, sumo, tempura, geishas, and ninjas."   8

Since the disaster, like many Japanese citizens posting blogs and Facebook status updates, Kanazawa has sought and published information about the nation's recovery efforts. "These tools are so effective in this disaster," she says. "People need to check for things such as the transportation situation and where the evacuation areas are. In Tōhoku, when someone tweeted 'We need 600 rice balls here,' they were delivered within an hour. Social media went from being a communication tool to a lifeline."   9

Brazil—and Beyond

In generations past, it would be difficult for a self-described life coach like Lygya Maya of Salvador, Brazil, to interact with a motivational-speaking giant like Tony Robbins, an American who has more than 200 books, audio CDs, and other products listed on Amazon.com. Perhaps she would have needed to take a trip to the U.S. in hopes of speaking with Robbins at one of his tour stops. Or write him a letter and hope he would answer with something beyond a polite thank you.   10

But this is the 21st century, and Maya takes full advantage of the digital age to engage with high-profile leaders such as Robbins and Mark Victor Hansen, co-author of the bestselling *Chicken Soup for the Soul* books. Robbins and Hansen are now Facebook friends with Maya, who they have advised and encouraged to push beyond perceived limitations in her work.   11

Such international collaborations have enabled Maya to create her 12
own signature style to market herself, which she calls a "Brazilian Carnival
Style" approach to guide clients to enjoying a happy, productive, and
empowering life. Maya now sees up to 300 clients a year in private sessions, and hosts as many as 500 group sessions annually.

"I use blogs, Facebook, Twitter, and Plaxo [an online address book] to 13
promote my business," Maya says. "I am about to start podcasting, as well
as making YouTube videos on every channel that I can find on the Internet.
Social media has opened up my business on many different levels. I am
now able to promote it literally to the world, free of charge."

Maya has also established more than 2,500 personal connections via 14
Facebook, LinkedIn, and other sites. She'll send tweets several times a day,
offering reflections like "When truthfully expressed, words reflect our core
value and spirit." All of this has helped Maya promote her budding empire
of services and products, which will soon include a book, *Cheeka Cheeka
BOOM Through Life!: The Luscious Story of a Daring Brazilian Woman*.
It's gotten to the point where—like some of her counterparts in the U.S.—
she must subcontract work just to keep up with it all.

"I'm about to hire a team to work with me on Twitter and all the social 15
media out there that we can use to support campaigns," Maya says. "You
must have a great team to share quality work. Otherwise, you will have
stress. This allows me to promote my services and products 24/7—and that
includes while I'm sleeping."

A Witness in Egypt

Amr Hassanein lists *Babel*, *Fantasia*, and *The Last Temptation of Christ* as 16
his favorite movies on his Facebook page. And his organizations/activities
of interest include Hands Along the Nile Development Services, a nonprofit
organization that promotes intercultural understanding between the U.S.
and his native Egypt. Now working as a freelance producer for ABC News,
Hassanein is also using Facebook as a vehicle to showcase his own firsthand accounts of political unrest in the Middle East. Recently, for example,
ABC sent him to Libya to assist with news coverage of the nation's conflict.

"My usage of social media tools is from a neutral side," says Hassanein, 17
sounding very much like an objective news reporter. "Social media makes
me feel like an observer. It gives me a sense of what's going on around me
at all times. The impact events here in Egypt, like the demonstrations, were
organized and known through Facebook."

Still, it's impossible to live through these times without getting caught 18
up in the politics. His sympathies remain with We Are All Khaled Said,

an anti-torture group that uses social media to allow voices of the Arab uprisings to be heard. (Sample Facebook post from the group: "Gaddafi has vowed it will be a 'long war' in Libya. Let's hope his [sic] wrong & Gaddafi's massacre of his people will end very soon.")

Hassanein recognizes that social media provides an opportunity to   19 deliver an unfiltered message to the world about local developments, as well as debunk stereotypes about people of the Middle East. Yet, aside from this bigger-picture purpose, these tools allow him to easily remain in close contact with loved ones and work associates.

Actions taken by the Egyptian government to block access to Facebook   20 and Twitter significantly backfired during its recent conflict, further fueling the resolve of the freedom movement, he says. "The impact was clear: What were normal demonstrations became a revolution. It made me think about the consequences of blocking people from information."

That said, some of the "anything goes" aspects of social media make   21 Hassanein feel uncomfortable. "When you watch a news channel that presents a direction you don't like," he says, "you have the ability not to watch. In social media, there is no uni-direction you can refuse or reject. People are the senders and the receivers. Inputs need to be self-filtering and self-censoring. For me, I will use my head."

An anti-Mubarak protestor holds a sign praising Facebook for helping to organize the protest in Tahrir Square, Cairo, Egypt.

Thinking about the Essay

1. What is McCafferty's thesis? What does he mean by "instant global communication" (paragraph 1)? How do the three people McCafferty profiles illuminate his thesis?

2. What is the allusion that the writer embeds in the title? How does this allusion influence the writer's tone?

3. McCafferty contributed this article to a magazine for technology and communications professionals. How does he adjust his style to address the interests of this audience? What is his purpose in attaching a photograph and a table?

4. How effective do you find the writer's decision to divide this essay into sections with subtitles? Justify your answer by referring to specific rhetorical strategies—for instance, classification—that you detect.

5. Evaluate McCafferty's conclusion. Why does he end the essay with a quotation?

Responding in Writing

6. Compose a classification essay in which you examine the types of social media tools available to people today and how these tools might contribute to globalization trends.

7. Argue for or against the proposition that social media tools can lead to social and political change.

8. Write a personal essay in which you discuss your own use of social media tools and what your motivation might be in maintaining a blog.

Networking

9. In a group of five, review the writer's table, "Blogs: Motivations for Writing and Readership Levels by Region." Then have each person list his or her own motivation for engaging in social media writing and communication. Draw up a list of all these reasons, and report to the class.

10. Check one of the blogs or websites mentioned in this article. Write a summary of your findings.

How to Raise a Global Kid

LISA MILLER

Lisa Miller is a staff writer at *New York* magazine. She is the former religion columnist for the *Washington Post*, former senior writer and religion editor of *Newsweek* magazine, and author of *Heaven: Our Enduring Fascination with the Afterlife*. She graduated from Oberlin College in 1984. In 2014, Miller was nominated for the National Magazine Award and featured in *The Best American Magazine Writing of 2014*. In the following essay, which appeared in the July 25, 2011, issue of *Newsweek*, Miller discusses the challenge facing American children who must have international experience in order to compete in the global economy.

Before Reading

Does your college offer study abroad opportunities? If so, do you plan to spend a term or academic year abroad? Do you think that study abroad programs help students to succeed in the global economy? Why or why not?

Happy Rogers, age 8, stands among her classmates in the schoolyard at dismissal time, immune, it seems, to the cacophonous din. Her parents and baby sister are waiting outside, but still she lingers, engrossed in conversation. A poised and precocious blonde, Hilton Augusta Parker Rogers, nicknamed Happy, would be at home in the schoolyard of any affluent American suburb or big-city private school. But here, at the elite, bilingual Nanyang Primary School in Singapore, Happy is in the minority, her Dakota Fanning hair shimmering in a sea of darker heads. This is what her parents have traveled halfway around the world for. While her American peers are feasting on the idiocies fed to them by junk TV and summer movies, Happy is navigating her friendships and doing her homework entirely in Mandarin. 1

Fluency in Chinese, she says—in English—through mouthfuls of spaghetti bolognese at a Singapore restaurant, "is going to make me better and smarter." 2

American parents have barely recovered from the anxiety attacks they suffered at the hands of the Tiger Mom—oh, no, my child is already 7 and she can't play a note of Chopin—and now here comes Happy's father, the multimillionaire American investor and author Jim Rogers, to give them something new to fret about. It is no longer enough to raise children who are brave, curious, hardworking, and compassionate. Nor is it sufficient to steer them toward the right sports, the right tutors, the right internships, and thus engineer their admittance to the right (or at least a good enough) college. According to Rogers, who in 2007 left New York's Upper West Side to settle in Singapore with his wife, Paige Parker, and Happy (Beeland Anderson Parker Rogers, called Baby Bee, was born the next year), parents who really care about their children must also ponder this: are we doing enough to raise "global" kids? 3

"I'm doing what parents have done for many years," Jim Rogers says. 4
"I'm trying to prepare my children for the future, for the 21st century.
I'm trying to prepare them as best I can for the world as I see it." Rogers
believes the future is Asia—he was recently on cable television flogging
Chinese commodities. "The money is in the East, and the debtors are in the
West. I'd rather be with the creditors than the debtors," he adds.

It has become a convention of public discourse to regard rapid 5
globalization—of economies and business; of politics and conflict; of fashion, technology, and music—as the great future threat to American prosperity. The burden of meeting that challenge rests explicitly on our kids. If they
don't learn—now—to achieve a comfort level with foreign people, foreign
languages, and foreign lands, this argument goes, America's competitive
position in the world will continue to erode, and their future livelihood and
that of subsequent generations will be in jeopardy. Rogers is hardly the only
person who sees things this way. "In this global economy, the line between
domestic and international issues is increasingly blurred, with the world's
economies, societies, and people interconnected as never before," said U.S.
Education Secretary Arne Duncan in remarks in the spring of 2010 at the
Asia Society in New York. "I am worried that in this interconnected world,
our country risks being disconnected from the contributions of other countries and cultures."

Despite Duncan's articulate urgency (and the public example of Rogers 6
and a few others like him), America is so far utterly failing to produce a
generation of global citizens. Only 37 percent of Americans hold a passport. Fewer than 2 percent of America's 18 million college students go
abroad during their undergraduate years—and when they do go, it's mostly
for short stints in England, Spain, or Italy that are more like vacations.
Only a quarter of public primary schools offer any language instruction
at all, and fewer high schools offer French, German, Latin, Japanese, or
Russian than they did in 1997. The number of schools teaching Chinese
and Arabic is so tiny as to be nearly invisible.

Meanwhile, 200 million Chinese schoolchildren are studying English. 7
South Korean parents recently threw a collective hissy fit, demanding that
their children begin English instruction in first grade, rather than in second.
Nearly 700,000 students from all over the world attended U.S. universities
during the 2009–10 school year, with the greatest increases in kids from
China and Saudi Arabia. "Not training our kids to be able to work and live
in an international environment is like leaving them illiterate," says David
Boren, the former U.S. senator and current president of the University of
Oklahoma. The gap between our ambition and reality yawns wide.

There is no consensus on remedies. According to a white paper issued 8
in 2009 by the Institute on International Education, most colleges and

universities say they want to increase participation in study-abroad programs, but only 40 percent are actually making concerted efforts to do so.
Long immersion programs are expensive, and in an environment of tough
statewide budget cuts, students and professors are too crunched for time
to make international experience a priority. Educators disagree on which
kinds of experiences are most advantageous for kids—or even what advantageous means. Is it enough for a teenager who has never traveled farther
than her grandma's house to get a passport and order a pint in a London
pub? Or does she have to spend a year in Beijing, immersed in Mandarin
and economic policy? Is the goal of foreign experience to learn a language
or gain some special expertise—in auto engineering or peace mediation?
Or is it to be of service to others by giving mosquito nets to poor children
in an African village?

Jim Rogers sees an America in decline, and his solution has been to   9
immerse himself in the countries and cultures that are ascendant. "We
think we're the world leader, but we're not," he says. "I don't like saying that. I'm an American. I vote. I pay taxes. But the level of knowledge
is not very high, and that's going to hurt us, I'm afraid." In the Rogers
family's five-bedroom bungalow, there is no TV. Instead, there are more
than a dozen globes to look at and maps to ponder, a nanny and a maid
who speak only Mandarin to the kids, bicycles to ride, and a new karaoke
machine so the girls can learn Chinese songs.

A generation ago and as far back as Thomas Jefferson, a certain kind   10
of child from a certain kind of family went abroad because it was done; a
sojourn in Europe was as crucial to becoming a cultivated person as knowing the works of Mozart or Rembrandt. The point was to see the Great
Museums, of course, but also to breathe the air—to learn to converse in
another tongue, to adapt to the rhythms of another place. Hemingway did
this, of course, but so did Benjamin Franklin and Johnny Depp. This is what
Pamela Wolf, who just returned to New York City with her husband and
children from a year in Barcelona, did. She enrolled her teenagers in an international school, where they made friends with kids from around the world
and learned to speak fluent Spanish. Her children have a global perspective
not only because of their language skills but also because arriving in a new
place, knowing no one, forced them to be resilient. "It's pushing yourself
out of your comfort zone," Wolf says. "It builds a very compassionate child.
While, yes, grades and academics are as important to me as anyone, you
need resilience to understand and have sympathy for other people."

Such lengthy sojourns, though, are available to only a few: the very   11
adventurous or the very rich. Wolf and her husband are both self-employed.
"Financially," she says, "we have the great privilege of earning money while
we're away."

Without resources and connections, a foreign experience can be a mis- 12
ery. Two years ago, Maribeth Henderson moved from San Antonio with her
husband, her college-age son, and her adopted 5-year-old daughter, Wei Wei,
to a remote part of China, in Guangdong province. Wei Wei didn't learn
much Mandarin—her school taught mainly Cantonese—and Henderson
felt lonely and alienated. "It was so Chinese that I couldn't assimilate and
feel comfortable," she says. "I couldn't speak the language; it was hard for
us to even order food in a restaurant. If you ordered a chicken, they would
literally hand you a chicken. You were lucky if it wasn't alive." Henderson
abandoned ship, returning to Texas with Wei Wei ahead of schedule and
leaving her husband and son in Guangzhou. Now, though, she's planning to try again. This summer she and Wei Wei will move to Beijing, and
Henderson hopes the big city will ameliorate her former isolation. About
her goal—helping Wei Wei learn Chinese—Henderson has no doubts. "For
children to be competitive and successful in a global economy," she says,
"it's important for them to be bilingual."

For parents who want to give their children global experience while 13
keeping them safely on the straight and narrow American path of PSATs,
SATs, and stellar extracurriculars, there's an ever-growing field of options.
Immersion schools have exploded over the past 40 years, growing from none
in 1970 to 440 today, according to the Center for Applied Linguistics, and
Mandarin, especially, is seen among type-A parents as a twofer: a child who
learns Mandarin starting at 5 increases her brain capacity and is exposed
to the culture of the future through language. (One mom in San Francisco
laughs when she recalls that her daughter learned about Rosa Parks and
the Montgomery bus boycott in Chinese.) The education entrepreneur Chris
Whittle and colleagues recently announced plans for the new Avenues school,
to open in New York City in September 2012 and designed to compete with
the city's most exclusive (and expensive) private schools. Its curriculum will
be fully bilingual—parents choose a Mandarin or Spanish track when their
kids are 3—providing the Happy Rogers experience but with all the conveniences of home. "We think that any child that graduates from high school
a monoglot is automatically behind," Whittle says. Fourteen months before
the school's doors open, Avenues has already received 1,200 applications.

Study abroad is now a prerequisite on some college campuses, and a few 14
professional schools, especially in business and engineering, have begun to
require international study as part of their curricula. Nursing students at a
community college in Utah must all spend a month at a hospital in Vietnam
as part of their training. But Margaret Heisel, director of the Center for
Capacity Building in Study Abroad, believes that a real global education
comes from a long stay in a strange place; it gives kids skills that no amount
of study can teach.

My own experience proves this point. During my sophomore year in 15 high school, my father, a university professor, moved our entire family to Amsterdam for his sabbatical year and enrolled my brothers and me in local public schools. During that glorious year, I rode my bike through city streets, learned to roll a cigarette one-handed, and eventually spoke Dutch like a 15-year-old native. (I can still say "That's so stupid" and "This is so boring.") We saw Stonehenge and the Rijksmuseum and drove to Burgundy for the grape harvest, but the real impact of that adventure was that I learned a degree of self-reliance—a 15-year-old girl needs to make friends and will cross any cultural boundary to do so—that I didn't know I had.

"I think it's liberating to some extent," Heisel says. "It touches people in 16 places that being in a familiar place doesn't. It requires versatility, flexibility. It's a different culture and it's pressing on kids in different ways." Baby Bee is equally at home on visits to the U.S. and in Singapore, where her father rides her to school each day on his personal pedicab. There she sings the Singapore national anthem and pledges the Singapore flag. "She's no different from the Chinese kids," says her teacher, Fu Su Qin. "And her Chinese is just as good."

Thinking about the Essay

1. Consider Miller's title and the promise it holds that readers will discover how to raise a global kid. Does Miller actually follow through on the promise implied by this title? Why or why not? Refer to specific aspects of the essay to justify your response.

2. What is the writer's thesis? Is this main idea stated or implied? Explain. What major topics inform Miller's thesis?

3. Why does Miller start her essay with a profile of Happy Rogers and her family? Which paragraphs constitute the writer's introduction? What is Miller's tone here and throughout the essay?

4. How does Miller employ the comparative method in order to organize her essay? What specific topics is she comparing and contrasting?

5. What conclusions does Miller draw about the challenges facing American students as they prepare for lives in a global economy?

Responding in Writing

6. Write a process paper in which you explain how you plan to prepare for the challenge of competing for work in an increasingly globalized world and economy.

7. In an argumentative essay, take up Miller's assertion that the United States is falling behind in the preparation of "global kids," agreeing or disagreeing with her opinion.

8. Find out more about "Tiger Mom" tactics, and write an essay about this topic and its relation to the education of global kids.

Networking

9. In groups of four or five, draft an article for your college newspaper in which you argue for increased opportunities to study abroad—or the creation of a study abroad program if one doesn't exist on your campus. Revise your paper, paying close attention to the logic and tone of your argument, before submitting the article for possible publication.

10. Consult the Institute for International Education's (IIE) website. Write a summary of your findings about the IIE's programs to strengthen international education.

The Noble Feat of Nike

Johan Norberg

Johan Norberg, a Swedish author, historian, and leading European intellectual, is the author of *In Defense of Global Capitalism* (2001) and writer and presenter of the recent documentary *Globalization Is Good*. Since 2007, Norberg has been associated with the Cato Institute, a conservative Washington, DC, think tank. He contributed this article to London's *The Spectator* in June 2003. In the essay, he takes issue with those who think that globalization is the invention of "ruthless international capitalists." In arguing his case, Norberg centers his discussion on one symbol of globalization—Nike—suggesting that we simply have to look at our "feet" to understand Nike's "feat" in advancing a benign form of globalization.

Before Reading

Check your sneakers. Where were they made? What do you think the workers earned to manufacture them? Do you think they were exploited? Explain your response.

Nike. It means victory. It also means a type of expensive gym shoe. In the minds of the anti-globalisation movement, it stands for both at once. Nike stands for the victory of a Western footwear company over the poor and dispossessed. Spongy, smelly, hungered after by kids across the world, Nike is the symbol of the unacceptable triumph of global capital.

A Nike is a shoe that simultaneously kicks people out of jobs in the West, and tramples on the poor in the Third World. Sold for 100 times more than the wages of the peons who make them, Nike shoes are hate-objects more potent, in the eyes of the protesters at this week's G8 riots, than McDonald's hamburgers. If you want to be trendy these days, you don't wear Nikes; you boycott them.

So I was interested to hear someone not only praising Nike sweatshops, but also claiming that Nike is an example of a good and responsible business. That someone was the ruling Communist party of Vietnam.   3

Today Nike has almost four times more workers in Vietnam than in the United States. I travelled to Ho Chi Minh to examine the effects of multinational corporations on poor countries. Nike being the most notorious multinational villain, and Vietnam being a dictatorship with a documented lack of free speech, the operation is supposed to be a classic of conscience-free capitalist oppression.   4

In truth the work does look tough, and the conditions grim, if we compare Vietnamese factories with what we have back home. But that's not the comparison these workers make. They compare the work at Nike with the way they lived before, or the way their parents or neighbours still work. And the facts are revealing. The average pay at a Nike factory close to Ho Chi Minh is $54 a month, almost three times the minimum wage for a state-owned enterprise.   5

Ten years ago, when Nike was established in Vietnam, the workers had to walk to the factories, often for many miles. After three years on Nike wages, they could afford bicycles. Another three years later, they could afford scooters, so they all take the scooters to work (and if you go there, beware; they haven't really decided on which side of the road to drive). Today, the first workers can afford to buy a car.   6

But when I talk to a young Vietnamese woman, Tsi-Chi, at the factory, it is not the wages she is most happy about. Sure, she makes five times more than she did, she earns more than her husband, and she can now afford to build an extension to her house. But the most important thing, she says, is that she doesn't have to work outdoors on a farm any more. For me, a Swede with only three months of summer, this sounds bizarre. Surely working conditions under the blue sky must be superior to those in a sweatshop? But then I am naively Eurocentric. Farming means 10 to 14 hours a day in the burning sun or the intensive rain, in rice fields with water up to your ankles and insects in your face. Even a Swede would prefer working nine to five in a clean, air-conditioned factory.   7

Furthermore, the Nike job comes with a regular wage, with free or subsidised meals, free medical services and training and education. The most persistent demand Nike hears from the workers is for an expansion of the factories so that their relatives can be offered a job as well.   8

These facts make Nike sound more like Santa Claus than Scrooge. But 9 corporations such as Nike don't bring these benefits and wages because they are generous. It is not altruism that is at work here; it is globalisation. With their investments in poor countries, multinationals bring new machinery, better technology, new management skills and production ideas, a larger market and the education of their workers. That is exactly what raises productivity. And if you increase productivity—the amount a worker can produce—you can also increase his wage.

Nike is not the accidental good guy. On average, multinationals in the 10 least developed countries pay twice as much as domestic companies in the same line of business. If you get to work for an American multinational in a low-income country, you get eight times the average income. If this is exploitation, then the problem in our world is that the poor countries aren't sufficiently exploited.

The effect on local business is profound: "Before I visit some foreign 11 factory, especially like Nike, we have a question. Why do the foreign factories here work well and produce much more?" That was what Mr. Kiet, the owner of a local shoe factory who visited Nike to learn how he could be just as successful at attracting workers, told me: "And I recognise that productivity does not only come from machinery but also from satisfaction of the worker. So for the future factory we should concentrate on our working conditions."

If I was an antiglobalist, I would stop complaining about Nike's bad 12 wages. If there is a problem, it is that the wages are too high, so that they are almost luring doctors and teachers away from their important jobs.

But—happily—I don't think even that is a realistic threat. With grow- 13 ing productivity it will also be possible to invest in education and healthcare for Vietnam. Since 1990, when the Vietnamese communists began to liberalise the economy, exports of coffee, rice, clothes and footwear have surged, the economy has doubled, and poverty has been halved. Nike and Coca-Cola triumphed where American bombs failed. They have made Vietnam capitalist.

I asked the young Nike worker Tsi-Chi what her hopes were for her 14 son's future. A generation ago, she would have had to put him to work on the farm from an early age. But Tsi-Chi told me she wants to give him a good education, so that he can become a doctor. That's one of the most impressive developments since Vietnam's economy was opened up. In ten years 2.2 million children have gone from child labour to education. It would be extremely interesting to hear an antiglobalist explain to Tsi-Chi why it is important for Westerners to boycott Nike, so that she loses her job, and has to go back into farming, and has to send her son to work.

The European Left used to listen to the Vietnamese communists when   15
they brought only misery and starvation to their population. Shouldn't
they listen to the Vietnamese now, when they have found a way to improve
people's lives? The party officials have been convinced by Nike that ruthless multinational capitalists are better than the state at providing workers
with high wages and a good and healthy workplace. How long will it take
for our own anticapitalists to learn that lesson?

Thinking about the Essay

1. Examine the writer's introduction. Why is it distinctive? How does Norberg
   "hook" us and also set the terms of his argument? Why is Nike an especially
   potent symbol around which to organize an essay on globalization?

2. Explain the writer's claim and how he defends it. Identify those instances in
   which he deals with the opposition. How effective do you think his argument is?
   Justify your answer.

3. What is the writer's tone in this essay? Why is the tone especially effective in
   conveying the substance of Norberg's argument?

4. Analyze the writer's **style** and how it contributes to his argument. Identify specific
   stylistic elements that you consider especially effective.

5. To a large extent, the writer bases his argument on direct observation. How can
   you tell that he is open-minded and truthful in the presentation of facts? What is
   the role of a newspaper or journal in claiming responsibility for the accuracy of
   this information?

Responding in Writing

6. Select a symbol of globalization and write an essay about it. You may use Nike
   if you wish, or Coca-Cola, McDonald's, or any other company that has a global
   reach.

7. Write a **rebuttal** to Norberg's essay. Try to answer him point by point.

8. Why have clothing manufacturing and other forms of manufacturing fled from the
   United States and other industrialized nations to less developed parts of the
   world? Write a causal analysis of this trend, being certain to state a thesis or
   present a claim that illustrates your viewpoint on the issue.

Networking

9. In groups of four, examine your clothes. List the countries where they were manufactured. Share the list with the class, drawing a global map of the countries
   where the various items were produced.

10. Check various Internet sites for information on Nike and its role in globalization.
    On the basis of your findings, determine whether or not this company is sensi-
    tive to globalization issues. Participate in a class discussion of this topic.

Globalization Rocked the Ancient World Too

Jared Diamond

Jared Diamond, an American scientist and author best known for his popular science books, has been described by *The Economist* as "America's best-known geographer." He is an internationally acclaimed professor and writer whose interests and expertise span many fields, including geography, evolutionary biology, ecology, physiology, history, and economics. Born in Boston in 1937, Diamond received his BA from Harvard University (1958) and a PhD from Cambridge University (1961). Currently he is a professor of geography at the University of California, Los Angeles (UCLA). Diamond is known for his work as a conservationist and as a director of the World Wildlife Fund. His field experience includes numerous expeditions to New Guinea and neighboring islands, where he helped to establish Indonesian New Guinea's national park system. His book *Guns, Germs, and Steel: The Fate of Human Societies* was awarded the Pulitzer Prize in 1998. He has also written the best-selling *Collapse: How Societies Choose to Fail or Succeed* (2004), *The World Until Yesterday* (2012), and *The Third Chimpanzee for Young People: On the Evolution and Future of the Human Animal* (2015). In this essay, which appeared in the *Los Angeles Times* on September 4, 2003, Diamond explores globalization from a unique historical perspective.

Before Reading

Do you think that the current debate over globalization is a new phenomenon, or might globalization have roots in older societies and civilizations?

We tend to think of globalization as uniquely modern, a product of 20th century advances in transportation, technology, agriculture and communications. But widespread dispersal, from a few centers, of culture, language, political ideas and economic systems—even genetically modified foods—is actually quite an ancient phenomenon.

Jared Diamond "Globalization Rocked the Ancient World Too" (*Los Angeles Times*, September 14, 2003). © 2003 by Jared Diamond. Reprinted by kind permission of the author.

The first wave of globalization began around 8500 BC, driven primar- 2
ily by genetically modified foods created in the Mideast and China, and to
a lesser extent Mexico, the Andes and Nigeria. As those foods spread to
the rest of the world, so did the cultures that created them, a process that
reshaped the ancient world in much the same way the U.S., Europe and
Japan are reshaping today's world.

Our ancient ancestors' method of genetically modifying food was of 3
course much different from the way it is done today. When humans lived as
hunters and gatherers, they had to make do with whatever wild plants and
animals they found. It turned out, though, that some of the wild species
upon which humans relied for food could be domesticated. Early farmers soon learned not only how to cultivate the resulting crops and raise
livestock but also how to select the traits they valued, thereby genetically
modifying foods.

In choosing to sow seeds from wild plants with particularly desirable 4
traits—often the result of mutations—early farmers changed genetically,
albeit unconsciously, the foods they raised.

Take the case of peas. Most wild pea plants carry a gene that makes 5
their pods pop open on the stalk, causing the peas to spill onto the ground.
It is no surprise that early farmers sought out mutant plants with a gene
for pods that stayed closed, which made for an easier harvest. As a consequence of their preference, by selecting, over many generations, seeds from
the plants that best served them, they ended up with a genetically modified
variety of peas.

Would-be farmers in some regions had a huge advantage. It turned 6
out that only a few species of wild plants and animals could be domesticated, most of them native to the Mideast, China, Mexico, the Andes or
Nigeria—precisely those places that became ancient centers of power. The
crops and livestock of those five restricted homelands of agriculture still
dominate our foods today. Many of the lands most productive for modern
agriculture—including California, Europe, Japan and Java—contributed
no species that were domesticated.

Ancient people lucky enough to live in one of the few areas with wild 7
plants that could be domesticated radically altered their societies. Hunters
and gatherers traded their nomadic lifestyles for safer, more settled lives in
villages near their gardens, orchards and pastures. Agricultural surpluses,
like wheat and cheese, could be stored for winter or used to feed inventors
and bureaucrats. For the first time in history, societies could support individuals who weren't directly involved in producing food and who therefore
had time to govern or to figure out how to smelt iron and steel. As a result
of all the extra food and stability, farming societies increased in population
density a thousandfold over neighboring hunter-gatherers.

Ultimately, ancient genetically modified foods conferred military and   8
economic might on the societies that possessed them. It was easy for armies
of 1,000 farmers, brandishing steel swords and led by a general, to kill or
drive out small bands of nomads armed only with wooden spears. The
result was globalization, as early farmers spread out from those first five
homelands, carrying their genes, foods, technologies, cultures, scripts and
languages around the world.

It is because of this first wave of globalization that almost every liter-   9
ate person alive today uses one of only two writing systems: an alphabet
derived from the first Mideastern alphabet or a character-based language
that grew out of Chinese. This is also why more than 90% of people alive
today speak languages belonging to just a half-dozen language families,
derived thousands of years ago from a half-dozen languages of the five
ancient homelands. The Indo-European family that includes English, for
example, originated in the Mideast. But then as now, there was also a cost:
Countless other ancient languages and cultures were eliminated as the
early farmers and their languages spread.

The first wave of globalization moved faster along east-west axes than   10
along north-south axes. The explanation is simple: Regions lying due east
or west of one another share the same latitude, and therefore the same day
length and seasonality. They are also likely to share similar climates, habitats and diseases, all of which means that crops, livestock and humans can
spread east and west more easily, since the conditions to which they have
adapted are similar. Conversely, crops, animals and technologies adapted
to one latitude spread only with difficulty north or south to another latitude with a different seasonality and climate.

There are certainly differences between modern globalization and that   11
first ancient wave. Today, crops are deliberately engineered in the labo-
ratory rather than unconsciously in the field. And globalizing influences
spread much more quickly by plane, phone and Internet than they did on
foot and horseback. But the basic similarity remains: Now, as then, a few
centers of innovation and power end up dominating the world.

Even in our modern wave of globalization, genetically modified crops   12
tend to spread along an east-west rather than a north-south axis. That's
because crops still remain as tied to particular climates as in ancient
times. Plant breeders at U.S. firms like Monsanto concentrate on genetically modifying wheat, corn and other temperate-zone crops rather than
coconuts, oil palms and other plants that grow in the tropics. That makes
good business sense for American plant breeders, because the rich farmers who can afford their products live in the temperate zone, not in the
tropics. But it also contributes to the widening gap between rich and poor
countries.

Does this mean that tropical Paraguay and Zambia are eternally cursed, 13
and that their citizens should accept poverty as fate? Of course not. Europeans and Americans themselves enjoy no intrinsic biological advantages:
They just had the good luck to acquire useful technologies and institutions
through accidents of geography. Anyone else who now acquires those same
things can reap the same benefits. Japan, Malaysia, Singapore, South Korea
and Taiwan already have; China and others are trying and will probably
succeed. In addition, some poor countries that don't acquire enough technology to become rich can still acquire enough technology (like a few nukes,
missiles, chemical weapons, germs or box-cutters) to cause a lot of trouble.

The biggest problem with today's wave of globalization involves differ- 14
ences between the First and Third worlds. Today, citizens in North America, Europe and Japan consume, on average, 32 times more resources (and
produce 32 times more waste) than the billions of citizens of the Third
World. Thanks to TV, tourism and other aspects of globalization, though,
people in less affluent societies know about our lifestyle, and of course they
aspire to it.

Vigorous debates are going on today about whether our world could 15
sustain double its present population (along with its consumption and
waste), or even whether our world's economy is sustainable at its present
level. Yet those aren't the biggest risks. If, through globalization, everyone
living on Earth today were to achieve the standard of living of an average
American, the effect on the planet would be some 10 times what it is today,
and it would certainly be unsustainable.

We can't prevent people around the world from aspiring to match our 16
way of life any more than the exporters of culture during the first wave of
globalization could expect other cultures not to embrace the farming way
of life. But since the world couldn't sustain even its present population if
all people lived the way that those in the First World do now, we are left
with a paradox. Globalization, most analysts feel, is unstoppable. But its
consequences may overtax the Earth's ability to support us. That's a paradox that needs resolving.

Thinking about the Essay

1. What is Diamond's claim, and how does he support it with evidence? What are
   the key fields of knowledge that he taps for facts and information?

2. Explain the tone of Diamond's essay and the way in which he establishes his
   authority as an expert. Do you think he is objective or subjective in the presentation of his argument? Justify your response by referring to specific words, sentences, and paragraphs.

3. Which paragraphs constitute Diamond's introduction? How does he link these
   paragraphs to the conclusion?

4. Do you think that Diamond's comparative method is effective? Why or why not? How is the comparative method reflected in the organization of the essay?

5. How does cause-and-effect analysis interact with Diamond's other key rhetorical strategies, notably illustration and comparison and contrast?

Responding in Writing

6. Respond in an argumentative essay to Diamond's assertion that globalization widens the gap between rich and poor nations. Be certain to provide adequate evidence to support your position.

7. Write an analysis of Diamond's essay that focuses on the types of evidence the writer uses to support his argument and the relative effectiveness of this strategy.

8. Compose an essay in which you present your opinion about genetically modified foods. Use sufficient evidence to support your thesis or claim.

Networking

9. With two other class members, write a letter to the editor of your college newspaper in which you discuss the impact of globalization on your campus.

10. Conduct research on the impact of globalization on the "First" and "Third" Worlds. Based on this research, compose a brief documented essay that lays out the conflicts between First and Third World nations over the impact of globalization on their societies and cultures.

Fear Not Globalization

JOSEPH S. NYE JR.

Joseph Samuel Nye Jr. was born in South Orange, New Jersey, in 1937. He received undergraduate degrees from Princeton University (1958) and Oxford University (1960) and a PhD from Harvard University (1964) in political science. Nye is University Distinguished Service Professor and former Dean of the Kennedy School of Government at Harvard University. A prolific writer and well-known authority in international relations, Nye has served in the US Department of State and on the committees of such prominent organizations as the Ford Foundation and the Carnegie Endowment for International Peace. His concept of "smart power" became popular with both the Clinton and Obama administrations, and in 2014 Nye was appointed to the Foreign Affairs Policy Board by Secretary of State John Kerry. A frequent guest on television news programs, Nye also writes frequently for *The New York Times*, *The Christian Science Monitor*, *Atlantic Monthly*, and *The New Republic*. His most recent book is *Is the American Century Over?* (2015). The title of the following essay, which appeared in *Newsday* on October 8, 2002, captures Nye's essential thesis about the forces of globalization in today's world.

Before Reading

Is globalization a force for good or bad? Will it turn all nations, cultures, and peoples into reflections of each other?

When anti-globalization protesters took to the streets of Washing-   1
ton recently, they blamed globalization for everything from hunger to the destruction of indigenous cultures. And globalization meant the United States.

The critics call it Coca-Colonization, and French sheep farmer Jose   2
Bove has become a cult figure since destroying a McDonald's restaurant in 1999.

Contrary to conventional wisdom, however, globalization is neither   3
homogenizing nor Americanizing the cultures of the world.

To understand why not, we have to step back and put the current   4
period in a larger historical perspective. Although they are related, the long-term historical trends of globalization and modernization are not the same. While modernization has produced some common traits, such as large cities, factories and mass communications, local cultures have by no means been erased. The appearance of similar institutions in response to similar problems is not surprising, but it does not lead to homogeneity.

In the first half of the 20th century, for example, there were some sim-   5
ilarities among the industrial societies of Britain, Germany, America and Japan, but there were even more important differences. When China, India and Brazil complete their current processes of industrialization and modernization, we should not expect them to be replicas of Japan, Germany or the United States.

Take the current information revolution. The United States is at the   6
forefront of this great movement of change, so the uniform social and cultural habits produced by television viewing or Internet use, for instance,

"Fear Not Globalization" by Joseph S. Nye, Jr. author of *The Paradox of American Power*. Reprinted by permission.

are often attributed to Americanization. But correlation is not causation. Imagine if another country had introduced computers and communications at a rapid rate in a world in which the United States did not exist. Major social and cultural changes still would have followed. Of course, since the United States does exist and is at the leading edge of the information revolution, there is a degree of Americanization at present, but it is likely to diminish over the course of the 21st century as technology spreads and local cultures modernize in their own ways.

The lesson that Japan has to teach the rest of the world is that even a   7 century and a half of openness to global trends does not necessarily assure destruction of a country's separate cultural identity. Of course, there are American influences in contemporary Japan (and Japanese influences such as Sony and Pokémon in the United States). Thousands of Japanese youths are co-opting the music, dress and style of urban black America. But some of the groups they listen to dress up like samurai warriors on stage. One can applaud or deplore such cultural transfers, but one should not doubt the persistence of Japan's cultural uniqueness.

The protesters' image of America homogenizing the world also reflects   8 a mistakenly static view of culture. Efforts to portray cultures as unchanging more often reflect reactionary political strategies than descriptions of reality. The Peruvian writer Mario Vargas Llosa put it well when he said that arguments in favor of cultural identity and against globalization "betray a stagnant attitude toward culture that is not borne out by historical fact. Do we know of any cultures that have remained unchanged through time? To find any of them one has to travel to the small, primitive, magico-religious communities made up of people . . . who, due to their primitive condition, become progressively more vulnerable to exploitation and extermination."

Vibrant cultures are constantly changing and borrowing from other   9 cultures. And the borrowing is not always from the United States. For example, many more countries turned to Canada than to the United States as a model for constitution-building in the aftermath of the Cold War. Canadian views of how to deal with hate crimes were more congenial to countries such as South Africa and the post-Communist states of Eastern Europe than America's First Amendment practices.

Globalization is also a two-edged sword. In some areas, there has been   10 not only a backlash against American cultural imports, but also an effort to change American culture itself. American policies on capital punishment may have majority support inside the United States, but they are regarded as egregious violations of human rights in much of Europe and have been the focus of transnational human rights campaigns. American attitudes toward climate change or genetic modification of food draw similar criticism.

More subtly, the openness of the United States to the world's diasporas both enriches and changes American culture.

Transnational corporations are changing poor countries but not   11
homogenizing them. In the early stages of investment, a multinational company with access to the global resources of finance, technology and markets holds the high cards and often gets the best of the bargain with the poor country. But over time, as the poor country develops a skilled workforce, learns new technologies, and opens its own channels to global finance and markets, it is often able to renegotiate the bargain and capture more of the benefits.

As technical capabilities spread and more and more people hook   12
up to global communications systems, the U.S. economic and cultural preponderance may diminish. This in turn has mixed implications for American "soft" power, our ability to get others to do what we want by attraction rather than coercion. Less dominance may mean less anxiety about Americanization, fewer complaints about American arrogance and a little less intensity in the anti-American backlash. We may have less control in the future, but we may find ourselves living in a world some-what more congenial to our basic values of democracy, free markets and human rights.

Thinking about the Essay

1. What is Nye's purpose in writing this article? How can you tell? What type of audience does Nye have in mind for his essay? Why does he produce such an affirmative tone in dealing with his subject?

2. Which paragraphs constitute Nye's introduction? Where does he place his thesis, and how does he state it?

3. Break down the essay into its main topics. How does Nye develop these topics? What strategies does he employ—for example, causal analysis, comparison and contrast, illustration—and where?

4. Analyze Nye's topic sentences for his paragraphs. How do they serve as clear guides for the development of his paragraphs? How do they serve to unify the essay?

5. How does Nye's concluding paragraph serve as an answer both to the issue raised in his introduction and to other concerns expressed in the body of the essay?

Responding in Writing

6. From your own personal experience of globalization, write an essay in which you agree or disagree with Nye's assertion that there is little to fear from globalization.

7. Try writing a rebuttal to Nye's argument, explaining why there is much to fear about globalization. Deal point by point with Nye's main assertions. Be certain to provide your own evidence in support of your key reasons.

8. Write an essay that responds to the following topic sentence in Nye's essay: "Vibrant cultures are constantly changing and borrowing from other cultures" (paragraph 9). Base your paper on personal experience, your reading, and your knowledge of current events.

Networking

9. With four other classmates, imagine that you have to teach Nye's essay to a class of high school seniors. How would you proceed? Develop a lesson plan that you think would appeal to your audience.

10. With the entire class, arrange an online chat about Nye's essay. As a focal point for your discussion, argue for or against the idea that he does not take the dangers of globalization seriously enough.

7 | Culture Wars: Whose Culture Is It, Anyway?

As we have seen in earlier chapters, the power and influence of the United States radiate outward to the rest of the world in many ways. Nowhere is this more visible than in the impact of various American cultural manifestations—ranging from food to clothing to music to television and film—on other countries. When a French farmer burns down a McDonald's, terrorists destroy a disco in Bali, or clerics in Iran attempt to ban Barbie dolls from stores, we sense the opposition to American cultural hegemony. Conversely, when Iranians do find ways to buy Barbies and also turn on their banned satellite systems to catch the latest episode of *Big Bang Theory*, or when street merchants in Kenya sell University of Michigan T-shirts, we detect the flip side of the culture wars—the mesmerizing power of American culture throughout the world. Sometimes it seems that American culture, wittingly or unwittingly, is in a battle for the world's soul.

We also have to acknowledge that the culture wars color American life as well. At home, debates over immigration, affirmative action, gay marriage, and much more impinge on our daily lives and dominate media presentations. It might be fashionable to say that we all trace our DNA to Africa and that ideally we are all citizens of the world, but the issue of what sort of culture we represent individually or collectively is much more complicated. Barack Obama might be the icon for the New American or the new Universal Person, but his slightest actions and words can prompt cultural controversy. American culture cuts many ways; it is powerful, but also strange and contradictory.

The culture wars take us to the borders of contradiction both at home and abroad. It is too facile to say that we are moving "beyond" monoculturalism at home or that the rest of the world doesn't have to embrace American culture if it doesn't want to. What is clear is that the very *idea* of American culture, in all its diversity, is so pervasive that it

Muslim tourists eat in a McDonald's restaurant in the Egyptian Red Sea resort of Sharmel-Sheikh.

Thinking about the Image

1. If McDonald's is stereotypically American, what is stereotypically Egyptian about this image? Why do you think the photographer is emphasizing those stereotypes?
2. Think about other images of globalization you have seen in this book. How effective is the "rhetoric" of globalization here?
3. Why is something so seemingly basic as food such a potent symbol of cultural meaning and pride? Does this photograph capture this symbolism effectively? Why or why not?

spawns numerous viewpoints and possibilities for resolution. After all, culture is a big subject: it embraces one's ethnic, racial, class, religious, sexual, and national identity. We can't be uncritical about culture. We have to understand how culture both molds and reflects our lives.

The writers in this chapter offer perspectives—all of them provocative and engaging—on national and transnational culture. They deal with the ironies of culture at home and the paradoxes of American cultural influence abroad.

Some of the writers engage in self-reflection, others in rigorous analysis. All refuse to view culture in simplistic terms. In reading them, you might discover that whether you grew up in the United States or another country, culture is at the heart of who you are.

Have Roots, Will Travel

LISA SEE

> Lisa See was born in Paris in 1955 but grew up in Los Angeles, where she lived with her mother who was also a writer. However, Lisa See spent a lot of time with her father's family in Chinatown, and most of her books are based on a biracial, bicultural Chinese experience. She graduated from Loyola Marymount University in 1979. She has long been intrigued by lost or forgotten stories or those that have been deliberately hidden. Her books include *On Gold Mountain: The One Hundred Year Odyssey of My Chinese-American Family* (1995) and international best sellers *Flower Net* (1997), *Snow Flower and the Secret Fan* (2005), and *Peony in Love* (2007). She now lives in Los Angeles, where she continues to write and work with various Chinese American cultural organizations; in this article, she reveals her strong feelings for her city.

Before Reading

How is the title contradictory? Is it an **oxymoron** to say that a person who puts down roots travels?

Many people are lured to Los Angeles because they think it has no history and they can escape their pasts and reinvent themselves. That's not me. My great-great-grandmother—a single mother with an entrepreneurial spirit—came here from Washington State to start her own business. My great-grandfather came from a small village in China and became the patriarch of Los Angeles' Chinatown. This makes me a fifth-generation Angeleno, and I'm pretty confident you won't meet many people like me. (In the interest of full disclosure, I was born in Paris, where my parents were students, but I don't count that six-week aberration.) My sons are sixth-generation Angelenos—as rare around here as snowflakes.

Lisa See, "Have Roots, Will Travel," *Smithsonian* 38.7 (Oct. 2007), 27–28, 30.

As a girl, I spent a lot of time with my grandparents and other relatives   2
in our family's antiques store in Chinatown. My grandparents used to take
me to a restaurant we called "the little place" to have what was then called
cha nau (and is now more popularly known as dim sum). Later we'd go
shopping along Spring Street: to the International Grocery for preserved
turnip, fermented tofu and sesame-seed candles; to the Sam Sing Butcher
Shop, with its life-size gold-leafed pig in the window; and to the Lime
House for Chinese custard pie.

But visiting my grandparents was about much more than things Chi-   3
nese. One block south of my family's store was El Pueblo, the city's birth-
place and home to Olvera Street—a tourist destination in the guise of an
"authentic" Mexican marketplace. Since 1781, El Pueblo has been a place
where art, culture, politics and rabble-rousers of every stripe have congre-
gated. But what most people don't know is that in addition to the original
Yagna Indian, Spanish and Mexican settlements, Los Angeles' first Chinatown stood here; not only did the whole city ripple out from El Pueblo, but my family did as well. My great-grandparents had a store here,
and my grandfather's restaurant, facing the original "Spanish plaza," was
only the seventh family-style Chinese restaurant in the city. I used to think
my grandmother liked to take me to El Pueblo for "Spanish" food—the
"polite" name for Mexican food in those days—but now I understand that
she liked to go there to remember her past.

Sometimes we'd continue on to Little Tokyo, where my grandmother   4
would buy interesting fabrics or pretty stationery. Other times we'd leave
the family store and head a couple of blocks north along Broadway and
then cut over to Hill Street to visit someone at the French Hospital, one of
only two vestiges of what had once been a vibrant Frenchtown. (Philippe's
restaurant, self-described home of the original French-dip sandwich, was
just across the street from my family's store.) Much of the property along
Broadway—today the main drag of Chinatown—is still owned by Italian
families; that area used to be Little Italy. Today, the descendants of those
pioneer families rent to immigrants from Vietnam, Cambodia, Laos and
China. I sometimes wonder if this single square mile or so has more layers
of people, cultures and food than any other in the country.

It seems that once my relatives got here, they just had to see, do, eat   5
and play their ways across the city . . . in good times and bad. My Chinese
great-grandfather loved cars and bought a new one every year, although
he never learned to drive. (His sons drove him around, and he let others
borrow his car to advertise their businesses.) My great-grandmother Jessie
and her husband, Harvey, were itinerant workers who followed harvests
and whatever other work they could get from Alaska down to the Mexican
border. Jessie's diary, written from 1905 to 1937, describes how, once she

moved to Los Angeles, she loved to get behind the wheel of some beat-up jalopy or other and drive hither, thither and yon to find bootleggers, go dancing or bail Harvey out of jail. (He ended up "on the nickel," living and dying homeless on Fifth Street.) All this driving—crisscrossing the city—took a long time back then, between breakdowns, dirt roads, flat tires, scarce gas stations and run-ins with the law. But this didn't stop them, nor did it stop my mother's parents after one came from Texas, the other from New York State. So I guess my desire to explore the city is genetic.

By the time I came along, in 1955, my parents lived on a "walk street"—a   6
street reserved for pedestrians—off Hyperion Avenue between the enclaves of Silver Lake and Echo Park. Once when I was a toddler, I sped out the screen door, zipped down the walk street, made a left at Hyperion and ambled along the sidewalk until a policeman spotted me. He took me back to my mom, who was horrified and embarrassed, but to this day she remains amused and bewildered by the fact that my nature was evident at such a young age.

I still feel the need to see what's out there. Like my parents, grandpar-   7
ents and great-grandparents before me, I love to get in my car, roll down the windows, turn up the radio and drive. (By now you must be thinking: No wonder Los Angeles has so much traffic! No wonder it has so much smog! What about global warming? And you'd have a point, although in my defense, I drive a Prius and explore a lot on foot too.)

My first memories are of a truly decrepit downtown tenement; now I   8
live in lush, celebrity-studded Brentwood. In all, I've lived in more than ten different parts of the city. Along the way, I've endured fires, floods, earth-quakes and landslides. I've met surfers and hippies, seen a neighborhood turn into a ghetto and encountered deer, coyotes, opossums, raccoons, every kind of rat and a mountain lion. I've crossed the city in search of the best Korean *bibimbap*, Salvadoran *pupusas* and Ethiopian food I eat with my fingers. I'm old enough to remember the Watts riot, and my sons remember what happened after the Rodney King verdict.

Here's the thing: all this diversity comes at a price, and it hasn't always   9
been a black-and-white, rich-and-poor or north-and-south-of-the-border issue. Los Angeles' first race riot occurred in Chinatown in 1871, when 19 Chinese men and boys were stabbed, hanged or shot to death. In 1945, on the day my aunt Sissee got married, my great-great-uncle was driving to church on the recently completed freeway. The kids got rowdy in the back seat, and one of my cousins (so many times removed) fell out of the car. It was fortunate he only broke his arm—the French Hospital wouldn't treat him because he was Chinese. In 1957 when my great-grandfather died, the City Council honored him as a Los Angeles pioneer, but one cemetery refused to bury him because he was Chinese. My parents were only the second mixed-race couple in my family to marry legally in this country;

California law banned marriage between Chinese and Caucasians until 1948. And that's just one family's story. I like to think we can learn from the past, but as the film *Crash* illustrated, we're constantly bumping into each other, and on any given day anything can happen in the City of Angels.

I'm a city commissioner now and serve on the El Pueblo de Los Angeles 10 Historical Monument Authority, which twice a month brings me back to my family's and my city's roots. Lately, after commission meetings, I've been walking to the block where my family had their store when I was growing up. Philippe's is still in business, and the double-dipped pork sandwich there is still the best. But these days I feel compelled to wend my way around the world by circling that single block, where I have the choice of takeout from Mexican, Filipino, Peruvian, Thai, Chinese or Texas barbecue restaurants. Then I get in my car and head home.

Sometimes I take the freeway, but often I head west on Sunset Boulevard 11 to travel through time, passing old neighborhoods with houses clinging to hillsides and bungalows swathed in Cecile Brunner roses, and then threading through the run-down decadence of Hollywood, with its prostitutes and by-the-hour motels, the fading hipness of the Sunset Strip and Beverly Hills, with its mansions and broad green lawns. Often, I don't see Los Angeles as it is—so much of it new, so much of it still trying to define itself—but as it was. I see the city of my childhood, the lingering echoes of my family and a history that's deep, complex and not always wonderful. It's a city beautiful, melancholy and triumphant, and it's my home.

Thinking about the Essay

1. Why does See like Los Angeles? Why does she like to go around this city? Identify and analyze her specific reasons.

2. In the essay, See uses sensory details—sight, sound, smell, taste—to recreate what she remembers from the past and what she observes as she drives around Los Angeles. How do they make the essay effective? For example, what would be the effect if paragraph 2 ended at the colon? Find and analyze sections in the essay where you think the descriptive details are especially effective.

3. A literary technique See uses is cataloging—lists of related items, as in paragraph 2. Analyze and evaluate her uses of cataloging.

4. Throughout her essay See uses comparison and contrast of the past and the present. Explain how the comparison and contrast controls the organization of the essay.

5. In paragraph 9, See comments that the diversity of Los Angeles "comes at a price." With a small group of classmates, discuss what she means by this statement, and then discuss if diversity continues to come at a price today. If your group decides that diversity does still come at a price, think of some specific examples to share with the entire class.

Responding in Writing

6. Think of a place you like to go to remember your past, as See says her grand-mother liked to go to El Pueblo to remember her past (paragraph 3). Using specific descriptive details and cataloging as See does in her essay, write an essay of personal reminiscence of the place as you remember it. You may also include how the place has changed from your memory of it in the past.

7. Write an essay in which you explain how diversity contributes to a city or a neighborhood or a college.

8. Write an essay in which you argue that diversity today does or does not come with a price. Provide specific evidence to support your position. Also use the three argumentative appeals—emotional, ethical, and logical—in your essay, and provide a refutation to the opposing position.

Networking

9. With a small group of your classmates, conduct some research into the city where your college is located. Gather statistics on variations in age, race, gender, ethnic groups, major types of jobs available, major types of entertainment, restaurants, sports, and/or other statistical information that your group is interested in. Write a summary of your findings and share it with the class.

10. The title "Have Roots, Will Travel" alludes to a Western series on television from 1957 to 1963 about Paladin, a gunslinger. Watch one or more episodes of this television program on the Internet. Also search for and listen to the "Ballad of Paladin." Write a synopsis or summary of the episodes that you watch, and a character sketch of the protagonist Paladin. Then write an essay in which you compare and contrast this program to a current television series and compare and contrast Paladin to the protagonist in the current television program.

Whose Culture Is It, Anyway?

HENRY LOUIS GATES JR.

Henry Louis Gates Jr. is one of the most respected figures in the field of African American studies. Born in 1950 in Keyser, West Virginia, he received a BA degree (summa cum laude) from Harvard University (1973) and MA (1974) and PhD degrees (1979) from Clare College, Cambridge. A recipient of numerous major grants, including the prestigious MacArthur Prize Fellowship, and currently head of Harvard's African American studies department, Gates in numerous essays and books argues for a greater diversity in arts, literature, and life. In one of his best-known works, *Loose Canons: Notes on the*

Culture Wars (1992), Gates states, "The society we have made simply won't survive without the values of tolerance. And cultural tolerance comes to nothing without cultural understanding." Among his many publications are *The Signifying Monkey: Toward a Theory of Afro-American Literary Criticism* (1988), which won both a National Book Award and an American Book Award; *Colored People, A Memoir* (1994); *The Future of the Race* (with Cornel West, 1996); *Wonders of the African World* (1999); and *In Search of Our Roots* (2009). In the following essay, which appeared originally in *The New York Times* on May 4, 1991, Gates analyzes the cultural diversity movement in American colleges and universities.

Before Reading

Gates argues elsewhere that we must reject "ethnic absolutism" of all kinds. What do you think he means by this phrase? Exactly how does a college or university—perhaps your institution—transcend this problem?

I recently asked the dean of a prestigious liberal arts college if his school 1 would ever have, as Berkeley has, a 70 percent non-white enrollment. "Never," he replied. "That would completely alter our identity as a center of the liberal arts."

The assumption that there is a deep connection between the shape of 2 a college's curriculum and the ethnic composition of its students reflects a disquieting trend in education. Political representation has been confused with the "representation" of various ethnic identities in the curriculum.

The cultural right wing, threatened by demographic changes and the 3 ensuing demands for curricular change, has retreated to intellectual pro-tectionism, arguing for a great and inviolable "Western tradition," which contains the seeds, fruit and flowers of the very best thought or uttered in history. (Typically, Mortimer Adler has ventured that blacks "wrote no good books.") Meanwhile, the cultural left demands changes to accord with population shifts in gender and ethnicity. Both are wrongheaded.

I am just as concerned that so many of my colleagues feel that the ratio- 4 nale for a diverse curriculum depends on the latest Census Bureau report as I am that those opposed see pluralism as forestalling the possibility of a communal "American" identity. To them, the study of our diverse cultures must lead to "tribalism" and "fragmentation."

The cultural diversity movement arose partly because of the frag-   5
mentation of society by ethnicity, class and gender. To make it the culprit
for this fragmentation is to mistake effect for cause. A curriculum that
reflects the achievement of the world's great cultures, not merely the
West's, is not "politicized"; rather it situates the West as one of a community of civilizations. After all, culture is always a conversation among
different voices.

To insist that we "master our own culture" before learning others—as   6
Arthur Schlesinger Jr. has proposed—only defers the vexed question: What
gets to count as "our" culture? What has passed as "common culture" has
been an Anglo-American regional culture, masking itself as universal. Significantly different cultures sought refuge underground.

Writing in 1903, W. E. B. Du Bois expressed his dream of a high culture   7
that would transcend the color line: "I sit with Shakespeare and he winces
not." But the dream was not open to all. "Is this the life you grudge us," he
concluded, "O knightly America?" For him, the humanities were a conduit
into a republic of letters enabling escape from racism and ethnic chauvi-
nism. Yet no one played a more crucial role than he in excavating the long
buried heritage of Africans and African-Americans.

The fact of one's ethnicity, for any American of color, is never neutral: 8
One's public treatment, and public behavior, are shaped in large part by
one's perceived ethnic identity, just as by one's gender. To demand that
Americans shuck their cultural heritages and homogenize themselves into a
"universal" WASP culture is to dream of an America in cultural white face,
and that just won't do.

So it's only when we're free to explore the complexities of our hyphen-   9
ated culture that we can discover what a genuinely common American
culture might actually look like.

Is multiculturalism un-American? Herman Melville didn't think so. As   10
he wrote: "We are not a narrow tribe, no. . . . We are not a nation, so much
as a world." We're all ethnics; the challenge of transcending ethnic chau-
vinism is one we all face.

We've entrusted our schools with the fashioning and refashioning of a   11
democratic polity. That's why schooling has always been a matter of political judgment. But in a nation that has theorized itself as plural from its
inception, schools have a very special task.

Our society won't survive without the values of tolerance, and cul-   12
tural tolerance comes to nothing without cultural understanding. The challenge facing America will be the shaping of a truly common public culture,
one responsive to the long-silenced cultures of color. If we relinquish the
ideal of America as a plural nation, we've abandoned the very experiment
America represents. And that is too great a price to pay.

Thinking about the Essay

1. Gates poses a question in his title. How does he answer it? Where does he state his thesis?

2. The essay begins with an anecdote. How does it illuminate a key aspect of the problem Gates analyzes?

3. Gates makes several references to other writers—Mortimer Adler, Arthur Schlesinger Jr., W. E. B. Du Bois, and Herman Melville. Who are these figures, and how do they provide a frame or context for Gates's argument?

4. How does the writer use comparison and contrast and causal analysis to advance his argument?

5. How does the concluding paragraph serve as a fitting end to the writer's argument?

Responding in Writing

6. Write a comparative essay in which you analyze the respective approaches to multiculturalism by Amartya Sen and Gates.

7. Gates speaks of "our hyphenated culture" (paragraph 9). Write a paper examining this phrase and applying it to your own campus.

8. Are you on "the cultural left" or "the cultural right" (to use Gates's words in paragraph 3), or somewhere in the middle? Write a personal essay responding to this question.

Networking

9. Form four working groups of classmates. Each group should investigate the ethnic composition of your campus, courses, and programs designed to foster pluralism and multiculturalism and the institution's policy on affirmative action. Draft a document in which you present your findings and conclusions concerning the state of the cultural diversity movement on your campus.

10. Search the Web for sites that promote what Gates terms "'universal' WASP culture" (paragraph 8). What sort of ideology do they promote? Where do they stand in terms of the culture wars? What impact do you think they have on the course of contemporary life in the United States?

Manifest Destiny

Luis Alberto Urrea

Luis Alberto Urrea was born in Tijuana, Mexico, to a Mexican father and an American mother. His father slowly learned English, and his mother never learned to speak Spanish, so Luis grew up in a mixed linguistic and cultural environment. He was the first member of his family to attend and graduate from college, earning degrees from the University of California at

San Diego and the University of Colorado. He has written critically acclaimed essays, novels, and poems about Mexican immigration into the United States from the unique and credible perspective of one who has lived on both sides of the border. He writes realistically about poverty-stricken Mexicans and explores the sympathy and pain all humans feel for others who are suffering. In 2005, Urrea was a finalist for the Pulitzer Prize for Nonfiction for *The Devil's Highway: A True Story*, and is a member of the Latino Literature Hall of Fame. In this essay he narrates a trip he took with his family through what Americans call the West, but he from his Mexican heritage calls the North.

Before Reading

What does the phrase "manifest destiny" mean? Have you studied manifest destiny in a history or social science class? If you remember the meaning of this phrase, write it down. If you do not remember the meaning, look it up and write down the definition and its role in the development of the United States. Keep this definition in mind as you read this essay.

This is how I came to be standing inside a sodbuster's hut at the edge of the Badlands, breathing 1876 air and hearing Spanish in my mind . . . 1

Maybe it was Jim Morrison's fault. Maybe it was Okie Bob's. I have always had a mystical urge toward the biggest, emptiest, western landscapes—they promise mysteries and verities, room to spit and walk about. I spent barrio boyhood Sunday mornings with Okie Bob's corral of cowboy movies and old western music in vivid black and white on channel six. But my nights? They belonged to The Lizard King. "The West . . . is the best," he intoned. "Get here and we'll do the rest." Psychedelic cowboy tunes on the edge of the continental shelf. 2

I was as west as one could get in the Lower 48; westering beyond San Diego would drop you right in the water. All that fascinating frontier stuff was actually east of my west. Unless it was south. 3

In Spanish, "frontier" is *frontera*. All the Tijuana license plates had FRONT on them, which I thought meant Tijuana was at the head of some great charge. Turns out, it was. *Frontera* does not only mean "frontier" in Spanish. It also means "border." Pioneers and buckaroos, settlers and desperados was headin' for me from two different directions. Here came The Virginian . . . and The Sinaloan. 4

Luis Alberto Urrea, "Manifest Destiny," *Orion*, May/June 2012 (reprinted in *Utne* May/June 2013, 56–57).

It is telling that, although we allegedly live in Chicago now, my family 5
lives 35 miles west of the city. The West remains the best in my mind, and I
drag the fam on epic drives almost every year. I feel relief when I cross the
Mississippi, and shivers of delight crossing the Missouri. When the land
turns red and black and craggy, I feel echoes in my bones. I hear America
singing, as Walt Whitman said, though my kids hear The Killers and Nine
Inch Nails, their earbuds going *sst-sst-sst-sst.*

We head to South Dakota, toward my Lakota brothers at Pine Ridge. 6
I always hanker to see my Oglala homeboys, Duane and Horses. Horses
tells me stories about how Sioux boys used to be migrant farmworkers
beside the Kerouac-era Messkins. "Why do you think guys at Pine Ridge
are named Pedro?" he asks. Though there they say *Pee-dro.*

I remember Duane visiting me once in Colorado, and a local yelling 7
from a passing truck, "Go back where you came from!" And Duane, shoot-
ing back, "Where to, South Dakota?"

And Horses once, on the phone, three beers down: "You think the 8
Indian wars are over? The cavalry's still chasing indigenous guys around
the territories."

Cornfields. Pecan logs. Plastic buffalo beside I-90. Jackalopes. The West 9
is the best. I rush out into the empty horizon, and go deeper in.

My mom's people availed themselves of traditional Manifest Destiny— 10
rolling west from their English roots. But my dad's people were the Original Illegal Immigrants, Spanish conquistadores. The Urrea brothers came
and took South America, then headed north. Their ancient roots seem to be
in the Visigoth invaders of Iberia. We are migratin' fools.

Once into Mexico, *el destino manifesto* sent them north again. Toward 11
the frontier that was later retranslated by the Treaty of Guadalupe Hidalgo
into the present border. Thus, my inevitable entry: Mom's migration met
Dad's and we washed up on the farthest beach.

This may seem like old history to you, but Newt is on CNN right now 12
calling Spanish a ghetto language, and Mitt was on last night telling us to
self-deport, and all candidates seem to get real traction on the backs of the
"invading hordes," on beaner border-jumpers, though the evidence shows
that we are at zero net immigration.

I remember when Slow Turtle, elder of the Wampanoag, came to my 13
college and said, "You boat people keep overcrowding my continent."
On my endless speaking tour, people like to counter my comments with
the inevitable, "Yeah, my family was immigrants, too, but we came here
legally." And I ask, "Who stamped their visas, Crazy Horse or Geronimo?"

I feel unworthy of the Black Hills, of the vast Badlands. Is it weird to 14
want to embrace a bison? (Well, I'll be the first to admit it is kind of foolish.) I'm a liberal patriot: don't tread on me, *cabrones*!

There is a rainbow arching from the emerald prairies to the glowing   15
whiteness of the Badlands—the dark violet sky behind makes the hoodoos
and monuments seem to be glowing from within. It's a scene that would
be too archetypal and rich for the postmodernists with whom I teach. It's
so unironic. But, as David Quammen once wrote, God gets carried away,
to his credit.

There are the signs along the road: *SEE! ORIGINAL SODBUSTER*   16
HUTS! And: *FEED! PRAIRIE DOGS!* Well now, our next detour is
decided upon—Maw and Paw want to see real sodbuster huts, and the
kids can toss peanuts to the 'dogs.

I used to work with a relief organization on the south side of the fron-   17
tera. We worked among beggars, orphans, prostitutes, drug addicts, street
gangs, killers, and prisoners. We fed widows and killed lice. It was some
rough country—it was Deadwood, in Spanish. The detritus and ruin of a
contested frontier.

What was interesting to me always was the debased grandeur of hope.   18
The beauty of scraping together castoff wood and paper and somehow
building a shelter against the wind and the beasts and your roving enemies.
The stink of these shacks, the endemic gray-black color that seeped in. The
newspapers on the walls to keep out the cold. The vermin that fell out of
the roofs. The wobbly handcrafted tables these small families gathered at
by candlelight to pick over their plates of beans.

These huts were scattered across a dirt landscape devoid of grass or   19
flowers. The city of Tijuana piled dead animals at the edge of their settlement and set fire to the carcasses. Run-over dogs, poisoned goats, dead
cows and horses burned in great bony pyres. And the wind never stopped.

My wife and I storm up the path toward the sodbuster homes while   20
the kids, giddy with the whistling little wag-tail dogs, spend all our loose
change on peanuts.

We bend to get in the door of the first hut, sunk into a slight hillock.   21
Still musty with the phantom odors of sleepers and cooking fires and sweat
and hope, the little hut is redolent in a ghosty way. The table is off plumb
and has clearly been hammered together from wagon parts. And the floor
is hard-swept dirt. It feels like church; we start to whisper.

And the dust is gray-black. The newspapers are still on the walls. And   22
beetles fall out of the ceiling. And for a moment I lose my bearings. I know
it. I know that smell. I know that dust. I have met those beetles. I have sat
on that crooked and dirty old bed.

We hurry out and rush to the next hut. And the haunted feelings inten-   23
sify. The soft shock. That small still voice of revelation comes upon me
there on the bare fields of the sodbuster settlement. This is the same story.

The depraved and filthy huts of the Tijuana garbage-pickers, poised on the edge of their *frontera*, are exactly the same constructions as these noble and brave huts poised on the edge of their frontier. The garbage-picker is simply part of the wrong story—those settlers are heading north, which is the wrong direction. These good people were heading west. It is our national story. Our drama. Our heritage. And it is beautiful.

Of course, nobody checked their footnotes with Duane or Horses.   24

Continuing on our westward journey, we take a detour into Custer   25
State Park. It is overrun by bikers, all of them heading for Sturgis. We come to a crossroad with hills on one side, prairies behind us, and shadowy forest ahead. All around our van, a run of Hells Angels, flying their colors, rumble on their Harleys. We all pause at the stop sign and become aware of a deeper rumbling than the bike engines. Suddenly, a real-life stampede of buffalo breaks out of the trees and charges between and around us in a tidal crashing of hooves. Angels yelling, "Oh my God!" The van shaking and rolling. The kids flying from window to window, shouting. America's shaggy heart has burst open around us.

We are all laughing. But why do I have tears running down my cheeks?   26
Why can I not breathe?

Once the bison are gone, we drive on, into the West again.   27

Thinking about the Essay

1. How does the title "Manifest Destiny" relate to Urrea's narrative? One critic has said that the tone of his narrative is ironic and that the title is ironic. Check the definition of *tone* and *irony* as well as the history of irony, beginning with the Horatian and Juvenlian classical forms of irony, and discuss what you think the critic meant. Is Urrea's irony Horatian or Juvenalian?

2. Is the essay easy to follow? What devices does the author use to connect the sections and make the essay coherent? What unifies the essay? What is Urrea's thesis? Is his overall purpose expository or argumentative? Why?

3. This essay was published in *Orion Magazine*. Go to the *Orion* website and read its history and mission. Who is the intended audience of this publication? How is Urrea's essay appropriate for the readers of this magazine?

4. Analyze Urrea's comparison and contrast of the sodbusters' huts on the edge of the Badlands to the huts of the people he worked with on the frontera in Mexico. What descriptive details does he use to help the readers sense the situation of the people who live in these dwellings?

5. Urrea uses a variety of allusions in his essay. Paragraph 5 illustrates this: "I Hear America Singing," a poem by Walt Whitman; and The Killers, and Nine Inch Nails, popular bands. Are you familiar with all these references? Find and research other allusions in this essay. Why do you think the author uses these allusions? What do these references tell you about Urrea's view of his readers?

Responding in Writing

6. Identify a situation with which you are familiar that you think should be changed—altered or abolished. Brainstorm about this situation. It may be personal, academic, legal, racial, social, or something else. Then write an essay in which you use irony to convince your readers that the situation should be changed. Use your classmates as your intended readers.

7. Write an essay in which you analyze Urrea's view of immigration in America. In your essay, include discussion of the various streams of immigrants into the "new" world that he discusses or alludes to.

8. Using the evidence in Urrea's essay as a springboard for your thoughts and writing, write an essay in which you propose a solution to the problems on the border between the United States and Mexico. Try to convince your audience to agree with your proposal(s).

Networking

9. With a small group of your classmates, research the history of irony, and trace its uses today. For example, Weird Al Yankovic used irony in his 2014 best-selling monologues and videos. Then discuss why irony is still a popular form of writing today. Summarize your findings and your discussion, and share them with your class.

10. Do an Internet search for and watch the video "An Evening with Luis Urrea," an interview at the 14th Annual Writer's Symposium by the Sea, Writing Beyond Boundaries to hear him speak about his own background and how it has affected his writing. Summarize what he says, and discuss how his background has influenced him.

It's a Mall World After All

Mac Margolis

Mac Margolis lives in Rio de Janeiro and is currently a *Bloomberg View* contributor. He has reported on Latin America for *Newsweek* and frequently contributed to *The Economist, The Washington Post*, and *Foreign Policy*. In the following piece, which appeared in the December 5, 2005, *Newsweek International*, columnist Mac Margolis defends a much maligned and distinctively American export to the world by looking at the variety of its manifestations around the world and its almost inadvertent role as a social and political institution. Margolis is a recipient of the Maria Moors Cabot Prize for outstanding reporting on Latin America—the oldest international award in journalism.

Before Reading

In what sense do you regard malls as an institution? Do you associate malls with democratic or other values?

When the Los Angeles firm Altoon + Porter Architects set out to   1
design a shopping arcade in Riyadh, Saudi Arabia, a few years ago, it faced a delicate mission: to raise a glitzy pleasure dome full of Western temptations in the maw of fundamentalist Islam. Not that the Saudis were consumer innocents; King Khalid airport in Riyadh fairly hums with wealthy Arabs bound for the lavish shops of Paris and London. But the trick was to lure women buyers—the royalty of retail—who are not allowed to shed their veils in public. "Women can't be expected to buy anything if they can't try it on," says architect Ronald Altoon, managing partner of the firm. So Altoon + Porter came up with an ecumenical solution: the Kingdom Centre, a three-story glass-and-steel Xanadu of retail with an entire floor—Women's Kingdom—devoted exclusively to female customers. "We took the veil off the women and put it on the building," says Altoon.

The modest proposal paid off. In Women's Kingdom, Saudi women   2
can shop, schmooze, dine or even loll about at the spa without upsetting the sheiks or subverting Sharia, the country's strict Islamic laws. Normally the third level of any mall is a dud, but it's become the most profitable floor in the whole arcade. The Kingdom Centre may not be revolutionary; no one is burning veils at the food court. Still, it represents a small but meaningful freedom for Saudi women. And its success points to the irrepressible global appetite for consumer culture, as well as to the growing role that the right to shop plays in fostering democratization and development.

It's been more than two decades since John B. Hightower, the director   3
of New York City's South Street Seaport Museum, a combination cultural center and shopping arcade, brazenly declared that "shopping is the chief cultural activity of the United States." Since then, it has also become one of America's chief exports: shopping malls, once a peculiarly American symbol of convenience and excess, now dot the global landscape from Santiago to St. Petersburg and Manila to Mumbai. In 1999, India boasted only three malls. Now there are 45, and the number is expected to rise to 300 by 2010. The pint-size Arab Emirate of Dubai, sometimes known as the Oz of malls, clocked 88.5 million mall visitors last year; nearly 180 million Brazilians

mob shopping arcades every month—almost as many as in the United States. Where elephants and giraffes once gamboled along the Mombasa road leading into Nairobi, the African mall rat is now a far more common sight, with four gleaming new malls to scavenge in at the Kenyan capital and three more in the works. And no one can keep pace with China, where foreign investors are scrambling to get a piece of a real-estate boom driven in part by mall mania. "The same energy and dynamism that the shopping industry brought to North America 30, 40 years ago is now reaching overseas," says Michael Kercheval, head of the International Council of Shopping Centers, an industry trade association and advisory group. "Now it's reached the global masses."

Indeed, the planet appears deep in the grip of the retail version of   4
an arms race. For years, the West Edmonton Mall in Alberta, Canada, with 20,000 parking spaces, an ice-skating rink, a miniature-golf course and four submarines (more than in the Canadian Navy) on display, had reigned as the grandest in the world. Last October it was overtaken by the $1.3 billion Golden Resources Shopping Center in northwest Beijing, with 20,000 employees and nearly twice the floor space of the Pentagon. Developers in Dubai are breaking ground on not one but two malls they claim will be even bigger, one of which boasts a man-made, five-run ski slope. Yet all these have been eclipsed by the behemoth South China Mall, which opened its doors in the factory city of Dongguan this year. By the end of the decade, China is likely to have at least seven of the world's 10 largest malls—many of them equipped with hotels, on the theory that no one can possibly see everything in a single day.

To those who malign malls as the epitome of all that is wrong with   5
American culture, their spread is like a pestilence upon the land. Dissident scholars churn out one dystopian tract—"One Nation Under Goods," "The Call of the Mall"—after another. Critics despair of whole nations willing to cash in their once vibrant downtowns and street markets for a wasteland of jerry-built nowhere, epic traffic jams and marquees ablaze with fatuous English names (Phoenix High Street, Palm Springs Life Plaza and Bairong World Trade Center Phase II). To some, this is an assault on democracy itself. "Shopping malls are great for dictatorships," says Emil Pocock, a professor of American studies at Eastern Connecticut State University, who takes students on field trips to malls to study consumer society. "What better way to control folks than to put them under a dome and in enclosed doors?" The "malling of America," in the words of author and famous mall-basher William Kowinski, has become the malling of the world.

As it turns out, that may not be such a bad thing. Rather than presage   6
or hasten the decline of the traditional downtown, as many critics fear, the rise of the mall is actually serving as a catalyst for growth, especially

in developing nations. In China, the booming retail sector has sucked in a fortune in venture capital and spawned dozens of joint ventures with international investors looking to snap up Chinese urban properties. In late July, the Simon Property Group, a major U.S. developer, teamed up with Morgan Stanley and a government-owned Chinese company to launch up to a dozen major retail centers throughout China over the next few years. Malls are a leading force in driving India's $330 billion retailing industry, which already accounts for a third of national GDP and recently over-took Russia's. Similarly, a burst of consumer spending in the Philippines—thanks to overseas nationals who send between $6 billion and $7 billion back every year—has fueled a real-estate boom, led by megamalls.

Most developing-world malls are integrated in the heart of the inner cities instead of strewn like beached whales along arid superhighways. "In China, 80 percent of shoppers walk to the mall," says Kercheval of the ICSC. In some megacities, including New Delhi, Nairobi and Rio, urban sprawl has flung customers into outlying neighborhoods, many of which spring up around brand-new shopping centers. That means malls are no longer catering just to the elite. "We used to talk exclusively about A-class shoppers," says Kercheval. "Now we are seeing the arrival of B-, C- and D-class customers. The developing-world mall is becoming more democratic." 7

In many places, malls are welcome havens of safety and security. In Rio, where teenagers (especially young men) are the main victims of street crime, parents breathe easier when they know their kids are at play in the mall, some of which deploy 100 or more private police. "Safety is one of our biggest selling points," says Paulo Malzoni Filho, president of the Brazilian Association of Shopping Centers. "When I enter into one of these malls, it feels like I have landed in a foreign country," says Parag Mehta, a regular at the Inorbit mall in the busy northern Mumbai suburb of Malad. 8

And as malls break new ground around the world, the one-size-fits-all business model created in North American suburbia is giving way to region-alized versions. Malls may conjure up the specter of a flood of U.S. brands and burgers, but in reality, local palates and preferences often prevail. On a recent evening in Beijing's Golden Resources Shopping Center, Kentucky Fried Chicken and Papa John's were nearly deserted, while the Korean restaurant just around the corner was packed. Chile has long welcomed foreign investors, yet the leading retailers at malls in Santiago are two local chains, Falabella and Almacenes Paris. In San Salvador, capital of El Salva-dor, the Gallerias shopping arcade houses a Roman Catholic church that holds mass twice a day—an intriguing metaphysical twist on the concept of the anchor store. In many developing countries, malls have attracted banks, art galleries, museums, car-rental agencies and even government services 9 such as passport offices and motor-vehicle departments, becoming de facto villages instead of just shopping centers.

For residents of the developing world, malls increasingly serve as sur-   10 rogate civic centers, encouraging social values that go beyond conspicuous spending. China is home to some 168 million smokers, but they are not allowed to partake at the smoke-free malls. That's not the only environmental plus; many Chinese malls are equipped with a soft-switching system that stabilizes the electrical current and conserves energy. In the Middle East, arcades such as Riyadh's Kingdom Centre are among the few public spaces where women can gather, gab or just walk about alone in public. "Malls are not just places to shop, they are places to imagine," says Xia Yeliang, a professor at Beijing University's School of Economics. "They bring communities together that might not otherwise encounter one another and create new communities."

For some societies, malls even offer a communal respite from the past.   11 In Warsaw, where World War II demolished most of the historic shopping district—and dreary chockablock communist-era architecture finished the job—one of the most revered public spaces around is the local mall. "For decades Poles dressed up for Sunday mass," says Grzegorz Makowski, a sociologist at Warsaw University and expert on consumer culture. "Now they dress for a visit to the shopping mall."

Still, for some critics, no amount of social or economic development   12 can hide the fact that all modern malls are at heart temples of rampant consumerism. Jan Gehl, a leading Danish champion of urban renaissance and a professor of architecture at the Royal Academy of Fine Arts in Copenhagen, likes to show his students pictures of malls around the world and ask them where each one is located. Many look so indistinguishable that they can't tell. (Only now are some clues beginning to appear.) Even Victor Gruen, the Viennese Jewish émigré who fled Hitler's Europe and created the first indoor-shopping arcade in the Minneapolis suburbs in the 1950s, eventually grew disgusted by the soulless concrete-box-with-parking monstrosities rendered in his name. "I refuse to pay alimony to these bastards of development," he growled during a 1978 speech in London, fleeing back to Europe. By then there was no escape; malls were already marching on the Old World.

Half a century on, some of the resistance to malls speaks more to nos-   13 talgia for an illusory past than a rejection of the present. Ancient Turkey certainly had its bazaar rats. And what is the contemporary shopping center if not a souk with a Cineplex? "Maybe the mall is just a modern and more comfortable version of what has always been," says Stephen Marshall of the Young Foundation, a London think tank. "It's quite possible the ancients would have seen our malls with all that technology as terrific places."

Certainly mall developers seem to have learned from their early excesses. 14
Instead of garish bunkers with blind walls and plastic rain forests, newer
malls boast sculpture gardens, murals, belvederes and gentle lighting. Lush
creepers, great ferns, cacti and feathery palms tumble down the interior
of the Fashion Mall, a boutique arcade, in Rio de Janeiro. The Kingdom
Centre in Riyadh won an international design award in 2003. And while
"big" may still be beautiful in mallworld, more and more developers are
launching arcades built to modest scale, deliberately emulating yesterday's
main streets or the Old World piazzas they replaced. This may not be the
much-vaunted consumer's arcadia the mallmeisters had always hoped for,
but global malls seem oddly to come closer to the bold democratic ideal
than the originals ever did. And when it rains, everybody stays dry.

Thinking about the Essay

1. Highlight three passing allusions that occur in the essay (the allusion to Xanadu
   in the opening paragraph, for example). Is there a chain of association between
   the series of allusions you see in the essay?

2. Why does Margolis focus on the "ecumenical solution" devised by the architectural firm Altoon + Porter in his beginning paragraph? How does this illustration
   serve to set up the other examples in the essay?

3. Where in the essay does Margolis address critics of malls as a cultural phenomenon? What is his response to these critics?

4. How does Margolis connect the "right to consumer culture" with democratic
   rights and values? Do you feel he is successful in making this connection?
   Why or why not?

5. Margolis concludes the piece by asserting that "global malls seem oddly to
   come closer to the bold democratic ideal than the originals ever did." Where
   in the essay has Margolis considered those precedents? Do you feel he has
   offered enough historical evidence to support his conclusion?

Responding in Writing

6. Do you see evidence in your own community that mall developers "have learned
   from their early excesses"? Write a brief critique of the architectural style and
   layout of your local mall.

7. Respond to Margolis's observation in paragraph 11 that malls "offer a communal respite from the past." Do you see this as a stereotypically American attitude
   toward the past? Would you characterize what malls offer as a "respite from the
   past" or as an "escape from the past"?

8. In a brief essay, reflect on the reasons for your own resistance to or enthusiasm
   for malls. Would you describe your feelings in terms of nostalgia for a past model
   in the process of being replaced or in terms of progress? What is the nature of
   this progress? What is lost or gained in the move to a new model of commerce?

Networking

9. In groups of three or four, list at least three "social values" (i.e., not consumer values) that are promoted or made possible by your local mall.

10. Go online and look up images of at least five different malls located in five different countries. What signs of individual character do you see?

Does the World Still Care About American Culture?

RICHARD PELLS

Richard Pells, who was born in Kansas City, Missouri, in 1941, studied at Rutgers University (BA, 1963) and Harvard University (MA, 1964; PhD, 1969). A professor of history at the University of Texas at Austin, Pells specializes in twentieth-century American cultural and intellectual history. His books include *Radical Visions and American Dreams* (1973), *Not Like Us: How Europeans Have Loved, Hated, and Transformed American Culture Since World War II* (1997), and *Modernist America: Art, Music, Movies, and the Globalization of American Culture* (2011). In the following article from the March 6, 2009, issue of *The Chronicle of Higher Education*, Pells examines the causes behind the decline of global interest in American culture.

Before Reading

Do you accept the premise that the rest of the world is less interested in American culture today than it was during most of the twentieth century?

For most of the 20th century, the dominant culture in the world was   1
American. Now that is no longer true. What is most striking about attitudes toward the United States in other countries is not the anti-Americanism they reflect, or the disdain for former President George W. Bush, or the opposition to American foreign policies. Rather, people abroad are increasingly indifferent to America's culture.

Richard Pells, "Does the World Still Care About American Culture?" Originally appeared in *The Chronicle of Higher Education*, March 6, 2009, Volume 55, Issue 26, p. B4. Reprinted by permission of the author.

American culture used to be the elephant in everyone's living room. 2
Whether people felt uncomfortable with the omnipresence of America's
high or popular culture in their countries, they could not ignore its power
or its appeal. American writers and artists were superstars—the objects of
curiosity, admiration and envy. Today they are for the most part unnoticed
or regarded as ordinary mortals, participants in a global rather than a distinctively American culture.

America's elections still matter to people overseas. As someone who 3
has taught American studies in Europe, Latin America and Asia, I received
e-mail messages from friends abroad asking me who I thought would win
the presidency in November. But I rarely get queries about what I think of
the latest American movie. Nor does anyone ask me about American novelists, playwrights, composers or painters.

Imagine any of these events or episodes in the past happening now: 4
In 1928, fresh from having written "Rhapsody in Blue" and the "Piano
Concerto in F Major," George Gershwin traveled to Paris and Vienna.
He was treated like an idol. As America's most famous composer, he met
with many of the leading European modernists: Schoenberg, Stravinsky,
Prokofiev, Ravel. At one point, Gershwin asked Stravinsky if he could take
lessons from the great Russian. Stravinsky responded by asking Gershwin
how much money he made in a year. Told the answer was in six figures,
Stravinsky quipped, "In that case . . . I should study with you."

In the 1930s, Louis Armstrong and Duke Ellington toured through- 5
out Europe, giving concerts to thousands of adoring fans, includ-
ing members of the British royal family. In the 1940s and '50s, Dave
Brubeck, Miles Davis, Dizzy Gillespie, Benny Goodman and Charlie
Parker often gave concerts in Western and Eastern Europe, the Soviet
Union, the Middle East, Africa, Asia and Latin America. The Voice of
America's most popular program in the 1960s was a show called Music
USA, specializing in jazz, with an estimated 100 million listeners around
the world. In the 1940s and '50s as well, Leonard Bernstein was invited
to conduct symphony orchestras in London, Moscow, Paris, Prague, Tel
Aviv and Milan.

If you were a professor of modern literature at a foreign university, 6
your reading list had to include Bellow, Dos Passos, Faulkner, Hemingway
and Steinbeck. If you taught courses on the theater, it was obligatory to
discuss *Death of a Salesman*, *The Iceman Cometh*, *Long Day's Journey
Into Night* and *A Streetcar Named Desire*.

If you wanted to study modern art, you did not—like Gene Kelly in 7
An American in Paris—journey to the City of Light (all the while singing
and dancing to the music of Gershwin) to learn how to become a painter.
Instead you came to New York, to sit at the feet of Willem de Kooning and

Jackson Pollock. Or later you hung out at Andy Warhol's "factory," surrounded by celebrities from the arts and the entertainment world.

If dance was your specialty, where else could you find more creative 8 choreographers than Bob Fosse or Jerome Robbins? If you were an aspiring filmmaker in the 1970s, the movies worth seeing and studying all originated in America. What other country could boast of such cinematic talent as Woody Allen, Robert Altman, Francis Ford Coppola, George Lucas, Martin Scorsese and Steven Spielberg?

Of course, there are still American cultural icons who mesmerize a global 9 audience or whose photos are pervasive in the pages of the world's tabloid newspapers. Bruce Springsteen can always pack an arena wherever he performs. The Broadway musical *Rent* has been translated into more than 20 languages. Hollywood's blockbusters still make millions of dollars abroad. America's movie stars remain major celebrities at international film festivals.

But there is a sense overseas today that America's cultural exports are 10 not as important, or as alluring, as they once were. When I lecture abroad on contemporary American culture, I find that few of America's current artists and intellectuals are household names, luminaries from whom foreigners feel they need to learn. The cultural action is elsewhere—not so much in Manhattan or San Francisco but in Berlin (the site of a major film festival) and Mumbai (the home of Indian filmmakers and media entrepreneurs who are now investing in the movies of Spielberg and other American directors). The importance of Mumbai was reinforced, spectacularly, when *Slumdog Millionaire* won the Oscar for best picture.

What accounts for the decline of interest in American art, literature and 11 music? Why has American culture become just another item on the shelves of the global supermarket?

The main answer is that globalization has subverted America's influ- 12 ence. During the 1990s, many people assumed that the emergence of what they called a global culture was just another mechanism for the "Americanization" of the world. Be it Microsoft or McDonald's, Disney theme parks or shopping malls, the movies or the Internet, the artifacts of American culture seemed ubiquitous and inescapable.

Yet far from reinforcing the impact of American culture, globalization has 13 strengthened the cultures of other nations, regions and continents. Instead of defining what foreigners want, America's cultural producers find themselves competing with their counterparts abroad in shaping people's values and tastes. What we have in the 21st century is not a hegemonic American culture but multiple forms of art and entertainment—voices, images and ideas that can spring up anywhere and be disseminated all over the planet.

American television programs like *Dallas* and *Dynasty* were once the 14 most popular shows on the airwaves, from Norway to New Zealand. Now many people prefer programs that are locally produced. Meanwhile, cable and satellite facilities permit stations like Al-Jazeera to define and interpret the news from a Middle Eastern perspective for people throughout the world.

Since 2000, moreover, American movies have steadily lost market share   15
in Europe and Asia. In 1998, the year *Titanic* was released abroad, American films commanded 64 percent of the ticket sales in France. Ten years later, Hollywood's share of the French market has fallen to 50 percent. Similarly, in 1998, American films accounted for 70 percent of the tickets sold in South Korea. Today that figure has fallen to less than 50 percent.

As in the case of television programs, audiences increasingly prefer   16
movies made in and about their own countries or regions. Indian films are now more popular in India than are imports from Hollywood. At the same time, American moviegoers are increasingly willing to sample films from abroad (and not just in art houses), which has led to the popularity in the United States of Japanese cartoons and animated films as well as recent German movies like *The Lives of Others*.

After World War II, professors and students from abroad were eager to   17
study in the United States. America was, after all, the center of the world's intellectual and cultural life. Now, with the rise of continental exchange programs and the difficulties that foreign academics face obtaining U.S. visas, it is often easier for a Dutch student to study in Germany or France or for a Middle Eastern student to study in India, than for either of them to travel to an American university. That further diminishes the impact of American culture abroad.

Crowds, especially of young people, still flock to McDonald's—   18
whether in Beijing, Moscow or Paris. But every country has always had its own version of equally popular fast food. There are wurst stands in Germany and Austria, fish-and-chips shops in England, noodle restaurants in South Korea and Singapore, kabob outlets on street corners in almost any city (including in America), all of which remain popular and compete effectively with the Big Mac.

Finally, cellphones and the Internet make information and culture   19
instantly available to anyone, without having to depend any longer on American definitions of what it is important to know. Indeed, globalization has led not to greater intellectual and political uniformity but to the decentralization of knowledge and culture. We live today in a universe full of cultural options, and we are therefore free to choose what to embrace and what to ignore.

I am not suggesting that America's culture is irrelevant. It remains   20
one—but only one—of the cultural alternatives available to people abroad and at home. Moreover, it is certainly conceivable that President Barack Obama will improve America's currently dreadful image in the world,

encouraging people to pay more attention not only to American policies but also to American culture—which the Bush administration, despite its efforts at cultural diplomacy, was never able to do.

But it is doubtful that America will ever again be the world's preemi-   21
nent culture, as it was in the 20th century. That is not a cause for regret. Perhaps we are all better off in a world of cultural pluralism than in a world made in America.

Thinking about the Essay

1. What claim does Pells establish in his introductory paragraph? What minor propositions does he provide to support his claim?

2. Where does Pells inject information about himself into this essay? What is his purpose? Do you think his strategy is effective? Justify your response.

3. Does Pells ever establish a clear definition of American culture, or does he force us to induce it? Explain. Could there be alternative definitions of American culture that compete with Pells's understanding of the word? Why or why not?

4. Trace the pattern of cause and effect that Pells establishes. According to Pells, what are the primary and secondary causes for the decline of global interest in American culture?

5. Pells alludes to numerous cultural figures and artistic works in this essay. What expectations does he have of his audience here? Would readers be less likely to relate to his essay—or accept his argument—if they were not familiar with Gene Kelly or had not read or seen *The Iceman Cometh*? Explain.

Responding in Writing

6. Write an argumentative essay in which you attempt to refute Pells's claim that the world is losing interest in American culture. Provide supporting points and examples to buttress your argument.

7. Write a causal analysis of the impact of globalization on the dissemination of American culture around the world.

8. Reverse Pells's claim and write an essay contending or explaining why Americans are far more interested in the cultures of other nations and regions than they were in the past.

Networking

9. Working in small groups, develop a list of all the references and allusions in Pells's essay and then identify as many as possible. Based on this list, establish what your group thinks that Pells means by American culture.

10. Conduct online research on one American musician, writer, artist, filmmaker, or actor mentioned in the essay—for example, Louis Armstrong, Ernest Hemingway, or Woody Allen—and explore the reception of this individual overseas. What conclusions can you draw from your research?

On Seeing England for the First Time

JAMAICA KINCAID

Jamaica Kincaid was born Elaine Potter Richardson in 1949 in St. John's, Antigua, in the West Indies. After immigrating to the United States, she became a staff writer for *The New Yorker*, with her short stories also appearing in *Rolling Stone*, *The Paris Review*, and elsewhere. She has taught at Harvard University and other colleges, including Claremont McKenna College, where she currently teaches in the summer. Kincaid has compiled a distinguished body of fiction and nonfiction, notably *Annie John* (1985), *A Small Place* (1988), *Lucy* (1991), *The Autobiography of My Mother* (1996), and *Among Flowers: A Walk in the Himalaya* (2005). The stories collected in *At the Bottom of the River* (1984) won the Morton Dauwen Zabel Award from the American Academy of Arts and Letters. Although Kincaid has turned in her writing to the relatively peaceful world of gardening, the typical tone of her fiction and essays is severely critical of the social, cultural, and political consequences of colonialism and immigration. In "On Seeing England for the First Time," published in *Transition* in 1991, Kincaid thinks about the time when Great Britain was associated with the forces of globalization throughout the world.

Before Reading

It was once said that the sun never sets on the British Empire. What does this statement mean? Could the same be said of the United States today?

When I saw England for the first time, I was a child in school sitting at a desk. The England I was looking at was laid out on a map gently, beautifully, delicately, a very special jewel; it lay on a bed of sky blue—the background of the map—its yellow form mysterious, because though it looked like a leg of mutton, it could not really look like anything so familiar as a leg of mutton because it was England—with shadings of pink and

1

"On Seeing England for the First Time" by Jamaica Kincaid, *Transition: An International Review*, 51. Copyright © 1991, pp. 32–40. *Transition* by Congress for Cultural Freedom; International Association for Cultural Freedom; W.E.B. Du Bois Institute for Afro-American Research. Copyright 1991. Reproduced with permission of Indiana University Press in the format Textbook via Copyright Clearance Center.

green, unlike any shadings of pink and green I had seen before, squiggly veins of red running in every direction. England was a special jewel all right, and only special people got to wear it. The people who got to wear England were English people. They wore it well and they wore it everywhere: in jungles, in deserts, on plains, on top of the highest mountains, on all the oceans, on all the seas, in places where they were not welcome, in places they should not have been. When my teacher had pinned this map up on the blackboard, she said, "This is England"—and she said it with authority, seriousness, and adoration, and we all sat up. It was as if she had said, "This is Jerusalem, the place you will go to when you die but only if you have been good." We understood then—we were meant to understand then—that England was to be our source of myth and the source from which we got our sense of reality, our sense of what was meaningful, our sense of what was meaningless—and much about our own lives and much about the very idea of us headed that last list.

At the time I was a child sitting at my desk seeing England for the first time, I was already very familiar with the greatness of it. Each morning before I left for school, I ate a breakfast of half a grapefruit, an egg, bread and butter and a slice of cheese, and a cup of cocoa; or half a grapefruit, a bowl of oat porridge, bread and butter and a slice of cheese, and a cup of cocoa. The can of cocoa was often left on the table in front of me. It had written on it the name of the company, the year the company was established, and the words "Made in England." Those words, "Made in England," were written on the box the oats came in too. They would also have been written on the box the shoes I was wearing came in; a bolt of gray linen cloth lying on the shelf of a store from which my mother had bought three yards to make the uniform that I was wearing had written along its edge those three words. The shoes I wore were made in England; so were my socks and cotton undergarments and the satin ribbons I wore tied at the end of two plaits of my hair. My father, who might have sat next to me at breakfast, was a carpenter and cabinet maker. The shoes he wore to work would have been made in England, as were his khaki shirt and trousers, his underpants and undershirt, his socks and brown felt hat. Felt was not the proper material from which a hat that was expected to provide shade from the hot sun should be made, but my father must have seen and admired a picture of an Englishman wearing such a hat in England, and this picture that he saw must have been so compelling that it caused him to wear the wrong hat for a hot climate most of his long life. And this hat—a brown felt hat—became so central to his character that it was the first thing he put on in the morning as he stepped out of bed and the last thing he took off before he stepped back into bed at night. As we sat at breakfast a car might go by. The car, a Hillman or a Zephyr, was made in England.

The very idea of the meal itself, breakfast, and its substantial quality and quantity was an idea from England; we somehow knew that in England they began the day with this meal called breakfast and a proper breakfast was a big breakfast. No one I knew liked eating so much food so early in the day; it made us feel sleepy, tired. But this breakfast business was Made in England like almost everything else that surrounded us, the exceptions being the sea, the sky, and the air we breathed.

At the time I saw this map—seeing England for the first time—I did not say to myself, "Ah, so that's what it looks like," because there was no longing in me to put a shape to those three words that ran through every part of my life, no matter how small; for me to have had such a longing would have meant that I lived in a certain atmosphere, an atmosphere in which those three words were felt as a burden. But I did not live in such an atmosphere. My father's brown felt hat would develop a hole in its crown, the lining would separate from the hat itself, and six weeks before he thought that he could not be seen wearing it—he was a very vain man— he would order another hat from England. And my mother taught me to eat my food in the English way: the knife in the right hand, the fork in the left, my elbows held still close to my side, the food carefully balanced on my fork and then brought up to my mouth. When I had finally mastered it, I overheard her saying to a friend, "Did you see how nicely she can eat?" But I knew then that I enjoyed my food more when I ate it with my bare hands, and I continued to do so when she wasn't looking. And when my teacher showed us the map, she asked us to study it carefully, because no test we would ever take would be complete without this statement: "Draw a map of England." 3

I did not know then that the statement "Draw a map of England" was something far worse than a declaration of war, for in fact a flat-out declaration of war would have put me on alert, and again in fact, there was no need for war—I had long ago been conquered. I did not know then that this statement was part of a process that would result in my erasure, not my physical erasure, but my erasure all the same. I did not know then that this statement was meant to make me feel in awe and small whenever I heard the word "England": awe at its existence, small because I was not from it. I did not know very much of anything then—certainly not what a blessing it was that I was unable to draw a map of England correctly. 4

After that there were many times of seeing England for the first time. I saw England in history. I knew the names of all the kings of England. I knew the names of their children, their wives, their disappointments, their triumphs, the names of people who betrayed them; I knew the dates on which they were born and the dates they died. I knew their conquests and was made to feel glad if I figured in them; I knew their defeats. I knew the 5 details of the year 1066 (the Battle of Hastings, the end of the reign of the Anglo-Saxon kings) before I knew the details of the year 1832 (the year slavery was abolished). It wasn't as bad as I make it sound now; it was worse. I did like so much hearing again and again how Alfred the Great, traveling in disguise, had been left to watch cakes, and because he wasn't used to this the cakes got burned, and Alfred burned his hands pulling them out of the fire, and the woman who had left him to watch the cakes screamed at him. I loved King Alfred. My grandfather was named after him; his son, my uncle, was named after King Alfred; my brother is named after King Alfred. And so there are three people in my family named after a man they have never met, a man who died over ten centuries ago. The first view I got of England then was not unlike the first view received by the person who named my grandfather.

This view, though—the naming of the kings, their deeds, their disap-   6
pointments—was the vivid view, the forceful view. There were other views, subtler ones, softer, almost not there—but these were the ones that made the most lasting impression on me, these were the ones that made me really feel like nothing. "When morning touched the sky" was one phrase, for no morning touched the sky where I lived. The mornings where I lived came on abruptly, with a shock of heat and loud noises. "Evening approaches" was another, but the evenings where I lived did not approach; in fact, I had no evening—I had night and I had day and they came and went in a mechanical way: on, off; on, off. And then there were gentle mountains and low blue skies and moors over which people took walks for nothing but pleasure, when where I lived a walk was an act of labor, a burden, some-thing only death or the automobile could relieve. And there were things that a small turn of a head could convey—entire worlds, whole lives would depend on this thing, a certain turn of a head. Everyday life could be quite tiring, more tiring than anything I was told not to do. I was told not to gossip, but they did that all the time. And they ate so much food, violating another of those rules they taught me: do not indulge in gluttony. And the foods they ate actually: if only sometime I could eat cold cuts after the-ater, cold cuts of lamb and mint sauce, and Yorkshire pudding and scones, and clotted cream, and sausages that came from up-country (imagine, "up-country"). And having troubling thoughts at twilight, a good time to have troubling thoughts, apparently; and servants who stole and left in the middle of a crisis, who were born with a limp or some other kind of defor-mity, not nourished properly in their mother's womb (that last part I fig-ured out for myself; the point was, oh to have an untrustworthy servant); and wonderful cobbled streets onto which solid front doors opened; and people whose eyes were blue and who had fair skins and who smelled only of lavender, or sometimes sweet pea or primrose. And those flowers with

those names: delphiniums, foxgloves, tulips, daffodils, floribunda, peonies; in bloom, a striking display, being cut and placed in large glass bowls, crystal, decorating rooms so large twenty families the size of mine could fit in comfortably but used only for passing through. And the weather was so remarkable because the rain fell gently always, only occasionally in deep gusts, and it colored the air various shades of gray, each an appealing shade for a dress to be worn when a portrait was being painted; and when it rained at twilight, wonderful things happened: people bumped into each other unexpectedly and that would lead to all sorts of turns of events—a plot, the mere weather caused plots. I saw that people rushed: they rushed to catch trains, they rushed toward each other and away from each other; they rushed and rushed and rushed. That word: rushed! I did not know what it was to do that. It was too hot to do that, and so I came to envy people who would rush, even though it had no meaning to me to do such a thing. But there they are again. They loved their children; their children were sent to their own rooms as a punishment, rooms larger than my entire house. They were special, everything about them said so, even their clothes; their clothes rustled, swished, soothed. The world was theirs, not mine; everything told me so.

If now as I speak of all this I give the impression of someone on the 7 outside looking in, nose pressed up against a glass window, that is wrong. My nose was pressed up against a glass window all right, but there was an iron vise at the back of my neck forcing my head to stay in place. To avert my gaze was to fall back into something from which I had been rescued, a hole filled with nothing, and that was the word for everything about me, nothing. The reality of my life was conquests, subjugation, humiliation, enforced amnesia. I was forced to forget. Just for instance, this: I lived in a part of St. John's, Antigua, called Ovals. Ovals was made up of five streets, each of them named after a famous English seaman—to be quite frank, an officially sanctioned criminal: Rodney Street (after George Rodney), Nelson Street (after Horatio Nelson), Drake Street (after Francis Drake), Hood Street, and Hawkins Street (after John Hawkins). But John Hawkins was knighted after a trip he made to Africa, opening up a new trade, the slave trade. He was then entitled to wear as his crest a Negro bound with a cord. Every single person living on Hawkins Street was descended from a slave. John Hawkins's ship, the one in which he transported the people he had bought and kidnapped, was called *The Jesus*. He later became the treasurer of the Royal Navy and rear admiral.

Again, the reality of my life, the life I led at the time I was being shown 8 these views of England for the first time, for the second time, for the one-hundred-millionth time, was this: the sun shone with what sometimes seemed to be a deliberate cruelty; we must have done something to deserve that. My dresses did not rustle in the evening air as I strolled to the theater (I had no evening, I had no theater; my dresses were made of a cheap cotton, the weave of which would give way after not too many washings). I got up in the morning, I did my chores (fetched water from the public pipe for my mother, swept the yard), I washed myself, I went to a woman to have my hair combed freshly every day (because before we were allowed into our classroom our teachers would inspect us, and children who had not bathed that day, or had dirt under their fingernails, or whose hair had not been combed anew that day, might not be allowed to attend class). I ate that breakfast. I walked to school. At school we gathered in an auditorium and sang a hymn, "All Things Bright and Beautiful," and looking down on us as we sang were portraits of the Queen of England and her husband; they wore jewels and medals and they smiled. I was a Brownie. At each meeting we would form a little group around a flagpole, and after raising the Union Jack, we would say, "I promise to do my best, to do my duty to God and the Queen, to help other people every day and obey the scouts' law."

Who were these people and why had I never seen them, I mean really 9 seen them, in the place where they lived? I had never been to England. No one I knew had ever been to England, or I should say, no one I knew had ever been and returned to tell me about it. All the people I knew who had gone to England had stayed there. Sometimes they left behind them their small children, never to see them again. England! I had seen England's representatives. I had seen the governor general at the public grounds at a ceremony celebrating the Queen's birthday. I had seen an old princess and I had seen a young princess. They had both been extremely not beautiful, but who of us would have told them that? I had never seen England, really seen it, I had only met a representative, seen a picture, read books, memorized its history. I had never set foot, my own foot, in it.

The space between the idea of something and its reality is always wide 10 and deep and dark. The longer they are kept apart—idea of thing, reality of thing—the wider the width, the deeper the depth, the thicker and darker the darkness. This space starts out empty, there is nothing in it, but it rapidly becomes filled up with obsession or desire or hatred or love—sometimes all of these things, sometimes some of these things, sometimes only one of these things. The existence of the world as I came to know it was a result of this: idea of thing over here, reality of thing way, way over there. There was Christopher Columbus, an unlikable man, an unpleasant man, a liar (and so, of course, a thief) surrounded by maps and schemes and plans, and there was the reality on the other side of that width, that depth, that darkness. He became obsessed, he became filled with desire, the hatred came later, love was never a part of it. Eventually, his idea met the longed-for reality. That the idea of something and its reality are often two completely different things is something no one ever remembers; and so when they meet and find that they are not compatible, the weaker of the two, idea or reality, dies. That idea Christopher Columbus had was more powerful than the reality he met, and so the reality he met died.

And so finally, when I was a grown-up woman, the mother of two chil- 11 dren, the wife of someone, a person who resides in a powerful country that takes up more than its fair share of a continent, the owner of a house with many rooms in it and of two automobiles, with the desire and will (which I very much act upon) to take from the world more than I give back to it, more than I deserve, more than I need, finally then, I saw England, the real England, not a picture, not a painting, not through a story in a book, but England, for the first time. In me, the space between the idea of it and its reality had become filled with hatred, and so when at last I saw it I wanted to take it into my hands and tear it into little pieces and then crumble it up as if it were clay, child's clay. That was impossible, and so I could only indulge in not-favorable opinions.

There were monuments everywhere; they commemorated victories, 12 battles fought between them and the people who lived across the sea from them, all vile people, fought over which of them would have dominion over the people who looked like me. The monuments were useless to them now, people sat on them and ate their lunch. They were like markers on an old useless trail, like a piece of old string tied to a finger to jog the memory, like old decoration in an old house, dirty, useless, in the way. Their skins were so pale, it made them look so fragile, so weak, so ugly. What if I had the power to simply banish them from their land, send boat after boatload of them on a voyage that in fact had no destination, force them to live in a place where the sun's presence was a constant? This would rid them of their pale complexion and make them look more like me, make them look more like the people I love and treasure and hold dear, and more like the people who occupy the near and far reaches of my imagination, my history, my geography, and reduce them and everything they have ever known to figurines as evidence that I was in divine favor, what if all this was in my power? Could I resist it? No one ever has.

And they were rude, they were rude to each other. They didn't like each 13 other very much. They didn't like each other in the way they didn't like me, and it occurred to me that their dislike for me was one of the few things they agreed on.

I was on a train in England with a friend, an English woman. Before we 14 were in England she liked me very much. In England she didn't like me at all. She didn't like the claim I said I had on England, she didn't like the views I had of England. I didn't like England, she didn't like England, but she didn't like me not liking it too. She said, "I want to show you my England, I want to show you the England that I know and love." I had told her many times before that I knew England and I didn't want to love it anyway. She no longer lived in England; it was her own country, but it had not been kind to her, so she left. On the train, the conductor was rude to her; she asked something, and he responded in a rude way. She became ashamed. She was ashamed at the way he treated her; she was ashamed at the way he behaved. "This is the new England," she said. But I liked the conductor being rude; his behavior seemed quite appropriate. Earlier this had happened: we had gone to a store to buy a shirt for my husband; it was meant to be a special present, a special shirt to wear on special occasions. This was a store where the Prince of Wales has his shirts made, but the shirts sold in this store are beautiful all the same. I found a shirt I thought my husband would like and I wanted to buy him a tie to go with it. When I couldn't decide which one to choose, the salesman showed me a new set. He was very pleased with these, he said, because they bore the crest of the Prince of Wales, and the Prince of Wales had never allowed his crest to decorate an article of clothing before. There was something in the way he said it; his tone was slavish, reverential, awed. It made me feel angry; I wanted to hit him. I didn't do that. I said, my husband and I hate princes, my husband would never wear anything that had a prince's anything on it. My friend stiffened. The salesman stiffened. They both drew themselves in, away from me. My friend told me that the prince was a symbol of her Englishness, and I could see that I had caused offense. I looked at her. She was an English person, the sort of English person I used to know at home, the sort who was nobody in England but somebody when they came to live among the people like me. There were many people I could have seen England with; that I was seeing it with this particular person, a person who reminded me of the people who showed me England long ago as I sat in church or at my desk, made me feel silent and afraid, for I wondered if, all these years of our friendship, I had had a friend or had been in the thrall of a racial memory.

I went to Bath—we, my friend and I, did this, but though we were together, I was no longer with her. The landscape was almost as familiar as my own hand, but I had never been in this place before, so how could that be again? And the streets of Bath were familiar, too, but I had never walked on them before. It was all those years of reading, starting with Roman Britain. Why did I have to know about Roman Britain? It was of no real use to me, a person living on a hot, drought-ridden island, and it is of no use to me now, and yet my head is filled with this nonsense, Roman Britain. In Bath, I drank tea in a room I had read about in a novel written in the eighteenth century. In this very same room, young women wearing those dresses that rustled and so on danced and flirted and sometimes disgraced

15

themselves with young men, soldiers, sailors, who were on their way to Bristol or someplace like that, so many places like that where so many adventures, the outcome of which was not good for me, began. Bristol, England. A sentence that began "That night the ship sailed from Bristol, England" would end not so good for me. And then I was driving through the countryside in an English motorcar, on narrow winding roads, and they were so familiar, though I had never been on them before; and through little villages the names of which I somehow knew so well though I had never been there before. And the countryside did have all those hedges and hedges, fields hedged in. I was marveling at all the toil of it, the planting of the hedges to begin with and then the care of it, all that clipping, year after year of clipping, and I wondered at the lives of the people who would have to do this, because wherever I see and feel the hands that hold up the world, I see and feel myself and all the people who look like me. And I said, "Those hedges" and my friend said that someone, a woman named Mrs. Rothchild, worried that the hedges weren't being taken care of properly; the farmers couldn't afford or find the help to keep up the hedges, and often they replaced them with wire fencing. I might have said to that, well if Mrs. Rothchild doesn't like the wire fencing, why doesn't she take care of the hedges herself, but I didn't. And then in those fields that were now hemmed in by wire fencing that a privileged woman didn't like was planted a vile yellow flowering bush that produced an oil, and my friend said that Mrs. Rothchild didn't like this either; it ruined the English countryside, it ruined the traditional look of the English countryside.

It was not at that moment that I wished every sentence, everything I 16 knew, that began with England would end with "and then it all died; we don't know how, it just all died." At that moment, I was thinking, who are these people who forced me to think of them all the time, who forced me to think that the world I knew was incomplete, or without substance, or did not measure up because it was not England; that I was incomplete, or without substance, and did not measure up because I was not English. Who were these people? The person sitting next to me couldn't give me a clue; no one person could. In any case, if I had said to her, I find England ugly, I hate England; the weather is like a jail sentence, the English are a very ugly people, the food in England is like a jail sentence, the hair of English people is so straight, so dead looking, the English have an unbearable smell so different from the smell of people I know, real people of course, she would have said that I was a person full of prejudice. Apart from the fact that it is I—that is, the people who look like me—who made her aware of the unpleasantness of such a thing, the idea of such a thing, prejudice, she would have been only partly right, sort of right: I may be capable of prejudice, but my prejudices have no weight to them, my prejudices have no force behind them, my prejudices remain opinions, my prejudices remain my personal opinion. And a great feeling of rage and disappointment came over me as I looked at England, my head full of personal opinions that could not have public, my public, approval. The people I come from are powerless to do evil on grand scale.

The moment I wished every sentence, everything I knew, that began   17 with England would end with "and then it all died, we don't know how, it just all died" was when I saw the white cliffs of Dover. I had sung hymns and recited poems that were about a longing to see the white cliffs of Dover again. At the time I sang the hymns and recited the poems, I could really long to see them again because I had never seen them at all, nor had anyone around me at the time. But there we were, groups of people longing for something we had never seen. And so there they were, the white cliffs, but they were not that pearly majestic thing I used to sing about, that thing that created such a feeling in these people that when they died in the place where I lived they had themselves buried facing a direction that would allow them to see the white cliffs of Dover when they were resurrected, as surely they would be. The white cliffs of Dover, when finally I saw them, were cliffs, but they were not white; you would only call them that if the word "white" meant something special to you; they were dirty and they were steep; they were so steep, the correct height from which all my views of England, starting with the map before me in my classroom and ending with the trip I had just taken, should jump and die and disappear forever.

Thinking about the Essay

1. Based on your careful reading of this essay, summarize Kincaid's understanding of cultural imperialism. Does the fact that she writes about England and not the United States diminish the importance of her argument? Explain.

2. Kincaid divides her essay into two major parts. What is her intention? What is the effect?

3. Kincaid establishes several contrasts between England and Antigua. What are they? How does this comparative method serve to organize the essay?

4. The writer's paragraphs tend to be quite long. Analyze the way she develops her introductory and concluding paragraphs. Also examine the longest paragraph in the essay (paragraph 6), and explain how she achieves coherence in the presentation of her ideas.

5. How does Kincaid's use of the personal voice—the "I" point of view—affect the tone and purpose of her essay? By adopting this personal perspective, what does Kincaid want the audience to infer about her and her experience of cultural imperialism?

Responding in Writing

6. Write an account of your early education. What did you learn about the country where you were born and its relationship to the rest of the world? How did your early education influence or mold your global understanding today?

7. Write an essay analyzing Kincaid's various views on England and what they ultimately mean to her. Has she convinced you about her perspective on the subject? Why or why not? Be certain to deal with her concluding paragraph and her reference to the "white cliffs of Dover."

8. Imagine that you live in a country that has a history of colonization. (Perhaps you or your family has actually experienced this condition.) What would your attitude toward the colonizing or globalizing power be? Write a paper exploring this real or imaginary situation.

Networking

9. With three other class members, draw up a complete list of the contrasts that Kincaid establishes between Antigua and England. Arrive at a consensus about why she is so preoccupied with England—not just as a child but also as an adult writing about the experience. Select one member of your group as a representative in a class panel discussion that talks about these contrasts.

10. Go online and research information about Antigua. Evaluate Kincaid's impressions of her native island with what you have learned about it.

The Clash of Civilizations: Is Conflict Avoidable?

The spread around the world of Coca-Cola, Hollywood films, and rock and roll—all the trappings of American popular culture—combined with the broader economic and political forces generated by America's superpower status has helped fuel what we call the "clash of civilizations." The phrase, coined by the American political scientist Samuel Huntington, suggests that we are in a new era in which the forces of globalization have brought entire civilizations, rather than separate nations, into conflict with each other. The nature of this conflict goes to the heart of what we mean by cultural identity—who am I, and where do I belong?—and how we see ourselves in relation to our civilization and other civilizations we come into contact with.

According to Huntington, whose article appeared in the summer 1993 issue of *Foreign Affairs* and subsequently in an expanded book, *The Clash of Civilizations and the Remaking of World Order* (1996), the world can be divided into seven or perhaps eight contemporary civilizations: Western, Latin American, Islamic, Sinic or Chinese (which includes China, Taiwan, Korea, and Vietnam), Japanese, Hindu, Orthodox (Russia, Serbia, and Greece), and African. "Human history," writes Huntington, "is the history of civilizations. It is impossible to think of the development of humanity in any other terms." Historically there have been numerous conflicts between and among these civilizations. However, Huntington's thesis is that with the rise of the West since 1500, other civilizations—notably the Islamic and Chinese—have resented this "rise" and reacted against it. Furthermore, in the inevitable cycles of history, other civilizations will rise in reaction to the dominance of the Western world and become dominant themselves, thus leading to a new clash with global consequences.

Huntington's broad thesis has come under scrutiny and attack on all sides, and some of his critics appear in this chapter. Yet it could be argued that what we see most clearly in the world today—the conflict between

AP Photo/Amit Shabi

Palestinian schoolgirls walk past Israeli soldiers in Hebron, one of the most contested and violent cities of the West Bank—a region jointly controlled by Israel and the Palestinian Authority. The tomb of Abraham, considered the patriarch of both Judaism and Islam, is located in Hebron; rivalries here extend for millennia.

Thinking about the Image

1. What elements make this photograph especially compelling? Consider the expressions on the faces of the schoolgirls, the size and positioning of the soldiers, and the details of the setting.
2. Do you think that the photographer reinforces conventional depictions of the Arab–Israeli conflict in the American media, or is the photographer trying to present a different perspective? Explain your response.
3. Do you believe that the photographer advances an argument concerning Israel's occupation of the West Bank? Why or why not?

the Western and Islamic worlds or the gradual ascendancy of China as the next major world power—confirms Huntington's basic claim. Conversely, if you think that reality actually contradicts Huntington's thesis, then you could argue that Western forms of culture, democracy, and modernization actually are cutting across all civilizations and triumphing over them. The social scientist Benjamin Barber maintains that there will be raging conflicts among civilizations in the future, but that "McWorld," as he terms the West, will triumph over "Jihad." Thus Western civilization will not decline but will defeat the forces of fundamentalism and totalitarianism.

The essays in this chapter deal with the clash of civilizations from a variety of perspectives. We can't deny that conflicts among civilizations exist; some are religious, others ethnic, still others cultural. The writers invite us to consider our own loyalties, and whether we associate with one culture, nation, or civilization or with many. Are there commonalities among civilizations, or must we be forever in conflict? Must we always deal with threats to our gods, our ancestors, our civilization? Or, in a world of seven billion people, are there tangible signs that we needn't think of "inferior" and "superior" civilizations but rather of a world showing signs of heightened tolerance, integration, and harmony? The way we answer these questions will determine the fabric of future civilizations.

American Dream Boat

K. OANH HA

> K. Oanh Ha was born in Vietnam in 1973. As she relates in the following essay, she left Vietnam with her family in July 1979, journeying with other "boat people" to the United States. Raised in California, she is a graduate of UCLA with a BA in English and American literature. She has covered globalization for KQED radio in San Francisco since 2005. In 2010, Ha joined Bloomberg News as its Vietnam bureau chief. Her stories explore the business of globalization as well as its social and cultural impact. Prior to working in radio, she was a staff writer for the *San Jose Mercury News*. She is working on a novel that is based loosely on her family's escape from Vietnam. In this personal narrative, published in *Modern Maturity* in 2002, Ha provides a gentle affirmation of how—when it comes to love—civilizations need not clash.

Before Reading

Have you dated someone whose background represents a culture or civilization entirely different from yours? If not, do you know of a couple who signify this coming together of civilizations? How do you—or they—work out any "clashes"?

The wedding day was only two weeks away when my parents called   1
with yet another request. In accordance with Vietnamese custom, they fully expected Scott Harris, my fiancé, and his family to visit our family on

K. Oanh Ha, "American Dream Boat," *Modern Maturity*, May–June 2002, pp. 45–47, 84. Copyright © 2002. Reprinted by permission of the author.

the morning of the wedding, bearing dowry gifts of fruit, candies, jewelry, and a pig, in an elaborate procession.

"But it's not going to mean anything to Scott or his family. They're not Vietnamese!" I protested. My parents were adamant: "Scott is marrying a Vietnamese. If he wants to marry you, he'll honor our traditions." 2

Maybe there's no such thing as a stress-free wedding. Small or large, there's bound to be pressure. But our February 12 wedding was a large do-it-yourselfer that required a fusion of Vietnamese and American traditions—a wedding that forced me and my parents to wrestle with questions about our identities, culture, and place in America. After nearly 20 years here, my family, and my parents in particular, were determined to have a traditional Vietnamese wedding of sorts, even if their son-in-law and Vietnam-born, California-raised daughter are as American as they can be. 3

And so I grudgingly called Scott that night to describe the wedding procession and explain the significance of the ritual. It's a good thing that he is a patient, easygoing man. "I'll bring the pig," he said, "but I'm worried it'll make a mess in the car." 4

"Oh! It's a *roasted pig*," I told him, laughing. 5

I was six years old when my family fled Vietnam in July 1979, just one family among the thousands who collectively became known as the "boat people," families who decided it was better to risk the very real possibility of death at sea than to live under Communist rule. But, of course, I never understood the politics then. I was just a child following my parents. 6

My memories are sketchy. There was the time that Thai pirates wielding saber-like machetes raided our boat. Two years ago, I told my mother, Kim Hanh Nguyen, how I remembered a woman dropping a handful of jewelry into my rice porridge during the raid with the instructions to keep eating. "That was no woman," my mother said. "That was me!" When we reached the refugee camp in Kuala Lumpur, my mother used the wedding ring and necklace to buy our shelter. 7

In September 1980, we arrived in Santa Ana, California, in Orange County, now home to the largest Vietnamese community outside of Vietnam. Those who had left in 1975, right after the end of the war and the American withdrawal, had been well-educated, wealthy, and connected with the military. My family was part of the wave of boat people—mostly middle-class and with little education—who sought refuge in America. 8

For nearly a year after we arrived, we crowded into the same three-bedroom apartment, all 13 of us: brothers, sisters, cousins, uncles, aunts, sisters-in-law, and my father's mother. There were only four of us children in my immediate family then, three born in Vietnam and one born shortly after our resettlement in the U.S. 9

We started school and watched Mr. Rogers on PBS in the afternoons, 10 grew to love hamburgers and ketchup and longed to lose our accents. We older kids did lose our accents—and those who came later never had accents to begin with because they were born here. When we first came, I was the oldest of three children, all born in Vietnam. Now I have seven siblings, 22 years separating me from my youngest brother, who will start kindergarten in the fall.

In some ways, I was the stereotypical Asian nerd. I took honors classes, 11 received good grades, and played the violin and cello. But there was a part of me that also yearned to be as American as my blond-haired neighbors across the street. I joined the school's swim and tennis teams, participated in speech competitions (which were attended by mostly white students) and worshipped Esprit and Guess. My first serious boyfriend was white but most of my friends were Asians who were either born in the U.S. or immigrated when they were very young. None of us had accents and we rarely spoke our native languages around one another. The last thing we wanted to be mistaken for was FOBs—fresh off the boat. I even changed my name to Kyrstin, unaware of its Nordic roots.

I wanted so badly to be a full-fledged American, whatever that meant. 12 At home though, my parents pushed traditional Vietnamese values. I spent most of my teenage years baby-sitting and had to plead with my then overly strict parents to let me out of the house. "Please, please. I just want to be like any other American kid."

My parents didn't understand. "You'll always be Vietnamese. No one's 13 going to look at you and say you're an American," was my mother's often-heard refrain.

I saw college as my escape, the beginning of the trip I would undertake 14 on my own. We had come to America as a family but it was time I navigated alone. College was my flight from the house that always smelled of fish sauce and jasmine tea.

At UCLA, I dated the man who would become my husband. Though 15 he's 17 years older than I am, my parents seemed to be more concerned with the cultural barriers than our age difference. "White Americans are fickle. They don't understand commitment and family responsibility like we Asians do," I was told.

Soon after I announced my engagement, my father, Minh Phu Ha, and 16 I had a rare and intimate conversation. "I'm just worried for you," he said. "All the Vietnamese women I know who have married whites are divorced from them. Our cultures are too far apart."

My father, I think, is worried that none of his kids will marry 17 Vietnamese. My sisters are dating non-Vietnamese Asians while my brother is dating a white American. "It's just that with a Vietnamese son-in-law, I can talk to him," my father explained to me one day. "A Vietnamese son-in-law would call me 'Ba' and not by my first name."

Although my parents have come to terms with having Scott as their 18 son-in-law and to the prospect of grandchildren who will be racially mixed, there are still times when Scott comes to visit that there are awkward silences. There are still many cultural barriers.

I still think of what it all means to marry a white American. I worry 19 that my children won't be able to speak Vietnamese and won't appreciate that part of their heritage. I also wonder if somehow this is the ultimate fulfillment of a latent desire to be "American."

Vietnamese-Americans, like Chinese-Americans, Indian-Americans, 20 and other assimilated immigrants, often speak of leading hyphenated lives, of feet that straddle both cultures. I've always been proud of being Vietnamese. As my family and I discussed and heatedly debated what the wedding event was going to look like, I began to realize just how "American" I had become.

And yet there was no denying the pull of my Vietnamese roots. Four 21 months before the wedding, I traveled back to Vietnam for the second time since our family's escape. It was a trip I had planned for more than a year. I was in Saigon, the city of my birth, to research and write a novel that loosely mirrors the story of my own family and our journey from Vietnam. The novel is my tribute to my family and our past. I'm writing it for myself as much as for my younger siblings, so they'll know what our family's been through.

I returned to Vietnam to connect with something I can't really name 22 but know I lost when we left 20 years ago. I was about to start a new journey with the marriage ahead, but I needed to come back to the place where my family's journey began.

Scott came along for the first two weeks and met my extended family. 23 They all seemed to approve, especially when he showed he could eat pungent fish and shrimp sauce like any other Vietnamese.

During my time there I visited often with family members and talked 24 about the past. I saw the hospital where I was born, took a walk through our old house, chatted with my father's old friends. The gaps in the circle of my hyphenated life came closer together with every new Vietnamese word that I learned, with every Vietnamese friend that I made.

I also chose the fabric for the tailoring of the *ao dai*, the traditional 25 Vietnamese dress of a long tunic over flowing pants, which I would change into at the reception. I had my sisters' bridesmaid gowns made. And I had a velvet ao dai made for my 88-year-old maternal grandmother, *Bâ Ngoai*, to wear to the wedding of her oldest grandchild. "My dream is to see you on your wedding day and eat at your wedding feast," she had told me several times.

Bâ Ngoai came to the U.S. in 1983, three years after my family landed 26
in Orange County as war refugees. As soon as we got to the United States,
my mother filed immigration papers for her. Bâ Ngoai made that journey
at age 73, leaving the only home she had known to be with my mother, her
only child. Bâ Ngoai nurtured and helped raise us grandchildren.

I had extended my stay in Vietnam. Several days after my original 27
departure date, I received a phone call. Bâ Ngoai had died. I flew home
carrying her ao dai. We buried her in it.

In Vietnamese tradition, one is in mourning for three years after the loss 28
of a parent or grandparent. Out of respect and love for the deceased, or *hieu*,
decorum dictates that close family members can't get married until after the
mourning period is over. But my wedding was only a month and a half away.

On the day we buried my grandmother, my family advised me to burn 29
the white cloth headband that symbolized my grief. By burning it, I ended
my official mourning.

Through my tears I watched the white cloth become wispy ashes. My 30
family was supportive. "It's your duty to remember and honor her," my
father told me. "But you also need to move forward with your life."

On the morning of our wedding, Scott's family stood outside our house 31
in a line bearing dowry gifts. Inside the house, Scott and I lighted incense in
front of the family altar. Holding the incense between our palms, we bowed
to my ancestors and asked for their blessings. I looked at the photo of Bâ
Ngoai and knew she had to be smiling.

Thinking about the Essay

1. How do you interpret the title? What aspects of the essay does it capture?

2. There are several characters in this essay. Who are they? How are they described? What sort of persona does Ha create for herself as the "I" narrator?

3. Why does Ha begin the essay in the present and then shift to the past? Trace the narrative pattern throughout her essay.

4. Often when you write a personal essay, it is valuable to create a central conflict. What is the conflict (or conflicts) in this selection? How does Ha develop and resolve it? Does this conflict lead to a thesis? Why or why not?

5. Explain the various moods and tones that Ha imbues her narrative with. Do they "clash" or not? Are they finally reconciled? Justify your response.

Responding in Writing

6. In a brief essay, explain why Ha's essay tells us about the clash of civilizations and how we might resolve it.

7. Write a narrative essay in which you tell of a relationship in which the people come from different civilizations. You can base this essay on personal

experience, the experience of family or friends, or a situation drawn from television or film.

8. Do you think that the narrator and her husband will have a happy marriage? Why or why not? Cite what you have learned about them in the essay as support for your response.

Networking

9. In a group of four, discuss the relationship between Scott and "Kyrstin" Oanh. Do you think it is healthy and viable, or do you sense potential problems? Summarize your decision for the rest of the class.

10. Search the Internet for more information on the Vietnamese boat people. Where have they settled in the United States? How do they preserve their culture and civilization? How often do they intermarry with Americans outside their background? Discuss your findings with the class.

The Light

Hisham Matar

Hisham Matar is a Libyan novelist, poet, and essayist who was born in New York City in 1950, the son of an official who worked for the Libyan mission to the United Nations. At the age of three, Hisham returned with his parents to Tripoli, but in 1979 his father fled to Cairo with the family to avoid persecution by the Gaddafi regime. (Libyan agents kidnapped his father in Cairo in 1990; he has not been seen since.) In 1986, Matar moved to London, where he completed an undergraduate degree in architecture and an MA in design. His debut novel, *In the Country of Men*, was shortlisted for England's prestigious Man Booker Prize in 2006. Matar's second novel, *Anatomy of a Disappearance*, was published in 2011 while he was a visiting professor at Barnard College in New York. Matar's essays have appeared in several major journals in the United States and Great Britain. In this essay from the September 12, 2011, issue of *The New Yorker*, Hisham uses a vivid poetic style to expose conflicts between and within clashing civilizations.

Before Reading

Can a landscape—a sunny seashore or a bleak stretch of terrain—affect one's thoughts and emotions? Can the environment also influence one's cultural and political behavior? Why or why not?

There is an hour in the Arab Mediterranean when the sun, as if in a state   1
of indecision, hovers a palm's length above the horizon. What a few
hours earlier was a blinding star is now weak enough to look at directly.
Its sideways light holds everything in a soft orange glow: the color of reticence and doubt, the color of my generation of Libyans and the historical
moment we inherited. But it also signals hope, the possibility of a different
future, where we might one day live free from totalitarian rule, and independent of the intrusive foreign powers that colluded with our dictators.
For our entire lives we have been held between these two forces, and this
late-afternoon light, different from anywhere else in the world, seemed
suggestive both of our entrapment and of our yearning.

We lived out our lives in a theatre of the macabre and the absurd.   2
We would listen to endless speeches, and we would clap. We endured
the disappearances, the assassinations, and never managed to completely
ignore the sweet-colored posters of our grinning leaders. On the outside,
the countries we admired, Europe and America, paid us the insult of
befriending our dictators and, when it came to our suffering, looking
the other way. It did not escape us that these external powers exercised
a new form of political control over our affairs. We called it "remote-
control colonialism." I still remember a speech by the late Egyptian President Anwar al-Sadat. I was a boy, and we were by the sea. Someone
was grilling fish—I remember the smell of fish. Of the speech itself, all
that remains in my head is one line, spoken by Sadat in the tone of an
irritated adult: "99.9 per cent of the playing cards are with America."
I remembered the shared silence among the people sitting around me,
and what it meant—the realization that America's blessing was needed
for all Egypt's dealings with the world. Even I understood the metaphor:
the "playing cards" were not only our present but also our future—in
short, our fate.

Save for a few extraordinary exceptions—Palestine, for example—my   3
generation was born well after foreign occupiers had left our lands. Yet
the independence we inherited was elusive, as elusive as our late afternoons. The older and bloodier our dictators became, the more grandi-
ose was their language. To maintain their legitimacy, they liked to recall
darker times, when the "boot of the European pressed on our necks."
The words they chose, their posturing, smothered us. Our leaders were
not only violent; they also corrupted our imagination. Dictatorship is the
triumph of kitsch, as Ryszard Kapuscinski noted, and my generation has

been aggressively and comprehensively exposed to the conning powers of this sort of bloodstained kitsch. Our lives have been lived within its logic. It decided what we read, watched, and heard. It influenced even the words we chose to express love, or how we felt about the moon and the sunset. It intervened whenever we veered off the path. It spoke in one note, monotonous and intolerant. When we hesitated, it did not explain; it simply repeated its orders, with greater ferocity. Worst of all, we slowly learned to obey.

Even when I was a young boy playing in the garden of our house in 4
Tripoli in the late afternoon, while my family and the whole world, it seemed, napped, I found that afternoon light both mesmeric and unsettling. It was only during this hour that the audacious yet cynical political language of our leaders fell silent. It was the hour most appropriate for contemplating the conundrum we were in; for realizing that the dictator had perfected his art and that, paradoxically, now that we were "independent," foreign intrusion in our politics and our economics was even more sinister, because it seemed impossible to resist. These circumstances inspired self-loathing in us, a sort of Beckettian pessimism: We can't be tools, we are tools, we will be tools.

One of the more perverse symptoms of this despair was extremism: 5
inarticulate, devastating, and violent. It expressed, in the most grotesque way, our hopelessness as well as the bleak landscape of our political imagination. It disturbed us and silenced us, making us even more reticent in the modern world. In hindsight, shame was not an inappropriate response.

Like picadors taunting a wounded bull, we watched as all the Western 6
silliness that we were already used to grew more heightened. We saw Western commentators become hysterical whenever the subject of Islam came up. Reductive interpreters of Arab life and history, people such as Bernard Lewis, were suddenly in vogue again. But, at last, when our isolation and our despondency became utterly desperate, we rose.

The Arab Spring is a powerful and compelling response not only to an 7
age of tyranny but also to the remnant chains of imperial influence. The final outcome—if there ever is such a thing as a final outcome in history—of our revolutions remains unclear. We might not succeed in building a better future. But no one can question the authenticity of our desire, or how much we are prepared to sacrifice for the opportunity to gain self-determination, dignity, and justice. Although the light persists, it is no longer melancholy. It suddenly seems an ally, its weak warmth on the skin comforting. When the sun sets now, our nights are calm. And we pray; farewell to the abyss.

Thinking about the Essay

1. In what way is the title for the essay symbolic? What types of **figurative language** does Matar use to develop and enhance his key symbol? How does his focus on the light of the Arab Mediterranean produce a specific mood?

2. State Matar's claim or major proposition. Where does his claim appear most clearly? What minor propositions does he develop?

3. What purpose might he have for incorporating anecdotes from his childhood?

4. Explain the allusions to Anwar al-Sadat (paragraph 2), Ryszard Kapuscinski (paragraph 3), "Beckettian pessimism" (paragraph 4), and Bernard Lewis (paragraph 6). How do these allusions contribute to your understanding of the writer and his goal in composing this essay?

5. Analyze the comparative framework of this essay. What are the main elements and ideas that Matar compares and contrasts?

Responding in Writing

6. Write an expository essay in which you respond to Matar's statement, "The Arab Spring is a powerful and compelling response not only to an age of tyranny but also to the remnant chains of imperial influence."

7. Argue for or against the proposition that environment is destiny.

8. Write a narrative and descriptive essay in which you tell of a time and event that helped you to understand conflicts between peoples, cultures, and civilizations.

Networking

9. In small groups, discuss the interaction of poetry and prose in "The Light." Evaluate the success of Matar's approach to writing, and share your evaluation with the class.

10. With several classmates, create a Facebook group that raises awareness about current political conditions in one nation affected by the Arab Spring.

America's 'Oh Sh*T' Moment

NIALL FERGUSON

Niall Ferguson was born in 1964 in Scotland. In 1985, he received his PhD from Magdalen College, Oxford. A writer and television commentator on contemporary international politics and economics, he is currently the Laurence A. Tisch Professor of History at Harvard University, a resident faculty member of the Minda de Gunzburg Center for European Studies, a Senior Research Fellow of Jesus

College, Oxford University, and a Senior Fellow of the Hoover Institution, Stanford University. His publications include the internationally acclaimed *The Pity of War: Explaining World War One* (1999), *Empire: The Rise and Demise of the British World Order and the Lessons for Global Power* (2003), *Colossus: The Rise and Fall of the American Empire* (2004), and *Civilization: The West and the Rest* (2011), which in 2012 was made into a PBS television series. Ferguson champions *counterfactual history*, also known as speculative or hypothetical history, which practices imagining what might have happened in history to understand what actually happened. To him individuals, not great forces, make history. In this 2011 article he projects the sharp decline of America and suggests how to avoid the imminent collapse.

Before Reading

What is an "oh sh*t moment"? Whether or not you have heard or read that phrase before, write down your connotation of the words and what you think they might mean.

Don't call me a "declinist." I really don't believe the United States—or Western civilization, more generally—is in some kind of gradual, inexorable decline.   1

But that's not because I am one of those incorrigible optimists who agree with Winston Churchill that the United States will always do the right thing, albeit when all other possibilities have been exhausted.   2

In my view, civilizations don't rise, fall, and then gently decline, as inevitably and predictably as the four seasons or the seven ages of man. History isn't one smooth, parabolic curve after another. Its shape is more like an exponentially steepening slope that quite suddenly drops off like a cliff.   3

If you don't know what I mean, pay a visit to Machu Picchu, the lost city of the Incas. In 1530 the Incas were the masters of all they surveyed from the heights of the Peruvian Andes. Within less than a decade, foreign invaders with horses, gunpowder, and lethal diseases had smashed their empire to smithereens. Today tourists gawp at the ruins that remain.   4

The notion that civilizations don't decline but collapse inspired the anthropologist Jared Diamond's 2005 book, *Collapse*. But Diamond   5

Niall Ferguson, "America's Oh Sh*t Moment", (*Newsweek*, November 7/14, 2011), 36–39.

focused, fashionably, on man-made environmental disasters as the causes of collapse. As a historian, I take a broader view. My point is that when you look back on the history of past civilizations, a striking feature is the speed with which most of them collapsed, regardless of the cause.

The Roman Empire didn't decline and fall sedately, as historians used   6
to claim. It collapsed within a few decades in the early fifth century, tipped over the edge of chaos by barbarian invaders and internal divisions. In the space of a generation, the vast imperial metropolis of Rome fell into disrepair, the aqueducts broken, the splendid marketplaces deserted.

The Ming dynasty's rule in China also fell apart with extraordinary   7
speed in the mid-17th century, succumbing to internal strife and external invasion. Again, the transition from equipoise to anarchy took little more than a decade.

A more recent and familiar example of precipitous decline is, of course,   8
the collapse of the Soviet Union. And, if you still doubt that collapse comes suddenly, just think of how the postcolonial dictatorships of North Africa and the Middle East imploded this year. Twelve months ago, Messrs. Ben Ali, Mubarak, and Gaddafi seemed secure in their gaudy palaces. Here yesterday, gone today.

What all these collapsed powers have in common is that the complex   9
social systems that underpinned them suddenly ceased to function. One minute rulers had legitimacy in the eyes of their people; the next they didn't.

This process is a familiar one to students of financial markets. Even   10
as I write, it is far from clear that the European Monetary Union can be salvaged from the dramatic collapse of confidence in the fiscal policies of its peripheral member states. In the realm of power, as in the domain of the bond vigilantes, you're fine until you're not fine—and when you're not fine, you're suddenly in a terrifying death spiral.

Remember that poster that used to hang in every college dorm, of a   11
runaway steam train that has crashed through the wall of a rail station and hit the street below, nose first? The caption was: "Oh sh*t!" I believe it's time to ask how close the United States is to the "Oh sh*t!" moment—the moment we suddenly crash downward like that train.

The West first surged ahead of the Rest after about 1500 thanks to a   12
series of institutional innovations that I call the "killer applications":

1. *Competition.* Europe was politically fragmented into multiple monarchies and republics, which were in turn internally divided into competing corporate entities, among them the ancestors of modern business corporations.
2. *The Scientific Revolution.* All the major 17th-century breakthroughs in mathematics, astronomy physics, chemistry, and biology happened in Western Europe.

3. *The Rule of Law and Representative Government.* An optimal system of social and political order emerged in the English-speaking world, based on private-property rights and the representation of property owners in elected legislatures.
4. *Modern Medicine.* Nearly all the major 19th- and 20th-century break-throughs in health care were made by Western Europeans and North Americans.
5. *The Consumer Society.* The Industrial Revolution took place where there was both a supply of productivity-enhancing technologies and a demand for more, better, and cheaper goods, beginning with cotton garments.
6. *The Work Ethic.* Westerners were the first people in the world to combine more extensive and intensive labor with higher savings rates, permitting sustained capital accumulation.

For hundreds of years, these killer apps were essentially monopolized by Europeans and their cousins who settled in North America and Australasia. They are the best explanation for what economic historians call "the great divergence": the astonishing gap that arose between Western standards of living and those in the rest of the world. 13

In 1500 the average Chinese was richer than the average North American. By the late 1970s the American was more than 20 times richer than the Chinese. Westerners not only grew richer than "Resterners." They grew taller, healthier, and longer-lived. They also grew more powerful. By the early 20th century, just a dozen Western empires—including the United States—controlled 58 percent of the world's land surface and population, and a staggering 74 percent of the global economy. 14

Beginning with Japan, however, one non-Western society after another has worked out that these apps can be downloaded and installed in non-Western operating systems. That explains about half the catching up that we have witnessed in our lifetimes, especially since the onset of economic reforms in China in 1978. 15

Now, I am not one of those people filled with angst at the thought of a world in which the average American is no longer vastly richer than the average Chinese. Indeed, I welcome the escape of hundreds of millions of Asians from poverty, not to mention the improvements we are seeing in South America and parts of Africa. But there is a second, more insidious cause of the "great reconvergence," which I do deplore—and that is the tendency of Western societies to delete their own killer apps. 16

Ask yourself: who's got the work ethic now? The average South Korean works about 39 percent more hours per week than the average American. The school year in South Korea is 220 days long, compared with 180 days here. And you don't have to spend too long at any major U.S. university to know which students really drive themselves: the Asians and Asian-Americans. 17

The consumer society? Did you know that 26 of the 30 biggest shop- 18 ping malls in the world are now in emerging markets, mostly in Asia? Only three are in the United States. And, boy, do they look forlorn these days, as maxed-out Americans struggle to pay down their debts.

Modern medicine? Well, we certainly outspend everyone else. As a 19 share of gross domestic product, the United States spends twice what Japan spends on health care and more than three times what China spends. Yet life expectancy in the U.S. has risen from 70 to 78 in the past 50 years, compared with leaps from 68 to 83 in Japan and from 43 to 73 in China.

The rule of law? For a real eye-opener, take a look at the latest World 20 Economic Forum (WEF) Executive Opinion Survey. On no fewer than 15 of 16 different issues relating to property rights and governance, the United States fares worse than Hong Kong. Indeed, the U.S. makes the global top 20 in only one area: investor protection. On every other count, its repu- tation is shockingly bad. The U.S. ranks 86th in the world for the costs imposed on business by organized crime, 50th for public trust in the ethics of politicians, 42nd for various forms of bribery and 40th for standards of auditing and financial reporting.

What about science? It's certainly true that U.S.-based scientists con- 21 tinue to walk off with plenty of Nobel Prizes each year. But Nobel win- ners are old men. The future belongs not to them but to today's teenagers. Here's another striking statistic. Every three years the Organization of Economic Cooperation and Development's Program for International Stu- dent Assessment tests the educational attainment of 15-year-olds around the world. The latest data on "mathematical literacy" reveal that the gap between the world leaders—the students of Shanghai and Singapore—and their American counterparts is now as big as the gap between U.S. kids and teenagers in Albania and Tunisia.

The late, lamented Steve Jobs convinced Americans that the future 22 would be "Designed by Apple in California. Assembled in China." Yet statistics from the World Intellectual Property Organization show that already more patents originate in Japan than in the U.S., that South Korea overtook Germany to take third place in 2005, and that China is poised to overtake Germany too.

Finally, there's competition, the original killer app that sent the frag- 23 mented West down a completely different path from monolithic imperial China. Well, the WEF has conducted a comprehensive Global Competi- tiveness survey every year since 1979. Since the current methodology was adopted in 2004, the United States' average competitiveness score has fallen from 5.82 to 5.43, one of the steepest declines among developed economies. China's score, meanwhile, has leapt up from 4.29 to 4.90.

And it's not only that we're becoming less competitive abroad. Perhaps 24
more disturbing is the decline of meaningful competition at home, as the
social mobility of the postwar era has given way to an extraordinary social
polarization. You don't have to be an Occupy Wall Street leftist to believe
that the American super-rich elite—the 1 percent that collects 20 percent
of the income—has become dangerously divorced from the rest of society,
especially from the underclass at the bottom of the income distribution.

But if we are headed toward collapse, what would an American "Oh 25
sh*t!" moment look like? An upsurge in civil unrest and crime, as happened in the 1970s? A loss of faith on the part of investors and a sudden
Greek-style leap in government borrowing costs? How about a spike of
violence in the Middle East, from Iraq to Afghanistan, as insurgents cap-
italize on our troop withdrawals? Or a paralyzing cyberattack from the
rising Asian superpower we complacently underrate?

Is there anything we can do to prevent such disasters? Social scien- 26
tist Charles Murray calls for a "civic great awakening"—a return to the
original values of the American republic. He's got a point. Far more than
in Europe, most Americans remain instinctively loyal to the killer applications of Western ascendancy, from competition all the way through to the
work ethic. They know the country has the right software. They just can't
understand why it's running so damn slowly.

What we need to do is to delete the viruses that have crept into our 27
system: the anticompetitive quasi monopolies that blight everything from
banking to public education; the politically correct pseudosciences and soft
subjects that deflect good students away from hard science; the lobbyists
who subvert the rule of law for the sake of the special interests they represent—to say nothing of our crazily dysfunctional system of health care,
our overleveraged personal finances and our newfound unemployment
ethic.

Then we need to download the updates that are running more success- 28
fully in other countries, from Finland to New Zealand, from Denmark to
Hong Kong, from Singapore to Sweden.

And finally we need to reboot our whole system. 29

I refuse to accept that Western civilization is like some hopeless old 30
version of Microsoft DOS, doomed to freeze, then crash. I still cling to the
hope that the United States is the Mac to Europe's PC, and that if one part
of the West can successfully update and reboot itself, it's America.

But the lesson of history is clear. Voters and politicians alike dare not 31
postpone the big reboot. Decline is not so gradual that our biggest problems can simply be left to the next administration, or the one after that.

If what we are risking is not decline but downright collapse, then the 32
time frame maybe even tighter than one election cycle.

Thinking about the Essay

1. Now that you have read the essay, consider the title again. Define an "oh sh*t moment." How does this moment apply to the economic and political situation of America? According to Ferguson, how close is America to reaching its "oh sh*t moment"? What solutions does he offer to avert the impending disaster for the United States?

2. What is Ferguson's thesis? In what paragraphs does he state the thesis? Why do you think he chose to use deductive organization instead of inductive organization with the main point at the end? Is this organization appropriate for his intended audience, readers of *Newsweek*?

3. What is Ferguson's purpose in this essay? Generally, is it to inform, to explain, or to convince? Specifically, what is he trying to inform, explain, or convince his readers of? Is his purpose optimistic or pessimistic? What is the plausibility or probability of his solutions' being implemented?

4. Ferguson employs a variety of methods of development or rhetorical modes in this essay, including exemplification, enumeration, definition, negation, comparison and contrast, cause and effect, and problem to solution. Find and analyze each of these methods in Ferguson's essay. For what purpose does he use each mode?

5. The author uses computer language and references to metaphorically present the problem and solutions. Trace and analyze his use of this implied comparison in the essay. Is this metaphor effective for Ferguson's purpose and audience? Explain.

Responding in Writing

6. In paragraph 17, Ferguson compares university students in the United States to Asian students, and concludes that U.S. students have lost the work ethic and the drive to excel in their studies. Using students and situations at your college with which you are familiar, agree or disagree with Ferguson on this point.

7. Write an essay in which you analyze Ferguson's explanation of America's "oh sh*t moment" and his proposed solution to the problem. Then state and explain your agreement or disagreement with Ferguson's argument.

8. Write an essay about a problem with which you are familiar—perhaps something on your campus, in your neighborhood or your city, on a job or internship, in your own family or the family of someone you know, or a contemporary national or global problem. Analyze the problem, and propose a solution.

Networking

9. Ferguson refers to the World Economic Forum (WEF) Executive Opinion Survey to support his position that the United States and indeed the Western countries are slipping from their position of power and leadership in the world. With a group of classmates, study the latest WEF report. Do the statistics and evidence in this recent survey support Ferguson's claim? Be specific in your answers, and

provide examples to support your generalizations. Summarize your discussion, and share it with your class.

10. In 2011, Niall Ferguson recorded a video on "The 6 Killer Apps of Prosperity," available on Ted Talks at http://www.ted.com. In this talk, Ferguson poses the proposition that history is a "curious" thing, and he investigates not only what has happened but also why. Listen to the talk, and have a discussion with your classmates about how economics helps us understand history.

When Afghanistan Was at Peace

Margaret Atwood

Margaret Atwood, born in 1939, is a Canadian novelist, poet, short story writer, essayist, and literary critic whose work explores the troubled contours of the modern world. Atwood's second collection of poetry, *The Circle Game* (1966), was published to critical acclaim. Equally impressive is a distinguished series of novels, including *Life Before Man* (1979), *The Handmaid's Tale* (1986), *Cat's Eye* (1988), *The Blind Assassin* (2000), *The Penelopiad* (2005), and *The Year of the Flood* (2009). Atwood's writing often blends the intensely personal experience with global realities. In "When Afghanistan Was at Peace," published in October 2001 in *The New York Times Magazine*, Atwood describes a world ruined by clashing civilizations.

Before Reading

Reflect on what you know about Afghanistan. How many "civilizations" have attempted to conquer and control it? Why is the United States fighting in Afghanistan today? What problems do you foresee for Afghanistan's future?

In February 1978, almost 23 years ago, I visited Afghanistan with my   1
spouse, Graeme Gibson, and our 18-month-old daughter. We went there almost by chance: we were on our way to the Adelaide literary festival in Australia. Pausing at intervals, we felt, would surely be easier on a child's time clock. (Wrong, as it turned out.) We thought Afghanistan would make a fascinating two-week stopover. Its military history impressed us—neither Alexander the Great nor the British in the 19th century had stayed in the country long because of the ferocity of its warriors.

"Don't go to Afghanistan," my father said when told of our plans.   2
"There's going to be a war there." He was fond of reading history books.
"As Alexander the Great said, Afghanistan is easy to march into but hard
to march out of." But we hadn't heard any other rumors of war, so off
we went.

We were among the last to see Afghanistan in its days of relative peace—   3
relative, because even then there were tribal disputes and superpowers in
play. The three biggest buildings in Kabul were the Chinese Embassy, the
Soviet Embassy and the American Embassy, and the head of the country
was reportedly playing the three against one another.

The houses of Kabul were carved wood, and the streets were like a liv-   4
ing "Book of Hours": people in flowing robes, camels, donkeys, carts with
huge wooden wheels being pushed and pulled by men at either end. There
were few motorized vehicles. Among them were buses covered with ornate
Arabic script, with eyes painted on the front so the buses could see where
they were going.

We managed to hire a car in order to see the terrain of the famous and   5
disastrous British retreat from Kabul to Jalalabad. The scenery was breathtaking: jagged mountains and the "Arabian Nights" dwellings in the val-
leys—part houses, part fortresses—reflected in the enchanted blue-green of
the rivers. Our driver took the switchback road at breakneck speed since
we had to be back before sundown because of bandits.

The men we encountered were friendly and fond of children: our curly-   6
headed, fair-haired child got a lot of attention. The winter coat I wore had
a large hood so that I was sufficiently covered and did not attract undue
notice. Many wanted to talk; some knew English, while others spoke
through our driver. But they all addressed Graeme exclusively. To have
spoken to me would have been impolite. And yet when our interpreter
negotiated our entry into an all-male teahouse, I received nothing worse
than uneasy glances. The law of hospitality toward visitors ranked higher
than the no-women-in-the-teahouse custom. In the hotel, those who served
meals and cleaned rooms were men, tall men with scars either from dueling
or from the national sport, played on horseback, in which gaining posses-
sion of a headless calf is the aim.

Girls and women we glimpsed on the street wore the chador, the long,   7
pleated garment with a crocheted grill for the eyes that is more comprehensive than any other Muslim cover-up. At that time, you often saw chic
boots and shoes peeking out from the hem. The chador wasn't obligatory
back then; Hindu women didn't wear it. It was a cultural custom, and since
I had grown up hearing that you weren't decently dressed without a girdle
and white gloves, I thought I could understand such a thing. I also knew
that clothing is a symbol, that all symbols are ambiguous and that this one

might signify a fear of women or a desire to protect them from the gaze of strangers. But it could also mean more negative things, just as the color red can mean love, blood, life, royalty, good luck—or sin.

I bought a chador in the market. A jovial crowd of men gathered around, amused by the spectacle of a Western woman picking out such a non-Western item. They offered advice about color and quality. Purple was better than light green or the blue, they said. (I bought the purple.) Every writer wants the Cloak of Invisibility—the power to see without being seen—or so I was thinking as I donned the chador. But once I had put it on, I had an odd sense of having been turned into negative space, a blank in the visual field, a sort of antimatter—both there and not there. Such a space has power of a sort, but it is a passive power, the power of taboo. 8

Several weeks after we left Afghanistan, the war broke out. My father was right, after all. Over the next years, we often remembered the people we met and their courtesy and curiosity. How many of them are now dead, through no fault of their own? 9

Six years after our trip, I wrote *The Handmaid's Tale*, a speculative fiction about an American theocracy. The women in that book wear outfits derived in part from nuns' costumes, partly from girls' schools' hemlines and partly—I must admit—from the faceless woman on the Old Dutch Cleanser box, but also partly from the chador I acquired in Afghanistan and its conflicting associations. As one character says, there is freedom to and freedom from. But how much of the first should you have to give up in order assuring the second? All cultures have had to grapple with that and our own—as we are now seeing—is no exception. Would I have written the book if I never had visited Afghanistan? Possibly. Would it have been the same? Unlikely. 10

Thinking about the Essay

1. Does Atwood provide a thesis sentence in this essay? Why or why not? How does her title imply a thesis? If you were writing a thesis sentence of your own for this essay, what would it be?

2. What is Atwood's purpose in writing this narrative essay? Consider that this essay was published shortly after the events of 9/11. Is narration an appropriate strategy for her purpose? Why or why not?

3. Narrative essays typically use description to flesh out the story. Find descriptive details that Atwood provides, and explain what these details contribute to the overall effect.

4. Analyze the point of view in this essay. Is Atwood an observer, a participant, or both? Is she neutral or involved? Support your opinion.

5. Consider the relationship of the introductory paragraphs to the conclusion. Why does Atwood use the introduction and conclusion to expand the time frame of her main narrative?

Responding in Writing

6. Write an **editorial** for your college newspaper supporting or attacking the role of Western powers in Afghanistan today.

7. Imagine that you are traveling to Afghanistan on assignment for a newspaper. Report back, telling readers about what you see and where you go. Feel free to research the subject prior to writing the essay.

8. What does Atwood say about the clash of civilizations in this essay? Answer this question by analyzing the strategies she uses to convey her thesis.

Networking

9. In groups of two or three, pool your knowledge of Afghanistan. Prepare a brief report to be presented to the class.

10. In her essay, Atwood alludes to some of the nations and civilizations that have tried to conquer Afghanistan over the centuries. Conduct a library or Internet search on the history of Afghanistan and how it has been a crossroads in the clash of civilizations. Prepare a brief report on your findings.

Fundamentalism Is Here to Stay

Karen Armstrong

Karen Armstrong, born in 1944 in England, is one of the most highly regarded commentators on religion in North America and Europe. She currently teaches Christianity at the Leo Baeck College Centre for Jewish Education in London. Armstrong joined a Catholic convent at the age of seventeen but left her order after seven years. Her experience as a nun, and her departure from the Catholic Church, are recounted in the autobiographical *Through the Narrow Gates* (1982). Armstrong now describes herself as a "freelance monotheist" and compares religion to a raft: "Once you get across the river, moor the raft and go on. Don't lug it with you if you don't need it anymore." Armstrong's recent books include *The Battle for God: A History of Fundamentalism* (2001), *Islam: A Short History* (2001), *The Great Transformation: The Beginning of Our Religious Traditions* (2006), *The Case for God* (2009), and *Fields of Blood: Religion and the History of Violence* (2014). In the following essay, which appeared on globalagendamagazine.com in 2005, Armstrong defines religious fundamentalism as a reaction to—and a clash with—the perceived values of a secular modernity.

Before Reading

How do you define **fundamentalism**? Do you see the fundamentalist impulse as a feature common to all religions? Are there differences in degree or kind?

In the middle of the 20th century, it was generally assumed that secularism was the coming ideology and that religion would never again play a major role in world events. Today, religion dominates the headlines, and this is due in no small part to the militant piety that has developed in every single major world faith over the past century.   1

We usually call it "fundamentalism." Fundamentalist groups have staged revolutions, assassinated presidents, carried out terrorist atrocities and become an influential political force in strongly secularist nations. There has, for example, been much discussion about the role of Protestant fundamentalism in the recent American elections. It is no longer possible to dismiss fundamentalism as a passing phase.   2

Fundamentalism Is Not . . .

We should begin by defining what fundamentalism is not. First, it should not be equated with religious conservatism. Leading American religious revivalist Billy Graham, for example, is not a fundamentalist.   3

Second, fundamentalism should not be linked automatically with violence. Only a tiny proportion of fundamentalists worldwide take part in acts of terror. The rest are simply struggling to live what they regard as a good religious life in a world that seems increasingly inimical to faith.   4

Third, fundamentalism is not an exclusively Islamic phenomenon. There are fundamentalist Jews, Christians, Hindus, Buddhists, Sikhs and Confucians, who all challenge the secular hegemony of the modern world. In fact, Islam developed a fundamentalist strain long after it had erupted in Judaism and Christianity.   5

Fundamentalism Is . . .

So what is fundamentalism? It is essentially a revolt against modern secular society. Wherever a western polity has been established that separates religion and politics, fundamentalist movements have sprung up in protest. Whatever the politicians or the pundits claim, people worldwide are demonstrating that they want to see religion reflected more prominently in public life. As part of their campaign, fundamentalists tend to withdraw from mainstream society to create enclaves of pure faith.   6

Typical examples are the Ultra-orthodox Jewish communities in New 7
York or the fundamentalist Christianity of Bob Jones University in South
Carolina. Here fundamentalists build a counterculture, in conscious defi-
ance of the godless world that surrounds them, and from these communities some undertake a counteroffensive designed to drag God or religion
back to centre stage from the wings to which they have been relegated in
modern secular culture.

This campaign is rarely violent. It usually consists of a propaganda 8
or welfare effort. In the United States, for example, the fundamentalist
riposte attempts to reform school textbooks or to get Christian candidates
elected to government posts. But if warfare is endemic in a region and has
become chronic—as in the Middle East or Afghanistan—fundamentalists
can get sucked into the violence that pervades the whole of society. In this
way, originally secular disputes such as the Arab-Israeli conflict have been
sacralized, on both sides.

The Road to Modernity

The ubiquity of the fundamentalist revolt shows that there is widespread 9
disappointment with modernity. But what is it about the modern world
that has provoked such rage and distress? In the 16th century, the peoples
of the west began to develop a new type of civilization unprecedented in
world history. Instead of basing their economy on a surplus of agricultural
produce, as did all premodern cultures, they relied increasingly on technology and the constant reinvestment of capital, which freed them from the
inherent limitations of agrarian society. This demanded radical change at
all levels of society—intellectual, political, social and religious. A wholly
new way of thinking became essential, and new forms of government had
to evolve to meet these altered conditions. It was found by trial and error
that the best way of creating a productive society was to create a secular,
tolerant, democratic polity.

It took Europe some 300 years to modernize, and the process was 10
wrenching and traumatic, involving bloody revolutions, often succeeded
by reigns of terror, brutal holy wars, dictatorships, cruel exploitation of the
workforce, the despoliation of the countryside, and widespread alienation
and anomie.

We are now witnessing the same kind of upheaval in developing coun- 11
tries presently undergoing modernization. But some of these countries have
had to attempt this difficult process far too rapidly and are forced to follow
a western program, rather than their own.

This accelerated modernization has created deep divisions in develop- 12
ing nations. Only an elite has a western education that enables them to

understand the new modern institutions. The vast majority remains trapped in the premodern ethos. They experience the incomprehensible change as profoundly disturbing, and cling to traditional religion for support. But as modernization progresses, people find that they cannot be religious in the old way and try to find new means of expressing their piety. Fundamentalism is just one of these attempts, and it therefore develops only after a degree of modernization has been achieved.

The modern spirit that developed in the west had two essential characteristics: independence and innovation. Modernization in Europe and America proceeded by declarations of independence on all fronts—religious, political and intellectual—as scientists and inventors demanded the freedom to develop their ideas without interference from religious or political authorities. Further, despite the trauma of modernization, it was exciting, because the western countries were continually meeting new challenges and creating something fresh. But in some developing countries, modernization came not with independence, but with colonial dependence and subjugation, and the west was so far ahead that these could not innovate but only imitate. So they find it difficult to develop a truly modern spirit. A nation such as Japan, which was not colonized, was able to make its own distinctive contribution to the modern economy in a way that some Middle Eastern countries have not been able to do.

A Fight for Survival

Culture is always contested, and fundamentalists are primarily concerned with saving their own society. Protestant fundamentalists in the United States want America to be a truly Christian nation, not a secular, pluralist republic. In Palestine, Hamas began by attacking the Palestine Liberation Organization, because it wanted the Palestinian resistance to be inspired by an Islamic rather than a secular polity. Osama bin Laden started by targeting the Saudi royal family and such secularist rulers as Saddam Hussein. Only at a secondary stage—if at all—do fundamentalists begin to attack a foreign foe. Thus fundamentalism does not represent a clash between civilizations, but a clash within civilizations.

Perhaps the most important factor to understand about this widespread religious militancy is its rootedness in a deep fear of annihilation. Every fundamentalist movement I have studied in Judaism, Christianity and Islam is convinced that modern secular society wants to wipe out religion—even in America. Fundamentalists, therefore, believe they are fighting for survival, and when people feel that their backs are to the wall, some can strike out violently. This profound terror of annihilation is not as paranoid as it may at first appear. Jewish fundamentalism, for example, gained fresh momentum after World War II, when Hitler had tried to exterminate European Jewry, and after the 1973 October War, when Israelis felt vulnerable and isolated in the Middle East.

In some Muslim countries, modernization has usually been so accelerated   16 that secularism has been experienced as an assault. When Mustafa Kemal Ataturk created modern secular Turkey, he closed down all the madrasahs (traditional institutes for higher education in Islamic studies) and abolished the Sufi orders. He also forced all men and women to wear Western dress. Reformers such as Ataturk wanted their countries to look modern. In Iran, the shahs used to make their soldiers walk through the streets with their bayonets out, tearing off women's veils and ripping them to pieces. In 1935, Shah Reza Pahlavi gave his soldiers orders to shoot at unarmed demonstrators in Mashhad (one of the holiest shrines in Iran), who were peacefully protesting against obligatory Western clothes. Hundreds of Iranians died that day. In such circumstances, secularism was not experienced as liberating and civilized, but as wicked, lethal and murderously hostile to faith.

The main fundamentalist ideology of Sunni Islam developed in the con-   17 centration camps in Egypt in which president Jamal Abd al-Nasser had incarcerated thousands of members of the Muslim Brotherhood in the late 1950s, without trial and often for doing nothing more incriminating than attending a meeting or handing out leaflets. One of these prisoners was Sayyid Qutb, who was executed by Nasser in 1966. Qutb went into the camp as a moderate and a liberal. But in these vile prisons, watching the Brothers being executed and subjected to mental and physical torture, and hearing Nasser vowing to relegate Islam to a marginal role in Egypt, he came to regard secularism as a great evil. He developed an ideology of committed armed struggle against this threat to the faith. His chief disciple today is Osama bin Laden.

Thus fundamentalism usually develops in a symbiotic relationship with   18 a secularism that is experienced as hostile and invasive. Every fundamentalist movement I have studied in each of the three monotheistic traditions has developed in direct response to what is perceived as a secularist attack. The more vicious the assault, the more extreme the fundamentalist riposte is likely to be. Because fundamentalists fear that secularists want to destroy them, aggressive and military action will only serve to confirm this conviction and exacerbate their fear, which can spill over into ungovernable rage.

Thus membership of al-Qaeda has increased since the recent Gulf   19 War. The offensive has convinced many Muslims that the West has really inaugurated a new crusade against the Islamic world. In the United States, Protestant fundamentalists in the smaller towns and rural areas often feel "colonized" by the alien ethos of Harvard, Yale and Washington, DC. They feel that the liberal establishment despises them, and this has resulted in a fundamentalism that has gone way beyond Jerry Falwell and the Moral Majority of the 1970s. (Falwell is an American fundamentalist Baptist pastor, televangelist and founder of the Moral Majority—a group dedicated to promoting its conservative and religious Christian-centric beliefs via support of political candidates.) Some groups, such as the Christian Reconstructionists, look forward to the imminent destruction of the federal government; the blazing towers of the World Trade Center would not be alien to their ideology. When liberals deplore the development and persistence of fundamentalism in their own societies and worldwide, they should be aware that the excesses of secularists have all too often been responsible for this radical alienation.

Here to Stay

Fundamentalism is not going to disappear, as secularists once imagined   20
that religion would modestly retreat to the sidelines and confine itself to private life. Fundamentalism is here to stay, and in Judaism, Christianity and Islam, at least, it is becoming more extreme. Fundamentalism is not confined to the "other" civilizations. A dangerous gulf has appeared, dividing many societies against themselves. In the Middle East, India, Pakistan, Israel and the United States, for example, fundamentalists and secular liberals form two distinct camps, neither of which can understand the other.

In the past, these movements were often dismissed with patrician dis-   21
dain. This has proved to be short-sighted. We have to take fundamentalism very seriously. Had the US made a greater effort to understand Shiite Islam, for example, it might have avoided unnecessary errors in the lead-up to the Iranian Revolution of 1978 to 79. The first step must be to look beneath the bizarre and often repulsive ideology of these movements to discern the disquiet and anger that lie at their roots. We must no longer deride these theologies as the fantasies of a lunatic fringe, but learn to decode their ideas and imagery. Only then can we deal creatively with fears and anxieties that, as we have seen to our cost, no society can safely ignore.

Thinking about the Essay

1. Why does Armstrong define fundamentalism first by stating what it is not? How do you respond to this tactic as a reader?

2. Where does Armstrong shift in the essay from definition to process analysis? How does Armstrong link the historical and economic factors that gave rise to modernity with the secular values that came to be associated with modernity? How is fundamentalism a response to modernity as both a process and a set of values?

3. Why does Armstrong make a point, throughout the essay, of dissociating the concept of fundamentalism from violence?

4. What examples does Armstrong give to acknowledge the militancy of twentieth-century attempts at rapid modernization? Do these examples strengthen or weaken her definition of fundamentalism? How has Armstrong prepared for this acknowledgment earlier in the essay?

5. Describe the symbiotic relationship between fundamentalist terrorism and secular modernity.

Responding in Writing

6. Respond to the term *militant piety*, which some would read as an oxymoron. How can piety take this form? In a brief essay, consider some examples of militant piety and explain why the term would, in your opinion, apply in each case.

7. Fundamentalism, according to Armstrong, "does not represent a clash between civilizations, but a clash within civilizations." However, Amartya Sen claims that the problem is "categorizing people of the world according to a unique, allegedly commanding system of classification" and that this categorization is "crude and inconsistent." Write an essay in which you briefly analyze the argument of each essayist, and then explain which has the more valid argument.

8. In a brief essay, offer some advice to American foreign policy makers on how to promote modernization in a Middle Eastern nation (such as Iraq) so that it will not be experienced or perceived as an "assault."

Networking

9. In groups of three or four, make a list of three religious leaders or public figures in the United States whose views everyone in the group agrees would qualify as "fundamentalist" (according to Armstrong's definition). Share the list with the class, and justify the application of the label to each person on the list.

10. Go online and read at least three reviews of Armstrong's *The Battle for God: A History of Fundamentalism*. Do any of the reviewers take exception to her definition of *fundamentalism*?

A World Not Neatly Divided

Amartya Sen

Amartya K. Sen, the 1998 Nobel Prize winner in economics, was born in 1933 in Santiniketan, India. After studying at Presidency College in Calcutta, Sen immigrated to England, where he received BA (1955), MA (1959), and PhD (1959) degrees from Trinity College, Cambridge. Master of Trinity College since 1998, Sen also has taught at Oxford University, the London School of Economics, Harvard University, and

Cornell University. Sen is credited with bringing ethical considerations into the study of economics. He has done groundbreaking work in establishing techniques for assessing world poverty and the relative wealth of nations, the causes of famine, and the economic impact of health and education on developing societies. His study, *Collective Choice and Social Welfare* (1970), in which he uses the tools of economics to study such concepts as fairness, liberty, and justice, brings to economic theory a dimension of moral philosophy that has made Sen an influential figure in contemporary thought. Other notable works include *Poverty and Famines: An Essay on Entitlement and Deprivation* (1981), *On Ethics and Economics* (1987), *Development as Freedom* (1999), *The Argumentative Indian: Writings on Indian History, Culture and Identity* (2005), *The Idea of Justice* (2009), *and Peace and Democratic Society* (2011). As this essay from *The New York Times*, published on November 23, 2001, demonstrates, Sen commands a lucid prose style that enables him to make complex issues accessible to general readers. Here, he argues for a more nuanced approach to the idea of civilization than the one posed by Samuel Huntington.

Before Reading

Is it necessary to divide the world into various types of civilizations? What is the purpose of such classification, and what are the possible results?

When people talk about clashing civilizations, as so many politicians   1
and academics do now, they can sometimes miss the central issue. The inadequacy of this thesis begins well before we get to the question of whether civilizations must clash. The basic weakness of the theory lies in its program of categorizing people of the world according to a unique, allegedly commanding system of classification. This is problematic because civilizational categories are crude and inconsistent and also because there are other ways of seeing people (linked to politics, language, literature, class, occupation or other affiliations).

The befuddling influence of a singular classification also traps those   2
who dispute the thesis of a clash: To talk about "the Islamic world" or

"the Western world" is already to adopt an impoverished vision of humanity as unalterably divided. In fact, civilizations are hard to partition in this way, given the diversities within each society as well as the linkages among different countries and cultures. For example, describing India as a "Hindu civilization" misses the fact that India has more Muslims than any other country except Indonesia and possibly Pakistan. It is futile to try to understand Indian art, literature, music, food or politics without seeing the extensive interactions across barriers of religious communities. These include Hindus and Muslims, Buddhists, Jains, Sikhs, Parsees, Christians (who have been in India since at least the fourth century, well before England's conversion to Christianity), Jews (present since the fall of Jerusalem), and even atheists and agnostics. Sanskrit has a larger atheistic literature than exists in any other classical language. Speaking of India as a Hindu civilization may be comforting to the Hindu fundamentalist, but it is an odd reading of India.

A similar coarseness can be seen in the other categories invoked, like "the Islamic world." Consider Akbar and Aurangzeb, two Muslim emperors of the Mogul dynasty in India. Aurangzeb tried hard to convert Hindus into Muslims and instituted various policies in that direction, of which taxing the non-Muslims was only one example. In contrast, Akbar reveled in his multiethnic court and pluralist laws, and issued official proclamations insisting that no one "should be interfered with on account of religion" and that "anyone is to be allowed to go over to a religion that pleases him." 3

If a homogeneous view of Islam were to be taken, then only one of these emperors could count as a true Muslim. The Islamic fundamentalist would have no time for Akbar; Prime Minister Tony Blair, given his insistence that tolerance is a defining characteristic of Islam, would have to consider excommunicating Aurangzeb. I expect both Akbar and Aurangzeb would protest, and so would I. A similar crudity is present in the characterization of what is called "Western civilization." Tolerance and individual freedom have certainly been present in European history. But there is no dearth of diversity here, either. When Akbar was making his pronouncements on religious tolerance in Agra, in the 1590's, the Inquisitions were still going on; in 1600, Giordano Bruno was burned at the stake, for heresy, in Campo dei Fiori in Rome. 4

Dividing the world into discrete civilizations is not just crude. It propels us into the absurd belief that this partitioning is natural and necessary and must overwhelm all other ways of identifying people. That imperious view goes not only against the sentiment that "we human beings are all much the same," but also against the more plausible understanding that we are diversely different. For example, Bangladesh's split from Pakistan was not connected with religion, but with language and politics. 5

Each of us has many features in our self-conception. Our religion, important as it may be, cannot be an all-engulfing identity. Even a shared 6 poverty can be a source of solidarity across the borders. The kind of division highlighted by, say, the so-called "anti-globalization" protesters—whose movement is, incidentally, one of the most globalized in the world—tries to unite the underdogs of the world economy and goes firmly against religious, national or "civilizational" lines of division.

The main hope of harmony lies not in any imagined uniformity, but in   7
the plurality of our identities, which cut across each other and work against sharp divisions into impenetrable civilizational camps. Political leaders who think and act in terms of sectioning off humanity into various "worlds" stand to make the world more flammable—even when their intentions are very different. They also end up, in the case of civilizations defined by religion, lending authority to religious leaders seen as spokesmen for their "worlds." In the process, other voices are muffled and other concerns silenced. The robbing of our plural identities not only reduces us; it impoverishes the world.

Thinking about the Essay

1. How does Sen begin his essay? What is his argument, and how does he present it in the opening paragraph?

2. Sen uses several illustrations to support his argument about "singular classification." Locate three of these examples and explain how they advance his claim.

3. Any discussion of types—whether types of civilizations or types of teachers—lends itself to classification. How does Sen use classification and **division** to organize his argument and his essay?

4. What transitional devices serve to unify this essay?

5. Does Sen's concluding paragraph serve to confirm his thesis or claim? Explain your answer.

Responding in Writing

6. What is so wrong about "singular classification," especially when considering nations, cultures, and civilizations? Write a response to this question, referring to Sen's essay in the process.

7. Write a complete analysis of the ways in which Sen composes his argument in "A World Not Neatly Divided."

8. Write a comparative paper analyzing the essays by Sen and Bharati Mukherjee.

Networking

9. In small groups, select a city, region, country, or civilization, and then draw up a list of traits or attributes—a singular classification—illuminating your subject. Present the list to class members, and as a group discuss the advantages and disadvantages of singular classification.

10. Conduct online research on an international city. Then write a travel blurb stressing both the singular nature of this city and also its diversity.

CHAPTER 6

9 | The Age of Terror: What Is the Just Response?

Just as changes in U.S. demographics, patterns of cultural interaction, the forces of globalization, and the "clash" of civilizations have brought us into expanding contact with the peoples of the world, current events remind us that this new world can be exceedingly dangerous. Indeed, in the years since the September 11, 2001 attack, we have had to reorient our thinking about numerous critical issues: the war on terrorism; the erosion of our sense of individual and collective security; the need to achieve a balance between individual rights and common security. Above all, we now face the ethical, political, and historical challenge of dealing with the reality that although the United States is still the world's major superpower, other superpowers—notably China and India—are emerging as global rivals. There are people and nations who hate America's standing in the world. And hatred and cruelty, as Isaac Bashevis Singer, a winner of the Nobel Prize for Literature, once observed, only produce more of the same.

The 9/11 terrorist attack was so profoundly unnerving that virtually all of us can remember where we were when the planes hijacked by terrorists crashed into New York's World Trade Center and the Pentagon in Washington, DC. This was a primal national event, similar in impact to the raid on Pearl Harbor in 1941 or the assassinations of President John Kennedy and Martin Luther King Jr. in the 1960s. These prior events, whether taking the lives of thousands or just one, serve to define entire American generations. Today the United States faces a new defining event or, more accurately, an unfolding series of events—first called the "war on terror" but now that phrase (as Reza Aslan explores in an essay appearing in this chapter) has been dropped by the Obama administration. Nevertheless, we do seem to be living in an age of terror, and we have to find ways in which national and global communities can deal with this unnerving reality.

Be a superpower! Destroy the Axis of Evil! One of several board games reflecting our preoccupation with the war on terror.

Thinking about the Image

1. What is the designer's purpose in creating this image? What specific details support your response?
2. What is your first response to this image? Are you amused? Why or why not?
3. How do you think that the designer might respond to parents who object to this image, claiming that this "game" is inappropriate for children?
4. Go online and try to locate virtual games that exploit the "war on terror" theme. What can you conclude about terrorism's impact on Internet gaming and, more generally, on the contemporary mind?

In a sense, the September 11 attack and subsequent assaults—in Bali, Spain, England, France, Sweden, India, the Middle East, and elsewhere—have forced the United States to look inward and outward for intelligent and effective responses. Looking inward, we often have to deal with our own anger, insecurity, and hatred of other peoples who commit these crimes against unsuspecting humanity. These are primal emotions that affect our sense of personal identity. At the same time, we must understand how others around the world view our country and must gain knowledge of peoples and cultures we once knew little or nothing about. For example, are the terrorists who planned and launched the 9/11 attack a mere aberration—some delusional distortion of the great culture and civilization of Islam? Or do they reflect the consensus of the Arab street? Where do college students—who should be committed to liberal learning—go to find answers to such large and complex questions? What courses exist on your campus? What organizations foster transnational or global understanding?

Ultimately—as writers in this chapter and throughout the text suggest— we have to read across cultures and nations to understand this new age of terror and its many manifestations: narcoterrorism, cyberterrorism, genocide, and more. We have to reflect on our own backgrounds. We have to be candid about how our individual experience molds our attitudes toward "others"— most of whom are like us but some of whom want to do us harm. Liberal education, as the American philosopher William James stated at the beginning of the last century, makes us less fanatical. Against the backdrop of contemporary terrorism, we have to search for wisdom and for sustaining values.

Where Nothing Says Everything

SUZANNE BERNE

> Suzanne Berne, an American novelist, was born in Washington, DC, in 1961. She was educated at Wesleyan University and the Iowa Writers' Workshop. She has taught at several universities, most recently at Boston College, where she teaches creative writing. Her novels are *A Crime in the Neighborhood* (1997), *The Ghost at the Table* (1997), and *A Perfect Arrangement* (2001). She was awarded the 2014 Bailey's Prize for Women's Fiction for her most recent novel, *The Dogs of Littlefield* (2013). The following essay on her visit to the devastated World Trade Center in the aftermath of 9/11, published in *The New York Times* on April 21, 2002, has become a contemporary classic.

Before Reading

Do you see yourself as part of what some commentators call the "post-9/11 generation"? Why or why not? What, in fact, do you know about September 11, 2001?

On a cold, damp March morning, I visited Manhattan's financial dis- 1
trict, a place I'd never been, to pay my respects at what used to be the World Trade Center. Many other people had chosen to do the same that

day, despite the raw wind and spits of rain, and so the first thing I noticed when I arrived on the corner of Vesey and Church Streets was a crowd.

Standing on the sidewalk, pressed against aluminum police barricades, wearing scarves that flapped into their faces and woolen hats pulled over their ears, were people apparently from everywhere. Germans, Italians, Japanese. An elegant-looking Norwegian family in matching shearling coats. People from Ohio and California and Maine. Children, middle-age couples, older people. Many of them were clutching cameras and video recorders, and they were all craning to see across the street, where there was nothing to see. 2

At least, nothing is what it first looked like, the space that is now ground zero. But once your eyes adjust to what you are looking at, "nothing" becomes something much more potent, which is absence. 3

But to the out-of-towner, ground zero looks at first simply like a construction site. All the familiar details are there: the wooden scaffolding; the cranes, the bulldozers and forklifts; the trailers and construction workers in hard hats; even the dust. There is the pound of jackhammers, the steady beep-beep-beep of trucks backing up, the roar of heavy machinery. 4

So much busyness is reassuring, and it is possible to stand looking at the cranes and trucks and feel that mild curiosity and hopefulness so often inspired by construction sites. 5

Then gradually your eyes do adjust, exactly as if you have stepped from a dark theater into a bright afternoon, because what becomes most striking about this scene is the light itself. 6

Ground zero is a great bowl of light, an emptiness that seems weirdly spacious and grand, like a vast plaza amid the dense tangle of streets in lower Manhattan. Light reflecting off the Hudson River vaults into the site, soaking everything—especially on an overcast morning—with a watery glow. This is the moment when absence begins to assume a material form, when what is not there becomes visible. 7

Suddenly you notice the periphery, the skyscraper shrouded in black plastic, the boarded windows, the steel skeleton of the shattered Winter Garden. Suddenly there are the broken steps and cracked masonry in front of Brooks Brothers. Suddenly there are the firefighters, the waiting ambulance on the other side of the pit, the police on every corner. Suddenly there is the enormous cross made of two rusted girders. 8

And suddenly, very suddenly, there is the little cemetery attached to St. Paul's Chapel, with tulips coming up, the chapel and grounds miraculously undamaged except for a few plastic-sheathed gravestones. The iron fence is almost invisible beneath a welter of dried pine wreaths, banners, ribbons, laminated poems and prayers and photographs, swags of paper cranes, withered flowers, baseball hats, rosary beads, teddy bears. And flags, 9 flags everywhere, little American flags fluttering in the breeze, flags on posters drawn by Brownie troops, flags on T-shirts, flags on hats, flags streaming by, tied to the handles of baby strollers.

It takes quite a while to see all of this; it takes even longer to come up   10
with something to say about it.

An elderly man standing next to me had been staring fixedly across   11
the street for some time. Finally he touched his son's elbow and said:
"I watched those towers being built. I saw this place when they weren't
there." Then he stopped, clearly struggling with, what for him, was a double
negative, recalling an absence before there was an absence. His son,
waiting patiently, took a few photographs. "Let's get out of here," the man
said at last.

Again and again I heard people say, "It's unbelievable." And then they   12
would turn to each other, dissatisfied. They wanted to say something more
expressive, more meaningful. But it is unbelievable, to stare at so much
devastation, and know it for devastation, and yet recognize that it does not
look like the devastation one has imagined.

Like me, perhaps, the people around me had in mind images from tele-   13
vision and newspaper pictures: the collapsing buildings, the running office
workers, the black plume of smoke against a bright blue sky. Like me, they
were probably trying to superimpose those terrible images onto the indus-
trious emptiness right in front of them. The difficulty of this kind of mental
revision is measured, I believe, by the brisk trade in World Trade Center
photograph booklets at tables set up on street corners.

Determined to understand better what I was looking at, I decided to   14
get a ticket for the viewing platform beside St. Paul's. This proved no easy
task, as no one seemed to be able to direct me to South Street Seaport,
where the tickets are distributed. Various police officers whom I asked
for directions, waved me vaguely toward the East River, differing degrees
of boredom and resignation on their faces. Or perhaps it was a kind
of incredulousness. Somewhere around the American Stock Exchange,
I asked a security guard for help and he frowned at me, saying, "You want
tickets to the disaster?"

Finally I found myself in line at a cheerfully painted kiosk, watching   15
a young juggler try to entertain the crowd. He kept dropping the four red
balls he was attempting to juggle, and having to chase after them. It was
noon; the next available viewing was at 4 p.m.

Back I walked, up Fulton Street, the smell of fish in the air, to wan-   16
der again around St. Paul's. A deli on Vesey Street advertised a view of
the World Trade Center from its second-floor dining area. I went in and
ordered a pastrami sandwich, uncomfortably aware that many people
before me had come to that same deli for pastrami sandwiches who would

never come there again. But I was here to see what I could, so I carried my sandwich upstairs and sat down beside one of the big plate-glass windows.

And there, at last, I got my ticket to the disaster.   17

I could see not just into the pit now, but also its access ramp, which   18 trucks had been traveling up and down since I had arrived that morning. Gathered along the ramp were firefighters in their black helmets and black coats. Slowly they lined up, and it became clear that this was an honor guard, and that someone's remains were being carried up the ramp toward the open door of an ambulance.

Everyone in the dining room stopped eating. Several people stood up,   19 whether out of respect or to see better, I don't know. For a moment, everything paused.

Then the day flowed back into itself. Soon I was outside once more,   20 joining the tide of people washing around the site. Later, as I huddled with a little crowd on the viewing platform, watching people scrawl their names or write "God Bless America" on the plywood walls, it occurred to me that a form of repopulation was taking effect, with so many visitors to this place, thousands of visitors, all of us coming to see the wide emptiness where so many were lost. And by the act of our visiting—whether we are motivated by curiosity or horror or reverence or grief, or by something confusing that combines them all—that space fills up again.

Thinking about the Essay

1. Does Berne state her thesis or imply it? Justify your response.

2. What is Berne's primary purpose in this essay? How does her title relate to the purpose?

3. The writer uses vivid sensory details to set the scene at Ground Zero. How do these details create a specific mood? Why does this mood inform our understanding of the relationship between the writer, her text, and her audience?

4. Cite instances where Berne moves from description to reflection and meditation. What is the effect of this strategy?

5. This essay is rich in novelistic and stylistic techniques. Identify several of these techniques, and explain their effect.

Responding in Writing

6. There have been countless essays on 9/11, but Berne's is frequently anthologized. Write your own analysis and evaluation of her essay, explaining why so many readers consider it to be outstanding.

7. How would you explain 9/11 if you were taking a group of tourists to the site today? Write a reflective essay addressing this question.

8. Argue for or against the proposition that you can learn profound truths about yourself and the world by thinking about the current "age of terror."

Networking

9. In small groups, discuss the impact that Berne's essay has had on each member. Then distill your discussion into a 200-word summary that one member of the group presents to the class.

10. Locate websites of organizations that memorialize the events of 9/11. Take notes on these organizations, and then prepare a paper on their missions and programs.

Bin Laden's Final Triumph

Shiraz Maher

Shiraz Maher is a British citizen who was born in 1981 in Birmingham to British Pakistani parents. Holding degrees in history from the University of Leeds and University of Cambridge, he is a Senior Research Fellow at the International Center for the Study of Radicalisation, King's College London, and Adjunct at Johns Hopkins, researching and writing about Syrian and Iraqi conflicts as well as the Salafi-Jihadi ideology and organizations in the broader Middle East. He is working on an intellectual history of al-Qaeda, exploring the development of its political thought. As a young man, he lived the experience of the Western Jihadist in Hizbut Tahrir, a radical Islamist group, but left the UK radical Islamist movement and has since dedicated his life to countering it. He tries to help Westerners comprehend the allure of the Islamic State for young Westerners and the deadly peril it poses. His recent books include *Greenbirds: Measuring Importance and Influence in Syrian Foreign Fighter Networks*, coauthored with Joseph Carter and Peter Neumann, and *The Arab Spring and Its Impact on Supply and Production in Global Markets*. In this article, Maher traces the rise of the Islamic State.

Before Reading

What do you know about Bin Laden? Who was he? If you do not remember much about him, do some research to identify his beliefs and his place in contemporary history.

Had Osama Bin Laden lived to see the present state of the Middle East he would have been rather pleased. The realisation of his ultimate ambition is gripping the Levant with the announcement of a caliphate straddling parts of Syria and Iraq. Controlling a piece of land roughly the size of Jordan and bigger than either Israel or Lebanon, Islamic State's leader, Abu Bakr al-Baghdadi is demanding international attention unlike any of his predecessors.

Islamic State is perhaps the most aggressive invading force in the Levant since the Mongols. Moreover, it is being given a free hand to recast the contours of power in what remains one of the world's most sensitive (and volatile) geo-strategic locations. This is no accident. The implosion of both Syria and Iraq, coupled with western reluctance to intervene in what is seen as yet another Arabian calamity, has fuelled the sudden rise of Baghdadi's millenarian militia.

This is precisely what Bin Laden always envisioned. His main thesis on the failure of the Islamist project was that western interference in the Middle East prevented the rise of Islamic governments. Weaken the west's sphere of influence, he argued, and a caliphate would emerge.

Events helped crystallise this view. Shortly after the Afghan mujahedin's unlikely victory over the Soviet Union in the late 1980s, Saddam Hussein invaded Kuwait and King Fahd turned to the United States to defend Saudi Arabia against his Ba'athist neighbour. Bin Laden was left embittered by the experience after the House of Saud scuppered his hopes of using the mujahedin to repel Saddam from Kuwait.

The humiliation for returning jihadists did not end there. Many from North Africa and the Gulf found themselves imprisoned and persecuted on their return. It was soon clear that going home was not an option and many of the Afghan alumni subsequently began to congregate in Sudan under the patronage of the chairman of the ruling party, Hassan al-Turabi, who had formed a Sunni Islamist movement at the time.

For the Arab fighters it was a comedown from their intoxicating victories in the mountains of the Hindu Kush against one of the great superpowers.

In Sudan, these fighters largely continued pursuing Islamo-nationalist aims. The Egyptians focused on Egypt, the Algerians on Algeria, and the Libyans on Libya. However, Saudi Arabia captured everyone's attention. The arrival of US troops in the Arabian Peninsula—home to Islam's most holy sites and regarded as sacred soil by Islamists—assaulted the imagination. This is when the gear shift occurred, redirecting the focus of jihadist anger from the metropolis to the periphery.

Shiraz Maher, "Bin Laden's Final Triumph", *New Statesman* (Aug. 29–Sept. 4, 2014), 22–25.

In an interview with the London-based Arabic-language newspaper 8
al-Quds al-Arabi in 1996, Bin Laden explained: ". . . we believe that the
US government committed the biggest mistake when it entered a peninsula which no non-Muslim nation has ever entered for 14 centuries . . .
[America's] entry was arbitrary and a reckless action. They have entered into
a confrontation with a nation whose population is one billion Muslims."

Having settled in Sudan, Bin Laden campaigned for Islamic revival in 9
Saudi Arabia by establishing the Committee for Advice and Reform. This
organisation had registered offices in Holborn, London, and was led by
another veteran of the Afghan campaign, Khaled al-Fawwaz, who acted as
Bin Laden's representative in London.

Between 1994 and 1995 Bin Laden used his London address to send 10
a total of 14 letters to the Saudi government. All of these urged the Saudi
state to end co-operation with the United States. What he wanted instead
was a more isolationist and self-assured form of Islam—a purer interpretation of sharia law, an end to western economic influence and a more
Muslim-centred foreign policy.

Another letter by Bin Laden to King Fahd explained: "It is not reason- 11
able to keep silent about the transformation of our nation into an American
protectorate which is defiled by the soldiers of the Cross with their impure
feet in order to protect your crumbling throne and preserve oilfields in the
kingdom." He continued:

> Is it not right for the [Islamic] nation to wonder about who is 12
> behind instability and turbulence in the country? Is it the system
> that delivered the country into a state of chronic military debilita-
> tion in order to justify bringing the Jewish and Christian forces to
> defile the holy lands? Or is it the people who call for the prepara-
> tion of the nation, arming it to be strong enough to take matters
> into its hands, protecting its honour and religion, defending its
> holy sites, its land and dignity?

Fawwaz sent all of these letters on Bin Laden's behalf until he was 13
indicted by the United States for his alleged involvement in the 1998 bombings of the US embassies in Kenya and Tanzania. Bin Laden himself was
implicated in the attacks.

Although a rationale of revenge was the primary argument Bin Laden 14
put forward to justify the 11 September 2001 attacks, he also argued that
confronting the US directly would undermine and weaken Arab regimes
back home. Indeed, this is how al-Qaeda has sought to credit itself with the
Arab-world uprisings of 2011, otherwise referred to as the "Arab spring".

"The abandonment of America's allies one by one is the fallout of its 15
diminishing pride and arrogance after receiving the blows in New York,
Washington and Pennsylvania," argued Ayman al-Zawahiri, Bin Laden's

second-in-command, shortly after the fall of Hosni Mubarak in Egypt in February 2011. The 9/11 attacks had "directly caused America to lose influence over the [Arab] people because its grasp over the [Arab] regimes was weakened".

Fantastical though such a view may be, it explains al-Qaeda's grand strategy for effecting change.   16

* * * *

Nowhere was the policy of direct confrontation with the United States   17
more apparent than in Iraq. Led by Abu Musab al-Zarqawi, al-Qaeda in Iraq launched a deliberately brutalising campaign aimed at shocking the west. From Iraq, Zarqawi sought to traumatise western societies into ever more reticence about intervention. His campaign struck directly at those who had supported "Operation Iraqi Freedom", claiming 4,486 American lives in the process and a further 318 from allied forces. The civilian death toll was immeasurably higher.

Traumatising as these casualties were, it is the broader cultural ramifica-   18
tions of the conflict that have left an indelible scar on both our society and politicians. Large sections of the Arab world—not just those already consumed with a deep suspicion of the west—erupted in a fit of anti-Americanism after the Iraq war. Every death of a western solider was cheered, every suicide bombing applauded; a Nelsonian eye was turned to the excesses of al-Qaeda in Iraq.

This perversion enveloped the entire region, from the trendy guests at   19
Lebanese beach parties to the chattering classes of Dubai's bevelled hotel lobbies. It is this cultural disengagement by ordinary Arabs, otherwise wholly unaligned to jihadist groups, that has proved so shocking.

While the west recorded uneven results in Iraq, the campaign was   20
broadly a success for the global jihad movement. Zarqawi not only achieved a small foothold for his fighters in Iraq but also successfully redefined the balance of power within al-Qaeda. By 2005, his brutal campaign across Iraq had begun to alienate much of the regional support al-Qaeda previously enjoyed. This worried the central leadership. Ayman al-Zawahiri wrote to Zarqawi, chastising him for two things in particular: executing hostages and pursuing a bloody, sectarian conflict with the Shias. "Many of your Muslim admirers among the common folk are wondering about your attacks," he wrote. "Don't lose sight of the target."

The overtures had no impact. Zarqawi rebuked Zawahiri by insist-   21
ing that he was on the ground and therefore best placed to decide what strategy the group should pursue. This prompted a lasting shift in the internal dynamics of the jihad movement—proximity now confers legitimacy. Those on the periphery could never be better placed than Zarqawi to dictate the prevailing strategy.

That precedent directly fuelled the rise of Islamic State today. Since 22 Zarqawi's death in 2006, al-Qaeda in Iraq has drifted into greater autonomy, renaming itself as the Islamic State of Iraq (ISI) that year. Although still nominally tied to al-Qaeda, the ISI was a largely independent group.

Relations finally unravelled with the onset of the Syrian civil war. Syr- 23 ian fighters from ISI led by Abu Muhammad al-Jawlani moved back into the country and established Jabhat al-Nusrah. They were supposed to serve as al-Qaeda's official representatives on the ground, though ISI could not resist direct involvement. Abu Bakr al-Baghdadi eventually ordered his own men into Syria, rebranding his group the Islamic State of Iraq and al-Sham (Isis) and ordering Jabhat al-Nusrah to disband.

Zawahiri was furious. He insisted that Baghdadi limit his ambitions to 24 Iraq and leave the Syrian campaign to Jawlani. It was not only the Qaeda leader who suggested this. Notable jihadist ideologues from around the world echoed these sentiments, including Abu Qatada, the radical Muslim preacher who was deported from London back to Jordan last year.

The disagreement opened up a chasm in the global jihad movement. 25 Both al-Qaeda and theoreticians associated with the group had urged Baghdadi to fall into line, only to be rebuffed. Invoking the primacy of proximity, as Zarqawi had done, spokesmen for Isis strongly rejected suggestions that the group was acting *ultra vires*. "The wars in Syria and Iraq are the same," explained Abu Muhammed al-Adnani, a leading spokesman for Isis. In both cases, the group insists, it is protecting Sunni Islam against Shia forces.

What is significant is how Isis has sought to justify itself to the broader 26 community of jihadi supporters. It is al-Qaeda and its ideologues—not Isis—that has betrayed the true spirit of what Osama Bin Laden always envisioned. And Isis is the rightful heir to his legacy, exploiting the power vacuum in the Levant to create an Islamic state.

The Isis leaders' frustration is understandable. They regard the cur- 27 rent US inaction in the region as stemming directly from the Americans' confrontation with them during the Iraq war from 2003. The spectre of that engagement continues to cast a long and enveloping shadow over western societies. It is precisely what Bin Laden had predicted would happen, which makes Zawahiri's reluctance to capitalise on it all the more inexplicable.

Withdrawing to Iraq would signal an acknowledgement of the bound- 28 aries set in the 1916 Sykes-Picot Agreement, a false aberration imposed on Muslims by "crusaders". Moreover, Adnani accuses Zawahiri of prioritising politics over jihad. Only this could explain why al-Qaeda did not exploit the uprisings in Tunisia, Egypt and Libya. The corollary is clear: al-Qaeda has lost its way under Zawahiri.

In many senses, Islamic State has now surpassed al-Qaeda altogether.   29
Whereas al-Qaeda is a terrorist organisation committed to confronting
the west violently, Islamic State has grander ambitions. Once a terrorist
group, it morphed into a sophisticated insurgency, and now operates its
own state.

The organisation is also investing heavily in winning public support.   30
It operates a broad range of social services, ensuring that people under its
authority have access to basic necessities such as health care, education and
fuel, as well as other public services. In July, during the Muslim festival of
Eid, it hosted recreational events, including pie-eating contests for children
and a tug on war for adults.

* * * *

When Khaled al-Fawwaz came to London as Osama Bin Laden's rep-   31
resentative in the late 1980s he was just one of many Islamist pouring
into the country. Others such as Abu Qatada, Abu Hamza and Omar Bak
Mohammed followed and, in the process they established a sophisticated
Islamist network across the UK.

In 1994 a major international conference promoting the caliphate was   32
held in London, gathering radical clerics from around the world. Some
early adherents of Islamism even went on to fight in Bosnia and Chechnya.
Others pursued more esoteric aims in states such as Yemen.

It is telling to chart the evolution of British Islamist discourse through   33
the 1990s. When the 1994 caliphate conference was convened, a large
part of proceedings was dedicated to discussing what the caliphate is and
whether it is obligated in Islam. By the end of the decade, the idea of the
caliphate was entrenched and the debate moved on. What Muslims discussed then was precisely how—not whether—the caliphate should be
revived. Seen in this way, it is clear that the roots of Islamist ideology run
deep in some parts of British Muslim life.

The caliphate is a broad concept bound up with another set of ideas,   34
too. At its core lies an alternative identity, the *umma*—a fraternity of the
faithful, in which loyalty and allegiance are defined through confessional
affiliation over civic ideals. It is the belief in the *umma* that has inspired as
many as 500 British men (and a handful of women) to pack their bags and
migrate to Syria.

British jihadists are not in Syria to melt into the background. They are   35
full and fervent participants in the conflict. In the past 12 months British
fighters have volunteered to be suicide bombers, executed prisoners of war,
and tortured detainees in their care.

Fighters from groups as diverse as Jabhat al-Nusrah, Ahrar al-Sham and   36
the Free Syrian Army have all told me of their concerns over the extremism

of British jihadists. They are regarded as some of the most vicious and vociferous. The issue emerged in sharp relief this past week with the murder of the American journalist James Foley, seemingly by a British executioner with a London accent.

Pressure is mounting on the Prime Minister to address the flow of   37 British fighters into groups such as Islamic State. The challenges are many, not least because there is a perception in some parts that the battle against Islamism has been won.

The main institutions promoting an Islamist agenda in this country—   38 the Muslim Council of Britain, the Muslim Association of Britain and the Federation of Islamic Organisations in Europe, among others—have been beaten back. So, too, have the most prominent preachers of radical ideology. At the same time, hardline organisations such as al-Muhajiroun and Hizb ut-Tahrir have fallen into obscurity.

To an extent, it can be said that there has been a decline in Islamist   39 agitation in the public sphere. Yet this success does not represent the whole picture. Because Islamist ideas have flourished in parts of the UK for more than two decades they remain a potent and pervasive force. That explains how a generation of men not even born during the 1994 caliphate conference has come to embrace the Syrian jihad so eagerly.

In 2011 David Cameron issued one of the clearest statements by any   40 politician of the need to inflect British values in the public sphere. In what popularly became known as the "Munich speech", the Prime Minister spoke of the need to build a strong civic identity to which all members of our society could subscribe. A few months later, Lord Carlile published his review into the Prevent counterterrorism strategy, adumbrating a new vision for the initiative.

Both the Prime Minister and Lord Carlile identified the role of   41 Islamist ideology as a primary driver of radicalisation. It was a marked departure from the cosseted approach adopted by their Labour predecessors in government, though much work remains to be done in this regard.

Dissuading young men not to join jihadist organisations in Syria and   42 Iraq is proving to be an arduous task. Where it was once thought that the domestic terrorism threat was being managed down, the revival of jihadist fortunes in Syria has extended its lifespan by another generation or two.

* * * *

The Islamic State surge is not the first time a jihadist organisation has   43 succeeded in taking swaths of land. It has happened before. Al-Qaeda and

Taliban forces held significant parts of Pakistan's North-West Frontier Province. In Somalia, al-Shabab has established itself in certain parts; Ansar Dine asserted itself over a significant area of northern Mali most recently.

What distinguishes Islamic State from its predecessors is that in every 44 one of those cases there was international momentum to unseat the jihadists. Western coalition forces worked with Pakistan to uproot militants from the tribal areas, while the African Union Mission in Somalia (AMISOM), backed by the UN, pushed back al-Shabab. In Mali, the French committed ground troops to overcome Ansar Dine and its affiliates.

There is no comparable momentum arrayed against Islamic State. 45 Neither the Iraqi nor the Syrian army is capable of overcoming it. Regional actors led by Saudi Arabia, Qatar and Turkey are unwilling to act and favour arming other rebel groups instead, a policy that has failed to deliver any meaningful results so far.

The western world looks on and sees only a conflict within Islam— 46 Sunni pitted against Shia—and asks why we should intervene. The post-9/11 campaigns in Afghanistan and Iraq appear not to have been worthwhile. This cognitive dissonance has allowed Abu Bakr al-Baghdadi to revive a caliphate in the heart of the Arab and Muslim world.

But public opinion is beginning to take notice of Islamic State. With 47 the execution of James Foley and the prominence of European (especially British) fighters in the conflict, it cannot be ignored. And yet, the belated approach of western policymakers has made Islamic State an entrenched entity. It is a state in every sense of the word. It maintains a treasury of billions of dollars, provides social services and has an army of skilled fighters with combat experience.

All this points to one conclusion, however depressing: Islamic State will 48 not be overcome without some form of western military intervention.

Thinking about the Essay

1. Most readers think that Bin Laden's assassination was his final defeat; however, Maher's title suggests that Bin Laden was not defeated but triumphant. How does the author support this suggestion of the title? What does he say was Bin Laden's thesis and vision of the Middle East? How far does the author say that Bin Laden's vision has come to fruition?

2. In order to comprehend what they read, readers must know the definition of unfamililar words or terms and how they fit into the context of a document. A few examples of such vocabulary words in this essay are *caliphate, the Levant, the Mongols, geostrategic, millenarian militia, mujahedin, Ba'athist House of Saud, scuppered, jihadist.* Look up the definitions of these and other unfamiliar words

you find. Think about the meanings of all the unfamiliar words and how a close reading by knowing the meanings of individual words in a piece of writing helps you to comprehend the overall essay better.

3. Maher uses chronological organization of ideas in the essay. How is this organizational pattern appropriate to the author's purpose? What is his purpose—to inform objectively or persuade by favoring one side or the other? Support your position in a discussion with a small group of classmates.

4. Moving step by step through the history of the last three decades, Maher traces the rise of the Islamic State. He also includes the causes and the effects of each step. What is Maher's conclusion concerning the Islamic State? Has he provided sufficient evidence to convince you that his stance is valid? Do you agree with his point, and do you think Western leaders will do what he suggests? Explain your position with specifics and examples.

5. Why is "dissuading young men not to join jihadist organisations" such an "arduous task"? Has Maher provided sufficient evidence to support this claim? Trace the reasons that he makes this claim. Do you agree?

Responding In Writing

6. Do you remember what you were doing on 9/11? Interview several people who do remember that day, and ask them for their responses. Collate their responses into an essay explaining how people responded on that day and how it affected them later.

7. Write an expository essay in which you analyze and explain the steps in the rise of the Islamist State, according to Maher.

8. Do you think Western media present an accurate or a biased view of Islamists? Research this question until you can formulate a valid answer. Then, using your research and specific examples from current media, write an argumentative essay in which you clearly state and explain your position and try to convince your classmates of your stance. Read and respond to several of your classmates' essays on this question.

Networking

9. Research the beliefs of Islam and the difference between the Shia and Sunni. Discuss your research with a small group of your classmates. Summarize your discussion and present it to all your classmates for discussion and response.

10. Read "Inside the Mind of the Western Jihadist" by Sohrab Ahmari from the 2014 Wall Street Journal at www.wsj.com. Summarize Ahmari's article and write a brief statement of what this article adds to your understanding of Shiraz Maher. Share your discoveries and responses with a small group of classmates, and then discuss them with the whole class. As a group, try to answer the question "Why are young Westerners drawn to the Islamic State?"

Reading a Death Warrant in Tehran

SHIRIN EBADI

> Shirin Ebadi is an Iranian lawyer, former judge, and
> human rights activist. She was born in Hamadan,
> Iran, in 1947, and trained for a legal career at the
> University of Tehran, where she received degrees in
> 1969 and 1971. Ebadi became the first woman to
> preside over an Iranian legislative court, but after the
> 1979 revolution, she came under increasing pressure
> from conservative clergy. Her work on behalf of
> women, political dissidents, and prisoners made her
> an international celebrity—but a thorn in the side of
> the Islamic Republic. In 2003, Ebadi received the
> Nobel Peace Prize for her efforts for democracy and
> human rights. Following threats to her life and break-
> ins at her office, Ebadi went into exile. In this essay
> from the April 9, 2006, issue of *The New York Times
> Magazine*, Ebadi recounts perhaps the most harrow-
> ing episode in her career as a human rights activist.

Before Reading

Would you defend victims of human rights violations even if your efforts threatened your safety? Why or why not?

In the fall of 2000, after a decade of defending victims in the courts of   1
Iran, I faced the most harrowing days of my career. The work I typically
handled—battered children, abused women, political prisoners—brought
me into daily contact with human cruelty, but the case at hand was different. The government had admitted partial complicity in a few of the
dozens of murders of intellectuals during the 1990's. Some were strangled
while running errands, others hacked to death at home. I represented the
family of two victims, a husband and wife.

The judge had granted us just 10 days to read the entire dossier, thou-   2
sands of pages. That would be our only access to the investigation's findings, our only chance to build our case. The disarray of the investigation,
the attempts to cover up the state's hand and the mysterious prison suicide
of a lead suspect compounded our difficulty in learning the truth. The
stakes could not have been higher. It was the first time that the Islamic
republic acknowledged it had murdered its critics—it said that a rogue

Dr. Shirin Ebadi, "Reading a Death Warrant in Tehran," *The New York Times Magazine*, April 9,
2006. © 2006 Dr. Shirin Ebadi. Used by kind permission of the author.

squad within the Ministry of Intelligence was responsible—and that a trial would be convened to hold the perpetrators accountable. We arrived at the courthouse tense with determination.

After surveying the sheer volume of files, stacks up to our heads, we   3
realized that we would have to read them concurrently and, therefore, except for one of us, out of order. The other lawyers allowed me to start at the beginning, so each page I hurriedly turned, my eyes were the first to see.

The sun shone through the dirty windowpane as we hunched over the   4
table, silent save for the rustle of papers. The significant passages, transcripts of interrogations of the accused killers, were buried in pages of bureaucratic filler. The material was dark with descriptions of the brutal murders—one killer told of crying out "Ya Zahra," in dark homage to the Prophet Muhammad's daughter, with each stab.

Around noon, our energy lagged, and we called to the young soldier   5
in the hall for some tea. The moment the tea arrived, we bent our heads down again. I had reached a page more detailed, and more narrative, than any previous section, and I slowed down to focus. It was the transcript of a conversation between a government minister and a member of the death squad during the worst wave of killings. When my eyes first fell on the sentence that would haunt me for years to come, I thought I had misread. I blinked once, but it stared back at me from the page: "The next person to be killed is Shirin Ebadi." Me.

My throat went dry. I read the line over and over again, the printed   6
words blurring before me. The only other woman in the room, Parastou Forouhar, whose parents had been brutally murdered, sat next to me. I pressed her arm and nodded toward the page. She bent her veiled head close and scanned from the top. "Did you read it? Did you read it?" she kept whispering. We read on together. My would-be assassin went to the minister of intelligence, requesting permission to carry out my killing. Not during the fasting month of Ramadan, the minister replied. But they don't fast anyway, the mercenary argued; these people have divorced God. It was through this belief—that the intellectuals, that I, had abandoned God— that they justified the killings as religious duty. In the grisly terminology of those who interpret Islam violently, the spilling of our blood was considered halal, permitted by God.

The door creaked open again. More tea, flavorless cups that cluttered   7
the table but kept us alert. I distracted myself by rearranging papers, my mind reeling. I wasn't scared, really. I remember an overwhelming disbelief. Why do they hate me so much? I wondered. How have I created enemies so eager to spill my blood that they cannot wait for Ramadan to end?

We didn't stop to talk about it then. We couldn't waste any precious   8
time. I sipped my tea and went on, though I turned the pages with difficulty.

It was only after we had finished for the day, as we passed through the courtyard outside, that I told the others. They shook their heads, murmured, "Alhamdolellah," thanks to God. I had evaded death.

I stepped into the welcoming cacophony of Tehran traffic, the wide streets overrun by wheezing old cars, and got a taxi home. I ran inside, peeled off my clothes and stayed under the shower for an hour, letting the water cascade over me, rinsing off the filth of those files. Only after dinner, after my daughters went to bed, did I tell my husband. So, something interesting happened to me at work today, I began. 9

Thinking about the Essay

1. What is the significance of the title? Does Ebadi write about one specific moment—the act of reading one document—or a series of related episodes? Explain.

2. Does Ebadi make a claim or develop an argument in this essay, or does she simply want to tell a personal story? Justify your response.

3. How does Ebadi develop and heighten the conflict underlying her narrative? At what point does the action reach a climax? Does she resolve the main conflict? Why or why not?

4. Where does Ebadi employ description to enhance the narrative? What is the effect?

5. Evaluate the concluding paragraph. Does the writer want to resolve the conflict or sustain it? Explain.

Responding in Writing

6. Write an expository essay explaining the impact of Ebadi's article on you. What do you learn about the writer? What was her purpose in designing this text? What impressions and conclusions do you draw from this critical reading of her article?

7. Write an argumentative essay in which you argue for or against the proposition that no government has a premium on human cruelty and the manipulation of terror—that, in fact, every nation engages in it. Support your major proposition with at least three minor propositions.

8. Can you ever justify killing a person as a religious duty? Answer this question in an argumentative essay.

Networking

9. In small groups, discuss the role of the intellectual in society. Should a given society tolerate all types of intellectuals, or should certain types be monitored, controlled, imprisoned, or killed? Report your findings to the class.

10. Go online and find out more about Shirin Ebadi. (She is on Facebook, one of several sources you might want to check.) Then compose a brief biography of Ebadi.

To Any Would-Be Terrorists

NAOMI SHIHAB NYE

Naomi Shihab Nye was born in 1952 in St. Louis, Missouri. Her family background is Palestinian American. She graduated from Trinity University (BA, 1974) and subsequently started a career as a freelance writer and editor. Today Nye is known for her award-winning poetry, fiction for children, novels, and essays. She has been a visiting writer at the University of Texas, the University of Hawaii, the University of California at Berkeley, and elsewhere. Among Nye's books are the prize-winning poetry collection *Different Ways to Pray* (1980); several other poetry volumes, including *Yellow Glove* (1986), *Fuel* (1998), and *You and Yours* (2005), incorporating poems dealing with Palestinian life; a book of essays, *Never in a Hurry* (1996); and a young adult novel, *Habibi* (1997). Among her many awards are the Peter I. B. Lavin Younger Poets Award from the Academy of American Poets and a Guggenheim Fellowship. Starting with the provocative title of the following essay, Nye speaks as a Palestinian American to an extremist audience that needs to "find another way to live."

Before Reading

If you had an opportunity to address a terrorist or terrorist group, what would you say, and how would you say it?

I am sorry I have to call you that, but I don't know how else to get your attention. I hate that word. Do you know how hard some of us have worked to get rid of that word, to deny its instant connection to the Middle East? And now look. Look what extra work we have.

Not only did your colleagues kill thousands of innocent, international people in those buildings and scar their families forever; they wounded a huge community of people in the Middle East, in the United States and all over the world. If that's what they wanted to do, please know the mission was a terrible success, and you can stop now.

Because I feel a little closer to you than many Americans could possibly feel, or ever want to feel, I insist that you listen to me. Sit down and listen.

I know what kinds of foods you like. I would feed them to you if you were right here, because it is very important that you listen.

I am humble in my country's pain and I am furious. 4

My Palestinian father became a refugee in 1948. He came to the United 5 States as a college student. He is 74 years old now and still homesick. He has planted fig trees. He has invited all the Ethiopians in his neighborhood to fill their little paper sacks with his figs. He has written columns and stories saying the Arabs are not terrorists; he has worked all his life to defy that word. Arabs are businessmen and students and kind neighbors. There is no one like him and there are thousands like him—gentle Arab daddies who make everyone laugh around the dinner table, who have a hard time with headlines, who stand outside in the evenings with their hands in their pockets staring toward the far horizon.

I am sorry if you did not have a father like that. 6

I wish everyone could have a father like that. 7

My hard-working American mother has spent 50 years trying to 8 convince her fellow teachers and choirmates not to believe stereotypes about the Middle East. She always told them, there is a much larger story. If you knew the story, you would not jump to conclusions from what you see in the news. But now look at the news. What a mess has been made.

Sometimes I wish everyone could have parents from different countries 9 or ethnic groups so they would be forced to cross boundaries, to believe in mixtures, every day of their lives. Because this is what the world calls us to do. WAKE UP!

The Palestinian grocer in my Mexican-American neighborhood paints 10 pictures of the Palestinian flag on his empty cartons. He paints trees and rivers. He gives his paintings away. He says, "Don't insult me" when I try to pay him for a lemonade. Arabs have always been famous for their generosity. Remember?

My half-Arab brother with an Arabic name looks more like an Arab 11 than many full-blooded Arabs do and he has to fly every week.

My Palestinian cousins in Texas have beautiful brown little boys. Many 12 of them haven't gone to school yet. And now they have this heavy word to carry in their backpacks along with the weight of their papers and books. I repeat, the mission was a terrible success. But it was also a complete, total tragedy, and I want you to think about a few things.

1.

Many people, thousands of people, perhaps even millions of people, in the 13 United States are very aware of the long unfairness of our country's policies regarding Israel and Palestine. We talk about this all the time. It exhausts us and we keep talking. We write letters to newspapers, to politicians, to each other. We speak out in public even when it is uncomfortable to do so, because that is our responsibility. Many of these people aren't even Arabs. Many happen to be Jews who are equally troubled by the inequity. I promise you this is true. Because I am Arab-American, people always express these views to me, and I am amazed how many understand the intricate situation and have strong, caring feelings for Arabs and Palestinians even when they don't have to. Think of them, please: All those people who have been standing up for Arabs when they didn't have to.

But as ordinary citizens we don't run the government and don't get   14
to make all our government's policies, which makes us sad sometimes. We believe in the power of the word and we keep using it, even when it seems no one large enough is listening. That is one of the best things about this country: the free power of free words. Maybe we take it for granted too much. Many of the people killed in the World Trade Center probably believed in a free Palestine and were probably talking about it all the time.

But this tragedy could never help the Palestinians. Somehow, miracu-   15
lously, if other people won't help them more, they are going to have to help themselves. And it will be peace, not violence, that fixes things. You could ask any one of the kids in the Seeds of Peace organization and they would tell you that. Do you ever talk to kids? Please, please, talk to more kids.

2.

Have you noticed how many roads there are? Sure you have. You must   16
check out maps and highways and small alternate routes just like anyone else. There is no way everyone on earth could travel on the same road, or believe in exactly the same religion. It would be too crowded: it would be dumb. I don't believe you want us all to be Muslims. My Palestinian grandmother lived to be 106 years old and did not read or write, but even she was much smarter than that. The only place she ever went beyond Palestine and Jordan was to Mecca, by bus, and she was very proud to be called a Hajji and to wear white clothes afterwards. She worked very hard to get stains out of everyone's dresses—scrubbing them with a stone. I think she would consider the recent tragedies a terrible stain on her religion and her whole part of the world. She would weep. She was scared of airplanes anyway. She wanted people to worship God in whatever ways they felt comfortable. Just worship. Just remember God in every single day and doing. It didn't matter what they called it. When people asked her how she felt about the peace talks that were happening right before she died, she puffed up like a proud little bird and said, in Arabic, "I never lost my peace inside." To her, Islam was a welcoming religion. After her home in

Jerusalem was stolen from her, she lived in a small village that contained a Christian shrine. She felt very tender toward the people who would visit it. A Jewish professor tracked me down a few years ago in Jerusalem to tell me she changed his life after he went to her village to do an oral history project on Arabs. "Don't think she only mattered to you!" he said. "She gave me a whole different reality to imagine—yet it was amazing how close we became. Arabs could never be just a 'project' after that."

Did you have a grandmother? Mine never wanted people to be pushed   17 around. What did yours want?

Reading about Islam since my grandmother died, I note the "tolerance"   18 that was "typical of Islam" even in the old days. The Muslim leader Khalidibn al-Walid signed a Jerusalem treaty which declared, "in the name of God . . . you have complete security for your churches which shall not be occupied by the Muslims or destroyed."

It is the new millennium in which we should be even smarter than we   19 used to be, right? But I think we have fallen behind.

3.

Many Americans do not want to kill any more innocent people anywhere   20 in the world. We are extremely worried about military actions killing innocent people. We didn't like this in Iraq, we never liked it anywhere. We would like no more violence, from us as well as from you. We would like to stop the terrifying wheel of violence, just stop it, right on the road, and find something more creative to do to fix these huge problems we have. Violence is not creative, it is stupid and scary, and many of us hate all those terrible movies and TV shows made in our own country that try to pretend otherwise. Don't watch them. Everyone should stop watching them. An appetite for explosive sounds and toppling buildings is not a healthy thing for anyone in any country. The USA should apologize to the whole world for sending this trash out into the air and for paying people to make it.

But here's something good you may not know—one of the best-selling   21 books of poetry in the United States in recent years is the Coleman Barks translation of Rumi, a mystical Sufi poet of the 13th century, and Sufism is Islam and doesn't that make you glad?

Everyone is talking about the suffering that ethnic Americans are going   22 through. Many will no doubt go through more of it, but I would like to thank everyone who has sent me a condolence card. Americans are usually very kind people. Didn't your colleagues find that out during their time living here? It is hard to imagine they missed it. How could they do what they did, knowing that?

4.

We will all die soon enough. Why not take the short time we have on   23
this delicate planet and figure out some really interesting things we might
do together? I promise you, God would be happier. So many people are
always trying to speak for God—I know it is a very dangerous thing to do.
I tried my whole life not to do it. But this one time is an exception. Because
there are so many people crying and scared and confused and complicated
and exhausted right now—it is as if we have all had a giant simultaneous
breakdown.

I beg you, as your distant Arab cousin, as your American neighbor,   24
listen to me.

Our hearts are broken: as yours may also feel broken in some ways, we   25
can't understand, unless you tell us in words. Killing people won't tell us.
We can't read that message.

Find another way to live. Don't expect others to be like you. Read   26
Rumi. Read Arabic poetry. Poetry humanizes us in a way that news, or
even religion, has a harder time doing. A great Arab scholar, Dr. Salma
Jayyusi, said, "If we read one another, we won't kill one another." Read
American poetry. Plant mint. Find a friend who is so different from you,
you can't believe how much you have in common. Love them. Let them
love you. Surprise people in gentle ways, as friends do. The rest of us will
try harder too. Make our family proud.

Thinking about the Essay

1. How does Nye address her primary audience—"would-be terrorists"? What
   tone or voice does she employ? What are some of the words and phrases she
   uses to get their attention? Of course, Nye also writes for a broader audience
   of readers—us. How does she make her message appealing to this larger
   audience?

2. Nye presents an elaborate argument in this essay. What is her central claim?
   What reasons or minor propositions does she give in support of her claim?
   How do the events of 9/11 condition the nature of her argument? What types
   of appeal does she make to convince her audience to think, feel, and act
   differently?

3. Examine the introductory paragraphs—paragraphs 1–12. Why does Nye
   use a first-person ("I") point of view? What is her purpose? What is the
   effect?

4. Analyze sections 1–4 of Nye's essay (paragraphs 13–26). What is the subject
   matter of each? How does the sequence of sections serve to advance the
   writer's argument? What transitional techniques permit essay coherence and
   unity?

5. Why is Nye's last paragraph a fitting conclusion to the essay? What elements from the body of the essay does this concluding paragraph reinforce and illuminate?

Responding in Writing

6. Write your own letter to any would-be terrorists. Address this audience in a personal voice. Use a variety of appeals to make your case.

7. In an analytical essay, examine the ways in which Nye tries to make her case in "To Any Would-Be Terrorists."

8. Write a letter to Naomi Shihab Nye in which you agree or disagree with the content of her essay.

Networking

9. Exchange your paper with another class member and evaluate it for content, grammar and syntax, organization, and tone. Make revisions based on your discussion.

10. Conduct online research on Rumi, and then write a paper explaining why Nye would allude to this figure in an essay on terrorism.

Why We Fight Wars

Paul Krugman

Paul Krugman, an American economist born in 1953 in Albany, New York, holds degrees from MIT and Yale, and is now Professor of Economics and International Affairs at Princeton and a columnist for the *New York Times*, *Fortune*, and *Slate*. Krugman is among the most influential economic thinkers in the United States. In addition to academic books and textbooks, he began writing for a more general audience in the '90s on issues he considered important to public policy. For example, in *The Age of Diminished Expectations* (1990) he wrote about the increasing U.S. income inequality, which he attributed in part to changes in technology, but primarily to a change in the political atmosphere toward conservativism. In 2008, he won the Nobel Memorial Prize in Economic Sciences for his contributions to new trade theory and new economic geography. The prize committee awarded this honor for his work explaining the patterns of world trade and the geographic concentration of wealth. In this article, he presents his views on the relationship between war and economics.

Before Reading

Why do you think we fight wars? List as many reasons as you can think of. Where did you get these ideas?

A century has passed since the start of World War I, which many people   1
at the time declared was "the war to end all wars." Unfortunately, wars just kept happening. And with the headlines from Ukraine getting scarier by the day, this seems like a good time to ask why.

Once upon a time wars were fought for fun and profit; when Rome   2
overran Asia Minor or Spain conquered Peru, it was all about the gold and silver. And that kind of thing still happens. In influential research sponsored by the World Bank, the Oxford economist Paul Collier has shown that the best predictor of civil war, which is all too common in poor countries, is the availability of lootable resources like diamonds. Whatever other reasons rebels cite for their actions seem to be mainly after-the-fact rationalizations. War in the preindustrial world was and still is more like a contest among crime families over who gets to control the rackets than a fight over principles.

If you're a modern, wealthy nation, however, war—even easy, victorious   3
war—doesn't pay. And this has been true for a long time. In his famous 1910 book "The Great Illusion," the British journalist Norman Angell argued that "military power is socially and economically futile." As he pointed out, in an interdependent world (which already existed in the age of steamships, railroads, and the telegraph), war would necessarily inflict severe economic harm even on the victor. Furthermore, it's very hard to extract golden eggs from sophisticated economies without killing the goose in the process.

We might add that modern war is very, very expensive. For example, by   4
any estimate the eventual costs (including things like veterans' care) of the Iraq war will end up being well over $1 trillion, that is, many times Iraq's entire G.D.P.

So the thesis of "The Great Illusion" was right: Modern nations can't   5
enrich themselves by waging war. Yet wars keep happening. Why?

One answer is that leaders may not understand the arithmetic. Angell,   6
by the way, often gets a bum rap from people who think that he was predicting an end to war. Actually, the purpose of his book was to debunk atavistic notions of wealth through conquest, which were still widespread in his time. And delusions of easy winnings still happen. It's only a guess, but it seems likely that Vladimir Putin thought that he could overthrow Ukraine's government, or at least seize a large chunk of its territory, on the cheap—a bit of deniable aid to the rebels, and it would fall into his lap.

Paul Krugman, "Why We Fight Wars," *New York Times* (Aug. 17, 2014) op ed page.

And for that matter, remember when the Bush administration predicted   7
that overthrowing Saddam and installing a new government would cost
only $50 billion or $60 billion?

The larger problem, however, is that governments all too often gain   8
politically from war, even if the war in question makes no sense in terms
of national interests.

Recently Justin Fox of the Harvard Business Review suggested that the   9
roots of the Ukraine crisis may lie in the faltering performance of the Russian
economy. As he noted, Mr. Putin's hold on power partly reflects a long run
of rapid economic growth. But Russian growth has been sputtering—and
you could argue that the Putin regime needed a distraction.

Similar arguments have been made about other wars that otherwise   10
seem senseless, like Argentina's invasion of the Falkland Islands in 1982,
which is often attributed to the then-ruling junta's desire to distract the
public from an economic debacle. (To be fair, some scholars are highly
critical of this claim.)

And the fact is that nations almost always rally around their leaders   11
in times of war, no matter how foolish the war or how awful the leaders.
Argentina's junta briefly became extremely popular during the Falklands
war. For a time, the "war on terror" took President George W. Bush's
approval to dizzying heights, and Iraq probably won him the 2004 election.
True to form, Mr. Putin's approval ratings have soared since the Ukraine
crisis began.

No doubt it's an oversimplification to say that the confrontation in   12
Ukraine is all about shoring up an authoritarian regime that is stumbling
on other fronts. But there's surely some truth to that story—and that raises
some scary prospects for the future.

Most immediately, we have to worry about escalation in Ukraine. All-   13
out war would be hugely against Russia's interests—but Mr. Putin may feel
that letting the rebellion collapse would be an unacceptable loss of face.

And if authoritarian regimes without deep legitimacy are tempted to   14
rattle sabers when they can no longer deliver good performance, think
about the incentives China's rulers will face if and when that nation's economic miracle comes to an end—something many economists believe will
happen soon.

Starting a war is a very bad idea. But it keeps happening anyway.   15

Thinking about the Essay

1. In this essay, Paul Krugman uses the rhetorical mode of cause and effect in the
   IBC (Introduction-Body-Conclusion) inductive structure. First, in the introduction
   to the essay, he poses a question, and then, in the body of the essay, he provides several answers with specific examples. Trace the thread of causes and

effects throughout his essay. Explain how the examples enhance the meaning. What is his final conclusion? Why do you think the conclusion to his essay is set off in a brief paragraph of two short sentences? Explain the meaning of this statement.

2. What is Krugman's thesis? Does he explicitly answer the question posed in the title? What is his purpose? Is his approach appropriate for the readers of *The New York Times*, where this column was published?

3. How does Krugman explain Russian Premier Vladimir Putin's attempt to overthrow the government of Ukraine? How is Putin's attempt related to the economics of Russia? How successful has Putin been in this attempt? Why should we worry about Putin's actions?

4. In paragraph 3, Krugman says, "it's very hard to extract golden eggs from sophisticated economies without killing the goose in the process." What does this allusion to golden eggs and the goose refer to? Explain what the allusion means in the context of the paragraph.

5. Overall, what is the relationship between war and economics, according to Krugman? Do you agree with him? With a small group of classmates, discuss the validity of his argument and his conclusion. Discuss specific contemporary events that support or refute his theory. Share your discussion with the class.

Responding in Writing

6. Write an essay in which you explain how national and/or global economics affects you—in jobs, in income, in spending. You might consider such things as the cost of gas, of food, of college, and so on.

7. Write an essay in which you analyze and evaluate the validity and plausibility of Krugman's economic theories. Include in your essay some research on Krugman's detractors, and answer or support their criticisms of Krugman's theories.

8. Krugman states that from an economic standpoint, war does not pay. Write an argumentative essay in which you agree or disagree with his statement. Include in your essay a summary of Krugman's argument and then present your view developed with specifics.

Networking

9. Krugman is a firm believer in Keynesian economics. Research John Maynard Keynes and his economic theory. Summarize his theory and how it has influenced economic theory and practice since he first published *The General Theory of Employment, Interest and Money* in 1936, during the Great Depression. Also research the comments of economists who disagree with Keynes—and Krugman and include your findings in your summary.

10. Go to www.nobelprize.org and listen to Krugman's lecture when he was awarded the Nobel Prize. Discuss his comments with a small group of classmates. What insights about the impact of economics on society can you glean from this speech? Summarize your discussion, and share it with your class.

Losing the "War on Terror"

Reza Aslan

Reza Aslan was born in Iran but immigrated to the United States when a teenager. Aslan has degrees from Santa Clara University, Harvard University, and the University of Iowa, and holds a PhD in Sociology, with a focus on the sociology of religion, from the University of California, Santa Barbara. A contributor to popular and scholarly periodicals, Aslan is also the author of *No God but God*: *The Origins, Evolution, and Future of Islam* (2005) and *How to Win a Cosmic War: God, Globalization, and the End of the War on Terror* (2009). In this essay from the April 8, 2009, edition of the *Los Angeles Times*, Aslan offers a critique of the "master narrative" of the war on terror.

Before Reading

Do you think that the "war on terror" is an accurate description of our common predicament, or can this phrase be a misleading or dangerous oversimplification of current global realities?

Secretary of State Hillary Rodham Clinton let slip last week that the Obama administration has finally abandoned the phrase "war on terror." Its absence had been noted by commentators. There was no directive, Clinton said, "it's just not being used." 1

It may seem a trivial thing, but the change in rhetoric marks a significant turning point in the ideological contest with radical Islam. That is because the war on terror has always been a conflict more rhetorical than real. There is, of course, a very real, very bloody military component in the struggle against extremist forces in the Muslim world, though one can argue whether the U.S. and allied engagements in Iraq, Afghanistan and beyond are an integral part of that struggle, a distraction from it or, worse, evidence of its subversion and failure. But to the extent that the war on terror has been posited, from the start, as a war of ideology—a clash of civilizations—it is a rhetorical war, one fought more constructively with words and ideas than with guns and bombs. 2

The truth is that the phrase "war on terror" has always been problematic, not just because "terror," "terrorism" and "terrorist" are wastebasket terms that often convey as much about the person using them as they do about the 3

Reza Aslan, "Losing the 'War on Terror,'" *Los Angeles Times*, April 8, 2009. Copyright © 2009 by Reza Aslan. Reprinted by permission of the author.

events or people being described, but because this was never meant to be a war against terrorism per se. If it were, it would have involved the Basque separatists in Spain, the Hindu/Marxist Tamil Tigers in Sri Lanka, the Maoist rebels in eastern India, Israeli ultranationalists, the Kurdish PKK, remnants of the Irish Republican Army and the Sikh separatist movements, and so on.

Rather, the war on terror, as conceived of by the Bush administration, was targeted at a particular brand of terrorism—that employed exclusively by Islamic entities. Which is why the enemy in this ideological conflict was gradually and systematically expanded to include not just the people who attacked the U.S. on Sept. 11, 2001, and the organizations that supported them, but an ever-widening conspiracy of disparate groups, such as Hamas in Palestine, Hezbollah in Lebanon, the Muslim Brotherhood in Egypt, the clerical regime in Iran, the Sunni insurgency in Iraq, the Kashmiri militants, the Taliban and any other organization that declared itself Muslim and employed terrorism as a tactic.   4

According to the master narrative of the war on terror, these were a monolithic enemy with a common agenda and a shared ideology. Never mind that many of these groups consider one another to be a graver threat than they consider America, that they have vastly different and sometimes irreconcilable political yearnings and religious beliefs, and that, until the war on terror, many had never thought of the United States as an enemy. Give this imaginary monolith a made-up name—say, "Islamofascism"— and an easily recognizable enemy is created, one that exists not so much as a force to be defeated but as an idea to be opposed, one whose chief attribute appears to be that "they" are not "us."   5

By lumping together the disparate forces, movements, armies, ideas and grievances of the greater Muslim world, from Morocco to Malaysia; by placing them in a single category ("enemy"), assigning them a single identity ("terrorist"); and by countering them with a single strategy (war), the Bush administration seemed to be making a blatant statement that the war on terror was, in fact, "a war against Islam."   6

That is certainly how the conflict has been viewed by a majority in four major Muslim countries—Egypt, Morocco, Pakistan and Indonesia— in a worldpublicopinion.org poll in 2007. Nearly two-thirds of respondents said they believe that the purpose of the war on terror is to "spread Christianity in the region" of the Middle East.   7

Indeed, if the war on terror was meant to be an ideological battle against groups such as Al Qaeda for the hearts and minds of Muslims, the consensus around the globe seems to be that the battle has been lost.   8

A September 2008 BBC World Service survey of 23 countries, including Russia, Australia, Pakistan, Turkey, France, Germany, Britain, the U.S., China and Mexico, found that almost 60% of all respondents said the war   9 on terror has either had no effect or that it has made Al Qaeda stronger. Forty-seven percent said they think that neither side was winning; 56% of Americans have that view.

It is time not just to abandon the phrase "war on terror" but to admit 10 that the ideological struggle against radical Islam could never be won militarily. The battle for the hearts and minds of Muslims will take place not in the streets of Baghdad or in the mountains of Afghanistan but in the suburbs of Paris, the slums of East London and the cosmopolitan cities of Berlin and New York.

In the end, the most effective weapon in countering the appeal of 11 groups such as Al Qaeda may be the words we use.

Thinking about the Essay

1. What is Aslan's thesis, and where does it appear?

2. What does Aslan mean by "rhetoric," and how does he connect this word to "ideology," "war on terror," and "master narrative"?

3. What types of illustration does Aslan use to structure his definition and analysis of such words as "terror," "terrorism," and "terrorist"? Would you say that Aslan's definitions are universally true or stipulative (that is, strictly personal and therefore limited in application)? Explain.

4. Identify the places where Aslan uses classification and division. How does classification operate in this essay as an organizing principle?

5. Consider the conclusion of this essay. Why does Aslan end with a single sentence? What is his purpose?

Responding in Writing

6. Write your own definition of "war on terror." Be certain to use a tone that captures your feelings about this term and about how people and groups respond to it.

7. Write an argumentative essay supporting or rejecting the concept "war on terror." Refer to Aslan's article in the course of your argument.

8. Aslan uses the phrase "radical Islam." Write your own extended definition of this term, explaining why or why not it is an accurate reflection of current global realities.

Networking

9. In groups of four or five, construct your own extended definition of "the master narrative of the war on terror" (paragraph 5). Share your definition with the class.

10. Locate a "war on terror" or a "radical Islam" website. What does this website say about current global conflicts and controversies? Report your findings in a class discussion.

10 | Global Aid: Can We Reduce Disease and Poverty?

Natural disasters, disease, and poverty continue to stalk the world in the twenty-first century. Moreover, the aftermath of Hurricane Katrina in 2005 was a reminder to many in the United States and around the world that major socioeconomic disparities exist even within a developed country. Poverty and a weak infrastructure made New Orleans and the surrounding region vulnerable to natural catastrophe, in much the same way that a compromised immune system invites disease. Observers compared the disaster in New Orleans to the humanitarian crises that result from floods and earthquakes in vulnerable, overpopulated Third World countries. But the fact is that most of the world's population lives under conditions like those found in the slums, shantytowns, and rural backwaters of the globe and in their counterparts in the United States.

We may like to think of such conditions as the provincial vestiges of a preindustrial world that, once exposed to the light of day, will naturally be assimilated into the modern world and corrected by the natural forces of progress. But globalization has also created new forms of poverty, isolation, and dependency. The new global economy has meant a return to what some would describe as an economics of colonial exploitation—although it is not clear who is exploiting whom, or even if "exploitation" is the correct label. Globalization has changed the relationship between "rich" and "poor" countries, but it is not clear whether the forces of a global free market will tend to bridge or widen the gap between rich and poor, or whether global commerce will strengthen the socioeconomic infrastructures of poor countries or mask and preserve their deficiencies. Without infrastructures of their own in place, the poorest nations in the world may become even more dependent on international aid to address poverty-related health problems. And while some blame these negative trends on the forces of an unregulated global free market, the philanthropic efforts of the Bill & Melinda Gates

Syrian refugees from Kobani flee from the attacks by the Islamic State into refugee camps in Turkey in September 2014.

Thinking about the Image

1. How would you describe your initial response to this image? For example, do you find the image to be optimistic or depressing? Explain your position.
2. How might your response be influenced by your attitudes toward gender, sexuality, race, religion, geography, or cultural background?
3. What point or argument do you think the photographer was trying to make?
4. Conduct research on the conflict in Syria, and then write a brief essay on one aspect of this problem. Insert at least three relevant images into the essay.

Foundation—which now spends nearly as much each year on global health projects as the World Health Organization—suggest that a corporate model of international aid may serve as a viable alternative to government-based infrastructures.

The essays in this chapter analyze global health and poverty issues in terms of a complex set of factors that have become even more challenging in recent decades with the phenomenon of globalization. For example, AIDS relief workers might distribute condoms to miners in South Africa, but the South African mines are run by unregulated transnational corporations, the miners are poor and underpaid migrant laborers, and their sex partners are often migrant workers who are forced into prostitution to feed and clothe their children. Often, the conditions that make people vulnerable to a disease are so closely connected with disease itself that cause and effect are nearly indistinguishable—hence, the term "nutritionally acquired immune deficiency syndrome" (NAIDS).

In the early nineteenth century, British economist Robert Malthus predicted that the world's population would eventually outrun the world's food supply and that hunger and famine were the natural mechanisms for adjusting supply with demand. Malthus, as many have pointed out, failed to take into account future technological innovations that would radically improve the efficiency of world food production. Today, world food supply exceeds demand. The problem of world hunger is a failure of distribution, not a failure to produce enough food. And many of the diseases that result from poverty and hunger can be treated or prevented, depending on the approach taken. Globalization reminds us that certain disparities are the result of structural failure, and that the magnitude of a natural disaster is often a function of an unnatural vulnerability.

Power to the Poor: Provide Energy to Fight Poverty

Morgan D. Bazilian

> Morgan D. Bazilian is lead energy specialist at the World Bank and deputy director of the Joint Institute for Strategic Energy Analysis. He holds a master's degree and a PhD in the techno-economic aspects of energy systems and has senior research affiliations at the University of Cambridge. Previously he worked on the United Nations Sustainable Energy for All initiative and served as chief of cabinet for the Minister of Energy in Ireland. He has been the lead climate change negotiator on low-carbon technology for the European Union and has served on the EU's energy research and development programs. His book *Analytical Methods for Energy Diversity and Security* (2008) is a standard reference in the area of energy policy. In this essay, Bazilian argues that "energy is a precondition to alleviating many other problems associated with poverty."

Before Reading

What is the future for energy development and use on this planet? How can you as an individual contribute to the wise use of energy now and in the future?

Imagine life without electricity. With no lights, electric stove, or water   1
pump, you must travel miles to fetch water and firewood, running a
particular risk of attack if you are a girl or a woman. At home, you cook
over a smoky stove or an open fire, raising your odds of getting lung and
heart disease. If you are pregnant, you may die in the dark, giving birth
at a clinic that lacks air conditioning and modern medical equipment.
Without vaccines, which require refrigeration, your children remain vulnerable to deadly diseases. At night, they study by the light of a kerosene
lamp, which causes burns when the fuel spills. Earning a living isn't easy,
either. No electricity means no sewing machines or rice mills, no pumps
for irrigating crops, and no way to keep drinks cold or keep a store open
at night. The lack of power keeps away bigger companies that might have
hired you.

Such is the plight of nearly half of the world's population. Some two   2
billion people lack electricity outright or have poor-quality service, and
nearly three billion rely on dirty fuels, such as firewood and animal dung,
for cooking and heating. Nearly 90 percent of those suffering from energy
poverty, as the problem is known, can be found in South Asia and sub
-Saharan Africa. In Liberia, to take one of the most extreme cases, just two

Faisal Mahmood/Reuters

A Pakistani child studies by candlelight during a power outage in April 2013.

percent of the population has regular access to electricity. And in Tanzania, nearly 50 percent of firms say that poor electricity service is a major constraint for doing business. They face an average of nearly nine power outages every month, leading to lost sales and poor productivity. In this area, the disparity between the developing world and the developed world could hardly be greater: the average American uses about 50 times as much power as the average Bangladeshi and about 100 times as much as the average Nigerian.

The problem has proved stubbornly persistent. Data from the World Bank show that although 1.7 billion people acquired access to electricity from 1990 to 2010, the gains barely outpaced population growth. They also accrued disproportionately to cities: today, about 85 percent of those without electricity live in rural areas far from any infrastructure. In sub -Saharan Africa especially, the scale of the challenge is daunting. Enabling people there to consume as much electricity as those in a middle-income region would require an increase in power generation of more than ten percent a year over two decades—an annual growth rate far greater than the historical two to three percent. Small wonder, then, that the International Energy Agency has forecast that in 20 to 30 years, the number of energy poor may remain close to where it stands today.

Although international donors have many compelling causes to choose from, reducing energy poverty should rank among the top. Energy is a precondition to alleviating many other problems associated with poverty, from poor health to lack of education to unemployment. The issue also reaches beyond the bounds of poverty to foreign policy, since a lack of energy access can foster instability. The good news is that governments, development agencies, and nonprofits have begun to ramp up spending on fighting energy poverty and have unveiled a slew of new initiatives, many of which have produced measurable improvements in the lives of the poor.

At the same time, those groups have tended to focus too much attention on small-scale fixes or incremental improvements. Such approaches can set ambitions too low, implicitly condemning billions of people to meager levels of energy use that will do little to lift them out of poverty. As Kandeh Yumkella, a senior UN official, has noted, "The provision of one light does nothing more than shine a light on poverty; the poor then only see more clearly that their floor is made of dirt."

Donors need to aim instead for the heart of the problem: governments in poor countries that are struggling to undertake effective and widespread energy programs. From the United States in the early twentieth century to postwar Germany and Japan to modern China, people have gained access to electricity and modern fuels thanks to concerted government leadership, massive public investments in infrastructure, good planning, well-trained work forces, supportive regulations, and financially viable institutions. There is no reason to believe that these fundamental ingredients matter less today.

Scaling Up

As governments in the developing world come to grips with the sheer size   7
of the challenge before them, they quickly realize that building energy infrastructure such as large power plants and transmission lines takes years or decades. In the meantime, small companies are stepping in with much-needed services, the most innovative of which often involve solar energy. Taking advantage of the recent plunge in the price of solar panels, companies are working with local banks to provide financing and servicing arrangements that are appropriate for the rural poor, which usually involve small up-front costs, modest monthly payments, and reliable maintenance agreements.

More and more families can now afford low-power systems that can   8
run a television or a few lights and take just a day or two to install. One Indian company, SELCO, has sold and maintained more than two million such systems, thanks largely to a sales approach that is tailored to poor customers. A related success story comes from Bangladesh, which has seen the fastest expansion of small-scale, off-grid solar power systems in the world. Over three million such systems were installed by 2014, a figure that is on track to double within the next three years. Credit goes principally to the Bangladeshi government, which created a dedicated agency that provides nongovernmental organizations and microfinance lenders with technical support and grants. Despite these advances, in India, nearly 300 million people still go without electricity. And in Bangladesh, over 60 percent of businesses rely on their own backup generators to keep the electricity flowing.

Although small-scale systems have helped millions of people take their   9
first steps up the energy ladder, they suffer from a number of technical and economic inefficiencies that larger systems can avoid. So-called mini-grids are one way to help make small-scale energy sources more practical. Originally designed for communities not yet linked to the main electrical grid, mini-grids can aggregate a whole village's infrastructure and power sources, making the system more efficient and easier to maintain than a series of individual systems. Because they often rely on a number of different technologies and can run independently from the main electrical grid, mini-grids are also resilient. As a result, the U.S. Department of Defense has installed them on several military bases from Texas to Hawaii, and hospitals, factories, and other sites that need reliable power are starting to adopt them, too. Those same features make them an attractive option in fragile and conflict-ridden states, where centralized systems can make easier targets for violence and are more likely to face long construction delays.

Still, mini-grids are best suited to specific conditions and have difficulty   10
competing with centralized power systems. Economies of scale explain
why centralized power systems became the norm around the world, replac-
ing smaller, isolated systems. Con Edison's present-day network in New
York City, with over 120,000 miles of electrical cables serving some three
million customers, is a far more efficient way to meet modern demands
than the lighting system that Thomas Edison established on Pearl Street in
1882. Energy systems in developing countries will no doubt take different
shapes from those in the developed world, and that is likely a good thing.
There will be a bigger role for distributed electricity generation and an
opportunity to benefit from advances in information and communications
technologies that make systems smarter. Nevertheless, large-scale power
plants will almost certainly remain an important part of the mix.

What It Takes

Given the scale of the problem, tackling energy poverty requires bold   11
government action. Historically, the process of expanding rural access to
electricity began with the public sector. Consider one of the most successful energy-poverty-alleviation programs in history: the U.S. government's
efforts to extend electricity access during the Great Depression as part of
President Franklin Roosevelt's New Deal. In 1930, roughly 65 percent of
U.S. households had electricity. As in many poor countries today, most people living in cities had electricity, but only around ten percent of those in the
countryside did. Private utilities were not delivering affordable power to
farmers and remained uninterested in building the expensive and low-return
infrastructure necessary to reach rural communities. In the Tennessee River
valley—a region that encompasses parts of Alabama, Georgia, Kentucky,
Mississippi, North Carolina, Tennessee, and Virginia—farmers lived without refrigerators and water heaters. With no modern water-management
systems, their crop yields suffered from relentless flooding.

Then the federal government acted. In 1933, Congress, invoking "the   12
interest of the national defense," created the Tennessee Valley Authority, which built several large dams in the region that not only produced
electricity but also helped improve flood control. And in 1935, Roosevelt
created the Rural Electrification Administration, which within five years
helped establish hundreds of rural electric cooperatives to serve hundreds
of thousands of customers. The National Academy of Engineering called
the electrification of the United States the greatest engineering achievement
in the twentieth century. And the Tennessee Valley Authority exists to this
day as one of the country's largest power providers and is a self-funded
corporation of the U.S. government employing more than 12,000 people.

Is Beauty Universal?
Global Body Images

Not every society worships supermodels, but most societies do have notions about what constitutes beauty. Whereas a washboard stomach might set the standard for beauty for certain people in the United States, there are cultures and constituencies elsewhere that value ample stomachs and hips as the ideal body type. What one society values as beauty might not appeal—indeed might seem ridiculous—to another.

Of course, the age of globalization has spawned a fusion of styles, customs, and attitudes concerning beauty and ideal body images. Fashion magazines, advertisements, and television commercials— whether in the United States, Dubai, Japan, or anywhere on the planet—project transcultural (if not universal) standards of beauty. For example, the fashions of Africa and India adorn the bodies of Americans, and a fondness for tattoos, appropriated from traditional societies by American teens, now seems to be spreading across continents like an unstoppable cultural virus.

The forces molding global definitions of beauty cannot escape the impact of American popular culture. Icons of American pop culture— whether Beyoncé or Britney Spears—have an exaggerated impact on the attitudes, body styles, and beauty images of people around the world. Of course, cultural differences concerning beauty and body image persist, but the impact of American culture on how others perceive beauty can be irresistible and (as Susan Bordo observes in this book) insidious.

This portfolio presents images of the body and beauty from several cultural and transnational perspectives. These images reveal societies in transition and traditional values affected by (and at times resisting) the forces of globalization.

Daphne Ouwersloot/Alamy

Male Beauty Contest.   Men in Central Africa compete in an effort to attract wives.

Considering the Image

1. How does the photograph encourage a fresh perspective on traditional African culture as well as global culture?

2. Do you think that the photographer wants to advance a claim about marriage rituals or simply present an exotic slice of life from some faraway culture? Justify your response.

China Newsphoto/Reuters/Corbis

Kindergarten Kids.   Children pose during a model contest held for kindergarten kids in Xiamen, east China's Fujian province.

Considering the Image

1. Identify the elements in this photograph that contribute to the overall effect. What aspects of the image do you find most effective?

2. What is your response to viewing these Chinese children dressed in Western clothing and posing as if they are models on a runway in New York or Paris? Do you find the scene amusing, charming, appalling, or what? Explain your reaction.

Dubai Britney.   Two Arab women in traditional black burkas walk past a picture of pop singer Britney Spears in a posh shopping center in Dubai.

Considering the Image

1. What is your reaction to this photograph? Why do you believe you respond in this manner? How might the two women in burkas and Britney Spears serve as competing cultural symbols that condition your response? If you or a family member actually wears a burka, chador, or head covering, how might your reaction differ from others in the class?

2. What "message" or argument, if any, does the photographer convey in this shot? Does the photographer advance positive or negative connotations of the women in burkas and/or Britney Spears? Might there be an element of satire in the scene? Explain your responses to these questions.

Morteza Nikoubazl/Reuters/Corbis

Persian Beauty.   An Iranian girl, surrounded by women in chadors, awaits admission to the Jamaran mosque in Tehran. The late Ayatollah Khomeini frequently conducted Friday prayers and made important speeches at this mosque.

Considering the Image

1. How does the photographer compose this image? Why does he bathe the girl in light while the people surrounding her are cast in shadows? What appeals to logos, ethos, and pathos do you detect?

2. Compare the representation of women in this image with those appearing in the Britney Spears photo. What similar and dissimilar cultural points do the two photographers want to make?

REUTERS/Michaela Rehle/Landov

Barbie at 50.   A model poses with the world's most popular "Barbie" doll turning 50 years old, during the press preview of the 60th International Toy Fair in Nuremberg, February 4, 2009.

Considering the Image

1. Describe the composition of this image. Why is Barbie so prominently centered in the photograph?
2. Compare this image with that of Britney Spears in this portfolio. In what ways are they similar? Do they make the same point or not? Justify your response.

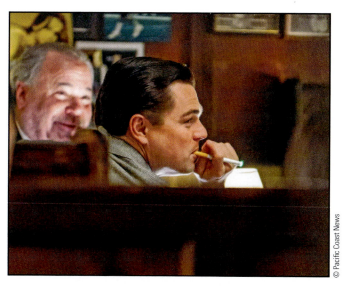

© Pacific Coast News

Celebrity Power.   Celebrities influence public opinion, behavior, and even morality. Here Leonardo DiCaprio smokes an electronic cigarette on set.

Considering the Image

1. Why does the photographer fill the frame with a close-up view of DiCaprio, largely excluding other elements? What is the effect?
2. Does the photograph suggest in any way that electronic smoking is acceptable in public? Why or why not?

China Photos/Getty Images News /Getty Images

Obese Girl Band.   Singers in a band named "Qianjin" (which in Chinese can mean both "girl" and "one ton") dance in celebration of the 2006 opening of a club for obese people in Beijing.

Considering the Image

1. Compare representations of women in this photograph with others in this portfolio, as well as with Susan Bordo's analysis in the essay that appears on pages 17–20.

2. An official at the Ministry of Health in China indicated that more than 200 million Chinese people are overweight. What cultural and economic values might serve to explain this phenomenon? How does the photograph articulate these values?

Indeed, expanding energy access works best when it is part of a 13 broader development plan. Beginning around 1980, both China and Thailand launched electricity programs that accompanied economy-wide reforms and managed to achieve universal electrification in two decades. In Vietnam, rural electrification formed part of the nationwide *doi moi* (renovation) reforms, which the government began in 1986. The measures included a gradual move from central planning to market mechanisms and an opening of the economy to trade and foreign investment, which laid a foundation on which the country's nascent energy sector could grow. Only later did the private sector begin participating.

Likewise, when Rwanda rolled out its energy-access efforts in 2009, it used 14 what it called a "sector-wide approach" that pooled aid from various sources together in a single program, one that was led by the Rwandan government but involved a range of stakeholders. The result: in just four years, the share of Rwanda's population with electricity roughly tripled. Every year, the country gains 60,000 new electrical connections, up from 1,000 annually before the reforms. Crucially, both Vietnam and Rwanda, like China and Thailand before them, recognized that efforts to combat energy poverty must go beyond the needs of rural households and aim to create wealth across the entire economy.

The Global Agenda

Most of the countries affected by energy poverty have already begun 15 reforming their energy sectors, have developed targets and strategies, and have launched dedicated agencies for expanding access to electricity and modern fuels. Still, they need some form of outside financial-risk mitigation and funding. Estimates for the price tag of expanding energy access globally range from $40 billion to $100 billion per year—big numbers, to be sure, but just a fraction of the total amount of capital spent in the energy sector. While public funding is necessary initially, it will ultimately be insufficient. In the long run, private investors will need to feel comfortable enough to dive into what are now very high-risk markets, if they exist at all. But the enormous demand is clear: a group of researchers led by Vijay Modi at Columbia University has shown that villagers in Mali and Uganda are willing to pay electricity rates that are nearly ten times as high as the rates that prevail in developed countries. It's hard to overstate the market opportunities that will arise once an additional billion-plus people gain access to energy. Glimpses of this are already apparent in some of sub -Saharan Africa's vibrant technology centers and in the explosive growth of the region's economy, which has more than doubled in size since 2000.

In light of the gains to be had, in 2013, the Obama administration 16 unveiled Power Africa, an initiative that provides funding and incentives for U.S. companies to bring their technologies to the region. The U.S. government committed $7 billion initially, and the private sector has since pledged about three times that amount. (The World Bank has also come on board, with $5 billion.) But Power Africa is no panacea. It's not clear whether it will outlast the Obama administration, and its initial focus on the private sector may be premature in some countries where the groundwork for public-private partnerships has yet to be laid.

Global goals also have a role, since they can help raise money, track   17
progress, and keep hold of the development community's often wandering attention. In 2012, the UN launched Sustainable Energy for All, an initiative that aims to ensure universal access to modern energy services by 2030. The UN is also working on a new round of targets, called the Sustainable Development Goals, to replace the Millennium Development Goals. The old goals didn't mention the eradication of energy poverty, but the new ones include it among the ranks of such aspirations as ending hunger and providing for universal education. The inclusion of energy issues on the list, which required no small feat of diplomacy, suggests that they are finally becoming part of the canon of traditional development economics.

The Geopolitics of Gigawatts

But goals alone won't trigger government action in the developing world;   18
only hardheaded policies can turn rhetoric into reality. Great powers such as the United States should consider the provision of energy not merely a matter of development but also a tool of geopolitics. Energy poverty counts as what the U.S. military calls a "threat multiplier," meaning that it can exacerbate existing challenges and contribute to instability. Providing electricity and modern fuels in the poorest countries can lower the risk of internal unrest and reduce the movement of people across borders. Indeed, some African governments have reacted to their increasingly vocal and young populations by unveiling promising new ventures to expand energy access. Since 2010, the Kenyan government has improved the electricity supply in Kibera, the largest slum in Nairobi, as part of a program that targets the areas of greatest social inequality.

Developed countries have all the more reason to act now in the wake   19
of new discoveries of oil and gas in East and West Africa. These finds have boosted government revenues, but the distribution of those revenues has, in some cases, exacerbated deep social and political problems. Take Nigeria, which is both one of the world's top oil exporters and home to one of the biggest populations without access to energy—90 million people. Decades of oil development in areas that still lack basic services have provided the

social, economic, and environmental drivers of violent conflict. Just as the United States has long been entangled in the energy security of the Middle East, it must now pay more attention to parts of sub-Saharan Africa. It should encourage countries there to govern the sector fairly and transparently and support efforts that funnel natural resource bounties toward addressing energy poverty.

Well-intentioned outsiders should remember that governments try- 20 ing to energize their territories need to take ownership of the efforts. The blueprints governments draw up with donor support need to respond to the specific national contexts and local needs; they should not be force-fed from afar. That's especially true when trying to balance the sometimes uncomfortable tradeoffs that can exist between addressing energy poverty and combating climate change. Governments in poor countries tend to focus on the former because of its immediacy, whereas wealthy governments are often more animated by the latter, given its global implications. Although clean energy technology has made enormous strides and will certainly play a very large role in the energy systems of tomorrow, donors will have to accept that in some cases, progress in energy access might come at the expense of the environment—as it did during the United States' electricity drive. That said, they should minimize these impacts as much as possible and make other concerns, such as food and water security, part of their calculus.

The economist Amartya Sen has argued that economic development 21 can be achieved only if the poor come to enjoy a set of freedoms including political participation, safety, and economic opportunity. Access to energy enables each of those fundamental rights, which is why efforts to eradicate poverty cannot afford to ignore it. True, the barriers that impede progress on ending energy poverty are formidable: scarce financial resources, competing priorities, weak institutions, and the sometimes misguided interventions on the part of outsiders. But they are well within the world's ability to overcome, and they are far less imposing than many of the technical obstacles humanity has already vanquished. The laws of physics operate the same in South Asia and sub-Saharan Africa as they do in Europe and North America. The needed materials are simple things, such as steel, concrete, copper, and glass.

Thinking about the Essay

1. What is the problem Bazilian sets up in the introduction to the essay? Is this technique effective to establish the problem and help readers understand it emotionally and cognitively?

2. How is the problem of energy related to poverty? To poor health? To education? To unemployment? To foreign policy? To climate change?

3. What solutions to energy poverty does Bazilian propose? What technical and economic inefficiencies impede progress in solving the problem of energy poverty? Is he optimistic or pessimistic about solving energy poverty? Does he convince you?

4. Three global goals are ending energy poverty, ending hunger, and providing universal education. How are the three goals interrelated?

5. Analyze the structure of Bazilian's essay. Is this structure appropriate and effective for his argument?

Responding in Writing

6. Using Bazilian's introduction as a sample, write a narrative essay (beginning in the morning and moving through your day until you go to bed) explaining what your life would be like if you had no electricity. What problems and disadvantages would you encounter? End with an explanation of the value of electricity in your life.

7. Write an essay analyzing the structure of Bazilian's argument. Identify, summarize, and explain the purpose of each section. Include identification, explanation, and effectiveness of the rhetorical strategies he uses in each section.

8. Write an argumentative essay in which you try to convince your classmates that each of us is responsible for conservation of energy. Include specific ways we can conserve energy.

Networking

9. Working with a small group of classmates, research the energy uses of a suburb in your area or of your university or a large manufacturing plant in your area. Discuss how energy could be used more wisely. Share your findings with the class.

10. Research some of the new policies and proposed innovation of the U.S. Department of Energy (DOE) and write a summary.

Is the Impact of Mobile Phones a Myth?

Tae Yoo

Tae Yoo was born in South Korea and holds a bachelor's degree in communications from Virginia Tech University. Currently she serves as senior vice president of corporate affairs at Cisco Systems Inc., a communications development and sales company. As the steward of Cisco's corporate social responsibility (CSR) programs, she directs Cisco's business, technical, and financial assets to create real social impact in communities around the world. In this essay, Yoo discusses global use of mobile phones and other communications devices.

Before Reading

How widespread is the use of mobile phones among your friends and family? What impact has the use of mobile phones had on them? How do you answer the question in the title: "Is the Impact of Mobile Phones a Myth?" Why?

At first glance, the numbers seem staggering. Global mobile phone penetration is 96 percent. In sub-Saharan Africa, where 47 percent of the population lives on less than $1.25 a day, mobile data use is expected to grow twentyfold by the end of 2019, according to a June 2014 mobility study by Ericsson. It is predicted there will be 930 million mobile subscriptions in sub-Saharan Africa by the end of 2019—nearly one for every resident. In India, 28 percent of citizens use a mobile phone, with an average of 2.54 devices per user. But such massive numbers can be deceiving. Mobile phones are often seen as a panacea for improving economic opportunity and public health worldwide. But in reality, we have a long way to go.

According to a Pew Research survey of 24 developing and emerging economies, only two countries had a critical mass of people using mobile phones to make or receive payments: Kenya (68 percent) and Uganda (50 percent). According to the report, "making or receiving payments is one of the least-used cell phone activities," with only 11 percent of the 24,263 people surveyed saying they use mobile devices for that purpose. Likewise, only 15 percent of respondents use mobile phones to get information about health and medicine. And while mobile adoption is high, Internet use is low. Only 40 percent of the world's population has access to the Internet at all. This is important, because research links Internet use to economic growth. For example, according to one 2010 report, a 10 percent increase in per capita GDP is associated with a 21.5 percent increase in Internet users per capita.

A couple of years ago I wrote about a young man named Stephen Ondicki, who lived in Kenya's second-largest slum. While his neighbors were earning less than $1 a day, Stephen was earning $8 a day running a computer repair shop. Stephen's success would have been impossible without a reliable and affordable broadband connection, which enabled him to take classes that prepared him to repair computers. For Stephen and others in developing countries, broadband connectivity is a powerful catalyst for economic and social advancement.

Yet, 4.2 billion people worldwide are not online. In developing   4
countries only 31 percent of people are online, and in the world's 49
least-developed countries, it is less than 10 percent, according to the International Telecommunication Union's 2013 Measuring the Information
Society Report. Smartphones, often a more affordable bridge to Internet
access, are still rare in emerging economies; while 59 percent of 18 to 29
year olds in Uganda own a cell phone, only 7 percent own a smartphone.
What are the obstacles? In many parts of the world, high-speed broadband access is simply too expensive. This may be due to a variety of factors, such as lack of competition, poor infrastructure, widespread poverty
or regulatory hurdles.

Basic mobile phones can circumvent lack of broadband access, but only   5
to a certain extent. Nelson Mandela said, "Education is the most powerful
weapon which you can use to change the world," yet use of mobile for education (m-learning) is still in its infancy and focused on basics like literacy.
For example, the nonprofit Worldreader delivers books on mobile devices
for free, using a compression technology to achieve high speeds even on
low-bandwidth networks. The service is available across the developing
world, with high use in sub-Saharan Africa and India.

Yes, mobile is powerful. But can it deliver the robust, specialized   6
training needed to fill in-demand jobs around the world—many of which
involve IT skills—and put 75 million unemployed young people to work?

None of this is meant to dismiss the global problem solvers who are   7
doing amazing work with mobile technology. The high mobile payment
rate in Kenya can be attributed to Safaricom's M-PESA, a system initially
designed to facilitate mobile microfinance loan payments but expanded
for broader use. Over 17 million Kenyans use M-PESA and around
25 percent of the country's GNP flows through it. Another example:
"micro-entrepreneurs" with Living Goods use mobile phones to market
low-cost health and hygiene products in their communities. They earn a
livelihood while improving public health.

But the reality is, while mobile phone use is widespread, it is not a silver   8
bullet for economic growth and individual livelihood. We must all work
together on two fronts: (1) capitalizing on skyrocketing mobile adoption
by developing and advancing truly transformational mobile tools that promote health, financial inclusion and skills development and (2) improving
access to high-speed broadband for all the world's people.

By "we," I mean corporations, governments, nonprofits and academia.   9
For example, Worldreader partnered with Australian application developer biNu to deliver its smart phone–like experience to low-end mobile
phones. Through its AppLab Incubator, the nongovernmental organization

(NGO) Grameen Foundation partners with private sector companies like MTN Uganda (telecommunications) and CARD Bank in the Philippines to develop, deliver and test mobile financial products for poor households. In a rural, isolated corner of Africa, Cisco partnered with USAID, local Internet service providers, and several NGOs such as NetHope, to bring high-speed Internet access to the world's largest refugee camp in Dadaab, Kenya. Thanks to this network, humanitarian organizations are saving money on communications and better serving the camp's residents, and refuges are getting educational and vocational training online at one of five community centers inside the camp.

When one person's livelihood changes, it can impact an entire fam-   10
ily, then a whole community. When something effective takes hold, it can change the world. Whether through a mobile device or a desktop computer, connectivity and creativity make it all possible.

Thinking about the Essay

1. How does Yoo answer the question she asks in the title? What specific evidence does she use to support her position? Is her evidence credible? Is her evidence sufficient? Is her evidence convincing?

2. What problem does she identify in the essay? What solutions does she pose? Do you think her suggestions for solving this global problem will work?

3. Yoo ends the essay by stating that "connectivity and creativity make it all possible." What does the pronoun *it* refer to? What is it that connectivity and creativity can make possible? Do you agree?

4. The author uses a variety of rhetorical strategies to develop, clarify, and convince. Explain how she uses each of the following strategies: statistics, examples, question and answer, cause and effect, problem to solution.

5. Explain how the author combines exposition and argument in the essay to convince her readers to agree with her assertions. How does she use the three argumentative appeals—ethical appeal, emotional appeal, and rational appeal?

Responding in Writing

6. Imagine your life without a mobile phone and without electronic access to the Internet. Write an essay in which you narrate and explain what your life would be like.

7. Write an essay in which you explain how electronic devices can contribute to global connectivity, communications, and creativity. Avoid unsupported generalizations; use specific rhetorical strategies and details to develop your exposition.

8. Write an essay in which you refute (present an opposing argument to) Yoo's argument. Share your refutation with a small group of classmates. With the members of your group, critique the effectiveness of each student's refutation. Also explain how Yoo would respond to each point of refutation.

Networking

9. Choose a column or article, a Facebook or Twitter account, or a blog written by someone from another country. Develop a discussion/conversation with this person. Let the writer know who you are and what your interest in him or her is. Ask questions that will help you know this person. Summarize what you learn, and share it with your class.

10. With a small group of classmates, list at least five other myths of contemporary society. The myths may be social, cultural, scientific, technical, academic, legal, or political; or they may be about health, sports, communications, education, fashion, body image, or something else. Choose one myth that your group agrees is a very significant myth today. Discuss specifically what this myth is, why the myth is significant today, what the causes and effects of the myth are, and what changes can be made to demythologize this belief. Summarize your discussion, and share it with the class.

A Year and a Day

EDWIDGE DANTICAT

Edwidge Danticat was born in Port-au-Prince, Haiti, in 1969, and raised by an aunt and uncle until she was twelve. At that point, she joined her parents in Brooklyn, New York. She received a BA from Barnard College (1990) and an MFA from Brown University (1993). Her novels and short story collections, which deal with the Haitian experience, include *Krik? Krak!* (1996), *The Farming of Bones* (1998), and *The Dew Breaker* (2004). Danticat has also published children's fiction, a memoir, and a collection of essays, *Create Dangerously* (2010). In 2009, Danticat received a prestigious MacArthur Fellows Program "Genius Grant." In this essay from the January 17, 2011, issue of *The New Yorker*, Danticat reflects on the disastrous earthquake that leveled Port-au-Prince a year earlier, resulting in hundreds of thousands of deaths and even greater numbers of displaced Haitians.

Before Reading

Would you be willing to volunteer your time or contribute money to alleviate the suffering of people victimized by a natural disaster? Why or why not?

In the Haitian vodou tradition, it is believed by some that the souls of
the newly dead slip into rivers and streams and remain there, under the
water, for a year and a day. Then, lured by ritual prayer and song, the souls
emerge from the water and the spirits are reborn. These reincarnated spirits
go on to occupy trees, and, if you listen closely, you may hear their hushed
whispers in the wind. The spirits can also hover over mountain ranges, or in
grottoes, or caves, where familiar voices echo our own when we call out their
names. The year-and-a-day commemoration is seen, in families that believe
in it and practice it, as a tremendous obligation, an honorable duty, in part
because it assures a transcendental continuity of the kind that has kept us
Haitians, no matter where we live, linked to our ancestors for generations.

1

By this interpretation of death, one of many in Haiti, more than two
hundred thousand souls went *anba dlo*—under the water—after the earthquake last January 12th. Their bodies, however, were elsewhere. Many were
never removed from the rubble of their homes, schools, offices, churches,
or beauty parlors. Many were picked up by earthmovers on roadsides and
dumped into mass graves. Many were burned, like kindling, in bonfires, for
fear that they might infect the living.

2

"In Haiti, people never really die," my grandmothers said when I was
a child, which seemed strange, because in Haiti people were always dying.
They died in disasters both natural and man-made. They died from political violence. They died of infections that would have been easily treated
elsewhere. They even died of chagrin, of broken hearts. But what I didn't
fully understand was that in Haiti people's spirits never really die. This has
been proved true in the stories we have seen and read during the past year,
of boundless suffering endured with grace and dignity: mothers have spent
nights standing knee-deep in mud, cradling their babies in their arms, while
rain pounded the tarpaulin above their heads; amputees have learned to
walk, and even dance, on their new prostheses within hours of getting them;
rape victims have created organizations to protect other rape victims; people have tried, in any way they could, to reclaim a shadow of their past lives.

3

My grandmothers were also talking about souls, which never really
die, even when the visual and verbal manifestations of their transition—
the tombstones and mausoleums, the elaborate wakes and church services,

4

the *desounen* prayers that encourage the body to surrender the spirit, the mourning rituals of all religions—become a luxury, like so much else in Haiti, like a home, like bread, like clean water.

In the year since the earthquake, Haiti has lost some thirty-five hundred people to cholera, an epidemic that is born out of water. The epidemic could potentially take more lives than the earthquake itself. And with the contagion of cholera comes a stigma that follows one even in death. People cannot touch a loved one who has died of cholera. No ritual bath is possible, no last dressing of the body. There are only more mass graves.

In the emerging lore and reality of cholera, water, this fragile veil between life and death for so many Haitians, has become a feared poison. Even as the election stalemate lingers, the rice farmers in Haiti's Artibonite Valley—the country's breadbasket—are refusing to step into the bacteria-infected waters of their paddies, setting the stage for potential food shortages and more possible death ahead, this time from hunger. In the precarious dance for survival, in which we long to honor the dead while still harboring the fear of joining them, will our rivers and streams even be trusted to shelter and then return souls?

A year ago, watching the crumbled buildings and crushed bodies that were shown around the clock on American television, I thought that I was witnessing the darkest moment in the history of the country where I was born and where most of my family members still live. Then I heard one of the survivors say, either on radio or on television, that during the earthquake it was as if the earth had become liquid, like water. That's when I began to imagine them, all these thousands and thousands of souls, slipping into the country's rivers and streams, then waiting out their year and a day before reemerging and reclaiming their places among us. And, briefly, I was hopeful.

My hope came not only from the possibility of their and our communal rebirth but from the extra day that would follow the close of what has certainly been a terrible year. That extra day guarantees nothing, except that it will lead us into the following year, and the one after that, and the one after that.

Thinking about the Essay

1. At what point in the essay do you begin to sense Danticat's main purpose? What is her purpose? What type of reader might her purpose appeal to? How does she frame her thesis around this purpose?

2. Danticat provides vivid descriptive details in this essay. Which details stand out for you? How does she create symbolic overtones with these details?

3. Explain what Danticat means by "a year and a day," and how she weaves this motif into the structure of the essay.

4. What is the relationship between the introductory and concluding paragraphs, specifically in terms of Danticat's thesis?

5. Describe the persona that Danticat creates for herself, her family, and the Haitian people.

Responding in Writing

6. In an essay of analysis, explore the theme of migrating souls that Danticat weaves into her text. Do you believe that souls live on after death? Answer this question and others posed by the writer's theme.

7. Argue for or against the proposition that religion or faith can make a natural disaster more acceptable to the surviving victims.

8. Write an expository essay in which you explain what you have learned about the Haitian people from a careful critical analysis of Danticat's text.

Networking

9. With another student, analyze the mood that Danticat creates in her essay. Then write a collaborative or joint essay explaining the techniques Danticat uses to create a dominant impression of Haiti and the Haitian people.

10. Search the Internet for information on the Haitian earthquake of 2010. Using at least three sources, write a brief research paper on one aspect of the earthquake or its aftermath.

What We're Afraid to Say About Ebola

Michael T. Osterholm

Born in 1953 in Minneapolis, Minnesota, Michael T. Osterholm is a public health scientist and biosecurity expert. He holds the McKnight Presidential Endowed Chair in Public Health at the University of Minnesota, and his areas of study include infectious disease, environmental health, and technological leadership. In 2005, he was appointed by Michael Leavitt, Secretary of the Department of Health and Human Services, to the newly established National Science Advisory Board on Biosecurity, and in 2008 he was appointed to the World Economic Forum Working Group on Pandemics. He is also an international leader in the growing concern over the use of biological weapons to target large civilian populations, a topic he reviews in his best-selling book *Living Terrors: What America Needs to Know to Survive the Coming Bioterrorist Catastrophe* (2001). In this article, he explains his dire concern over the possibility of the uncontrolled spread of Ebola.

Before Reading

What do you know about Ebola? Why are so many people afraid of this disease and even hesitant to talk about it?

The Ebola epidemic in West Africa has the potential to alter history as much as any plague has ever done.   1

There have been more than 4,300 cases and 2,300 deaths over the past six months. Last week, the World Health Organization warned that, by early October, there may be thousands of new cases per week in Liberia, Sierra Leone, Guinea and Nigeria. What is not getting said publicly, despite briefings and discussions in the inner circles of the world's public health agencies, is that we are in totally uncharted waters and that Mother Nature is the only force in charge of the crisis at this time.   2

There are two possible future chapters to this story that should keep us up at night.   3

The first possibility is that the Ebola virus spreads from West Africa to megacities in other regions of the developing world. This outbreak is very different from the 19 that have occurred in Africa over the past 40 years. It is much easier to control Ebola infections in isolated villages. But there has been a 300 percent increase in Africa's population over the last four decades, much of it in large city slums. What happens when an infected person yet to become ill travels by plane to Lagos, Nairobi, Kinshasa or Mogadishu—or even Karachi, Jakarta, Mexico City or Dhaka?   4

The second possibility is one that virologists are loath to discuss openly but are definitely considering in private: that an Ebola virus could mutate to become transmissible through the air. You can now get Ebola only through direct contact with bodily fluids. But viruses like Ebola are notoriously sloppy in replicating, meaning the virus entering one person may be genetically different from the virus entering the next. The current Ebola virus's hyper-evolution is unprecedented; there has been more human-to-human transmission in the past four months than most likely occurred in the last 500 to 1,000 years. Each new infection represents trillions of throws of the genetic dice.   5

If certain mutations occurred, it would mean that just breathing would put one at risk of contracting Ebola. Infections could spread quickly to every part of the globe, as the H1N1 influenza virus did in 2009, after its birth in Mexico.   6

Why are public officials afraid to discuss this? They don't want to be accused of screaming "Fire!" in a crowded theater—as I'm sure some will   7

Michael T. Osterholm, "What We're Afraid to Say About Ebola", (*New York Times*, Sept. 12, 2014), op ed page.

accuse me of doing. But the risk is real, and until we consider it, the world will not be prepared to do what is necessary to end the epidemic.

In 2012, a team of Canadian researchers proved that Ebola Zaire, the   8
same virus that is causing the West Africa outbreak, could be transmitted by the respiratory route from pigs to monkeys, both of whose lungs are very similar to those of humans. Richard Preston's 1994 best seller "The Hot Zone" chronicled a 1989 outbreak of a different strain, Ebola Reston virus, among monkeys at a quarantine station near Washington. The virus was transmitted through breathing, and the outbreak ended only when all the monkeys were euthanized. We must consider that such transmissions could happen between humans, if the virus mutates.

So what must we do that we are not doing?   9

First, we need someone to take over the position of "command and   10
control." The United Nations is the only international organization that can direct the immense amount of medical, public health and humanitarian aid that must come from many different countries and nongovernmental groups to smother this epidemic. Thus far it has played at best a collaborating role, and with everyone in charge, no one is in charge.

A Security Council resolution could give the United Nations total   11
responsibility for controlling the outbreak, while respecting West African nations' sovereignty as much as possible. The United Nations could, for instance, secure aircraft and landing rights. Many private airlines are refusing to fly into the affected countries, making it very difficult to deploy critical supplies and personnel. The Group of 7 countries' military air and ground support must be brought in to ensure supply chains for medical and infection-control products, as well as food and water for quarantined areas.

The United Nations should provide whatever number of beds are   12
needed; the World Health Organization has recommended 1,500, but we may need thousands more. It should also coordinate the recruitment and training around the world of medical and nursing staff, in particular by bringing in local residents who have survived Ebola, and are no longer at risk of infection. Many countries are pledging medical resources, but donations will not result in an effective treatment system if no single group is responsible for coordinating them.

Finally, we have to remember that Ebola isn't West Africa's only prob-   13
lem. Tens of thousands die there each year from diseases like AIDS, malaria and tuberculosis. Liberia, Sierra Leone and Guinea have among the highest maternal mortality rates in the world. Because people are now too afraid of contracting Ebola to go to the hospital, very few are getting basic medical care. In addition, many health care workers have been infected with Ebola, and more than 120 have died. Liberia has only 250 doctors left, for a population of four million.

This is about humanitarianism and self-interest. If we wait for vaccines and   14
new drugs to arrive to end the Ebola epidemic, instead of taking major action
now, we risk the disease's reaching from West Africa to our own backyards.

Thinking about the Essay

1. What is Osterholm's purpose in this essay? Is he presenting the truth or just
   scare tactics? Will his essay lessen or increase fear of Ebola?

2. Analyze how Osterholm uses each of the following rhetorical techniques to
   achieve his purpose: analysis and division, cause and effect, comparison and
   contrast, and exemplification.

3. Explain the two possible paths for the future of Ebola according to Osterholm.
   Then summarize his proposal for solving these problems and ending the epidemic. What should we do that is not being done now? Is his solution a viable
   one? Is it plausible? Why or why not?

4. Osterholm uses two metaphors to stress the severity of this epidemic: "throws
   of the genetic dice" (paragraph 5) and "screaming 'Fire!'" (paragraph 7). What
   is the meaning of each of these figures of speech in the context of this essay?

5. Osterholm ends his essay with the statement that the need for action now
   is "about humanitarianism and self-interest" (paragraph 14). Are these two
   terms contradictory? How can anything be about both humanitarianism and
   self-interest? Explain what the author means.

Responding in Writing

6. Osterholm comments that "with everyone in charge, no one is in charge" (paragraph 10). Think of an experience that illustrates this statement. Write an essay
   in which you first explain the meaning of the statement, and then narrate the
   illustrative experience.

7. Summarize Osterholm's argument on how to prevent the spread of the Ebola
   virus, and discuss the viability of his proposal.

8. Write an essay in which you explain why people are afraid of Ebola and what they
   can do to lessen their fear. Provide sufficient evidence to convince your audience
   that your suggestions are viable.

Networking

9. An epidemic scare that occurred after Osterholm wrote this essay was the
   spread of measles that began at Disneyland in California in 2015. With a small
   group of classmates, research this problem—how it began, how it spread, what
   issues it brought to people's attention, and how it has been resolved so far.
   Summarize your findings and then discuss them with your class.

10. Research the origin of Ebola, how it spreads, and how it is treated. What do
    other researchers and experts in infectious diseases say is the probable future
    for Ebola? Write a report summarizing your research.

The Singer Solution to World Poverty

Peter Singer

Peter Singer, the Ira W. DeCamp Professor of Bioethics at Princeton University's Center for Human Values, is one of the most influential—and assuredly the most controversial—philosophers of his generation. Born in Melbourne, Australia, in 1946 and educated at the University of Melbourne (BA, 1967) and University College, Oxford (BPhill, 1971), Singer has been a prolific writer and lecturer on such contentious social and ethical issues as infanticide, euthanasia, animal liberation, genetic engineering, and reproductive technologies. His books, which have been translated into almost two dozen languages, include *Practical Ethics* (1974, 1993), *Animal Liberation: A New Ethics for Our Treatment of Animals* (1975, 1990), *Rethinking Life and Death* (1995), *One World: The Ethics of Globalization* (2002), and *The Life You Can Save: Acting Now to End World Poverty* (2009). The following essay, which appeared in *The New York Times Magazine* in 1999 and was reprinted in *Best American Essays* (2000), has provoked the sort of criticism and debate that characterize Singer's provocative ideas.

Before Reading

Is it immoral to spend your money on luxuries when you could use this cash to help feed a starving child? Justify your response.

In the Brazilian film *Central Station*, Dora is a retired schoolteacher who   1
makes ends meet by sitting at the station writing letters for illiterate people. Suddenly she has an opportunity to pocket $1,000. All she has to do is persuade a homeless 9-year-old boy to follow her to an address she has been given. (She is told he will be adopted by wealthy foreigners.) She delivers the boy, gets the money, spends some of it on a television set and settles down to enjoy her new acquisition. Her neighbor spoils the fun, however, by telling her that the boy was too old to be adopted—he will be

killed and his organs sold for transplantation. Perhaps Dora knew this all along, but after her neighbor's plain speaking, she spends a troubled night. In the morning Dora resolves to take the boy back.

Suppose Dora had told her neighbor that it is a tough world, other people have nice new TVs too, and if selling the kid is the only way she can get one, well, he was only a street kid. She would then have become, in the eyes of the audience, a monster. She redeems herself only by being prepared to bear considerable risks to save the boy.

At the end of the movie, in cinemas in the affluent nations of the world, people who would have been quick to condemn Dora if she had not rescued the boy go home to places far more comfortable than her apartment. In fact, the average family in the United States spends almost one-third of its income on things that are no more necessary to them than Dora's new TV was to her. Going out to nice restaurants, buying new clothes because the old ones are no longer stylish, vacationing at beach resorts—so much of our income is spent on things not essential to the preservation of our lives and health. Donated to one of a number of charitable agencies, that money could mean the difference between life and death for children in need.

All of which raises a question: In the end, what is the ethical distinction between a Brazilian who sells a homeless child to organ peddlers and an American who already has a TV and upgrades to a better one—knowing that the money could be donated to an organization that would use it to save the lives of kids in need?

Of course, there are several differences between the two situations that could support different moral judgments about them. For one thing, to be able to consign a child to death when he is standing right in front of you takes a chilling kind of heartlessness; it is much easier to ignore an appeal for money to help children you will never meet. Yet for a utilitarian philosopher like myself—that is, one who judges whether acts are right or wrong by their consequences—if the upshot of the American's failure to donate the money is that one more kid dies on the streets of a Brazilian city, then it is, in some sense, just as bad as selling the kid to the organ peddlers. But one doesn't need to embrace my utilitarian ethic to see that, at the very least, there is a troubling incongruity in being so quick to condemn Dora for taking the child to the organ peddlers while, at the same time, not regarding the American consumer's behavior as raising a serious moral issue.

In his 1996 book, *Living High and Letting Die*, the New York University philosopher Peter Unger presented an ingenious series of imaginary examples designed to probe our intuitions about whether it is wrong to live well without giving substantial amounts of money to help people who are hungry, malnourished or dying from easily treatable illnesses like diarrhea. Here's my paraphrase of one of these examples:

Bob is close to retirement. He has invested most of his savings in a very   7
rare and valuable old car, a Bugatti, which he has not been able to insure.
The Bugatti is his pride and joy. In addition to the pleasure he gets from
driving and caring for his car, Bob knows that its rising market value means
that he will always be able to sell it and live comfortably after retirement.
One day when Bob is out for a drive, he parks the Bugatti near the end of a
railway siding and goes for a walk up the track. As he does so, he sees that
a runaway train, with no one aboard, is running down the railway track.
Looking farther down the track, he sees the small figure of a child very
likely to be killed by the runaway train. He can't stop the train and the child
is too far away to warn of the danger, but he can throw a switch that will
divert the train down the siding where his Bugatti is parked. Then nobody
will be killed—but the train will destroy his Bugatti. Thinking of his joy in
owning the car and the financial security it represents, Bob decides not to
throw the switch. The child is killed. For many years to come, Bob enjoys
owning his Bugatti and the financial security it represents.

Bob's conduct, most of us will immediately respond, was gravely wrong.   8
Unger agrees. But then he reminds us that we, too, have opportunities to
save the lives of children. We can give to organizations like UNICEF or
Oxfam America. How much would we have to give one of these organizations to have a high probability of saving the life of a child threatened by
easily preventable diseases? (I do not believe that children are more worth
saving than adults, but since no one can argue that children have brought
their poverty on themselves, focusing on them simplifies the issues.) Unger
called up some experts and used the information they provided to offer
some plausible estimates that include the cost of raising money, administra-
tive expenses and the cost of delivering aid where it is most needed. By his
calculation, $200 in donations would help a sickly 2-year-old transform
into a healthy 6-year-old—offering safe passage through childhood's most
dangerous years. To show how practical philosophical argument can be,
Unger even tells his readers that they can easily donate funds by using their
credit card and calling one of these toll-free numbers: (800) 367-5437 for
UNICEF; (800) 693-2687 for Oxfam America.

Now you, too, have the information you need to save a child's life.   9
How should you judge yourself if you don't do it? Think again about Bob
and his Bugatti. Unlike Dora, Bob did not have to look into the eyes of the
child he was sacrificing for his own material comfort. The child was a complete stranger to him and too far away to relate to in an intimate, personal
way. Unlike Dora, too, he did not mislead the child or initiate the chain of
events imperiling him. In all these respects, Bob's situation resembles that
of people able but unwilling to donate to overseas aid and differs from
Dora's situation.

If you still think that it was very wrong of Bob not to throw the switch 10 that would have diverted the train and saved the child's life, then it is hard to see how you could deny that it is also very wrong not to send money to one of the organizations listed above. Unless, that is, there is some morally important difference between the two situations that I have overlooked.

Is it the practical uncertainties about whether aid will really reach the 11 people who need it? Nobody who knows the world of overseas aid can doubt that such uncertainties exist. But Unger's figure of $200 to save a child's life was reached after he had made conservative assumptions about the proportion of the money donated that will actually reach its target.

One genuine difference between Bob and those who can afford to 12 donate to overseas aid organizations but don't is that only Bob can save the child on the tracks, whereas there are hundreds of millions of people who can give $200 to overseas aid organizations. The problem is that most of them aren't doing it. Does this mean that it is all right for you not to do it?

Suppose that there were more owners of priceless vintage cars—Carol, 13 Dave, Emma, Fred and so on, down to Ziggy—all in exactly the same situation as Bob, with their own siding and their own switch, all sacrificing the child in order to preserve their own cherished car. Would that make it all right for Bob to do the same? To answer this question affirmatively is to endorse follow-the-crowd ethics—the kind of ethics that led many Germans to look away when the Nazi atrocities were being committed. We do not excuse them because others were behaving no better.

We seem to lack a sound basis for drawing a clear moral line between 14 Bob's situation and that of any reader of this article with $200 to spare who does not donate it to an overseas aid agency. These readers seem to be acting at least as badly as Bob was acting when he chose to let the runaway train hurtle toward the unsuspecting child. In the light of this conclusion, I trust that many readers will reach for the phone and donate that $200. Perhaps you should do it before reading further.

Now that you have distinguished yourself morally from people who 15 put their vintage cars ahead of a child's life, how about treating yourself and your partner to dinner at your favorite restaurant? But wait. The money you will spend at the restaurant could also help save the lives of children overseas! True, you weren't planning to blow $200 tonight, but if you were to give up dining out just for one month, you would easily save that amount. And what is one month's dining out, compared to a child's life? There's the rub. Since there are a lot of desperately needy children in the world, there will always be another child whose life you could save for another $200. Are you therefore obliged to keep giving until you have nothing left? At what point can you stop?

Hypothetical examples can easily become farcical. Consider Bob. How   16
far past losing the Bugatti should he go? Imagine that Bob had got his foot
stuck in the track of the siding, and if he diverted the train, then before it
rammed the car it would also amputate his big toe. Should he still throw
the switch? What if it would amputate his foot? His entire leg?

As absurd as the Bugatti scenario gets when pushed to extremes, the   17
point it raises is a serious one: only when the sacrifices become very significant indeed would most people be prepared to say that Bob does nothing
wrong when he decides not to throw the switch. Of course, most people
could be wrong; we can't decide moral issues by taking opinion polls. But
consider for yourself the level of sacrifice that you would demand of Bob,
and then think about how much money you would have to give away in
order to make a sacrifice that is roughly equal to that. It's almost certainly
much, much more than $200. For most middle-class Americans, it could
easily be more like $200,000.

Isn't it counterproductive to ask people to do so much? Don't we run   18
the risk that many will shrug their shoulders and say that morality, so conceived, is fine for saints but not for them? I accept that we are unlikely to
see, in the near or even medium-term future, a world in which it is normal
for wealthy Americans to give the bulk of their wealth to strangers. When
it comes to praising or blaming people for what they do, we tend to use a
standard that is relative to some conception of normal behavior. Comfortably off Americans who give, say, 10 percent of their income to overseas
aid organizations are so far ahead of most of their equally comfortable
fellow citizens that I wouldn't go out of my way to chastise them for not
doing more. Nevertheless, they should be doing much more, and they are
in no position to criticize Bob for failing to make the much greater sacrifice
of his Bugatti.

At this point various objections may crop up. Someone may say: 19
"If every citizen living in the affluent nations contributed his or her share
I wouldn't have to make such a drastic sacrifice, because long before such
levels were reached, the resources would have been there to save the lives of
all those children dying from lack of food or medical care. So why should
I give more than my fair share?" Another, related, objection is that the
Government ought to increase its overseas aid allocations, since that would
spread the burden more equitably across all taxpayers.

Yet the question of how much we ought to give is a matter to be   20
decided in the real world—and that, sadly, is a world in which we know
that most people do not, and in the immediate future will not, give substantial amounts to overseas aid agencies. We know, too, that at least in
the next year, the United States Government is not going to meet even the
very modest United Nations–recommended target of 0.7 percent of gross

national product; at the moment it lags far below that, at 0.09 percent, not even half of Japan's 0.22 percent or a tenth of Denmark's 0.97 percent. Thus, we know that the money we can give beyond that theoretical "fair share" is still going to save lives that would otherwise be lost. While the idea that no one need do more than his or her fair share is a powerful one, should it prevail if we know that others are not doing their fair share and that children will die preventable deaths unless we do more than our fair share? That would be taking fairness too far.

Thus, this ground for limiting how much we ought to give also fails. In the world as it is now, I can see no escape from the conclusion that each one of us with wealth surplus to his or her essential needs should be giving most of it to help people suffering from poverty so dire as to be life-threatening. That's right: I'm saying that you shouldn't buy that new car, take that cruise, redecorate the house or get that pricey new suit. After all, a $1,000 suit could save five children's lives. 21

So how does my philosophy break down in dollars and cents? An American household with an income of $50,000 spends around $30,000 annually on necessities, according to the Conference Board, a nonprofit economic research organization. Therefore, for a household bringing in $50,000 a year, donations to help the world's poor should be as close as possible to $20,000. The $30,000 required for necessities holds for higher incomes as well. So a household making $100,000 could cut a yearly check for $70,000. Again, the formula is simple: whatever money you're spending on luxuries, not necessities, should be given away. 22

Now, evolutionary psychologists tell us that human nature just isn't sufficiently altruistic to make it plausible that many people will sacrifice so much for strangers. On the facts of human nature, they might be right, but they would be wrong to draw a moral conclusion from those facts. If it is the case that we ought to do things that, predictably, most of us won't do, then let's face that fact head-on. Then, if we value the life of a child more than going to fancy restaurants, the next time we dine out we will know that we could have done something better with our money. If that makes living a morally decent life extremely arduous, well, then that is the way things are. If we don't do it, then we should at least know that we are failing to live a morally decent life—not because it is good to wallow in guilt but because knowing where we should be going is the first step toward heading in that direction. 23

When Bob first grasped the dilemma that faced him as he stood by that railway switch, he must have thought how extraordinarily unlucky he was to be placed in a situation in which he must choose between the life of an innocent child and the sacrifice of most of his savings. But he was not unlucky at all. We are all in that situation. 24

Thinking about the Essay

1. Why does Singer begin his essay with an allusion to a Brazilian film that you probably have not seen? Do you find his introduction effective?

2. Where does Singer's claim appear? What evidence does he use, or does he rely on hypothetical examples and situations? Explain.

3. Singer calls himself "a utilitarian philosopher" (paragraph 5). What does he mean by this term, and how does the essay reflect his ethical approach to the problem of poverty?

4. How does Singer deal with potential objections to his argument?

5. Do you find Singer's "solution" to be convincing? Why or why not?

Responding in Writing

6. Write an argumentative essay in which you agree or disagree with Singer's solution to world poverty.

7. Write an explanatory essay in which you present your own viewpoint on making charitable contributions to help alleviate poverty or disease. Singer, for example, donates 20 percent of his income to Oxfam, a famine relief agency, and also some of his royalties to other charities. Would you do the same if you were in a position to do so?

8. What range of private acts aside from the one that Singer presents could help alleviate poverty and disease? Write an essay responding to this question.

Networking

9. With two other class members, have a discussion of the issues raised by Singer in his essay and your personal response to them. Share your opinions with the rest of the class.

10. Locate the UNICEF or Oxfam website and summarize its content.

Technology Won't Feed the World's Hungry

Anuradha Mittal

Anuradha Mittal, a native of India, is founder and director of the Oakland Institute, a policy think tank that works to promote public participation and democratic debate on economic and social policy issues. Mittal is known internationally as an expert on trade, human rights, and agriculture issues. She has traveled widely as a public speaker and has appeared as guest and commentator on television and radio. Her articles on international public policy issues have appeared in

The New York Times and in other journals worldwide. In the following article, which appeared in the
July 12, 2001, issue of *Progressive Media Project*,
Mittal argues that biotechnology cannot solve the
problem of world hunger.

Before Reading

Do you see the debate over genetically engineered foods primarily in terms
of your choice as a consumer or in terms of the way such technology would
address world hunger?

D on't be misled. Genetically engineered food is not an answer to world   1
hunger.

The U.N. Development Program (UNDP) released a report last week   2
urging rich countries to put aside their fears of such food and help developing nations unlock the potential of biotechnology.

The report accuses opponents of ignoring the Third World's food needs.   3
It claims that Western consumers who do not face food shortages or nutritional deficiencies are more likely to focus on food safety and the loss of
biodiversity, while farming communities in developing countries emphasize
potentially higher yields and "greater nutritional value" of these crops.

But the UNDP has not done its homework.   4

In my country, India, for example, the debate pits mostly U.S.-trained   5
technocrats, seduced by technological fixes, against farmers and consumers
who overwhelmingly say no to these crops. The people who are to use the
modified seeds and eat the modified food often want nothing to do with
them.

The report rehashes the old myth of feeding the hungry through mira-   6
cle technology. As part of the 1960s Green Revolution, Western technology
created pesticides and sent them to developing countries for agricultural
use, which may have increased food production, but at the cost of poison-
ing our earth, air and water.

What's more, it failed to alleviate hunger. Of the 800 million hungry   7
people in the world today, more than 200 million live in India alone. It's
not that India does not produce enough food to meet the needs of its hungry. It's that organizations like the International Monetary Fund (IMF)
have slashed public services and social-safety nets so that the food can't
get to the needy.

More than 60 million tons of excess, unsold food grain rotted in India 8
last year because the hungry were too poor to buy it. In desperation, some
farmers burned the crops they could not market and resorted to selling
their kidneys and other body parts, or committing suicide, to end the cycle
of poverty.

A higher, genetically engineered crop yield would have done nothing 9
for them. And if the poor in India are not able to buy two meals a day, how
will they purchase nutritionally rich crops such as rice that is engineered to
contain vitamin A?

The report compares efforts to ban genetically modified foods with the 10
banning of the pesticide DDT, which was dangerous to humans but was
effective in killing the mosquitoes that spread malaria. The Third World
had to choose between death from DDT or malaria. It's appalling that even
today the debate in developed countries offers the Third World the option
of either dying from hunger or eating unsafe foods.

Malaria, like hunger, is a disease of poverty. When economic conditions 11
improve, it disappears, just as it did in the United States and Europe.

The focus ought to be on the root causes of the problem, not the symp- 12
tom. The hungry don't need a technological quick fix. They need basic
social change.

In the Third World, the battle against genetically engineered food is a 13
battle against the corporate concentration of our food system. Corporations are gaining control of our biodiversity and even our seeds. This is a
potential stranglehold on our food supply. In response, developing countries are imposing moratoriums on genetically engineered crops. Sri Lanka,
Thailand, Brazil, Mexico and China, among others, have already done so.

The UNDP has been snookered about genetically engineered food. The 14
rest of us shouldn't be.

Thinking about the Essay

1. How does Mittal frame her paragraph-long paraphrase of the claims of the UNDP
   within the opening paragraphs of the essay?

2. Does Mittal's reference to India as "my country" have any effect on her argument?
   Would the argument be as strong without the personal element? Why or why not?

3. How does Mittal characterize the advocates of biotechnology who are the
   authors of the UNDP report?

4. According to Mittal, what is the role that corporations play in the promotion of
   biotechnology? How does this claim change her characterization of the motives
   for promoting such technology?

5. How effective is the colloquial language of the two-sentence concluding paragraph? Are there other examples of such language in the essay?

Responding in Writing

6. In a brief essay, connect Mittal's argument with other arguments presented in this chapter about economic infrastructure as the root cause of world health problems.

7. Argue for or against the use of biotechnology as a solution to world hunger by invoking an analogy of your own that you believe characterizes the reaction of opponents or supporters of such technology. Why is this analogy appropriate?

8. Do you think that adequate public services and social safety nets exist in the United States that prevent the kind of failure of resource distribution Mittal describes in India? Why do people go hungry in the United States today? Is this hunger the result of a systemic failure? Answer these questions in an argumentative essay.

Networking

9. In small groups, discuss your reservations (or enthusiasms) about genetically engineered food. Do you feel that you are reacting according to your limited interests as a Western consumer? Why or why not?

10. Go online and engage in a discussion group debate over genetically engineered food from a global, hunger-relief point of view. Write a summary of the attitudes and rhetoric you encounter.

CHAPTER 1

The Fate of the Earth: Can We Preserve the Global Environment?

11

CHAPTER

I t is tempting to think that at one time—was it before 9/11, or before the explosion of the first atomic bomb, or before the Black Death?—the problems of the world were simpler and more manageable. But were they? After all, the Black Death of the thirteenth century liquidated more than a third of Europe's population. There have always been world conflicts and challenges that Earth's inhabitants have had to confront. So far we have survived; we have not destroyed the planet. However, as the writers in this chapter attest, the fate of the Earth is uncertain, for humanity continues to be a flawed enterprise.

What is certain is that for the last several decades we have been moving into a new era in global history. This new era, as the writers in earlier chapters have revealed, is both like and unlike previous historical epochs. We do not have to accept the thesis of Francis Fukuyama that we have reached the "end" of history. At the same time, we do have to acknowledge that new challenges—scientific, ecological, economic, political, and cultural—await us in the new millennium. Numerous local and global problems need our sustained attention. Over the past decade, in particular, we have come to recognize that we have relationships and obligations to the planet and its inhabitants. A dust storm originating in Africa can sweep across the Atlantic, affecting ecologies in other continents. A nuclear accident in Russia can affect the milk of cows in Nebraska. Even the cars that we purchase and drive—as one author in this chapter asserts—can have an impact on the world's climate.

Clearly, then, in this new millennial era, we are part of a global environment. We have mutual obligations not to waste natural resources, to respect the environment, to harness science and technology to human and nonhuman benefit, and so much more. This new era is not necessarily more corrosive than previous epochs, but the stakes do seem to be higher. We now have to comprehend our reciprocal relationships at the numerous

313

Tourists visiting a Bedouin village in the Egyptian desert clearly affect the local ecosystem and indigenous community.

Thinking about the Image

1. How does the photographer frame this shot? Who is in the foreground, and who is in the background? What is the dominant impression?
2. Are you amused or surprised by the dress of the tourists? Why or why not?
3. What kind of story does this photograph tell about the impact of tourism on landscape and indigenous culture?
4. What do you think is the point of view of the photographer toward the people on the camels? How can you tell?

crossroads of nature and civilization. The *process* of civilization wherein we harness our physical, creative, scientific, political, intellectual, and spiritual resources is well advanced. However, the current condition of the global environment, as the writers in this last chapter testify, demands our attention.

By and large, the writers in this chapter, all of whom deal with subjects of consequence—global warming, biotechnology, environmental degradation, population growth, weapons of mass destruction—are not doomsday prophets. In fact, while offering cautionary statements about our shortsightedness and wastefulness, they tend to find hope for the world's environment. Whether finding once again a small spot in Eden in a remote Amazon jungle or contemplating the consequences of driving an SUV, these writers try to establish a moral basis for the continuation of the species—not just our human species but all varieties of life on Earth. We are not caught in an endless spiral that will end in mass extinction. But we do have to harness what Albert Schweitzer called "the devils of our own creation." Ultimately, we must find ways to coexist on Earth with nature and all living things.

To Save Chimps

Jane Goodall

> British naturalist Jane Goodall, born in London in 1934, has spent much of her adult life in the jungles of Tanzania engaged in the study of chimpanzees. Fascinated by animals since childhood, Goodall, after graduating from school, traveled to Kenya to work with the famed paleontologist Louis Leakey, serving as his assistant on fossil-gathering trips to the Olduvai Gorge region. In 1960, at Leakey's urging, Goodall started a new project studying wild chimpanzees in the Gombe Stream Chimpanzee Reserve in Tanzania. In 1965, Cambridge University awarded Goodall a Ph.D. degree based on her thesis growing out of five years of research in the Gombe Reserve; she was only the eighth person in the university's history to earn a doctorate without having earned an undergraduate degree. Goodall has received dozens of major international awards from conservation societies and environmental groups, including the Albert Schweitzer Award, two Franklin Burr Awards from the National Geographic Society, and numerous honorary doctorates from universities around the world. Among her many books are the widely read *In the Shadow of Man* (1971), *The Chimpanzees of Gombe: Patterns of Behavior* (1986), *Hope for the Animals of the World* (2009), and a two-volume autobiography in letters, *Africa in My Blood* (2000) and *Beyond Innocence* (2001). She also has written books for children and participated in media productions based on her work. This essay from the fall 2006 issue of *WorldView* reflects one of Goodall's core beliefs— that saving animals matters.

Before Reading

Goodall suggests that family planning can protect animals and the environment. Do you agree or disagree, and why?

When I arrived at Gombe National Park in western Tanzania to study   1
chimpanzees 47 years ago, lush forest stretched for miles along Lake
Tanganyika's eastern shoreline and inland as far as I could see. Gradually,
over the years, growing populations of local people and refugees struggling
to survive in one of the world's poorest places have cut down the trees for
firewood, to build homes and to clear the land for farming. By 1980, the
trees outside the park had almost all gone. Much of the soil was exhausted.
Looking for new land to clear, people have moved to the very steepest
slopes of the escarpment, where heavy rains wash away the thin topsoil,
cause terrible soil erosion and deadly mudslides. Women walk further and
further from their villages in search of fuel wood, adding hours of labor to
already difficult days.

This situation, of course, is not only grim for people but desperate   2
also for the chimpanzees of Gombe. The deforestation around the tiny
35-square-kilometer park prevents the chimpanzees from going beyond
the park for food as they once did. And the availability of food is considerably reduced, particularly for the chimpanzee communities to the north
and south. These two groups are frequently exposed to human disease as
people press up to the park's boundaries. Moreover, when the northern
and southern chimpanzee communities seek food in the central part of the
park, they violate the territory of the central community. Brutal and often
deadly violence breaks out. This is a present-day crisis. In the long term, the
chimpanzees' future is even more grave; the genetic viability and overall
health of these chimpanzees are likely to be compromised since they are
unable to increase the gene pool by mating with chimps outside the park.

What can be done? It became clear that, to protect the chimpanzees   3
and their forest habitat, it would be necessary to help human populations
around Gombe. Thus, in 1994 the Jane Goodall Institute created the Lake
Tanganyika Catchment Reforestation and Education program. We call the
program TACARE, or Take Care.

We realized it would be important to first gain the trust of the villagers.   4
Our team of Tanzanian staff began by asking the people what they needed.
Not surprisingly, conservation was seldom listed on top: the villagers
were concerned with growing more food, with health and with education.
We started work with 12 villages and a grant from the European Union.
The program was so successful that we expanded it to 24 villages and
have acquired some major funding from the U.S. Agency for International
Development and several other donors. From the very first, TACARE was

Jane Goodall, "Save the Chimps," from *WorldView*, Fall 2006; 19, 3 Platinum Periodicals,
p. 27. *WorldView* by National Council of Returned Peace Corps Volunteers. Copyright 2006.
Reproduced with permission of Carnegie Council on Ethics and International Affairs in the
format Textbook via Copyright Clearance Center.

conceived as a holistic program and today has six areas of emphasis: community development, water and environmental sanitation, education, agriculture, forestry and health. We work with regional medical authorities to provide primary healthcare, basic information about hygiene and HIV-AIDS education.

Kigoma Region is one of the world's poorest regions. Largely due to   5
lack of education and inadequate health services, it has one of the highest fertility rates in the world, 4.8 percent, as well as high infant and maternal mortality. We launched our family planning activities in 1999 with a David and Lucile Packard Foundation grant to train local men and women as community-based distributors of family planning education and methods of birth control. Our long-term goal was to help the communities that surround Gombe improve the health of mothers and their babies, and to encourage spacing between births. We have 136 trained distributors who now serve in their villages by making house calls, speaking at family planning centers, and conducting private peer-counseling sessions. TACARE also raises awareness through village Family Planning Days, market speeches and public meetings. We use media and performance: plays and *ngoma*, or traditional singing and dancing, videos, calendars and T-shirts with project messages. We serve about 140,000, of which about half are women of child-bearing age.

To meet individual needs, TACARE provides a variety of family plan-   6
ning methods and services to both men and women who request them. They include oral contraceptives and condoms, as well as referrals for clinical long-term and permanent methods such as intra-uterine devices, Depo-Provera, Norplant or voluntary sterilization for men and women.

The institute is the only NGO in rural Kigoma to provide family plan-   7
ning services at the grassroots level. Our trained educator-distributors offer our best chance of succeeding. Our program director at TACARE, Mary Mavanza, says, "Before we began our health services, family planning was almost unheard of in the Kigoma region. Using community-based peers is the best way to open doors and minds." They are critical sources of support and information for the park's neighbors.

Aisha, who has four children, was breastfeeding her three-month-old   8
baby girl when she became pregnant. Her tribe's custom and taboos told her that if she weaned her baby early, she and the baby would weaken and possibly die. She decided to perform an abortion. She took strong local herbs during the daytime and that night experienced severe abdominal pains and heavy bleeding. Her alarmed husband ran to his neighbor, TACARE's local educator-distributor, for advice. Relatives paid the boat fare to rush Aisha to the hospital, where she remained two days. When she returned home, our community-based distributor gave her nutritional

advice and when she told him of her abortion, the distributor suggested birth control options. This mother of four children selected DepoProvera injections.

"My children are doing fine," says Aisha now, "and I have enough time 9 to care for my family." She has started a small-scale business selling fish in the market. "I am happy by knowing that I won't conceive unless I plan for it."

We hear of many similar voices. Women who are able to control the 10 timing of childbirth can now pursue education or help support their families through small businesses. Their status rises within their families and communities. One mother of six, Nyamwiza, started oral contraceptives with the support of her husband, and found more time to sell fish in the market. She joined TACARE's micro-finance program, which gives small loans—mostly to women—for environmentally sustainable businesses. With her first loan, Nyamwiza expanded her fish business and sold cassava flour. Her husband helped her open a small shop to sell sugar, kerosene, oil, cigarettes and matches. The couple can now pay school fees and buy shoes, uniforms and books for their children. She wants her children to complete secondary school, an uncommon achievement in Kigoma Region.

TACARE places major emphasis on helping women because experience 11 all over the world shows that as women's education levels rise, the family size lowers, so the ripple effects of family planning can be significant. We discovered that one of the reasons girls drop out of school when they reach puberty is the unhygienic latrines and a lack of privacy. So, we provide ventilated pit latrines to all schools.

Our family planning efforts still face significant challenges. The vil- 12 lagers of Kigoma Region have little exposure to the rest of the world and, therefore, tend to the traditional and the conservative. They prefer large families because more children mean more hands to help farm and fish, and the assurance of support in old age. Well-off families are traditionally large since it is considered a mark of prestige. Unfortunately, many are very poor families, which results in great hardship. A significant part or our job is taking our message about the educational and financial benefits of smaller families. A growing number of people understand the hardships posed by large families. Frequently they ask our community-based distributors why they did not come sooner.

While women instinctively appreciate having more control over their 13 fertility and childbirth, our distributors have to work harder to persuade men, who generally are reticent to even talk about family planning. So we seek them out on the fish landings and in the cafes.

Men's acceptance is sometimes hard-won. In Zashe village, one of our 14
distributors, Iddi Nanda, told me about a pregnant woman who came into
the local dispensary with a sick one-year-old strapped on her back. She
looked weak, too. When Iddi suggested family planning, she asked him to
talk to her husband, who was a pastor.

When Iddi went to the woman's house the next day, the husband ordered 15
Iddi to leave. After a few days, the wife went to Iddi and insisted he try
again. This time the pastor threatened Iddi. One day months later the husband came to Iddi's door and begged to enter, promising he would not harm
Iddi. The pastor's wife and children were all sick, he said, and he couldn't
care for his family and attend to church matters. He also realized how much
work his wife did each day. The pastor joined family planning services.

In just a few years, I can see how TACARE is benefiting the natural 16
environment. Woodlots have been established near the villages so women
no longer need to search out and hack at stumps of trees on the steep
slopes, stumps that could produce 20-foot trees in just five years. Forests
are growing again outside Gombe park. This regeneration is crucial in protecting the watershed and preventing erosion. It also means the chimpanzees will soon be able to seek out other remnant populations, increasing
the gene pool and providing hope for their long-term survival.

The program has won support from the Tanzanian government. 17
Recently, the Kigoma Regional Medical Office asked us to seek funding
to extend the service to all of the villages in the district and to nearby
Kasulu and Kibondo districts. We now receive significant support from
government agencies, including USAID-Tanzania, which in 2005 asked us
to co-host a workshop in Kigoma linking healthy families and healthy forests. More than 50 professionals took part, representing local and international NGOs working in the environment and development fields and local
governments. And, USAID-Tanzania has asked us to use our approach in
a pilot community-based program for people with AIDS in which our distributors would offer anti-retroviral therapy.

In 2004, I visited Kigoma and met with some TACARE participants. A 18
mother stood up in front of the group and told me she assumed she would
always struggle against poverty. With education in family planning, she
decided to delay having another child, and started a small business. She
began to realistically imagine a drastically different future.

"Thanks to TACARE, my children will be well-educated, they will be 19
well-fed, and they will be well-clothed," she said. "I want to thank TAC-
ARE for giving me my life." In the end, that is our goal: changing lives, one
at a time, knowing that even in a generation or even a decade our impact
will have grown exponentially.

Thinking about the Essay

1. How do you interpret the author's title in light of your reading of this essay? Is Goodall's essay about saving chimpanzees, improving the lives of Africans, or a combination of purposes? Explain.

2. Analyze Goodall's introductory paragraph. How does it set the stage for the rest of the essay?

3. What connections does Goodall draw between the lives of Africans and chimpanzees? How does she organize her essay around these subjects?

4. What is Goodall's thesis? Does she state it in one sentence or a series of sentences, or does she imply it? Justify your response.

5. Goodall divides her essay into three sections. What is the essential topic of each section? Does she achieve unity and coherence among the parts? Why or why not?

Responding in Writing

6. Argue for or against the proposition that Goodall in this essay succeeds in linking the fates of chimpanzees and their local African population.

7. Write a personal essay in which you narrate and describe what you have learned from a family pet or from the natural world.

8. Reread Goodall's essay, and write a précis of her argument.

Networking

9. Divide into groups of three and four and list examples of the destruction of natural habitats in the United States and around the world. Present your list to the class along with other groups.

10. Go online with another classmate and find out about TACARE and/or the Jane Goodall Institute. Share your findings in class discussion.

The Change Within

Naomi Klein

Naomi Klein is an environmentalist, social activist, and journalist, known for her anti-globalization, anti-war, anti-capitalism stance. She was born in 1970 in Canada and attended the University of Toronto but did not graduate. She is known for her criticism of corporate globalization and corporate capitalism. Her works include *No Logo* (2000), *The Shock Doctrine* (2007), and *This Changes Everything: Capitalism vs. the Climate* (2014). In this article, she asserts that we need a new way of thinking to combat climate change.

Before Reading

What do you know about climate change and the controversies related to it? How do you think we can combat it?

This is a story about bad timing. 1

One of the most disturbing ways that climate change is already playing 2
out is through what ecologists call "mismatch" or "mistiming." This is the
process whereby warming causes animals to fall out of step with a critical
food source, particularly at breeding times, when a failure to find enough
food can lead to rapid population losses.

The migration patterns of many songbird species, for instance, have 3
evolved over millennia so that eggs hatch precisely when food sources
such as caterpillars are at their most abundant, providing parents with
ample nourishment for their hungry young. But because spring now often
arrives early, the caterpillars are hatching earlier too, which means that
in some areas they are less plentiful when the chicks hatch, threatening
a number of health and fertility impacts. Similarly, in West Greenland,
caribou are arriving at their calving grounds only to find themselves out
of sync with the forage plants they have relied on for thousands of years,
now growing earlier thanks to rising temperatures. That is leaving female
caribou with less energy for lactation, reproduction and feeding their
young, a mismatch that has been linked to sharp decreases in calf births
and survival rates.

Scientists are studying cases of climate-related mistiming among 4
dozens of species, from Arctic terns to pied flycatchers. But there is one
important species they are missing—us. *Homo sapiens*. We too are suffering from a terrible case of climate-related mistiming, albeit in a cul-
tural-historical, rather than a biological, sense. Our problem is that the
climate crisis hatched in our laps at a moment in history when political
and social conditions were uniquely hostile to a problem of this nature and
magnitude—that moment being the tail end of the go-go '80s, the blastoff
point for the crusade to spread deregulated capitalism around the world.
Climate change is a collective problem demanding collective action the
likes of which humanity has never actually accomplished. Yet it entered
mainstream consciousness in the midst of an ideological war being waged
on the very idea of the collective sphere.

This deeply unfortunate mistiming has created all sorts of barriers to 5
our ability to respond effectively to this crisis. It has meant that corporate power was ascendant at the very moment when we needed to exert
unprecedented controls over corporate behavior in order to protect life

Naomi Klein, "The Change Within," *The Nation*, May 12, 2014, 19–21.

on earth. It has meant that regulation was a dirty word just when we needed those powers most. It has meant that we are ruled by a class of politicians who know only how to dismantle and starve public institutions, just when they most need to be fortified and reimagined. And it has meant that we are saddled with an apparatus of "free trade" deals that tie the hands of policy-makers just when they need maximum flexibility to achieve a massive energy transition.

Confronting these various structural barriers to the next economy is the critical work of any serious climate movement. But it's not the only task at hand. We also have to confront how the mismatch between climate change and market domination has created barriers within our very selves, making it harder to look at this most pressing of humanitarian crises with anything more than furtive, terrified glances. Because of the way our daily lives have been altered by both market and technological triumphalism, we lack many of the observational tools necessary to convince ourselves that climate change is real—let alone the confidence to believe that a different way of living is possible. 6

And little wonder: just when we needed to gather, our public sphere was disintegrating; just when we needed to consume less, consumerism took over virtually every aspect of our lives; just when we needed to slow down and notice, we sped up; and just when we needed longer time horizons, we were able to see only the immediate present. 7

This is our climate change mismatch, and it affects not just our species, but potentially every other species on the planet as well. 8

The good news is that, unlike reindeer and songbirds, we humans are blessed with the capacity for advanced reasoning and therefore the ability to adapt more deliberately—to change old patterns of behavior with remarkable speed. If the ideas that rule our culture are stopping us from saving ourselves, then it is within our power to change those ideas. But before that can happen, we first need to understand the nature of our personal climate mismatch. 9

Climate change demands that we consume less, but being consumers is all we know. Climate change is not a problem that can be solved simply by changing what we buy—a hybrid instead of an SUV, some carbon offsets when we get on a plane. At its core, it is a crisis born of overconsumption by the comparatively wealthy, which means the world's most manic consumers are going to have to consume less. 10

The problem is not "human nature," as we are so often told. We weren't born having to shop this much, and we have, in our recent past, been just as happy (in many cases happier) consuming far less. The problem is the inflated role that consumption has come to play in our particular era. 11

Late capitalism teaches us to create ourselves through our consumer 12
choices: shopping is how we form our identities, find community and
express ourselves. Thus, telling people that they can't shop as much as
they want to because the planet's support systems are overburdened can be
understood as a kind of attack, akin to telling them that they cannot truly
be themselves. This is likely why, of the original "Three Rs"—reduce, reuse,
recycle—only the third has ever gotten any traction, since it allows us to
keep on shopping as long as we put the refuse in the right box. The other
two, which require that we consume less, were pretty much dead on arrival.

Climate change is slow, and we are fast. When you are racing through 13
a rural landscape on a bullet train, it looks as if everything you are passing
is standing still: people, tractors, cars on country roads. They aren't, of
course. They are moving, but at a speed so slow compared with the train
that they appear static.

So it is with climate change. Our culture, powered by fossil fuels, is that 14
bullet train, hurtling forward toward the next quarterly report, the next
election cycle, the next bit of diversion or piece of personal validation via
our smartphones and tablets. Our changing climate is like the landscape
out the window: from our racy vantage point, it can appear static, but it is
moving, its slow progress measured in receding ice sheets, swelling waters
and incremental temperature rises. If left unchecked, climate change will
most certainly speed up enough to capture our fractured attention—island
nations wiped off the map, and city-drowning superstorms, tend to do that.
But by then, it may be too late for our actions to make a difference, because
the era of tipping points will likely have begun.

Climate change is place-based, and we are everywhere at once. The 15
problem is not just that we are moving too quickly. It is also that the terrain
on which the changes are taking place is intensely local: an early bloom-
ing of a particular flower, an unusually thin layer of ice on a lake, the late
arrival of a migratory bird. Noticing those kinds of subtle changes requires
an intimate connection to a specific ecosystem. That kind of communion
happens only when we know a place deeply, not just as scenery but also as
sustenance, and when local knowledge is passed on with a sense of sacred
trust from one generation to the next.

But that is increasingly rare in the urbanized, industrialized world. We 16
tend to abandon our homes lightly—for a new job, a new school, a new
love. And as we do so, we are severed from whatever knowledge of place
we managed to accumulate at the previous stop, as well as from the knowledge amassed by our ancestors (who, at least in my case, migrated repeatedly themselves).

Even for those of us who manage to stay put, our daily existence can 17
be disconnected from the physical places where we live. Shielded from the

elements as we are in our climate-controlled homes, workplaces and cars, the changes unfolding in the natural world easily pass us by. We might have no idea that a historic drought is destroying the crops on the farms that surround our urban homes, since the supermarkets still display miniature mountains of imported produce, with more coming in by truck all day. It takes something huge—like a hurricane that passes all previous high-water marks, or a flood destroying thousands of homes—for us to notice that something is truly amiss. And even then we have trouble holding on to that knowledge for long, since we are quickly ushered along to the next crisis before these truths have a chance to sink in.

Climate change, meanwhile, is busily adding to the ranks of the root- 18 less every day, as natural disasters, failed crops, starving livestock and climate-fueled ethnic conflicts force yet more people to leave their ancestral homes. And with every human migration, more crucial connections to specific places are lost, leaving yet fewer people to listen closely to the land.

Climate pollutants are invisible, and we have stopped believing in what 19 **we cannot see.** When BP's Macondo well ruptured in 2010, releasing torrents of oil into the Gulf of Mexico, one of the things we heard from company CEO Tony Hayward was that "the Gulf of Mexico is a very big ocean. The amount of volume of oil and dispersant we are putting into it is tiny in relation to the total water volume." The statement was widely ridiculed at the time, and rightly so, but Hayward was merely voicing one of our culture's most cherished beliefs: that what we can't see won't hurt us and, indeed, barely exists.

So much of our economy relies on the assumption that there is always 20 an "away" into which we can throw our waste. There's the away where our garbage goes when it is taken from the curb, and the away where our waste goes when it is flushed down the drain. There's the away where the minerals and metals that make up our goods are extracted, and the away where those raw materials are turned into finished products. But the lesson of the BP spill, in the words of ecological theorist Timothy Morton, is that ours is "a world in which there is no 'away.'"

When I published *No Logo* a decade and a half ago, readers were 21 shocked to learn of the abusive conditions under which their clothing and gadgets were manufactured. But we have since learned to live with it—not to condone it, exactly, but to be in a state of constant forgetfulness. Ours is an economy of ghosts, of deliberate blindness.

Air is the ultimate unseen, and the greenhouse gases that warm it are 22 our most elusive ghosts. Philosopher David Abram points out that for most of human history, it was precisely this unseen quality that gave the air its power and commanded our respect. "Called Sila, the wind-mind of the world, by the Inuit; Nilch'i, or Holy Wind, by the Navajo; Ruach, or rushing-spirit, by the ancient Hebrews," the atmosphere was "the most mysterious and sacred dimension of life." But in our time, "we rarely acknowledge the atmosphere as it swirls between two persons." Having forgotten the air, Abram writes, we have made it our sewer, "the perfect dump site for the unwanted by-products of our industries. . . . Even the most opaque, acrid smoke billowing out of the pipes will dissipate and disperse, always and ultimately dissolving into the invisible. It's gone. Out of sight, out of mind."

Another part of what makes climate change so very difficult for us 23 to grasp is that ours is a culture of the perpetual present, one that deliberately severs itself from the past that created us as well as the future we are shaping with our actions. Climate change is about how what we did generations in the past will inescapably affect not just the present, but generations in the future. These time frames are a language that has become foreign to most of us.

This is not about passing individual judgment, nor about berating our- 24 selves for our shallowness or rootlessness. Rather, it is about recognizing that we are products of an industrial project, one intimately, historically linked to fossil fuels.

And just as we have changed before, we can change again. After listen- 25 ing to the great farmer-poet Wendell Berry deliver a lecture on how we each have a duty to love our "homeplace" more than any other, I asked him if he had any advice for rootless people like me and my friends, who live in our computers and always seem to be shopping for home. "Stop somewhere," he replied. "And begin the thousand-year-long process of knowing that place."

That's good advice on lots of levels. Because in order to win this fight 26 of our lives, we all need a place to stand.

Thinking about the Essay

1. What is ecological "mismatch" or "mistiming"? What examples of this ecological phenomenon does Klein provide? What is the most important climate change mismatch? Why is it the most important? What is the good news about this significant mismatch?

2. What are the aspects of our personal climate mismatch that we as humans need to understand? Explain each.

3. What does the metaphor in the concluding paragraph mean? How does it relate to Klein's comments?

4. Is the purpose of Klein's article informative, expository, or argumentative? What is her thesis? Does she explicitly state her main point, or does she imply it?

5. One stylistic technique that Klein uses is balanced sentences employing parallelism (paragraphs 5, 7, and 20). Analyze how and why she repeats not only words but also sentence patterns. What is the effect of the balanced sentences?

Responding in Writing

6. Think of a place that has changed since you first saw it. Write an essay in which you describe how it looked in the past and how it looks now. Use specific descriptive details to help your readers see the place then and now. If you know the reasons for the change, include them in your essay.

7. Write an essay in which you analyze Klein's position on climate change—its causes, effects, and solutions.

8. In paragraph 23, Klein asserts that "ours is a culture of the perpetual present, one that deliberately severs itself from the past . . . as well as the future." Write an essay in which you explain what the author means, and then agree or disagree with this statement. The purpose of this argumentative essay is to convince your classmates that your stance is valid and they can understand why you have this opinion. Include specific examples from your experience, observation, and study to support your position.

Networking

9. To fully understand how well Klein achieves her purpose for her audience, do some research into the magazine *Nation*. Visit the website of *The Nation*, research its history, and scan some of the covers, cartoons, photographs, and articles from recent issues of the magazine. Make a list of the ideas and issues included. Who would be likely readers of this magazine? Is Klein's essay appropriate for these intended readers? Why? Summarize your research.

10. What is the meaning of "sense of place"? In a small group of classmates, research the meaning of this phrase. Each student in your group should read a different online article on sense of place and write a summary of the article. Then discuss the articles in your group and discuss how sense of place is related to climate change. Include the importance of sense of place in literature. Summarize your research and discussion, and participate in a class discussion of sense of place and how it relates to climate change.

We Can't Wish Away Climate Change

AL GORE

Al Gore (Albert Gore Jr.) is a former congressman, senator, and forty-fifth vice president of the United States. He was the Democratic candidate for the presidency in 2000, winning the popular vote but losing the electoral count when the Supreme Court in a 5–4 decision awarded Florida to George W. Bush. The son of a distinguished senator from Tennessee, Gore was born in 1948 and grew up in Washington, DC. He attended Harvard University (B.A., 1969) and served a tour of duty in Vietnam. A self-described "raging moderate," Gore became interested in environmental issues when he was in Congress, writing during that time the best-selling *Earth in the Balance: Ecology and the Human Spirit* (1992). After his defeat in the 2000 presidential race, Gore became one of the world's most prominent advocates of environmental protection. His book *An Inconvenient Truth* (2006) and companion film, which won the Academy Award for best documentary, were highly successful, helping Gore to earn a Nobel Peace Prize in 2007. He is also the author of *The Assault on Reason* (2007) and *Our Choice: A Plan to Solve the Climate Crisis* (2010). As a businessman, he is an investor in alternative energy companies. In this essay, which was published in *The New York Times* in 2010, Gore warns about the dangers associated with global warming.

Before Reading

Do you think that global warming or climate change represents a danger to life on this planet? Why or why not?

It would be an enormous relief if the recent attacks on the science of global warming actually indicated that we do not face an unimaginable calamity requiring large-scale, preventive measures to protect human civilization as we know it. 1

Of course, we would still need to deal with the national security risks of our growing dependence on a global oil market dominated by dwindling reserves in the most unstable region of the world, and the economic risks of sending hundreds of billions of dollars a year overseas in return for that oil. And we would still trail China in the race to develop smart grids, fast trains, solar power, wind, geothermal and other renewable sources of energy—the most important sources of new jobs in the 21st century. 2

But what a burden would be lifted! We would no longer have to worry that our grandchildren would one day look back on us as a criminal generation that had selfishly and blithely ignored clear warnings that their fate was in our hands. We could instead celebrate the naysayers who had doggedly persisted in proving that every major National Academy of Sciences report on climate change had simply made a huge mistake. 3

I, for one, genuinely wish that the climate crisis were an illusion. But
unfortunately, the reality of the danger we are courting has not been
changed by the discovery of at least two mistakes in the thousands of pages
of careful scientific work over the last 22 years by the Intergovernmental
Panel on Climate Change. In fact, the crisis is still growing because we are
continuing to dump 90 million tons of global-warming pollution every
24 hours into the atmosphere—as if it were an open sewer.   4

It is true that the climate panel published a flawed overestimate of the
melting rate of debris-covered glaciers in the Himalayas, and used information about the Netherlands provided to it by the government, which
was later found to be partly inaccurate. In addition, e-mail messages stolen from the University of East Anglia in Britain showed that scientists
besieged by an onslaught of hostile, make-work demands from climate
skeptics may not have adequately followed the requirements of the British
freedom of information law.   5

But the scientific enterprise will never be completely free of mistakes.
What is important is that the overwhelming consensus on global warming
remains unchanged. It is also worth noting that the panel's scientists—acting
in good faith on the best information then available to them—probably
underestimated the range of sea-level rise in this century, the speed with which
the Arctic ice cap is disappearing and the speed with which some of the large
glacial flows in Antarctica and Greenland are melting and racing to the sea.   6

Because these and other effects of global warming are distributed globally, they are difficult to identify and interpret in any particular location.
For example, January was seen as unusually cold in much of the United
States. Yet from a global perspective, it was the second-hottest January
since surface temperatures were first measured 130 years ago.   7

Similarly, even though climate deniers have speciously argued for several years that there has been no warming in the last decade, scientists
confirmed last month that the last 10 years were the hottest decade since
modern records have been kept.   8

The heavy snowfalls this month have been used as fodder for ridicule
by those who argue that global warming is a myth, yet scientists have long
pointed out that warmer global temperatures have been increasing the rate
of evaporation from the oceans, putting significantly more moisture into
the atmosphere—thus causing heavier downfalls of both rain and snow
in particular regions, including the Northeastern United States. Just as it's
important not to miss the forest for the trees, neither should we miss the
climate for the snowstorm.   9

Here is what scientists have found is happening to our climate: man-
made global-warming pollution traps heat from the sun and increases atmospheric temperatures. These pollutants—especially carbon dioxide—have   10

been increasing rapidly with the growth in the burning of coal, oil, natural gas and forests, and temperatures have increased over the same period. Almost all of the ice-covered regions of the Earth are melting—and seas are rising. Hurricanes are predicted to grow stronger and more destructive, though their number is expected to decrease. Droughts are getting longer and deeper in many mid-continent regions, even as the severity of flooding increases. The seasonal predictability of rainfall and temperatures is being disrupted, posing serious threats to agriculture. The rate of species extinction is accelerating to dangerous levels.

Though there have been impressive efforts by many business leaders, hundreds of millions of individuals and families throughout the world and many national, regional and local governments, our civilization is still failing miserably to slow the rate at which these emissions are increasing—much less reduce them. 11

And in spite of President Obama's efforts at the Copenhagen climate summit meeting in December, global leaders failed to muster anything more than a decision to "take note" of an intention to act. 12

Because the world still relies on leadership from the United States, the failure by the Senate to pass legislation intended to cap American emissions before the Copenhagen meeting guaranteed that the outcome would fall far short of even the minimum needed to build momentum toward a meaningful solution. 13

The political paralysis that is now so painfully evident in Washington has thus far prevented action by the Senate—not only on climate and energy legislation, but also on health care reform, financial regulatory reform and a host of other pressing issues. 14

This comes with painful costs. China, now the world's largest and fastest-growing source of global-warming pollution, had privately signaled early last year that if the United States passed meaningful legislation, it would join in serious efforts to produce an effective treaty. When the Senate failed to follow the lead of the House of Representatives, forcing the president to go to Copenhagen without a new law in hand, the Chinese balked. With the two largest polluters refusing to act, the world community was paralyzed. 15

Some analysts attribute the failure to an inherent flaw in the design of the chosen solution—arguing that a cap-and-trade approach is too unwieldy and difficult to put in place. Moreover, these critics add, the financial crisis that began in 2008 shook the world's confidence in the use of any market-based solution. 16

But there are two big problems with this critique: First, there is no readily apparent alternative that would be any easier politically. It is difficult to imagine a globally harmonized carbon tax or a coordinated 17 multilateral regulatory effort. The flexibility of a global market-based policy—supplemented by regulation and revenue-neutral tax policies—is the option that has by far the best chance of success. The fact that it is extremely difficult does not mean that we should simply give up.

Second, we should have no illusions about the difficulty and the   18
time needed to convince the rest of the world to adopt a completely new approach. The lags in the global climate system, including the buildup of heat in the oceans from which it is slowly reintroduced into the atmosphere, means that we can create conditions that make large and destructive consequences inevitable long before their awful manifestations become apparent: the displacement of hundreds of millions of climate refugees, civil unrest, chaos and the collapse of governance in many developing countries, large-scale crop failures and the spread of deadly diseases.

It's important to point out that the United States is not alone in its   19
inaction. Global political paralysis has thus far stymied work not only on climate, but on trade and other pressing issues that require coordinated international action.

The reasons for this are primarily economic. The globalization of the   20
economy, coupled with the outsourcing of jobs from industrial countries, has simultaneously heightened fears of further job losses in the industrial world and encouraged rising expectations in emerging economies. The result? Heightened opposition, in both the industrial and developing worlds, to any constraints on the use of carbon-based fuels, which remain our principal source of energy.

The decisive victory of democratic capitalism over communism in the   21
1990s led to a period of philosophical dominance for market economics worldwide and the illusion of a unipolar world. It also led, in the United States, to a hubristic "bubble" of market fundamentalism that encouraged opponents of regulatory constraints to mount an aggressive effort to shift the internal boundary between the democracy sphere and the market sphere. Over time, markets would most efficiently solve most problems, they argued. Laws and regulations interfering with the operations of the market carried a faint odor of the discredited statist adversary we had just defeated.

This period of market triumphalism coincided with confirmation by   22
scientists that earlier fears about global warming had been grossly understated. But by then, the political context in which this debate took form was tilted heavily toward the views of market fundamentalists, who fought to weaken existing constraints and scoffed at the possibility that global constraints would be needed to halt the dangerous dumping of global-warming pollution into the atmosphere.

Over the years, as the science has become clearer and clearer, some indus-   23
tries and companies whose business plans are dependent on unrestrained

pollution of the atmospheric commons have become ever more entrenched. They are ferociously fighting against the mildest regulation—just as tobacco companies blocked constraints on the marketing of cigarettes for four decades after science confirmed the link of cigarettes to diseases of the lung and the heart.

Simultaneously, changes in America's political system—including the replacement of newspapers and magazines by television as the dominant medium of communication—conferred powerful advantages on wealthy advocates of unrestrained markets and weakened advocates of legal and regulatory reforms. Some news media organizations now present showmen masquerading as political thinkers who package hatred and divisiveness as entertainment. And as in times past, that has proved to be a potent drug in the veins of the body politic. Their most consistent theme is to label as "socialist" any proposal to reform exploitive behavior in the marketplace. **24**

From the standpoint of governance, what is at stake is our ability to use the rule of law as an instrument of human redemption. After all has been said and so little done, the truth about the climate crisis—inconvenient as ever—must still be faced. **25**

The pathway to success is still open, though it tracks the outer boundary of what we are capable of doing. It begins with a choice by the United States to pass a law establishing a cost for global warming pollution. The House of Representatives has already passed legislation, with some Republican support, to take the first halting steps for pricing greenhouse gas emissions. **26**

Later this week, Senators John Kerry, Lindsey Graham and Joe Lieberman are expected to present for consideration similar cap-and-trade legislation. **27**

I hope that it will place a true cap on carbon emissions and stimulate the rapid development of low-carbon sources of energy. **28**

We have overcome existential threats before. Winston Churchill is widely quoted as having said, "Sometimes doing your best is not good enough. Sometimes, you must do what is required." Now is that time. Public officials must rise to this challenge by doing what is required; and the public must demand that they do so—or must replace them. **29**

Thinking about the Essay

1. How would you characterize Gore's tone in this essay? What is his purpose in using words like "unimaginable calamity" (paragraph 1), "naysayers" (paragraph 3), and "open sewer" (paragraph 4)? What additional examples of this sort of diction can you locate?

2. Why does Gore allude to the National Academy of Sciences and the Copenhagen climate summit, as well as to several politicians including President Obama and Winston Churchill? What is his purpose here?

3. Explain the way Gore constructs his argument. What is his claim, and how does he reinforce it? What minor propositions does he establish? What is the nature of his evidence? Finally, how does he refute or deal with opposing viewpoints?

4. Where does Gore employ causal analysis and comparison and contrast? How do these strategies reinforce his argument?

5. According to Gore, the American political system must change. How persuasive is the writer's opinion, and why?

Responding in Writing

6. Argue for or against the proposition that climate change is a danger to humankind.

7. Analyze Gore's essay as a model of journalistic opinion writing. Discuss style, tone, paragraph organization, and such argumentative strategies as appeals to reason, emotion, and ethics.

8. Write an essay offering your plan to address and solve climate change.

Networking

9. Help to arrange a class viewing of Gore's documentary film, *An Inconvenient Truth*. Afterward, discuss the film in relation to his essay.

10. Go online to find out more about the U.S. Congress and what it is doing (or not doing) to address the problem of climate change. Find out what your congressional representative's position is on the issue, and then compose an email to your representative expressing your own viewpoint.

Talking Trash

ANDY ROONEY

Andrew A. Rooney, better known as "Andy" from his regular appearances on *60 Minutes* and his syndicated columns in more than 200 newspapers, was one of the nation's best-known curmudgeons, a writer and commentator who was frequently at odds with conventional wisdom on various issues. Born in Albany, New York, in 1919, he attended Colgate University before serving in the U.S. Army from 1942 to 1945 as a reporter for *Stars and Stripes*. Rooney wrote, produced, and narrated programs for some of the major shows in television history: He wrote material for Arthur Godfrey from 1949 to 1955, and for Sam Levenson, Herb Shriner, Victor Borge, Gary Moore, and other celebrities who define many of the high points of early television comedy. Over the decades, Rooney also produced television essays, documentaries, and specials for ABC, CBS, and public television. A prolific writer, he was the author of more than a dozen books, including *My War* (1995), *Sincerely, Andy Rooney* (1999), *Common Nonsense* (2002), *Years of Minutes* (2003), and *60 Years of Wisdom and Wit* (2009). Known for his dry, unassuming, but acerbic wit (which from time to time got him in trouble with viewers and television studios), Rooney is at his best when convincing readers about simple truths. Andy Rooney died in 2011. In this essay, which appeared in 2002 in *Diversion*, he tells us the simple truth about our inability to moderate our wasteful ways.

Before Reading

Americans are perceived as being terribly wasteful. They discard food, appliances, clothing, and so much more that other peoples and societies would find useful. Do you agree or disagree with this profile of the wasteful American? And how do you fit into this picture?

Last Saturday I filled the trunk of my car and the passenger seats behind me with junk and headed for the dump. There were newspapers, empty cardboard boxes, bags of junk mail, advertising flyers, empty bottles, cans, and garbage. I enjoy the trip. Next to buying something new, throwing away something that is old is the most satisfying experience I know. 1

The garbage men come to my house twice a week, but they're very fussy. If the garbage is not packaged the way they like it, they won't take it. That's why I make a trip to the dump every Saturday. It's two miles from our house, and I often think big thoughts about throwing things away while I'm driving there. 2

How much, I got to wondering last week, does the whole Earth weigh? New York City alone throws away 24 million pounds of garbage a day. A day! How long will it take us to turn the whole planet Earth into garbage, throw it away, and leave us standing on nothing? 3

Oil, coal, and metal ore are the most obvious extractions, but any place there's a valuable mineral, we dig beneath the surface, take it out, and make it into something else. We never put anything back. We disfigure one 4 part of our land by digging something out and then move on to another spot after we've used up all its resources.

After my visit to the dump, I headed for the supermarket, where I bought $34 worth of groceries. Everything was packed in something—a can, a box, a bottle, a carton, or a bag. When I got to the checkout counter, the cashier separated my cans, boxes, cartons, bottles, and bags and put three or four at a time into other bags, boxes, or cartons. Sometimes she put my paper bags into plastic bags. One bag never seemed to do. If something was in plastic, she put that into paper.   5

On the way home, I stopped at the dry cleaner. Five of my shirts, which had been laundered, were in a cardboard box. There was a piece of cardboard in the front of each shirt and another cardboard cutout to fit the collar to keep it from getting wrinkled. The suit I had cleaned was on a throwaway hanger, in a plastic bag with a form-fitting piece of paper inside over the shoulders of my suit.   6

When I got home, I put the groceries where they belonged in various places in the kitchen. With the wastebasket at hand, I threw out all the outer bags and wrappers. By the time I'd unwrapped and stored everything, I'd filled the kitchen wastebasket a second time.   7

It would be interesting to conduct a serious test to determine what percentage of everything we discard. It must be more than 25%. I drank the contents of a bottle of Coke and threw the bottle away. The CocaCola Company must pay more for the bottle than for what they put in it. Dozens of things we eat come in containers that weigh more and cost the manufacturer more than what they put in them.   8

We've gone overboard on packaging, and part of the reason is that a bag, a can, or a carton provides a place for the producer to display advertising. The average cereal box looks like a roadside billboard.   9

The Earth could end up as one huge, uninhabitable dump.   10

Thinking about the Essay

1. What is Rooney's claim? Where does he state it? What evidence does he provide to support his claim?

2. Does Rooney, writing about a serious problem, maintain a serious tone in this essay? What evidence in the essay leads you to your view?

3. How does Rooney structure his argument? Does he provide enough supporting points to back up his major claim or proposition? Why or why not?

4. Is Rooney merely making value judgments about himself, or does he have a broader purpose? How do you know?

5. Explain the style of this essay. Are Rooney's language and sentence structure accessible or difficult? How does his style facilitate your reading and appreciation of the essay?

Responding in Writing

6. Argue for or against the proposition that we are a wasteful society. As Rooney does, organize your essay around your own personal experience or your knowledge of family and friends.

7. Write an imaginative essay about the year 2050. Center the essay on Rooney's last sentence: "The Earth could end up as one huge, uninhabitable dump."

8. Write a letter to your local congressional representative outlining the need for your community to do more about controlling its waste flow. Offer specific remedies for improvement.

Networking

9. Divide into groups of three or four, and jot down some of the instances of waste you have encountered on your campus. Compare your list with other group members' lists. Which problems seem to be most common? Which are singular? Share and discuss your results with the rest of the class.

10. Go online to research waste management. What is the current status of this movement in the United States? Which cities or regions are doing the best job of managing their waste problems? Present your findings in class discussion.

A Place That Makes Sense

BILL MCKIBBEN

Bill McKibben was born in Palo Alto, California, in 1960 and studied at Harvard University (B.A., 1982). His writing focuses on the global ecosystem and the human impact on it. Frequently, he brings moral and religious ideas to bear on the ways in which our behavior—from consumerism to industrial shortsightedness—degrades the natural world. McKibben says that with respect to nature and Earth's ecosystem, he tries "to counter despair." In books like *The End of Nature* (1989), *Hope, Human and Wild: True Stories of Living Lightly on the Earth* (1995), *Long Distance: A Year of Living Strenuously* (2000), *Enough: Staying Human in an Engineered Age* (2003), *Deep Economy: The Wealth of Communities and the Durable Future* (2007), *Earth: Making a Life on a Tough New Planet* (2010), and *Oil and Honey: The Education of an Unlikely Activist* (2013), McKibben balances a sense of alarm about our profligate waste of natural resources with a tempered optimism that we can revere and preserve our fragile planet. "What I have learned so far," McKibben observes, "is that what is sound and elegant and civilized and respectful of community is also environmentally benign." This essay by McKibben, which appeared in *The Christian Century* on September 23, 2008, poses a challenge: Are we living too large?

Before Reading

In his essay, McKibben asserts that "most places in the U.S. make so little sense" (paragraph 11). What do you think he means by this statement, especially as it relates to sustainable lifestyles and the environment?

Not far from Siena, in the Tuscan hill town of Montalcino, is the Abbey of Sant'Antimo. It was first built in—well, no one's certain. It was there by the ninth century. What you see now is a modern reconstruction, modern meaning 12th century. In other words, it's a part of the landscape. 1

And the landscape is a part of it. As I sat in the pews one afternoon earlier this summer, listening to the monks chant Nones in sonorous harmony, I kept looking past the altar to two windows behind. They framed prime views of the steeply raked farm fields in back of the sanctuary—one showed rows of dusty-leaved olive trees climbing a hill, the other rank upon rank of grapevines in their neat rows. With the crucifix in the middle they formed a kind of triptych, and it was easy to imagine not only the passion, but also one's cup running over with Chianti, one's head anointed with gleaming oil. 2

And easy enough, I think, to figure out why this Tuscan landscape is so appealing to so many. Its charm lies in its comprehensibility—its scale makes intuitive, visceral sense. If you climb one of the bell towers in the hill towns of Tuscany, you look out on a compassable world—you can see where the food that you eat comes from, trace the course of the rivers. It seems sufficient unto itself, as indeed it largely was once upon a time. And in the ancient churches it's easy to construct a vision of the medieval man or woman who once sat in the same hard pew—a person who understood, as we never can, his or her place in the universe. That place was bounded by the distance one could travel physically—save for the Crusade years, it was probably easy to live a life without ever leaving the district. (Florentines speak of living an entire life in view of the Duomo.) And it was bounded just as powerfully by the shared and deep belief in the theology of the church. You knew your place. 3

Which is a phrase with several meanings. You would have been deeply   4
rooted in that world—it's hard to imagine there the identity crises that are
routine in our world. You would have been considerably more rooted than
we're comfortable with. You knew your place in the sense that you were
born into it, and there was little hope of leaving if it didn't suit. Peasants
were peasants and lords were lords, and never the two met. Inequality was
baptized, questioning unlikely. The old medieval world made sense, but it
was often an oppressive sense—hence the 500-year project to liberate ourselves in every possible way.

And though Tuscany still looks comprehensible—and is thus a suit-   5
able backdrop for profitable tourism and powerful travel fantasy—it's
now mostly sham. The farms remain, largely supported by farm subsidies
from the European Union and the wine-buying habits of affluent foreigners. The villages are mostly emptied out, with only the old remaining—on
weekends traffic swells as Florentines and Romans head to the country
house. Even the churches are largely relics. Stop in for afternoon Mass
and you're likely to find three or four old women listening to an African
priest limp along in halting Italian—there aren't nearly the vocations necessary to fill these pulpits. Even the chanting monks at the Sant'Antimo
abbey are imports—a French brotherhood that took over the church a
decade ago.

Still, it's so alluring, this idea of rootedness. Especially for those of us   6
who live in places that make no sense at all. Where food travels 2,000 miles
and arrives at a Wal-Mart. Where God lives at a megachurch without the
tradition or culture to give worship much weight. How we thirst for places
that make sense.

Which is why it was such a pleasure, a few days later, to find myself   7
in a very different kind of church, this one compact, ultramodern, made
of glass. Oh, and Lutheran. The ground floor, on this Thursday, was a
day-care center filled with parents and kids; the second floor was all
offices; and the third housed the sanctuary, a kind of window-girded
nest. And when I looked out past the small cross, what I saw were the
canals and sidewalks of Hammarby Sjostad—another place that makes
sense. Real sense.

Hammarby Sjostad, a ten-minute ferry ride from the center of Stock-   8
holm, used to be an industrial brownfield, toxic and unpopulated. When
Sweden bid to host the 2004 Olympics, it was slated to become the Olympic Village; the bid failed, but the momentum for a new neighborhood
was enormous, and ground was broken seven or eight years ago. It was
designed from the start to be an ecological gem, where the average person
would live half again as lightly as the average Swede, who is already among
the most ecologically minded citizens of the developed world. The whole

place is a closed loop—food waste is turned into biogas, trash is burned for energy, water is recycled. None of it is outrageously high-tech; it's just all thought out.

And the fancy piping is actually only a small part of what makes the   9
place work. The town requires an uncoerced but very real willingness to cooperate, to be part of a community. For instance: by the lobby of each apartment is a series of portholes built into the wall, each one connected to a pneumatic tube. You put food waste in one, paper trash in the next and so on—everything is sucked off to the right processing center. But if you put plastic in with banana peels, the system breaks down. So there's a little graph above the chutes showing how many times each building screwed up the month before. Building 7 (five stories high like most of the blocks in the development), three errant bags. Building 8, one. Building 9, none at all.

Or say you want to wash your clothes. There's no washing machine in   10
your flat—much energy is saved by having a wash house shared by a few buildings. You walk in and wave your key over a sensor, and up pops a digital display. You use it to book a time in the next few days to do your wash in the high-tech machines.

It's a reminder of why most places in the U.S. make so little sense.   11
Cheap energy has led Americans to sprawl endlessly out. We rattle around enormous houses and enormous suburbs, distant from each other in every sense of the word. (The average American eats meals with friends, family or neighbors half as often as he or she did 50 years ago.) Cheap fossil fuel has turned us into the first people in human history who have essentially no need of each other—a kind of hyperindividualism has replaced community.

Waste tubes in Hammarby Sjostad require community cooperation to work properly.

There is very little automobile traffic in Hammarby Sjostad.

So maybe Hammarby Sjostad's way of doing things would chafe a 12
little—the American cry has become "Don't tell me what to do," and it's
hard to imagine us sharing washing machines with our neighbors. We don't
even want to travel together—or at least we didn't until high gas prices
began pulling us from our single-occupancy SUVs.

But the responsibilities come with deep pleasures. To stroll the streets 13
of this town is to realize that you've stumbled into a low-key paradise. On
a fine day it seems as if all 25,000 residents are out and about, strolling the
boardwalks and paths, oblivious to car traffic because it's almost nonexis-
tent. (Parking is expensive, and who needs it—there's a fast ferry to town
and a tram that comes by every few minutes.) The community was planned
with bars every few blocks, with a community kayak dock, with playing
fields and community centers, with shared barbecue pits. Swedes may not
be gregarious, but there's the steady hum of community—clusters of moms
pushing prams, for instance. (And if you want proof that this place works,
the number of families with kids is higher than expected—they're having
to build extra schools.) What I'm trying to say is, the place make sense.

The place makes sense in the world, as well. Here's the cost: the flats 14
are relatively small, between 600 and 1,000 square feet. That's two or
three rooms plus a modest kitchen and a balcony. You can't have endless
stuff because there's no room (everyone has storage space in the base-
ment, and there's a special room for bikes). So there's way less space than
we've come to consider normal—it's about like living in a trailer, maybe
a double-wide.

But that's OK. When the community is an extended home recreation 15
center, you don't need a special warren in your dwelling. What it means

is a resident of Hammarby Sjostad is able to live, more or less, at a level calculated to be sustainable for all of the world's 6 billion humans—as compared with the American lifestyle, which would require five additional earths if it were extended across all humanity. This is a place where people aren't drowning Bangladesh or spreading malarial mosquitoes or doing all the other things that come with living too large.

Which brings us back to the church. The state built it—Lutheranism   16 is the official religion in Sweden. And though I wasn't there on a Sunday, to judge by the number of chairs in the sanctuary, the congregation is a small percentage of the neighborhood. Still, there was a powerful sense that the gospel had been consulted in the construction of this town, if only instinctively. The rooted, practical gospel, the one that centers on loving your neighbor as yourself. I've never been in a place that made more sense.

Thinking about the Essay

1. McKibben published this essay in *The Christian Century*. What evidence do you find in the essay that suggests he writes for an audience interested in religious matters? What assumptions does he make about his intended audience? To what extent do you feel you are a member of that readership? Explain.

2. What exactly do the Abbey of Sant'Antimo and Hammarby Sjostad symbolize? How does McKibben develop these symbols? What comparative details emerge from his approach?

3. Why does McKibben present information on Tuscany in the first third of the essay, and then move to a town in Sweden? Is this strategy directly relevant to the subject he develops? Explain.

4. What is the author's argument? Where does he state his claim, and how effective is its placement? How does he employ personal experience, observation, and data to support his claim? Cite specific examples.

5. Explain the author's tone and how he achieves it. Is he optimistic or pessimistic about his subject? How do you know?

Responding in Writing

6. Write an essay explaining how you would design a town that offers an ecologically sustainable lifestyle.

7. Argue for or against the proposition that moral and religious considerations should override personal preferences when we make decisions that might affect our environment adversely.

8. Write an essay of extended definition in which you discuss the concept of "rootedness."

Networking

9. Divide into groups of three or four and discuss your views on "loving your neighbor as yourself" and how this concept might relate to environmental issues. Share your responses with the rest of the class. Also, mention whether your views were modified or changed during group discussion.

10. Go online and read messages of some of the professional newsgroups whose members are in the environmental movement. Select several messages regarding ecologically sustainable lifestyles, and write a report on your findings.

A Hole in the World

JONATHAN SCHELL

Jonathan Schell was born in New York City in 1943. Following graduate study in Far Eastern history at Harvard University and additional study in Tokyo, Schell accompanied an American forces operation in South Vietnam in the winter and spring of 1967 that resulted in the evacuation of an entire village after "pacification" failed. He wrote graphic descriptions of the destruction of Vietnamese villages in *The Village of Ben Suc* (1967) and *The Military Half: An Account of Destruction in Quang Ngai and Quang Tin* (1968). Just as his first two books excoriated the American presence in Vietnam, Schell in his third book, *The Time of Illusion* (1976), offered a critique of the Nixon administration and the Watergate scandal. Schell's next book, *The Fate of the Earth* (1982), still one of the most persuasive treatments of the dangers of nuclear war, became a best seller. Schell returned to the subject of nuclear proliferation in *The Gift of Time: The Case for Abolishing Nuclear Weapons* (1998) and *The Seventh Decade: The New Shape of Nuclear Danger* (2007). He was the peace and disarmament correspondent for *The Nation* and Harold Willens Peace Fellow at the Nation Institute. Schell died in 2014. In the following essay, published in *The Nation* on October 1, 2001, Schell uses the events of 9/11 to raise the even more frightening specter of nuclear destruction.

Before Reading

How has 9/11 made you more aware of the dangers posed by weapons of mass destruction? Do you carry this awareness with you, or does the prospect of an attack with a weapon of mass destruction seem remote and unthreatening? Explain your response.

O n Tuesday morning, a piece was torn out of our world. A patch of blue sky that should not have been there opened up in the New York skyline. In my neighborhood—I live eight blocks from the World Trade Center—the heavens were raining human beings. Our city was changed forever. Our country was changed forever. Our world was changed forever.

It will take months merely to know what happened, far longer to feel so much grief, longer still to understand its meaning. It's already clear, however, that one aspect of the catastrophe is of supreme importance for the future: the danger of the use of weapons of mass destruction, and especially the use of nuclear weapons. This danger includes their use by a terrorist group but is by no means restricted to it. It is part of a larger danger that has been for the most part ignored since the end of the cold war.

Among the small number who have been concerned with nuclear arms in recent years—they have pretty much all known one another by their first names—it was commonly heard that the world would not return its attention to this subject until a nuclear weapon was again set off somewhere in the world. Then, the tiny club said to itself, the world would awaken to its danger. Many of the ingredients of the catastrophe were obvious. The repeated suicide-homicides of the bombers in Israel made it obvious that there were people so possessed by their cause that, in an exaltation of hatred, they would do anything in its name. Many reports—most recently an article in *The New York Times* on the very morning of the attack—reminded the public that the world was awash in nuclear materials and the wherewithal for other weapons of mass destruction. Russia is bursting at the seams with these materials. The suicide bombers and the market in nuclear materials was that two-plus-two that points toward the proverbial necessary four. But history is a trickster. The fates came up with a horror that was unforeseen. No one had identified the civilian airliner as a weapon of mass destruction, but it occurred to the diabolical imagination of those who conceived Tuesday's attack that it could be one. The invention illumined the nature of terrorism in modern times. These terrorists carried no bombs—only knives, if initial reports are to be believed. In short, they turned the tremendous forces inherent in modern technical society—in this case, Boeing 767s brimming with jet fuel—against itself.

So it is also with the more commonly recognized weapons of mass   4
destruction. Their materials can be built the hard way, from scratch, as
Iraq came within an ace of doing until stopped by the Gulf War and as
Pakistan and India have done, or they can be diverted from Russian, or for
that matter American or English or French or Chinese, stockpiles. In the
one case, it is nuclear know-how that is turned against its inventors, in the
other it is their hardware. Either way, it is "blowback"—the use of a technical capacity against its creator—and, as such, represents the pronounced
suicidal tendencies of modern society.

This suicidal bent—nicely captured in the name of the still current   5
nuclear policy "mutual assured destruction"—of course exists in forms
even more devastating than possible terrorist attacks. India and Pakistan,
which both possess nuclear weapons and have recently engaged in one
of their many hot wars, are the likeliest candidates. Most important—
and most forgotten—are the some 30,000 nuclear weapons that remain
in the arsenals of Russia and the United States. The Bush Administration
has announced its intention of breaking out of the antiballistic missile
treaty of 1972, which bans antinuclear defenses, and the Russians have
answered that if this treaty is abandoned the whole framework of nuclear
arms control built up over thirty years may collapse. There is no quarrel
between the United States and Russia that suggests a nuclear exchange
between them, but accidents are another matter, and, as Tuesday's attack
has shown, the mood and even the structure of the international order can
change overnight.

What should be done? Should the terrorists who carried out Tuesday's   6
attacks be brought to justice and punished, as the President wants to
do? Of course. Who should be punished if not people who would hurl
a cargo of innocent human beings against a fixed target of other innocent human beings? (When weighing the efficiency—as distinct from the
satisfaction—of punishment, however, it is well to remember that the
immediate attackers have administered the supposed supreme punishment of death to themselves.) Should further steps be taken to protect the
country and the world from terrorism, including nuclear terrorism? They
should. And yet even as we do these things, we must hold, as if to life
itself, to a fundamental truth that has been known to all thoughtful people since the destruction of Hiroshima: There is no technical solution to
the vulnerability of modern populations to weapons of mass destruction.
After the attack, Secretary of Defense Rumsfeld placed U.S. forces on the
highest state of alert and ordered destroyers and aircraft carriers to take
up positions up and down the coasts of the United States. But none of
these measures can repeal the vulnerability of modern society to its own
inventions, revealed by that heart-breaking gap in the New York skyline.

This, obviously, holds equally true for that other Maginot line, the proposed system of national missile defense. Thirty billion dollars is being spent on intelligence annually. We can assume that some portion of that was devoted to protecting the World Trade Center after it was first bombed in 1993. There may have been mistakes—maybe we'll find out—but the truth is that no one on earth can demonstrate that the expenditure of even ten times that amount can prevent a terrorist attack on the United States or any other country. The combination of the extraordinary power of modern technology, the universal and instantaneous spread of information in the information age and the mobility inherent in a globalized economy prevents it.

Man, however, is not merely a technical animal. Aristotle pointed out   7 that we are also a political animal, and it is to politics that we must return for the solutions that hold promise. That means returning to the treaties that the United States has recently been discarding like so much old newspaper—the one dealing, for example, with an International Criminal Court (useful for tracking down terrorists and bringing them to justice), with global warming and, above all, of course, with nuclear arms and the other weapons of mass destruction, biological and chemical. The United States and seven other countries now rely for their national security on the retaliatory execution of destruction a million fold greater than the Tuesday attacks. The exit from this folly, by which we endanger ourselves as much as others, must be found. Rediscovering ourselves as political animals also means understanding the sources of the hatred that the United States has incurred in a decade of neglect and, worse, neglect of international affairs—a task that is highly unwelcome to many in current circumstances but nevertheless is indispensable to the future safety of the United States and the world.

It would be disrespectful of the dead to in any way minimize the   8 catastrophe that has overtaken New York. Yet at the same time we must keep room in our minds for the fact that it could have been worse. To lose two huge buildings and the people in them is one thing; to lose all of Manhattan—or much, much more—is another. The emptiness in the sky can spread. We have been warned.

Thinking about the Essay

1. This essay appeared less than a month after the 9/11 disaster. Do you think that the writer exploited the catastrophe, or is his purpose valid? Explain your response.

2. Schell's credentials as a specialist on nuclear proliferation are impressive. Is this essay geared to a highly intelligent audience or a more general one? Cite internal evidence to support your response.

3. How is the essay organized? Where does the introduction begin and end? What paragraphs constitute the body? Where is the conclusion? What markers assisted you in establishing these stages of essay development?

4. Reduce the logical structure of Schell's argument to a set of major and minor propositions. Is his conclusion valid in light of the underlying reasons? Explain.

5. What assertion in the essay do you most agree with, and why? Which assertion do you find dubious or unsupported, and why?

Responding in Writing

6. Write an essay in which you agree or disagree with Schell's statement that the danger of the use of weapons of mass destruction is "of supreme importance for the future" (paragraph 2).

7. Schell asserts that the United States has neglected its role in international affairs, including its abandonment of international treaties, thereby endangering the nation's security. Argue for or against his claim.

8. Write an analysis of Schell's style in this essay. Begin with the title itself and how it resonates throughout the essay. Discuss the impact of such graphic uses of language as "the heavens were raining human beings" (paragraph 1). Identify those stylistic techniques the author uses to persuade us to accept the logic of his position.

Networking

9. Divide into groups of between three and five, and create a simulation game *whereby* a specific city is threatened by a weapon of mass destruction. Imagine the steps taken to thwart the attack, and determine if these steps would be successful or not. Present your scenario to the class.

10. Do an Internet search for information on nuclear disarmament. Using the information retrieved, write a report on what various groups, agencies, and governments are doing to reduce and prevent the spread of nuclear weapons.

Conducting Research in the Global Era

Introduction

The *doing* of research is as important a process as the writing of a research paper. When scholars, professors, scientists, journalists, and students do research, they ask questions, solve problems, follow leads, and track down sources. The process of research as well as the writing of the research paper has changed radically over the last ten years, as the Internet now makes a whole world of resources instantly available to anyone. Skillfully navigating your way through this wealth of resources, evaluating and synthesizing information as you solve problems and answer questions, enhances your critical thinking and writing abilities and develops the tools you will need for professional success.

A research paper incorporates the ideas, discoveries, and observations of other writers. The information provided by these scholars, thinkers, and observers helps to support your own original thesis or claim about a topic. Learning how to evaluate, adapt, synthesize, and correctly acknowledge these sources in your research protects you from charges of plagiarism (discussed later). More importantly, it demonstrates to you how knowledge is expanded and created. Research and research writing are the cornerstone not only of the university but of our global information society.

The research paper is the final product of a process of inquiry and discovery. The topics and readings in this book bring together voices from all over the world, discussing and debating issues of universal importance. As you develop a topic, work toward a thesis, and discover sources and evidence, you will use the Internet to bring international perspectives to your writing. More immediately, your teacher will probably ask you to work in peer groups as you refine your topics, suggest resources to each other, and evaluate preliminary drafts of your final research paper. Although the primary—and ultimate—audience for your research paper is your teacher, thinking of your work as a process of discovery and a contribution to a larger global conversation will keep your perspective fresh and your interest engaged.

The Research Process

A research paper is the final result of a series of tasks, some small and others quite time-consuming. Be sure to allow yourself plenty of time for each stage of the research process, working with your teacher or a peer group to develop a schedule that breaks down specific tasks.

The four broad stages of the research process are

1. Choosing a topic
2. Establishing a thesis
3. Finding and evaluating evidence
4. Organizing and outlining your information

Stage One: Choosing a Topic

Reading and discussing the often urgent issues addressed in this book may have already given you an idea about a topic you would like to explore further. Your attention may also have been engaged by a television news report, an international website that presented an unexpected viewpoint, or a speaker who visited your campus. Even if your teacher assigns a specific topic area, finding—and nurturing—a genuine curiosity and concern about that topic will make the research process much more involving and satisfying. Some topics are too broad, too controversial (or not controversial enough), too current, or too obscure for an effective research paper.

Determining an Appropriate Research Topic

Ask yourself the following questions about possible topics for your research paper:

- Am I genuinely curious about this topic? Will I want to live with it for the next few weeks?
- What do I already know about this topic? What more do I want to find out?
- Does the topic fit the general guidelines my teacher has suggested?
- Can I readily locate the sources I will need for further research on this topic?

Exercise: Freewriting

Review your work as your class progresses, taking note of any readings in the text that particularly appealed to you or any writing assignments that you especially enjoyed. Create a new folder on your computer and label it "Research Paper." Create a new document and title it "Freewriting." Then write, without stopping, everything that intrigued you originally about that reading or that assignment. Use the questions on page 348 to prompt your thinking.

Browsing

Having identified a general topic area of interest, begin exploring that area by *browsing*. When you browse, you take a broad and casual survey of the existing information and resources about your topic. There are many resources to consult as you begin to dig deeper into your topic, nearly all of which can be found at your campus library. Begin at the reference desk by asking for a guide to the library's reference collection.

- *General Reference Texts*. These include encyclopedias, almanacs, specialized dictionaries, and statistical information.
- *Periodical Index*. Both in-print and online versions of periodical indices now exist (the electronic versions are often subscription-only and available only through academic and some public libraries). A periodical index lists subjects, authors, and titles of articles in newspapers, journals, and magazines. Some electronic versions include both abstracts (brief summaries) and full-text versions of the articles.
- *Library Catalog*. Begin your catalog browsing with a subject or keyword search. Identify the call number that appears most frequently for the books you are most likely to use—that number will point you to the library shelves where you'll find the most useful books for your topic.

Making a Global Connection

Unless you read another language, the information you find in books is not likely to be as international or immediate in perspective as what you can find in periodicals and online. For the most up-to-date information as well as a perspective from the nation or countries involved in your topic, your online and periodical research will probably be most useful.

- *Search Engines*. For the most current and broadest overview of a research topic, a search engine such as Google, Bing, or Yahoo! can provide you with an ever-changing—and dauntingly vast—range of perspectives. Many search engines, including these three, have international sites (allowing you to search in specific regions or countries) as well as basic translation services. At the browsing stage, spending time online can both stimulate your interest and help you focus your topic. Because websites change so quickly, however, be sure to print out a page from any site you think might be useful in the later stages of your research—that way, you'll have a hard copy of the site's URL (uniform resource locator, or Web address). If you're working on your own computer, create a new folder under "favorites" or "bookmarks" titled "Research Project," and file bookmarks for interesting sites there.

Stage Two: Establishing a Thesis

Moving from a general area of interest to a specific *thesis*—a claim you wish to make, an area of information you wish to explore, a question you intend to answer, or a solution to a problem you want to propose—requires thinking critically about your topic. You have already begun to focus on what specifically interests you about this topic in the freewriting exercise on page 348. The next step in refining your topic and establishing a thesis is to determine your audience and purpose for writing.

Determining Your Audience and Purpose

- Where have you found, through your browsing, the most interesting or compelling information about your topic? Who was the audience for that information? Do you consider yourself to be a part of that audience? Define the characteristics of that audience (e.g., concerned about the environment, interested in global economics, experienced at traveling abroad).
- Why are you most interested in this topic? Do you want to encourage someone (a friend, a politician) to take a specific course of action? Do you want to shed some light on an issue or event that not many people are familiar with?
- Try a little imaginative role playing. Imagine yourself researching this topic as a professional in a specific field. For example, if your topic is environmental preservation, imagine yourself as a pharmaceuticals researcher. What would your compelling interest in the topic be? What if you were an adventure traveler seeking new destinations—how would your approach to the topic of environmental preservation change?
- If you could have the undivided attention of anyone, other than your teacher, with whom you could share your knowledge about this topic, who would that person be and why?

Moving from a Topic to a Thesis Statement

Although choosing a topic is the beginning of the research *process*, it is not the beginning of your research *paper*. The course that your research will take and the shape that your final paper will assume are based on your *thesis statement*. A thesis statement is the answer to whatever question originally prompted your research. To narrow your topic and arrive at a thesis statement, ask yourself specific questions about the topic.

Using Questions to Create a Thesis Statement

General Topic	More Specific Topic	Question	Thesis Statement
Preserving the global environment	Preserving the rain forest	What is a creative way in which people could try to preserve the rain forest?	Ecotourism, when properly managed, can help the rain forest by creating economic incentives for the people who live there.
Economic security for women in the developing world	Creating economic opportunities for women in the developing world	What approaches could help women in the developing world establish economic security for themselves and their communities?	Microloans are a creative and empowering way of redistributing wealth that allows individual women to develop their own economic security.
AIDS in Africa	The incidence of AIDS in African women	How are international organizations working to stop the spread of AIDS among African women?	Improving literacy and educational opportunities for African girls and women will help to stem the spread of AIDS.
Dating and courtship between people of different religions	Dating behavior among second-generation American Hindu or Muslim teenagers	How are kids from conservative cultural or religious backgrounds negotiating between their family's beliefs and the pressures of American popular culture?	Encouraging multicultural events helps teenagers learn about each other's cultures and beliefs.

Stage Three: Finding and Evaluating Evidence

Developing a Working Bibliography

A working bibliography is a record of every source you consult as you conduct your research. Although not every source you use may end up cited in your paper, having a consolidated and organized record of *everything* you looked at will make drafting the paper as well as preparing the Works Cited list much easier. Some people use their computers for keeping a Works Cited list (especially if you do much of your research using online databases, which automatically create citations). For some people—even if many of your sources are online—index cards are much more portable and efficient. Index cards allow you to easily rearrange the order of your sources (according to priority, for example, or sources that you need to double-check). The cards let you jot down notes or summaries, and they slip into your book bag for a quick trip to the library.

Whether your working bibliography is on a computer or on index cards, always record the same information for each source you consult. Note that current Modern Language Association (MLA) guidelines stipulate italics rather than underlining. If you are preparing your working bibliography on a computer, use italics for book titles, magazine titles, and the like; use underlining on handwritten index cards.

Checklists for Working Bibliographies

Information for a book:

❑ Author name(s), first and last
❑ Book title
❑ Place of publication
❑ Publisher's name
❑ Date of publication
❑ Library call number
❑ Page numbers (for specific information or quotes you'll want to consult later)

Information for an article in a journal or magazine:

❑ Author name(s), first and last
❑ Article title
❑ Magazine or journal title
❑ Volume and issue number (when issue number is available)
❑ Date of publication
❑ Page numbers
❑ Library call number

Information for online sources:

❑ Author (if there is one)
❑ Title of an article or graphic on the web page
❑ Title of website, if different from the above

❏ Version or edition
❏ Publisher or sponsor of the site (if any)
❏ Date of publication (if available)
❏ Date of your online access
❏ URL (website address; not usually included in your Works Cited list unless it would be unlikely your reader could find the correct source or if your instructor requires one)

Some sites include information on how they prefer to be cited. You'll notice this information at the bottom of a main or "splash" page of a site, or you'll see a link to a "citation" page.

Sample working bibliography note: Article

Honey, Martha. "Protecting the Environment: Setting Green Standards for the Tourism Industry." *Environment* 45.1 (2003): 8–12.

Sample working bibliography note: Online source

World Tourism Association. "Global Code of Ethics for Tourism." <http:www.//world-tourism.org/projects/ethics/principles.html>.

Consulting Experts and Professionals

In the course of your research you may discover someone whose work is so timely, or opinions so relevant, that a personal interview would provide even more (and unique) information for your paper. Look beyond the university faculty for such experts—for example, if your topic is ecotourism, a local travel agent who specializes in ecotourism might be able to give you firsthand accounts of such locales and voyages. If your topic is second-generation teenagers balancing conservative backgrounds with American popular culture, hanging out with a group of such kids and talking with them about their lives will give you the kind of first-person anecdote that makes research writing genuinely fresh and original. Think of "expertise" as being about *experience*—not just a title or a degree.

Checklist for Arranging and Conducting Interviews

❏ Be certain that the person you wish to speak to will offer a completely unique, even undocumented, perspective on your topic. Interviewing someone who has already published widely on your topic is not the best use of your research time, as you can just as easily consult that person's published work.

❏ E-mail, telephone (at a business number, if possible), or write to your subject well in advance of your paper deadline. Explain clearly that you are a student writing a research paper, the topic of your paper, and the specific subject(s) you wish to discuss.

❏ An interview can be conducted via e-mail or over the telephone as well as in person. Instant messaging, because it can't be easily documented and doesn't lend itself to longer responses, is not a good choice.

❏ Write out your questions in advance!

Conducting Field Research

Field research involves traveling to a specific place to observe and document a specific occurrence or phenomenon. For example, if you were writing about the challenges and opportunities of a highly diverse immigrant community (such as Elmhurst, Queens), you might arrange to spend a day at a local school, park, or coffee shop. Bring a notebook, a digital camera, a tape recorder—anything that will help you capture and record observations. Although your task as a field researcher is to be *unbiased*—to objectively observe what is happening, keeping an open mind as well as open eyes— you'll want to always keep your working thesis in mind, too. For example, if your thesis is

> Allowing students in highly diverse American communities to create events that celebrate and respect their own cultural traditions within the general American popular culture helps to create understanding between teenagers and their immigrant parents

your field research might take you to a high school in an immigrant community to observe the interactions among teenagers. You'll want to record everything—both positive and negative, both expected and surprising—that you observe and overhear, but you won't want to get distracted by a teacher's mentioning the difficulties of coping with many different languages in the classroom. That's fascinating, but it's another topic altogether.

Checklist for Arranging and Conducting Field Research

❏ If your field research involves crossing a private boundary or property line—such as a school, church, hospital, or restaurant—be sure to contact the institution first to confirm that it's appropriate for you to visit. As with the guidelines for conducting a personal interview, inform the person with whom you arrange the visit that you are a student conducting field research and that your research is for a classroom paper.

❏ Respect personal boundaries. Some people might not want to be photographed, and others might be uneasy if they think you are taking notes on their conversation or behavior. If you sense that your presence is making someone uncomfortable, apologize and explain what you are doing. If the person is still uncomfortable, back off.

❏   When you use examples and observations from your field research in your research paper, do not use the first person as part of the citation. Simply describe what was observed and under what circumstances.

Not recommended: When I visited the dog park to see how the personalities of dogs reflect those of their owners, I was especially attracted to the owner of a bulldog named Max. When I introduced myself to Max's owner, George T., and explained my project to him, George agreed with my thesis and pointed out that the owners of large, athletic dogs like Rottweilers tended to be young men, and the owners of more sedentary dogs (like Max) seemed to be a little mellower.

Recommended: A visit to a local dog park revealed the ways in which the personalities of dogs reflect those of their owners. George T., the owner of a bulldog named Max, pointed out that the younger men at the park were accompanied by large, athletic dogs like Rottweilers, while more sedentary people (like George) tended to have mellower breeds such as bulldogs.

Assessing the Credibility of Sources

After browsing, searching, observing, and conversing, you will by now have collected a mass of sources and data. The next step is to evaluate those sources critically, using your working bibliography as a road map back to all the sources you have consulted to date. This critical evaluation will help you to determine which sources have the relevance, credibility, and authority expected of academic research.

Checklist for Assessing Source Credibility

❏   Do the table of contents and index of a book include keywords and subjects relevant to your topic? Does the abstract of a journal article include keywords relevant to your topic and thesis? Does a website indicate through a menu (or from your using the "search" tool) that it contains content relevant to your topic and thesis?

❏   How current is the source? Check the date of the magazine or journal and the copyright date of the book (the original copyright date, not the dates of reprints). Has the website been updated recently, and are its links current and functioning?

❏   How authoritative is the source? Is the author credentialed in his or her field? Do other authors refer to this writer (or website) in their work?

❏   Who sponsors a website? Is the site of a major media group, a government agency, a political think tank, or a special-interest group? If you are unsure, print out the home page of the site and ask your teacher or a reference librarian.

Taking Notes

Now that you have determined which sources are most relevant and useful, you can begin to read them with greater attention to detail. This is *active reading*—annotating, responding to, and taking notes on what you are reading. Taking careful notes will help you build the structure of your paper and will ensure accurate documentation later. As with the working bibliography, you can take notes either on your computer or on index cards. For online sources, you can cut and paste blocks of text into a separate word-processing document on your computer; just be certain to include the original URL and to indicate that what you have cut and pasted is a *direct quote* (which you might later paraphrase or summarize). Some researchers cut and paste material in a font or color that is completely different from their own writing, just to remind them of where specific words and concepts came from (and as protection against inadvertent plagiarism).

There are three kinds of notes you will take as you explore your resources:

- Summaries give you the broad overview of a source's perspective or information and serve as reminders of a source's content should you wish to revisit it later for more specific information or direct quotes.
- Paraphrases express a source's ideas and information in your own language.
- Direct quotations are best for when an author or subject expresses a thought or concept in language that is so striking, important, or original that to paraphrase it would be to lose some of its importance. Direct quotations are exact copies of an author's own words and are always enclosed in quotation marks.

Checklist for Taking Notes

- ❑ Take just one note (summary, paraphrase, or quotation) on each index card. Be sure to note the complete source information for a quote on the card (see the Checklists for Working Bibliographies on page 352 for what information is required).
- ❑ Cross-check your note cards against your working bibliography. Be sure that every source on which you take notes has a corresponding entry in the working bibliography.
- ❑ Write a subtopic at the top of each card, preferably in a bright color. Keep a running list of all of your subtopics. This will enable you to group together related pieces of information and determine the structure of your outline.

Sample note: Summary

Subtopic	Indigenous peoples and ecotourism
Author/title	Mastny, "Ecotourist trap"
Page numbers	94
Summary	The Kainamaro people of Guyana are actively involved with the development of ecotourism in their lands, ensuring that their cultural integrity takes precedence over financial gain.

Sample note: Paraphrase

Subtopic	Indigenous peoples and ecotourism
Author/title	Mastny, "Ecotourist trap"
Page numbers	94
Paraphrase	Actively involving indigenous peoples in ecotourism arrangements is important. A representative for the Kainamaro people of Guyana, Claudette Fleming, says that although this community first worried about maintaining their cultural integrity, they came to see that ecotourism would be a more beneficial way to increase their income and at the same time control their lands and culture than other industries such as logging.

Sample note: Direct quotation

Subtopic	Indigenous peoples and ecotourism
Author/title	Mastny, "Ecotourist trap"
Page numbers	94
Direct quotation	"The Kainamaro are content to share their culture and creativity with outsiders—as long as they remain in control of their futures and the pace of cultural change."

Understanding Plagiarism, Intellectual Property, and Academic Ethics

- *Plagiarism.* Plagiarism is passing off someone else's words, ideas, images, or concepts as your own. Plagiarism can be as subtle and accidental as forgetting to add an in-text citation or as blatant as "borrowing" a friend's paper or handing in something from a website with your own name on it. Most schools and colleges have explicit, detailed policies about what constitutes plagiarism, and the consequences of being caught are not pretty—you may risk anything from failure on a particular assignment to expulsion from the institution. There are two basic ways to avoid plagiarism: (1) Don't wait until the last minute to write your paper (which will tempt you to take shortcuts); and (2) give an in-text citation (see page 362) for absolutely everything you include in your research paper that didn't come out of your own head. It's better to be safe and overcite than to be accused of plagiarism. For a straightforward discussion of plagiarism, go to http://honorcouncil.georgetown .edu/whatisplagiarism.

- *Intellectual Property*. If you've ever considered wiping your hard drive clean of free downloaded music files out of the fear of being arrested or fined, then you've wrestled with the issue of intellectual property. Intellectual property includes works of art, music, animation, and literature—as well as research concepts, computer programs, and even fashion. Intellectual property rights for visual, musical, and verbal works are protected by copyright law. When you download, for free, a music track from the Internet, you are violating copyright law—the artist who created that work receives no credit or royalties for your enjoyment and use of his or her work. When you cut and paste blocks of a website into your own research paper without giving credit, you are also violating copyright law. To respect the intellectual property rights of anyone (or anything) you cite in your research paper, you carefully cite the source of the information. Using quotes from another writer, or images from another artist, in your own academic paper is legally defined as "fair use"—if you make it clear where the original material comes from.

- *Ethics and the Academic Researcher*. As you enter an academic conversation about your research topic, your audience—even if it's only your teacher—expects you to conduct yourself in an ethical fashion. Your ethos, literally, means "where you stand"—what you believe, how you express those beliefs, and how thoughtfully and considerately you relate to the "stances" of others in your academic community. In the professional academy, researchers in fields from medieval poetry through cell biology are expected to adhere to a code of ethics about their research. Working with the ideas and discoveries of others in their academic communities, they are careful to always acknowledge the work of their peers and the contributions that work has made to their own research. You should do the same. When you leave school, these basic ethical tenets remain the same. You wouldn't hand in another rep's marketing report as your own, you wouldn't claim credit for the successful recovery of another doctor's patient, and you wouldn't put your name on another reporter's story. To violate professional ethics is to break the trust that holds an academic or professional community together.

Stage Four: Organizing and Outlining Your Information

Now that you have gathered and evaluated a mass of information, the next step is to begin giving some shape and order to what you have discovered.

Writing an outline helps you to think through and organize your evidence, determine the strengths and weaknesses of your argument, and visualize the shape of your final paper. Some instructors will require you to hand in an outline along with your research paper. Even if an outline isn't formally required, it is such a useful and valuable step toward moving from a pile of index cards to a logical, coherent draft that you should plan to create one.

Checklist for Organizing Your Information

❏ Gather up all of your note cards and print out any notes you have taken on your computer. Double-check all of your notes to make sure that they include accurate citation information.

❏ Using your list of subtopics, group your notes according to those subtopics. Are some piles of cards enormous, while other topics have only a card or two? See if subtopics can be combined—or if any subtopics could be further refined and made more specific.

❏ Set aside any note cards that don't seem to "fit" in any particular pile.

❏ Find your thesis statement and copy it out on a blank index card. Go through the cards in each subtopic. Can you immediately see a connection between each note card and your thesis statement? (If not, set that note card aside for now.)

❏ Do not throw away any of the note cards, even if they don't seem to fit into your current research plan. You probably won't use every single note card in your paper, but it's good to have a continuing record of your work.

Basic Outlining

Many word-processing programs include an "outline" function, and your instructor may ask you to follow a specific format for your outline. An outline is a kind of road map for your thought processes, a list of the pieces of information you are going to discuss in your paper and how you are going to connect those pieces of information to each other as well as back to your original thesis. You can begin the outlining process by using the note cards you have divided into subtopics:

     I. Most compelling, important subtopic
       A. Supporting fact, quote, or illustration
       B. Another interesting piece of evidence that supports or illustrates the subtopic
         1. A direct quotation that further illustrates point B
         2. Another supporting point
           a. Minor, but still relevant, points

Another useful outlining strategy is to assign each subtopic a working "topic sentence" or "main idea." As you move into the drafting process, you can return to those topic sentences/main ideas to begin each paragraph.

The Writing Process

A research paper is more than a collection of strung-together facts. No matter how interesting and relevant each individual piece of information may be, your reader is not responsible for seeing how the parts make up a whole. Connecting the evidence, demonstrating the relationships between concepts and ideas, and proving how all of it supports your thesis are entirely up to you.

Drafting

The shape of your outline and your subdivided piles of index cards provide the framework for your rough draft. As you begin to write your essay, think about "connecting the dots" between each piece of evidence, gradually filling in the shape of your argument. Expect your arrangement of individual note cards or whole subtopics to change as you draft.

Remember that you are not drafting a final paper, and certainly not a perfect paper. The goal of drafting is to *organize* your evidence, to get a sense of your argument's strengths and weaknesses, and to test the accuracy of your thesis and revise it if necessary. Drafting is as much a thinking process as it is a writing process.

If you get "stuck" as you draft, abandon whatever subtopic you are working on and begin with another. Working at the paragraph level first—using the evidence on a subtopic's note card to support and illustrate the topic sentence or main idea of the subtopic—is a much less intimidating way to approach drafting a research paper.

Finally, as you draft, be sure that you include either an in-text citation (see page 362) or some other indication of *precisely* where each piece of information came from. This will save you time when you begin revising and preparing the final draft as well as the Works Cited list.

Incorporating Sources

As you draft, you will build connections between different pieces of evidence, different perspectives, and different authors. Learning how to smoothly integrate all those different sources into your own work, without breaking the flow of your own argument and voice, takes some practice. The most important thing to remember is to accurately indicate the source of every piece of information as soon as you cite it.

One way to smoothly integrate sources into your paper is through paraphrase. For example:

> The educational benefits of ecotourism can help future generations to respect the environment. "Helping people learn to love the earth is a high calling and one that can be carried out through ecotourism. Ecotourism avoids much of the counterproductive baggage that often accompanies standard education" (Kimmel 41).

In revision, this writer used paraphrase to move more gracefully from her main point to the perspective provided by her source:

> Teachers like James R. Kimmel have called the ecotourism experience a "nirvana" for educating their students. "Helping people learn to love the earth is a high calling and one that can be carried out through ecotourism," he observes, noting that the "counterproductive baggage" such as testing and grading are left behind (Kimmel 41).

This system of indicating where exactly an idea, quote, or paraphrase comes from is called parenthetical citation. In MLA and APA style, which are required by most academic disciplines (see pages 363–368), these in-text citations take the place of footnotes or endnotes.

Using Transition Verbs Between Your Writing and a Source

Using conversation verbs as transitions between your own writing and a direct quote can enliven the style of your paper. In the previous example, the writer uses the verb "observes" rather than just "states" or "writes." Other useful transitions include:

Arundhati Roy argues that . . .
Amy Tan remembers that . . .
Barbara Ehrenreich and Annette Fuentes compare the results of . . .
Al Gore admits that . . .
Naomi Shihab Nye insists that . . .
Hisham Matar vividly describes . . .

Revising and Polishing

The drafting process clarified your ideas and gave structure to your argument. In the revision process, you rewrite and rethink your paper, strengthening the connections between your main points, your evidence, and your thesis. Sharing your essay draft with a classmate, with your instructor, or with a tutor at your campus writing center will give you an invaluable objective perspective on your paper's strengths and weaknesses.

Checklist for Your Final Draft

❑ Have I provided parenthetical citations for every source I used?
❑ Do all of those parenthetical citations correspond to an item in my Works Cited list?
❑ Does my essay's title clearly and specifically state my topic?
❑ Is my thesis statement identifiable, clear, and interesting?
❑ Does each body paragraph include a topic sentence that clearly connects to my thesis?

❏ Do I make graceful transitions between my own writing and the sources I incorporate?

❏ When I shared my paper with another reader, was I able to answer any questions about my evidence or my argument using sources already at hand? Or do I need to go back to the library or online to "fill in" any questionable areas in my research?

❏ Does my conclusion clearly echo and support my thesis statement and concisely sum up how all of my evidence supports that thesis?

❏ Have I proofread for clarity, grammar, accuracy, and style?

❏ Is my paper formatted according to my instructor's guidelines? Do I have a backup copy on disk and more than one printed copy?

Documentation

From the beginning of your research, when you were browsing in the library and online, you have been documenting your sources. To document a source simply means to make a clear, accurate record of where exactly a piece of information, a quote, an idea, or a concept comes from, so that future readers of your paper can go back to that original source and learn more. As we have seen, careful attention to documentation is the best way to protect yourself against inadvertent plagiarism. There are two ways you document your sources in your paper: within the text itself (*in-text* or *parenthetical* citation) and in the Works Cited list at the end of your paper.

What Do I Need to Document?

- Anything I didn't know before I began my research
- Direct quotations
- Paraphrases
- Summaries
- Specific numerical data, such as charts and graphs
- Any image, text, or animation from a website
- Any audio or video
- Any information gathered during a personal interview

Parenthetical (In-Text) Citation

MLA style for documentation is most commonly used in the humanities and is the format discussed here. Keep in mind that different academic disciplines have their own documentation guidelines and styles, as do some organizations (many newspapers, for example, have their own "style guides"). An in-text citation identifies the source of a piece of information as part of your own sentence or within parentheses. In MLA style, the parenthetical information includes the author's last name and the page number (if appropriate) on which the information can be found in the original source. If your readers want to know more, they can then turn to your Works Cited page to find the author's full name and the complete bibliographic information for that source. Always place the in-text or parenthetical citation as close to the incorporated source material as possible—preferably within the same sentence.

Guidelines for Parenthetical (In-Text) Citation

Page numbers for a book

The end of the Second World War began Samuel Beckett's greatest period of creativity, which he referred to as "the siege in the room" (Bair 346). Bair describes the period immediately after the Second World War as a time of great creativity for Samuel Beckett (346).

In the first parenthetical citation, the author is not named within the student writer's text, so the parentheses include both the source author's name and the page number on which the information can be found. In the second example, the source author (Bair) is mentioned by name, so there is no need to repeat that name within the parentheses—only the page number is needed.

Page numbers for an article in a magazine or journal

Wheatley argues that "America has embraced values that cannot create a sustainable society and world" (25).

Page numbers for a newspaper article

Cite both the section letter (or description of the section) and the page.

Camera phones are leading to new questions about the invasion of privacy (Harmon sec. 4:3).
A spokesperson for the National Institutes of Health has described obesity as the greatest potential danger to the average American's health (Watts B3).

Website

Arts and Letters Daily includes links to opinions and essays on current events from English-language media worldwide.
Article 2 of the proposed Global Code of Ethics for Tourism describes tourism "as a vehicle for individual and collective fulfillment" *(world-tourism)*.

When an online source does not give specific "page," screen, or paragraph numbers, your parenthetical citation must include the name of the site.

Works Cited List

Gather your working bibliography cards, and be sure that every source you cite in your paper has a corresponding card. To construct the Works Cited list, you simply arrange these cards in alphabetical order, by author. The Works Cited page is a separate, double-spaced page at the end of your paper.

Formatting Your Works Cited List

- Center the title, Works Cited, at the top of a new page. Do not underline it, italicize it, or place it in quotation marks.
- Alphabetize according to the author's name, or according to the title (for works, such as websites, that do not have an author). Ignore words such as *the*, *and*, and *a* when alphabetizing.
- Begin each entry at the left margin. After the first line, indent all other lines of the entry by five spaces (one stroke of the "tab" key).
- Double-space every line.
- Place a period after the author, the title, the publishing information, and the medium of publication (Print, Web, CD-ROM, etc.).
- Italicize book and web page titles. Titles of articles, stories, poems, and parts of entire works in other media are placed in quotation marks.

Guidelines for Works Cited List

Book by one author

Ruiz, Teofilo F. *The Terror of History*. Princeton, NJ: Princeton UP: 2011. Print.

Multiple books by the same author

List the author's name for the first entry. For each entry that follows, replace the author's name with three hyphens.

Holzer, Harold. *Lincoln at Cooper Union*. New York: Simon and Shuster, 2004. Print.

—. *Lincoln: President-Elect*. New York: Simon and Shuster, 2008. Print.

Book with two or three authors/editors

Goodbody, Axel, and Kate Rigby, eds. *Ecocritical Theory*. Charlottesville: UP Virginia, 2011. Print.

Book with more than three authors/editors

Freeman, Arthur, James Pretzer, Barbara Fleming, and Karen M. Simon. *Clinical Applications of Cognitive Therapy*. 2nd ed. New York: Springer, 2004. Print.

Alternatively, in this case, you can use the first name only and add *et al.* ("and others").

Book or publication with group or organization as author

Modern Language Association. *MLA Handbook for Writers of Research Papers*. 7th ed. New York: MLA, 2009. Print.

Book or publication without an author

Chase's Calendar of Events 2012. New York: McGraw, 2012. Print.

Work in an anthology of pieces all by the same author

Thomas, Lewis. "The Youngest and Brightest Thing Around." *The Medusa and the Snail: More Notes of a Biology Watcher*. New York: Viking, 1979. Print.

Work in an anthology of different authors

Chase, Katie. "Man and Wife." *The Best American Short Stories* 2008. Ed. Salman Rushdie. Boston: Houghton, 2008. Print.

Work translated from another language

Eco, Umberto. *The Prague Cemetery*. Trans. Richard Dixon. New York: Houghton Mifflin Harcourt, 2012. Print.

Entry from a reference volume

For dictionaries and encyclopedias, simply note the edition and its date. No page numbers are necessary for references organized alphabetically, such as encyclopedias (and, obviously, dictionaries).

Merriam-Webster's Medical Desk Dictionary. Rev. ed. Boston: Cengage, 2006. Print.

"Carriera, Rosalba." *The Oxford Companion to Western Art*. Ed. Hugh Brigstoke. Oxford: Oxford UP, 2001. Print.

Article from a journal

Note that current MLA guidelines no longer make a distinction between journals that are numbered continuously (e.g., Vol. 1 ends on page 208, Vol. 2 starts on page 209) or numbered separately (i.e., each volume starts on page 1). No matter how the journal is paginated, all of them must contain volume *and* issue numbers. (To indicate the issue number, place a period and the number after the volume number.) One exception is journals with issue numbers only; simply cite the issue numbers alone as though they are volume numbers.

Blair, Kristen L. "New Media Affordances and the Connected Life." *CCC* 63.2 (Dec. 2011): 314–27. Print.

Enoch, Jessica. "Resisting the Script of Indian Education: Zitkala-Sa and the Carlisle Indian School." *College English* 65.1 (2002): 117–41. Print.

Article from a weekly or biweekly periodical

Denby, David. "War Horse." *New Yorker* 2 Jan. 2012: 78. Print.

Article from a monthly or bimonthly periodical

Perlin, John. "Solar Power: The Slow Revolution." *Invention and Technology* Summer 2002: 20–25. Print.

Article from a daily newspaper

Sciolino, Elaine. "The French, the Veil, and the Look." *New York Times* 17 Apr. 2011: 4. Print.

If the newspaper article goes on for more than one page, add a plus sign to the first page number.

Newspaper or periodical article with no author

"Groups Lose Sole Authority on Chaplains for Muslims." *New York Times* 14 Oct. 2003: A15. Print.

Unsigned editorial in a newspaper or periodical

"Monitoring Syria." Editorial. *Washington Post* 29 Dec. 2011: A16. Print.

Letter to the editor of a newspaper or periodical

Post, Diana. Letter. "U.S. Should Stand Against Rape." *Ms.* Fall 2011: 7. Print.

Film, video, DVD

If you are writing about a specific actor's performance or a specific director, use that person's name as the beginning of the citation. Otherwise, begin with the title of the work. Specify the medium of the recording (film, video, DVD, etc.).

Princess Mononoke. Dir. Hayao Miyazaki. Prod. Studio Ghibli, 1999. Miramax, 2001. Videocassette.

Eames, Charles and Ray. *The Films of Charles and Ray Eames, Volume 1: Powers of Ten.* 1978. Pyramid Home Video, 1984. Videocassette.

Television or radio broadcast

"Alone on the Ice." *The American Experience.* PBS. KRMA, Denver, 8 Feb. 1999. Television.

Arnold, Elizabeth. "The Birds of the Boreal." *National Geographic Radio Expeditions.* NPR. WNYC, New York, 14 Oct. 2003. Radio.

A sound recording

> Bukkene Bruse. "Wedding March from Osterdalen." *Nordic Roots* 2.
> Northside, 2000. CD.

Personal interview

Give the name of the person you interviewed, how the interview was conducted (phone, e-mail, etc.), and the date of the interview.

> Jackson, Janet. Telephone interview. 12 Sept. 2011.

> Clinton, Hillary. E-mail interview. 8 Aug. 2012.

Online sources

MLA no longer recommends the inclusion of URLs (Web addresses) in the Works Cited entries. However, you should include URLs when the reader probably cannot find the source without them or if your instructor requires them.

Web page/Internet site

Give the site title, the name of the site's author or editor (if there is one), electronic publication information, medium of publication (Web), your own date of access, and the site's URL, if needed. (If some of this information is not available, just cite what you can.)

> *Arts & Letters Daily*. Ed. Denis Dutton. 2003. Web. 2 Sept. 2003.

Document or article from an Internet site

Include the author's name, document title, information about a print version (if applicable), information about the electronic version, medium of publication (Web), date of access, and URL (if needed).

> Brooks, David. "The Organization Kid." *Atlantic Monthly* April 2001:
> 40–54. Web. 25 Aug. 2003.

Book available online

The citation is similar to the format for a print book, but include as much information as you can about the website as well as the date of your access to it.

> Einstein, Albert. *Relativity: The Special and General Theory*. Trans. Robert
> W. Lawson. New York: Henry Holt, 1920. *Bartleby.com: Great Books
> Online*. 2003. Ed. Steven van Leeuwen. Web. 6 Sept. 2003.

> Wheatley, Phillis. *Poems on Various Subjects, Religious and Moral*. Project
> *Gutenberg*. 2003. Ed. Michael S. Hart. Web. 6 Sept. 2003.

Database available online

> Bartleby Library. 2003. Ed. Steven van Leeuwen. Web. 28 Sept. 2003.

Source from a library subscription database

Academic and most public libraries offer their members access to subscription-only databases that provide electronic access to publications not otherwise available on free-access websites. According to current MLA guidelines, the name of the subscription service and the institution that provided the access need not be included in the Works Cited entry.

> Mastny, Lisa. "Ecotourist Trap." *Foreign Policy* Nov.–Dec. 2002: 94.
> *Questia*. Web. 10 Oct. 2003.

> Rossant, John. "The Real War Is France vs. France." *Business Week*
> 6 Oct. 2003: 68. *MasterFile Premier*. Web. 13 Oct. 2003.

Newspaper article online

> Zernike, Kate. "Fight Against Fat Shifts to the Workplace." *New York
> Times*. New York Times, 12 Oct. 2003. Web. 12 Oct. 2003.

Journal article online

> Salkeld, Duncan. "Making Sense of Differences: Postmodern History,
> Philosophy and Shakespeare's Prostitutes." *Chronicon: An Electronic
> History Journal* 3.1 (1999). Web. 5 Apr. 2003.

E-mail

Give the writer's name, the subject line (if any) enclosed in quotation marks, the date of the message, and the medium of transmission (e-mail).

> Stanford, Myles. "Johnson manuscripts online." Message to the author.
> 12 July 2003. E-mail.

Electronic posting to an online forum

Many online media sources conduct forums in which readers can respond to breaking news or ongoing issues. Citing from such forums is difficult because many people prefer to post anonymously; if the author's username is too silly or inappropriate, use the title of the post or the title of the forum to begin your citation and determine its place in the alphabetical order of your Works Cited list.

> Berman, Piotr. 6 Oct. 2003. "Is Middle East Peace Impossible?" Web. 13
> Oct. 2003. <http://tabletalk.salon.com/webx?13@@.596c5554>.

Leaking All over the Page

LAURA KIPNIS

"We were warned to expect 'dirty tricks,'" he tweeted. "Now we have the first one." He'd been set up, he told reporters. His lawyer attributed the allegations to "dark forces," part of a "greater plan" to discredit him (Harnden). The "we" (and "he") in question was Julian Assange, a thirty-nine-year-old Australian and founder of guerrilla media organization WikiLeaks, which dedicates itself to embarrassing governments and corporations through strategic leaks of classified and secret documents to the media. Assange has yet to be formally charged with anything, although he's currently under house arrest at the English country estate of one of his supporters and facing extradition to Sweden after allegedly sexually assaulting two women there. The women, both WikiLeaks supporters, did consent to have sex with him, but apparently not the kind of sex he had in mind. As one of them put it, "Not only was it the worst screw of my life, it was also violent" (qtd. in Davies).

The details of the police reports have, in turn, been strategically leaked to the media, generating a worldwide outbreak of commentary, argumentation, and conspiracy theories, as well as a $1.5 million book deal with American and British publishers for Assange's memoirs. Little known until recently, Assange, a digital age international scofflaw, is now an international celebrity. The quantity of information in circulation about him increases exponentially with each passing day: details on everything from his complexion (ghostly) to his relationship with his mother (complicated) to

The writer hooks the reader at the outset with an intriguing quote.

Citations in parentheses signal MLA style.

The writer provides background.

Laura Kipnis, "Leaking All over the Page," PMLA, Volume 126, Number 4, October 2011, pp. 1085–1091 (7). Publications of the Modern Language Association of America by Modern Language Association of America. Copyright 2011 in the format Textbook via Copyright Clearance Center.

his personality (egomaniacal, self-aggrandizing, charming one moment and autocratic the next—he himself says he's "somewhere on the autistic spectrum" [qtd. in Hosenbail]). Thanks to the assault allegations, now we even have play-by-play accounts of his sexual style: caddish or criminal, depending on whom you ask.

One problem in writing about contemporary scandal, I've found, having recently completed a book on the subject I started a decade ago, is the unending barrage of new material coupled with the rapid exhaustion rate of the example pool. "Are you going to include this new scandal or that one?" everyone you know queries so helpfully every time another ingenue self-implodes or the latest billion-dollar Ponzi scheme is exposed, until the prospective manuscript starts resembling one of those Jorge Luis Borges stories about the infinite book with an indefinite number of pages containing every known instance and scrap of information relating to its ostensible subject, driving writers, readers, and librarians to despair.

The writer establishes her authority and her thesis.

Given the shelf-life issue, no doubt Assange will be superseded by a hundred new scandals long before these remarks hit print. But at the moment he's impossible to ignore, which is the sine qua non of a good scandal: somehow you can't look away. This one also happens to put conventional political affiliations and divisions up for grabs: it's not just feminists against leftists; it's leftists against First Amendment advocates and Pentagon Papers–era First Amendment advocates against WikiLeaks-era First Amendment advocates and feminists accusing other feminists of being rape apologists. No less a public-sphere feminist than Naomi Wolf has ridiculed the rape accusations against Assange as motivated by "hurt feelings" at best ("Julian Assange"), despite having created a miniscandal a few years back herself by accusing Harold Bloom of groping her thigh some twenty years earlier, when she'd been his student ("Sex"). Has she somehow forgotten this? Among the reasons high-profile scandal cases are magnets for so much social commentary is the infinitely useful opportunities for disavowal and disidentification they create.

The writer begins an extended definition and analysis of celebrity scandal. The writer refers to experts for support.

As a self-appointed scandal theorist, and one not tethered to any particular academic discipline (my long-ago formal education was in art), I must start, when confronted with such a superb trove of material, by asking, Now what? One of the attractions of scandal as a subject is how little of theoretical interest has been written on it to date: it's pretty much virgin terrain, despite the vast amount of social real estate it occupies. You're forced to make your methodology up as you go along, feeling your way through pitch-black sewers on hands and knees, grasping at glimmers of insight. There's no recipe; each case necessarily generates its own techniques. The method, such as it is, emerges from the contours and particulars of the scandals themselves.

> The writer establishes a breezy, self-effacing tone.
> The writer provides a basic thesis concerning scandal theory.

A concern about such procedures, obviously, is that the transgressions and embarrassments of the particular scandal might seep into the writing of the case or color the analysis. Still, transforming scandalizers into characters in a narrative does demand some level of authorial identification, some imagined proximity to their particular logic or illogic. (Perhaps this approach borrows more from novelists than social critics.) Another concern is not knowing exactly where you'll end up—you can lose your bearings or your overview of the situation, as have the protagonists themselves, of course, which is what got them into such a mess in the first place. You may discover alien dimensions in your own thinking that aren't what you intended to stand for; your instincts may lead you astray. You may not even subscribe to your own conclusions in the end. Occasionally, practical decisions must be made: am I really willing to say "X" or "Y" in print?

> The writer explores issues and problems in developing a theory of celebrity scandal.

It's not that there isn't any critical distance but that critical proximity can be more useful. I'd go so far as to say that drawing on your worst impulses is the only way to understand contemporary scandals and the instant celebrities they create. Speaking of worst impulses, I confess that my interest in the Assange case probably had less to do with its sociopolitical dimensions than its parabolic ones: the pleasant shapeliness of a moral fable peeking through the tawdry details.

> The writer makes a strong emotional claim about her interest in scandal.

Assange used exposé for what he sees as political purpose, only to have exposé turned against him for feminist purposes. Note the satisfying formal symmetry, the chiastic structure, the O. Henry twist: he who exposes the secrets of the powerful shall have his own powerful secrets similarly exposed.

Please don't think that I'm in favor of governmental payback or dirty tricks, should those turn out to have been in play. (Assange's lawyer did initially suggest the whole thing had been a "honey trap," though Assange himself later poo-pooed the idea [Davies].) Whatever it is that draws me to the biographical and psychological excesses being paraded through the public square, I fear it has as much to do with the tropes, puns, homologies, and literary resonances in these narratives as the sociological ones, which could be a form of excess in its own right.

I suspect, however, that this surplus is exactly what's so captivating about scandal. You're going around, minding your own business, and these split-off fragments of other people's repressions and wishes come hurtling at you from the social ether like messages in a bottle, one bedeviled psyche flagging down another, scattering coded clues and demanding to be deciphered. There's this intersubjective gravitational pull. But then what, methodologically speaking? Conventional modes of sociopolitical analysis yield banalities, yet following the path of fascination propels you into the murk of the unknown. For writers, there's always a certain queasy thrill in projecting fascinations and attractions you don't entirely understand into the public arena, though if your subject matter is other people's dirty secrets and public self-immolations and your method is following errant interpretative instincts and seeing where they lead, what dirty secrets are you yourself exposing in the process? No doubt more of them than you care to know.

The cases I've found myself compelled by haven't tended to be the highest-profile or glitziest ones; they've been closer to home, episodes in which someone relatively ordinary, though perhaps professionally accomplished, is thrust into celebrity or notoriety by

The writer analyzes the reasons why we are attracted to scandal.

following some desire or obsession or grudge where it leads while remaining curiously indifferent to potential social consequences. Through some brew of inadvertency or compulsion or recklessness, the blunder is brought to light (as such things generally are), frequently wrecking the scandalizer's life in the process.

But scandals are also public performances: they're about people enacting their tangled, furtive longings and grudges on a national and sometimes international scale, scattering unconsciousness around in public for everyone else to trip over, violating norms and taboos with imagined impunity as though superegos didn't exist. Often there's a theatrical whiff about these psychodramas: the curtain opens on a bizarre private world of chaos and misjudgment, and the rest of us are thrust into the role of audience. It's a role we play to the hilt: commenting on the action like a Greek chorus, dissecting motives like amateur psychoanalysts, maybe nervously pondering our own susceptibility to life-wrecking inchoateness. Every scandal reproduces this complicatedly codependent relationship between a scandal protagonist and a scandal public, precisely because scandal requires an audience: if no one paid attention, scandal would cease to exist. In short, we all have crucial roles to play in scandal formation: scandalizers screw things up in showy, provocative ways while the rest of us luxuriate in the warm glow of imaginary imperviousness that other people's life-destroying stupidities invariably provide, castigating transgressors for their moral failings while disavowing any similar propensities of our own.

The writer develops the proposition that scandal is public performance and self-deception.

Of course, disavowing such propensities is how scandalizers come to find themselves in the midst of a scandal in the first place. The uniting feature in most scandal cases is some major blind spot, some form of splitting. How else can a socialized being so completely suspend awareness of social punishment, be so incapable of thinking a couple of steps ahead? This element of self-obliviousness, and what it implies about the willingness of otherwise rational people to volunteer for public pillorying, is not exactly reassuring. But are we in the audience so much more self-knowledgeable? One suspects not. I'm pretty sure that my own capacity for self-knowledge is nothing to gloat about.

But how would I know? As the psychologist Herbert Fingarette points out in his rather alarming 1969 study *Self-Deception*, it's not just that "spelling things out" (38) to oneself is an acquired skill (like driving a car, as he puts it [41]) but that there can be overriding reasons to avoid doing it and to avoid becoming conscious that you're avoiding doing it. Self-examination isn't a very reliable talent, as it turns out; the available techniques are spotty at best. As the novelist-critic J. M. Coetzee frets in his essay "Confession and Double Thoughts," it's impossible to know whether the "truth" you discover in your occasional feeble attempts at self-examination is anything close to truth and not just some self-serving fiction, since the "unexamined, unexaminable principle" governing your conclusions "may not be a desire for the truth but a desire *to be a particular way*" (221)—to seem rational and coherent to yourself, for instance. In other words, all the self-examination in the world isn't going to help you if you're bent on self-deception or if one part of you is bent on deceiving another part, which is no doubt true of any of us at least some of the time. That's what having an unconscious means, and thanks for nothing.

As we know, scandal in the Internet age offers an embarrassment of riches when it comes to proving this point. The Internet and scandal are Siamese twins joined at the forehead, with the most excruciatingly private details about other people's inner lives and desires and failures of self-management archived online forever, to do with what you will. And the details are so weirdly gripping! Roland Barthes, writing about the odd biographical details that particularly pierced him in old photographs (the punctum, in his often cited term), refers to them as "part-objects," which "flatter a certain fetishism of mine." They nourish his "amorous preference" for certain kinds of knowledge, providing him—at least some facet of him—with delight (30).

The writer mentions the impact of the Internet on scandal.

As usual, Barthes had the courage of his fetishes, though as fetishes go, let's just say his tended to be fairly dignified ones. For my part, such delights are also tinged with discomfiture. They're rabbit holes, plummeting you into the muckiness of someone else's interiority, where you paddle around frantically trying to get your bearings.

The writer offers a self-referential comment.

Take the details in the leaked police reports on Assange. The allegation is that during a ten-day stay in Stockholm, Assange had sexual encounters with two women, both WikiLeaks supporters, that started as consensual but became coercive to the point of rape. One of the women, identified as Miss A, had arranged Assange's trip to Sweden and let him stay in her apartment. She charges that he pulled off her clothes and snapped her necklace, and though she more or less went along with all this, she protested when she realized Assange was trying to have unprotected sex with her. When she tried to put a condom on him, he stopped her by pinning her arms. He finally agreed to use the condom but then deliberately ripped it, she accuses, and ejaculated without withdrawing. Assange denies all this, countering that he continued to sleep in her flat with her permission for the following week; if he'd assaulted her, why would she allow him to stay? Miss A concurs that he stayed but says that they'd stopped having sex because he'd exceeded the limits of what she could accept. However, he approached her one day at her apartment, naked from the waist down, and rubbed against her. Nevertheless, after this encounter, Miss A still threw a party for Assange at her flat (Davies).

The writer develops case studies relating to the Assange scandal.

Then Assange met a second woman, Miss W, at a seminar arranged by Miss A. When the two of them began having sex at her flat, Assange also refused to wear a condom; like Miss A, Miss W refused to have sex without one. Assange gave up and fell asleep, but during the night they woke up and had sex after he reluctantly agreed to use a condom. In the morning Miss W woke up to find Assange again having sex with her, and when she asked if he was wearing a condom, he said no. Miss W had never had unprotected sex before, she said, and the leaks from a police interview with her former boyfriend confirm this. According to the ex, it would have been unthinkable for her. Despite these conflicts, both women allegedly continued to see Assange during the remainder of his stay (Burns and Somaiya).

When the two women eventually learned of their similar experiences with Assange and that he'd been seeing both of them at the same time, they went to the police to see if they could compel him to take an HIV test, which he'd already refused to do, saying he didn't have the time. The police said they couldn't force him to take a test and that the women's statements would have to be passed on to a prosecutor for further action to be taken. (In Sweden "unlawful coercion" is prosecutable under rape statutes.) That night the story was leaked to Swedish papers. When journalists asked Assange for his reaction, his response was that the sex had been consensual. When asked if he was promiscuous, he replied, "I'm not promiscuous. I just really like women" (qtd. in Mostrous).

For some reason these slightly perturbing details keep playing though my mind like an annoying song. Then we have the homology between Assange's alleged aversion to condoms and his political commitment to leaks. As it happens, leakiness was one of the themes in my scandal book, *How to Become a Scandal*, spurred on by Freud: "No mortal can keep a secret. If his lips are silent, he chatters with his fingertips; betrayal oozes out of him at every pore" (77–78). Notice how *viscous* Freud makes the whole thing sound—betrayal doesn't trickle or drip or bleed; it *oozes*, mucouslike (or worse). The point seems to be that human beings can't help spilling clues all over the place about the mess of embarrassing conflicts and metaphysical anguishes lodged within. The viscosity of the substance in question should interest anyone who's ever struggled to quash some delinquent libidinal urge; presumably this would be everyone.

The leaky-vessel problem struck me as a useful starting point for a book on scandals, and certain people's proclivities for getting into them. Why? All I can tell you is that leakiness kept *seeking me out*.

The writer develops the extended metaphor of scandal theory as a narrative of "leakiness."

It even turned out (as I realized only after the book went to press) that diapers figured in *two* of the scandal cases I wrote about, speaking of leakiness. In one an astronaut drove cross-country to attack a romantic rival, supposedly wearing adult diapers along the way to avoid making rest stops (25–67); in another a renowned judge threatened his ex-lover while impersonating a fat, diabetic, diaper-wearing detective from Texas (68–109). Scandal cases often do seem to contain these strangely antic elements, as though an invisible screenwriter with a penchant for bad puns were working behind the scenes. What's a diaper, after all, but the perfect symbol for incontinent feelings, for being out of control? Consider the usual idioms for falling afoul of social codes: getting yourself in "deep shit," winding up with your life "in the toilet." These scandal protagonists couldn't have found a better symbol if they'd tried. (Or had they? The unconscious has a particular sense of humor, not to mention a potty mouth, or so it's been said; Freud wrote a classically unfunny book on the subject.) The diaper motif rather brilliantly distills the scandalizer's situation down to its essence, since what's an adult in diapers but someone whose self-management skills have critically failed?

This isn't very dignified territory, to say the least. Also, you start wondering what unknown elements are leaking through your prose onto the page. It struck me numerous times in the course of writing on scandal how many alarming similarities there are between writing and scandal, poised as writers so often are between the murky chasms of unknowingness and whatever thin protections against it form or style provide (so you hope). If the terrain of scandal is especially riddled with compulsion, neurosis, and a thousand other unflattering propensities, so is writing about it. Writing on scandal means writing about unconsciousness, along with every variety of ugly feeling, compulsion, self-destruction, and failed self-knowledge. But the only method really adequate to the subject is letting your mind veer where it wants to and risking some embarrassing leakage yourself.

This isn't a tidy procedure. But as Fingarette laments, regarding the waywardness of his own investigations into self-deception, "As is characteristic when paradox lies at the heart of things, there is a particular slipperiness about this object of investigation" (13). Slipperiness, leakiness—clearly we're into some damp terrain.

As celebrity studies emerges as an academic discipline, the question of what to do with all the embarrassing scandal effluvia will have to be addressed. A certain amount of dampness is inevitable for anyone who embarks on such a path. Yielding to the logic—or illogic—of these leaky narratives, favoring a poetics of proximity over critical distance, transports investigators to unexpected and possibly alarming places. Of course, the usual methods of academic critique come with their own risks: banality, generality, overfamiliarity—in other word, dryness.

Which brings me back to the Assange case. After Assange left Sweden, the police issued an international arrest warrant compelling him to return to Sweden for hearings. Whether the allegations will hold up or whose version of these events is true doesn't really matter for the purposes of scandal: scandal details don't have to be true to be scandalous. The substrata of meanings and associations that accrue around the narratives give them their social resonance, not their factuality. Yet by what method are these substrata to be excavated?

The historian Sean Wilentz has impugned Assange for being offended by any actions that are cloaked, which Wilentz regards as simpleminded (qtd. in Italie). Condoms, cloaks . . . something in the scandal theorist perks to attention. Assange is accused of ripping a condom? Obviously—isn't he committed to penetrating every security protocol he can? Aha! There's that punster-symbologist, working behind the scenes again. The language of scandal is especially plastic, stretching this way and that and sullying everything in its path, transforming anything it encounters into material. Although Barthes doesn't mention it in

The writer prepares for her conclusion.

In her conclusion, the writer offers a reflection on scandal theory and the language of scandal.

Camera Lucida, another definition of the word *punctum*, according to *Wiktionary*, is "the sharp tip of any part of the anatomy." It can also be a tiny orifice, as defined in *Oxford Dictionaries*, like the small opening that allows tears to drain from eyes. Reading this, the scandal theorist's antenna again perks up: more leakiness. Let Barthes's remark that the punctum isn't necessarily in good taste stand as a warning to others who might venture down this road.

Works Cited

Barthes, Roland. *Camera Lucida: Reflections on Photography*. Trans. Richard Howard. New York: Hill, 1982. Print.

Burns, John F., and Ravi Somaiya. "Confidential Swedish Police Report Details Allegations against WikiLeaks Founder." *New York Times*. New York Times, 18 Dec. 2010. Web. 24 Dec. 2010.

Coetzee, J. M. "Confession and Double Thoughts: Tolstoy, Rousseau, Dostoevsky." *Comparative Literature* 37.3 (1985): 193–232. Print.

Davies, Nick. "10 Days in Sweden: The Full Allegations against Julian Assange." *Guardian*. Guardian News and Media, 17 Dec. 2010. Web. 28 Dec. 2010.

Fingarette, Herbert. *Self-Deception*. 1969. Berkeley: U of California P, 2000. Print.

Freud, Sigmund. "Fragment of an Analysis of a Case of Hysteria." 1905. *Standard Edition*. Vol. 7. London: Hogarth, 1961. 64–94. Print.

Harnden, Toby. "Julian Assange's Arrest Warrant: A Diversion from the Truth?" *Telegraph*. Telegraph Media Group, 22 Aug. 2010. Web. 28 Dec. 2010.

Hosenbail, Mark. "Special Report: Julian Assange versus the World." *Reuters*. Reuters, 13 Dec. 2010. Web. 28 Dec. 2010.

Italie, Hillel. "Authors, Historians Debate Leaks of WikiLeaks." *Pantagraph.com*. Pantagraph, 4 Dec. 2010. Web. 9 June 2011.

Kipnis, Laura. *How to Become a Scandal: Adventures in Bad Behavior*. New York: Metropolitan, 2010. Print.

Mostrous, Alexi. "People Power Will Come to My Rescue, WikiLeaks Founder Predicts." *Times*. News Intl. Trading, 21 Dec. 2010. Web. 28 Dec. 2010.

The writer presents her citations in MLA format.

"Punctum." *Oxford Dictionaries Online*. Oxford UP, n.d. Web. 1 July 2011.

"Punctum." *Wiktionary*. Wikimedia, n.d. Web. 1 July 2011.

Wolf, Naomi. "Julian Assange Captured by World's Dating Police." *Huffington Post*. TheHuffingtonPost, 7 Dec. 2010. Web. 28 Dec. 2010.

—. "Sex and Silence at Yale." *New York Magazine*. New York Media, 1 Mar. 2004. Web. 28 Dec. 2010.

Glossary of Rhetorical Terms

allusion A reference to a familiar concept, person, or thing.

analytical essay An essay that defines and describes an issue by breaking it down into separate components and carefully considering each component.

annotation Marking up a text as you read by writing comments, questions, and ideas in the margins.

argument A *rhetorical strategy* that involves using persuasion to gain a reader's support for the writer's position.

assertion A statement that a writer claims is true without necessarily providing objective support for the *claim*.

audience The assumed readers of a text.

brainstorming An idea-generation strategy. Write your topic, a keyword, or your *thesis* at the top of a blank piece of paper or computer screen, and for ten or fifteen minutes just write down everything you associate with, think of, or know about that topic.

causal analysis A *rhetorical strategy* that examines the relationships between events or conditions and their consequences.

cause-and-effect analysis See *causal analysis*.

claim In *argument*, a statement that the author intends to support through the use of reasons, evidence, and appeals.

classification A rhetorical strategy that divides a subject into categories and then analyzes the characteristics of each category. See also *division*.

cognitive styles Different and individual approaches to thinking and understanding, especially in regard to how we process language and text.

coherence A characteristic of effective writing, achieved through careful organization of ideas and the skillful use of *transitions*.

colloquial language Informal language not usually found in an academic essay but appropriate in some cases for purposes of *illustration*.

comparison and contrast Two strategies that are often used to complement one another in the same essay. Comparison examines the similarities between two or more like subjects; contrast examines the differences between those subjects.

composing process The work of writing, moving from notes and ideas through multiple *drafts* to a "final" essay. All writers develop their own composing process as they become more comfortable with writing.

conflict A struggle between two opposing forces that creates suspense, tension, and interest in a *narrative*.

conventions The expectations general readers have of specific kinds of writing.

deduction An *argument* that begins with a clearly stated *claim* and then uses selected evidence to support that claim. See also *induction*.

definition/extended definition A writing strategy that describes the nature of an abstract or concrete subject. Extended definition is a kind of essay based on that definition, expanding its scope by considering larger issues related to the subject (for example, the different ways in which different groups of people might define a term like *freedom*).

description A kind of writing based on sensory observations (sight, hearing, smell, touch) that allows readers to imaginatively re-create an experience.

diction The "style" of language, either written or spoken, from which inferences about the speaker's education, background, and origins can be made. Your choice of diction in a piece of writing depends on your intended *audience* and your *purpose*.

discourse Dialogue or conversation. In the study of rhetoric, *discourse* refers to the ways a specific group of people, organization, or institution speaks to and about itself.

division A *rhetorical strategy* that breaks a subject down into smaller parts and analyzes their relationship to the overall subject.

drafting Moving from notes and an outline to the general shape and form of a "final" essay. Writers often go through multiple drafts of an essay, moving ideas around, tinkering with the language, and double-checking facts.

editorialize An "editorial" in a newspaper offers the collective opinion of the newspaper's management on a *topical* issue. Writers "editorialize" when they offer opinions on a subject of topical interest. Unlike the approach of an *argument*, editorializing writers do not always consider the viewpoints of their opponents.

evidence In *argument*, the facts and expert opinions used to support a *claim*.

exemplification See *illustration*.

exposition A type of writing in which you explain or convey information about a subject.

expository essay An essay that seeks to explain something by combining different *rhetorical strategies*, such as *classification* and *description*.

extended definition See *definition*.

figurative language Imaginative language that compares one thing to another in ways that are not necessarily logical but that are nevertheless striking, original, and "true." Examples of figurative language are *metaphor*, *simile*, and *allusion*.

illustration Also called *exemplification*. The use of examples to support an essay's main idea. A successful illustrative essay uses several compelling examples to support its *thesis*.

imagery Descriptive writing that draws on vivid sensory descriptions and *figurative language* to re-create an experience for a reader.

induction In *argument*, a strategy that uses compelling evidence to lead an *audience* to an inevitable conclusion. See also *deduction*.

invective Angry or hostile language directed at a specific person (or persons).

irony A *rhetorical strategy* that uses language to suggest the opposite of what is actually being stated. Irony is used frequently in works of *satire* and works of humor.

major proposition See *claim*.

metaphor The comparison of two unlike things to one another for *figurative* effect.

minor proposition In *argument*, the position a writer goes on to defend through *reasons* and *evidence*. See also *claim*.

motif A simple theme (often a phrase or an image) that is repeated throughout a narrative to give it a deeper sense of *unity* and to underscore its basic idea.

narration/narrative A type of writing that tells a story. In an essay, *narration* is often used to describe what happened to a person or place over a certain period of time.

op-ed style Named for the "opinion and editorial" pages of newspapers, "op-ed style" describes brief *arguments* written for a general *audience* that are supported by *evidence* commonly accepted as "true" or "expert."

oxymoron Contradictory words that are combined to produce a paradoxical phrase.

paraphrase Stating another author's opinions, ideas, or observations in your own words. When you paraphrase, you still give full credit (through in-text citation) to the original author.

persona The voice of the author of an essay or story, even if that voice never uses the first person or gives any further details about its "self." Your persona, in an academic essay, might be that of a concerned citizen, a sociological researcher, or a literary critic.

personal essay An essay written in the first person (the "I" point of view) that uses personal experience to illustrate a larger point.

persuasion A *rhetorical strategy*, often used in *argument*, that seeks to move readers to take a course of action or to change their minds about an issue.

point of view The perspective and attitude of a writer or narrator toward the subject.

précis A *summary* of the relevant facts, statements, and *evidence* offered by an essay, especially an *argument*.

prewriting Any idea-generation strategy that gets you "warmed up" for drafting an essay.

process analysis A kind of essay that describes, in chronological order, each step or stage of the performing of an action (a "how-to" essay).

prologue A brief statement or introduction to a longer work (originally, the introduction to a play spoken by one of the actors).

proposition A *thesis* statement, or *claim*, that suggests a specific action to take and seeks the support of readers to take that action. A proposition is supported by *evidence* demonstrating why this course of action is the best to take. See also *major proposition* and *minor proposition*.

purpose The reason a writer takes on a subject, as well as the goal the writer hopes to achieve.

reader response theory Loosely defined, the idea that every reader brings an individual approach and background of knowledge to a text and responds to a text in a unique way.

reasons In *argument*, *evidence* you offer that your reader will accept as legitimate support for your claim. See also *minor proposition*.

rebuttal In *argument*, a considered response to an opposing point of view.

reflective essay An essay in which you examine and evaluate your own actions or beliefs, learning more about yourself in the process.

refutation In *argument*, proof that someone (usually the opposition) is incorrect.

revision The stage in the writing process in which you revisit your draft, reading and rewriting for clarity and *purpose*, adding or subtracting relevant *evidence*, and perhaps sharing your essay with additional readers for comment.

rhetoric The deliberate and formal use of language, usually in writing, to illustrate an idea or demonstrate a truth. The writer of rhetoric always has in mind an *audience* and a *purpose*.

rhetorical strategies Key patterns that writers employ to organize and clarify their ideas and opinions in an essay.

satire Writing that uses humor, often mocking, to call attention to stupidity or injustice and inspire social change. Satirists call attention to the foibles of groups, institutions, and bureaucracies rather than of individual people.

sensory detail Details based on the five senses (touch, sight, smell, taste, sound) that enhance descriptive writing.

simile A style of *figurative language* that compares two unlike things using "like" or "as." See also *metaphor*.

stipulative definition Creating, based on your own experience and opinions, a definition of a term (generally an abstract term, such as *globalization*) for the purposes of your own *argument*.

style A writer's own unique sense for, and use of, language, *imagery*, and *rhetoric*. Some writers are immediately recognizable by their style; other times, a writer needs to consider *audience* and *purpose* when developing an appropriate style for a particular rhetorical task.

summary As a critical reading strategy, the brief restating (in your own words) of an essay's *thesis*, main points, and *evidence*. Summarizing can help you better understand the logic of a writer's argument and the way an essay is organized. See also *précis*.

symbol Something that stands for, or represents, something else. All numbers and letters are symbols, in that they stand for concepts and sounds.

thesis In an essay, a brief statement that concisely states the writer's subject and opinion on that subject.

tone The writer's "voice" in an essay that, through the use of *diction* and *figurative language*, as well as other *rhetorical strategies*, conveys the writer's feelings about the subject.

topical Relating to an issue or subject drawn from current events or that is of immediate interest to the *audience*.

topic sentence The sentence encapsulating the focus, or main idea, of each paragraph of an essay.

transition The language used to connect one idea to the next in an essay. Skillful use of transitions helps to give an essay *coherence*, allowing the reader to smoothly follow the writer's train of thoughts as well as to clearly see the connections between those thoughts and supporting *evidence*.

unity A quality of good writing that goes beyond *coherence* to an overall sense of completion. A writer achieves unity when the reader feels that not a word needs to be added to (or taken away from) the essay.

usage In rhetorical studies, the ways in which language is commonly used in speaking and writing.

visual texts Anything that conveys an idea without necessarily using language (photographs, advertisements, cartoons, graffiti, etc.).

voice See *tone*.

warrant In *argument*, a plausible *assertion* that a reader must agree with in order to accept the *claim*.

Glossary of Globalization Terms

acculturation The adoption by one culture of features from another, often as a result of conquest or colonialization—for example, the use of French as a primary language in many former French colonies in Africa.

anarchy The absence of any authority; total individual freedom.

assimilation The adoption of a society's culture and customs by immigrants to that society. At both an individual and a group level, the process is gradual and often reciprocal.

balkanization (From the breakup of the countries of the Balkan Peninsula, in Europe, into hostile and frequently warring nations after World War I.) To break apart into smaller, hostile nations or entities, as in the division of the former Yugoslavia and the breakup of the former Soviet Union.

bilingualism/multilingualism Functional literacy in two or more languages; policies that promote the acquisition of more than one language.

biotechnology The application of science, especially genetic engineering, to living organisms in order to effect beneficial changes.

borderless economy Through alliances such as NAFTA and the European Union, the movement toward the free trade of goods and services across national borders.

capital The resources (money, land, raw materials, etc.) used to produce goods and services for the open market.

capitalism Economic system based on the ownership and exchange of goods and services by private individuals, in which individual accumulation of resources is relatively unchecked by governmental regulations.

caste An ancient Indian system of social hierarchy, now much in decline, that held that social status was inherited and could not be changed. The term is more broadly used to indicate a class of people who cannot move up the social hierarchy.

centrist Politically inclined toward moderation and compromise.

civil liberties Guarantees of certain rights, such as freedom of speech and right of assembly. In the United States, these rights are upheld by the Constitution (although they are also frequently challenged in society as well as in the courts).

Cold War From 1945 to 1991, a period of tensions and hostilities between the Soviet Union and its Warsaw Pact allies and the United States and its NATO allies. The era was marked by massive arms proliferation and mutual paranoia and distrust.

collectivity The sharing of resources and responsibilities among a community or social group, rather than dividing and accumulating individually.

colonialism/postcolonial From the sixteenth through the mid-twentieth century, the conquest and ruling of peoples in Asia, Africa, and South America by European nations.

commercialization The transformation of a concept or idea into something that can be marketed, bought, and sold.

communism Political ideology based on the public ownership of resources and centralized planning of the economy. Based on the philosophy of Karl Marx (1818–1883), who sought alternatives to what he saw as the exploitation of the working classes by the rise of industrialization.

conservative In the United States, referring to a political ideology that supports individual liberties and minimal governmental involvement in the economy. Also, a social inclination toward traditional morals and values and a resistance to change.

consumerism Until recently, policies and practices meant to protect consumers from bad business practices. Has come to mean a lifestyle focused on the accumulation of material goods at the expense of other values.

Creole Refers to both languages and peoples, with different specific implications depending on the geographical region discussed. Generally, refers to a people or language that is the result of a mingling of cultures, races, and ethnicities, often due to colonization.

culture The shared customs, traditions, and beliefs of a group of people. These shared values are learned by members of the group from each other, and members of a specific culture share, create, contribute to, and preserve their culture for future generations.

democracy A political system through which enfranchised citizens (people who are acknowledged by the state as citizens and have been granted the right to vote) determine governmental courses of action through elections.

developing world Nations, especially those formerly colonized or under imperialist domination, now moving toward industrialization and economic and political stability.

diaspora Originally applied to Jewish people living outside of Israel; now applied to groups of people "dispersed" or widely scattered from their original homelands.

disarmament Originally a Cold War term used to describe ongoing negotiations between the superpowers to limit and eventually dismantle weapons systems; now describes the diplomatic work of convincing nations to stop or reverse the production of weapons (especially nuclear).

disenfranchised See *enfranchisement.*

ecosystem The fragile web of relationships between living beings and their environment.

emigration Leaving one country for another. See also *immigration*.

enfranchisement The granting of the right to vote to an individual or a group. To be "disenfranchised" is to have no vote, and by extension no voice in determining your own or your community's governance.

ethnic/ethnicity Referring to a shared sense of common religion, race, national, and/or cultural identity.

ethnic cleansing An organized effort to force or coerce an ethnic group from a region. In recent history, efforts at ethnic cleansing in places like Rwanda and Serbia have led to *genocide*.

ethnocentrism The belief that one's own culture or ethnic identification is superior to that of others.

ethnology The anthropological study of cultures.

Eurocentric/Eurocentrism A worldview that believes European or Western values to be superior.

expatriate Someone who lives in a country where he or she is not a citizen.

fascism An extremely repressive political ideology that exercises complete control over individual and civil liberties through the use of force.

feminism The theory that women should have the same political, economic, and social rights as men.

free-market economy An economic system in which individuals, acting in their own self-interest, make decisions about their finances, employment, and consumption of goods and services. In a free-market economy, the government provides and regulates common services such as defense, education, and transportation.

free trade Unrestricted trade of goods and services between countries, free from tariffs (which artificially inflate the prices of imported goods) and quotas (which limit the importation of certain goods in order to protect a country's own industries).

fundamentalism Reactionary movement to establish traditional religious values and texts as the primary and/or governing ideology in a society.

genocide The organized destruction of a group of people because of their race, religion, or ethnicity.

global village Term coined in the 1960s by media critic Marshall McLuhan to describe the ability of new communications technologies to bring peoples together.

global warming A gradual increase in global temperature and resulting changes in global climate, caused by the accumulation of "greenhouse gases" from the burning of fossil fuels and the deterioration of the ozone layer (which shields the earth from ultraviolet rays).

globalization The consolidation of societies around the world due to international trade, economic interdependence, the reach of information technologies, and the possible resulting loss of local traditions, languages, values, and resources.

GMO (genetically modified organism) A living entity (plant, animal, or microbe) that has been altered in some way through the intervention of genetic engineering.

hegemony The domination of one state, entity, or social group over another.

homogenous Referring to a society or culture of very limited diversity whose citizens share very similar racial and/or ethnic backgrounds.

human rights The Universal Declaration of Human Rights ratified by the United Nations in 1948 seeks to guarantee that all human beings have a fundamental dignity and basic rights of self-determination.

ideology A belief system that determines and guides the structure of a government and its relation to its citizens.

immigration The movement of people from their homeland to a new nation. See also *emigration*.

imperialism/empire The economic and cultural influence, and occasionally domination, of nations or peoples by stronger nations. The motives of "imperialist" nations are usually economic (seeking raw resources, opening new markets for trade) and/or ideological (e.g., in the nineteenth century, the British imperialist idea that England had a "duty" to bring "civilization" to other parts of the globe).

indigenous Referring to peoples understood to be "natives" or original inhabitants of lands now threatened by urbanization or other factors. Opponents of globalization argue that the cultures of indigenous peoples are under particular threat from the forces of globalization.

industrialization The transformation of an economy from agricultural to industrial, often followed by urbanization.

information age Term coined by media scholar Marshall McLuhan in 1964 to discuss the rapidly expanding reach (at the time, through television, radio, and print) of technologies that spread information.

information technology Any electronic technology that enhances the production and dissemination of textual, visual, and auditory content, such as computers and cellular telephones.

liberal Implying a political and social tolerance of different views and lifestyles. In the United States, applies to a political preference for increased governmental involvement, especially in matters of social welfare.

Luddite From an early nineteenth century anti-industrialization movement in England; now describes a person who is opposed to technological progress because of its possible dehumanizing effects.

marginalization The effects of social and governmental policies that leave some members of a society disenfranchised, unable to seek or participate in common resources (such as education and health care), and/or unable to freely express themselves and their views.

Marxism A philosophy based on the work of political economist Karl Marx (1818–1883) from which socialism and communism are derived. Marxist political thought focuses on the relationships between economic resources, power, and ideology, with the goal of redistributing resources equitably.

mestizo A Hispanic American of mixed European and indigenous ancestry.

monocultural Referring to a culture that is homogenous and resists diversification.

multiculturalism The belief that all cultures have intrinsic worth and that the diversity of cultures within a society is to be encouraged and celebrated.

multilateralism Cooperation between two or more nations on international issues.

NAFTA (North American Free Trade Agreement) An agreement between the United States, Canada, and Mexico that reduces governmental intervention in trade and investment between these countries.

nationalism Personal and communal feelings of loyalty to a nation; patriotism.

NATO (North Atlantic Treaty Organization) Defense alliance originally created in 1949 to counter the potential threat of the Soviet Union and its Warsaw Pact allies; now includes some of those former enemies in its membership.

naturalization The granting of citizenship, with its rights and privileges, to an immigrant.

NGO (nongovernmental organization) Organizations such as the International Red Cross, Doctors Without Borders, and the International Olympic Committee that provide aid or promote international cooperation without the specific involvement or oversight of governments.

patriarchy A society or worldview that subordinates women.

pluralism Encouragement by a society of competing and divergent political viewpoints.

political asylum Protection guaranteed by a government to refugees fleeing persecution in their own country because of their political beliefs or activism.

polygamy In some cultures, the practice of marrying more than one wife.

polyglot A person who speaks several languages, or referring to a community or culture in which several languages are spoken.

pop culture Values, traditions, and shared customs and references generated by the mass media, as opposed to values based on religion or ideology.

privatization The sale and transfer of formerly government-owned assets (such as utilities) to private corporations.

progressive Referring to a political inclination toward active reform, especially in social justice.

protectionism A government's efforts to protect its own agricultural and manufacturing industries from international competition. See also *free trade*.

race A group of people who have ancestry, physical characteristics, and cultural traditions in common. There is no genetic or "scientific" basis for the defining or classifying of an individual's "race."

rogue state A controversial term coined by the United States to describe states that act irrationally and that pose particular dangers to the United States and its allies. During the Clinton administration, the term was briefly replaced with "state of concern." Some opponents of globalization describe the United States itself as a "rogue state" for taking military, economic, and environmental actions without the participation or consideration of other states.

social justice A popular movement to redistribute wealth, resources, and political power more equitably among the members of a society.

socialism A political ideology based on considerable government involvement in the economy and other social institutions.

sovereignty The power of a state to govern itself and to defend its own interests.

Stalinism Referring to the methods of Joseph Stalin, general secretary of the Communist Party of the USSR and ruler of the Soviet Union from 1922 to 1953. A brutal dictator, his economic policies of forcing rapid industrialization and collectivization of agriculture resulted in massive suffering.

superpower During the Cold War, term used to describe both the United States and the Soviet Union.

terrorism The use of random violence, especially against civilian targets, by ideologically motivated groups or individuals in an attempt to create social upheaval and to achieve recognition of their agenda.

Third World Term generally applied to nations moving toward industrialization and economic stabilization; the term *developing world* is now more commonly used.

totalitarianism An extremely repressive political system that attempts to completely control every aspect of a society through the use of force.

transnational A corporation or entity that conducts business and policy across national borders and has interests in several different nations.

urbanization The massive shift of a nation's peoples from rural, agrarian communities to large urban areas, usually as a result of industrialization.

utopia An idealized, speculative nation or system of government.

welfare state A nation that assumes primary governmental responsibility for the health, education, and social security of its citizens, often in exchange for heavy individual tax burdens.

Index

393